S0-BEH-653

# REFORMED THOUGHT AND SCHOLASTICISM

## THE ARGUMENTS FOR THE EXISTENCE OF GOD IN DUTCH THEOLOGY, 1575-1650

# STUDIES IN THE HISTORY OF CHRISTIAN THOUGHT

EDITED BY
HEIKO A. OBERMAN, Tübingen

IN COOPERATION WITH
HENRY CHADWICK, Cambridge
JAROSLAV PELIKAN, New Haven, Conn.
BRIAN TIERNEY, Ithaca, N.Y.
E. DAVID WILLIS, Princeton, N.J.

VOLUME XXIX

**JOHN PLATT**

## REFORMED THOUGHT AND SCHOLASTICISM

### THE ARGUMENTS FOR THE EXISTENCE OF GOD IN DUTCH THEOLOGY, 1575-1650

LEIDEN
E. J. BRILL
1982

# REFORMED THOUGHT AND SCHOLASTICISM

## THE ARGUMENTS FOR THE EXISTENCE OF GOD IN DUTCH THEOLOGY, 1575-1650

BY

JOHN PLATT

LEIDEN
E. J. BRILL
1982

Platt, John — Reformed thought and scholasticism: the arguments for the existence of God in Dutch theology, 1575-1650 / by John Platt. — Leiden: Brill. — (Studies in the history of christian thought; vol. 29)

UDC 26

ISBN 90 04 06593 8



PRINTED IN THE NETHERLANDS

# CONTENTS



## PART I

## THE BACKGROUND



## PART II

## THE ARGUMENTS FOR THE EXISTENCE OF GOD AMONG ORTHODOX DUTCH THEOLOGIANS



## PART III

## NATURAL THEOLOGY IN THE CONTROVERSIES BETWEEN REMONSTRANTS AND CONTRA-REMONSTRANTS

# ACKNOWLEDGEMENTS

This study originated as an Oxford doctoral thesis under the Board of the Faculty of Theology and my first debt of gratitude is to the latter for the award of the Denyer and Johnson Senior Studentship in 1972 which made possible the extended stay in the Netherlands where I not only laid the foundations for this work but also met Professor Dr. G. J. Hoenderdaal and Professor Dr. G. H. M. Posthumus Meyjes of Leiden University, both of whom have been most helpful. Thanks are also due to the supervisors of my thesis and especially to the Revd. Dr. J. O'Higgins, S. J., of Campion Hall whose clear-headed guidance was always of great assistance. I must express my gratitude to Professor H. A. Oberman for accepting this work for publication in this distinguished series.

The Master and Fellows of my college were kind enough to give me leave of absence in Hilary Term, 1975 and again in Trinity Term, 1980; the latter when I was preparing this book for the press whilst on my second long visit to Holland, made possible on this occasion by a generous bursary from Leiden University.

The bulk of my research was carried out in the Bodleian Library and that of Leiden University to whose staffs I am greatly obliged. Pembroke itself is extremely fortunate in its college office and I am particularly grateful to Mrs. Susan Ousley for the cheerful efficiency with which she prepared the typescript for publication.

Finally I have to thank my wife without whose constant support and encouragement nothing would have been accomplished.

Pembroke College,
Oxford,
1980.

J.E.P.

# ABBREVIATIONS

| | |
|---|---|
| BWPGN | *Biographisch Woordenboek van Protestantsche Godgeleerden in Nederland*, The Hague, (1907)-1949. |
| CR | *Corpus Reformatorum*, Brunswick, 1834- |
| LCC | Library of Christian Classics, Vol. 20, *Calvin: The Institutes of the Christian Religion*, (Books I i-III xix) edited by J. T. McNeill, translated by F. L. Battles, London, 1961. |
| NAK | *Nederlands Archief voor Kerkgeschiedenis*. |
| NNBW | *Nieuw Nederlandsch Biographisch Woordenboek*, Leiden, 1911-37. |
| PRE | *Realencyclopädie für protestantische Theologie und Kirche*, 3rd Edition, Leipzig, 1898-1908. |
| ST | *Summa Theologiae*, Blackfriars' edition, London 1963- |
| WA | *D. Martin Luthers Werke*, Weimar, 1883- |

# PART I

# THE BACKGROUND

CHAPTER ONE

# INTRODUCTION

This investigation seeks to make a modest contribution to the debate on the changes which took place in Reformed theology in the period following the death of Calvin. The transition from the latter's theology to that of Reformed scholastic orthodoxy which took place during our period is an undoubted fact which has provoked contrasting reactions on the part of subsequent students who may, broadly speaking, be divided into two opposing parties.

In the one group are those who point to the contrast between 'reformation' and 'orthodoxy' and see this as a process of sad deterioration. Olivier Fatio, a member of the other party, has succinctly summarized the views of his opponents: "le passage de la doctrine réformée à la dogmatique orthodoxe est un processus d'objectivation croissante des découvertes existentielles du début de la Réforme...... Ces auteurs opposent dynamisme à statisme, créativité à redite, règne de la grâce à ontologisation de la connaissance de Dieu et à systématisation de l'Ecriture, pour qualifier la différence entre la période précédant la mort de Calvin et celle qui la suit."[1] For his part, Fatio acknowledges in Daneau, whom he holds up as representative of the Reformed theologians immediately following Calvin, "une certaine rationalisation extérieure de l'œuvre", which he regards as "inévitable avec le processus de scolarisation et d'établissement."[2] The emphasis here is clearly on "extérieure"; all are agreed that there was a change in the manner in which Reformed theology was presented, the crucial question is whether or not there are points at which the external changes in presentation affected the 'internal' doctrines thus expounded.

Fatio has sought to circumvent such an investigation, urging "il faut renoncer à séparer avec Weber, le *reformatorisch* de l'*orthodox*, car dans l'œuvre d'un Daneau ou dans celle de ses contemporains les deux éléments sont constamment imbriqués l'un dans l'autre. Cela implique que l'on renonce à étudier — et à critiquer — ces auteurs en partant d'un *a priori* dogmatique qui a déterminé au préalable ce qui est spécifiquement

[1] O. Fatio, *Méthode et Théologie. Lambert Daneau et les débuts de la scolastique réformée*, Geneva, 1976, p. IX.

[2] *Ibid.*, p. X.

*reformatorisch*."[3] Such a renunciation would seem to be well nigh impossible since the Reformation did effect an enormous change in both the method and content of theology and this not least in conscious protest against and rejection of the contemporary theology of the schools. However much certain modern scholars may point to rationalist elements in Calvin's works, there is a world of difference from that of scholasticism. Thus, when in the generation immediately following his death, his successors are found making increasing use of scholastic methods, we are surely perfectly entitled, indeed positively obliged, to consider whether such usage affected the substance of their doctrine so as to bring about a return to the very positions against which the Reformers had rebelled. Furthermore, in doing this it is hard to see how we can avoid identifying the 'reformed' element in their thought, though, of course, it should be possible to conduct the investigation without the sort of prejudice which stands ready to condemn any deviation from some cherished ideal of pristine Reformed purity. This study concentrates on Natural Theology, one of the most sensitive of topics in which modern scholars have notoriously allowed their present, often passionately held, convictions to determine their view of the past.

The issue of nature and grace lay at the heart of the Reformers' protest against the contemporary scholastic theology.[4] The medieval schoolmen had a positive view of the relationship, "grace presupposes nature", and although the latter was not considered adequate in itself but required supplementing, nonetheless "grace does not abolish nature but perfects it." For Luther, on the other hand, man's nature was so corrupt that there could be no effective knowledge of God from this source. In fact the Reformer's crucial message was the abolition of the grace-nature framework in favour of that of grace alone. "Therefore true theology and the knowledge of God is in Christ crucified."[5] As we shall see in the course of our subsequent discussion of Melanchthon's views[6], Luther did not deny that the natural man could have some knowledge of God, His existence and His attributes, but such knowledge was utterly inadequate and could provide no foundation upon which to build.

When we turn to Calvin and, in particular, to his discussion of the issue at the beginning of the first book of the *Institutes*, we find that he too

[3] *Ibid.*, pp. XI-XII.

[4] See W. van 't Spijker's excellent summary article, "Natuur en Genade in de Reformatorische Theologie", *Theologia Reformata*, 22, 1979, pp. 176-90.

[5] "Ergo in Christo crucifixo est vera theologia et cognitio Dei." (Heidelberg Disputation, 1518, *WA.*, 1, p. 362.)

[6] See below, p. 19.

recognizes, indeed insists upon, man's natural knowledge of God. However, the very moment Calvin introduces this he makes clear its essentially negative purpose; "There is within the human mind, and indeed by natural instinct, an awareness of divinity. This we take to be beyond controversy. To prevent anyone from taking refuge in the pretence of ignorance, God himself has implanted in all men a certain understanding of his divine majesty."[7] Equally, Calvin sets the same negative sign against the other natural sense of the knowledge of God, the external one set out in chapter five, entitled "The Knowledge of God shines forth in the Fashioning of the Universe and the Continuing Government of it"; prefacing his account of it thus: "But upon his individual works he has engraved unmistakable marks of his glory, so clear and so prominent that even unlettered and stupid folk cannot plead the excuse of ignorance."[8]

At this point the two opposing schools which we mentioned above diverge in their interpretation. Thus one of the older generation of Calvin scholars, B. B. Warfield, sees these two sources, innate belief and the witness of the created and providential ordering of nature and history, as being arguments for the existence of God which he identifies with the two such employed by the earliest fathers of the Church.[9] Warfield's concern with the matter goes much further and so we find him writing that the *Institutes* "concerns itself with the so-called proofs of the divine existence as means through which we rather obtain knowledge of what God is, than merely attain to knowledge that God is", and he allows himself to speculate "whether, had we from him a professed instead of a merely incidental treatment of the topic, the metaphysical arguments would have remained lacking in his case as in theirs ...."[10] As, by metaphysical, Warfield is here clearly referring to varieties of the ontological argument,[11] we can only assent to his conjectural conclusion, "it seems very possible that as foreign to his *a posteriori* method (cf. I.v.9) they lay outside his scheme of proofs."[12]

---

[7] *Institutes*, I, iii, 1, *LCC.*, p. 43.

[8] *Institutes*, I, v. 1, *LCC.*, p. 5.

[9] B. B. Warfield, "Calvin's Doctrine of the Knowledge of God" and "Calvin's Doctrine of God", in *The Princeton Theological Review*, Vol. 7, 1909, pp. 219-325, and pp. 381-436, see especially pp. 395-6. These articles are reprinted in B. B. Warfield, *Calvin and Calvinism*, New York, 1931, pp. 29-30 and pp. 133-185.

[10] Warfield, *op. cit.*, pp. 391, 396.

[11] "Metaphysical proofs of the existence of God such as those adduced by Augustine, Anselm, and Descartes, were quite foreign to the theology of the first three centuries." (*Ibid.*, p. 396).

[12] *Ibid.*, p. 397.

Warfield's attempt to read such a concern for the arguments in Calvin has been firmly rejected by T. H. L. Parker: "We must disagree with B. B. Warfield, who, after asserting that Calvin points us to the works of God rather than to the proofs of his existence, yet leaves the door open for them to re-enter into Reformed theology by stressing Calvin's 'practical religious motive'. The inference presumably is that this motive is purely one of method, and incidental, and that there was a Calvin who allowed a speculative motive and the proofs that go with it. If so, it was not the Calvin whose theological works we have. Although Warfield speaks of Calvin's 'special interest in the theistic argument' and says that 'he asserts their (i.e. the proofs') validity most strenuously' (*Calvin and Calvinism*, New York, 1931, p. 31 and n. 8), he does not say where all this activity is to be found. In point of fact, of course, it comes from reading back into Calvin another motive and other thoughts, culled from the course of scholastic Calvinism, which not only are not to be found in Calvin, but also do violence to the motive of his theology. Neither chapter 1 nor chapter 5 of book I ought to be interpreted as supplying the Calvinian equivalent to St. Thomas' 'demonstrations'".[13]

However, the manner in which, especially in chapter five, Calvin sets out God's revelation in nature and history, can still prompt a reaction of the sort which we find in a modern scholar who is well aware of Calvin's essentially negative stance. Thus E. A. Dowey writes: "Had we not approached this subject through the preceeding discussion, we might now think to find ourselves in the presence of some kind of rational theist. Calvin never forgets for a moment that sin has blinded man to the revelation in creation, but since *sin* does it, the revelation itself is not harmed. Man's receiving apparatus functions wrongly. In the description of how it should function Calvin uses in simplified form some arguments from nature that would do credit to Herbert of Cherbury. .... the rational quality of the arguments we are about to analyze and the active contribution to them of the human mind on the level of ordinary logic are unmistakable. .... In this sin-negated natural theology, the arguments from design and from sufficient cause are held up as norms for the mind ..."[14]

Parker added an appendix to the revised edition of his own work in order to criticize Dowey. In particular, as regards the natural knowledge of God, he feels that the latter "will nevertheless give it a too positive function and thus carry over such knowledge as a valuable component of

[13] T. H. L. Parker, *Calvin's Doctrine of the Knowledge of God*, 2nd ed., Grand Rapids, Michigan, 1959.

[14] E. A. Dowey, *The Knowledge of God in Calvin's Theology*, New York, 1952, p. 73.

Christian preaching.''[15] In response, Parker underlines the profound centrality of Calvin's concept of inexcusability drawn from Romans 1,20 and 2,1, concluding that ''the only 'apologetic' use that Calvin allows to the revelation in creation is a very different one from what modern apologetics sees as its task. There is no question of its providing a stepping-stone towards the truth, of its proving a foundation to build on. In itself, apart from the Scriptures, it has merely made every man objectively inexcusable before God....''.[16]

As the above summary of the dispute between modern scholars clearly shows, arguments for the existence of God are central to any investigation into the extent to which natural theology is being employed. Are such arguments used at all? If so, which and in what context? We have already talked of scholasticism and will have frequent cause to do so again, but this is a somewhat ''slippery'' phenomenon to grasp.[17] At least in the matter of the arguments for God's existence we can bring a sharper focus to bear since the schoolmen's own use of such arguments is readily to hand and can enable us to see the degree to which any subsequent theologian is reverting to such usage.

It is with such questions in mind that a large part of this study is devoted to the examination of the use made of the arguments for the existence of God in one particular area of Reformed theology, the Dutch, in the period from the foundation of the first Protestant university there in 1575 to 1650. Honesty compels the present writer to own that his choice of the northern Netherlands has been greatly influenced by personal interests and predelictions, but, on any reading, Dutch theology was a force to be reckoned with at this time and can lay as good a claim as any to reflect the state of Reformed theology as a whole. The upper limit of our period is not arbitrarily fixed by the mid-point of the seventeenth century but because, as Dibon[18] has convincingly demonstrated in his study of the philosophical teaching in the Dutch universities, the positive impact of Cartesianism can be pretty precisely dated then. Since this impact was quickly felt in

---

[15] Parker, *op. cit.*, p. 121.

[16] *Ibid.*, p. 125.

[17] Whilst we may be perfectly happy to accept such a succinct definition of the term as is given, for example in the *Dictionnaire de Théologie Catholique*, ''on doit donc dire que la scolastique est essentiellement une méthode de spéculation théologique et philosophe visant à la pénétration rationelle et à la systématisation des verités révélées à l'aide des concepts philosophiques.'' (Vol. 14. Part 2, Paris, 1941, col. 1691), it is frequently difficult to assess whether and to what extent a particular theologian is ''scholastic.''

[18] P. Dibon, *L'Enseignement philosophique dans les Universités néerlandaises à l'époque précartésienne (1575-1650)*, Amsterdam, 1954.

theology and not least in the matter of the arguments for the existence of God, it makes good sense for us to accept the same restriction to the pre-Cartesian era.

Serious scholars of the sixteenth and seventeenth centuries quickly become aware of the complexities of the thought of the period and, whilst welcoming such contributions to the intellectual history of the times as R. H. Popkin's study of Scepticism,[19] are compelled to attribute much of the clarity of the thesis argued therein to a resolute concentration upon certain selected features of the issue to the virtual exclusion of factors which do not fit into the determined pattern. An example of this in Popkin's case is his failure to see the extent to which early modern scepticism arose as an ally to religious belief against the threat posed by the inexorable determinism of Aristotelian rationalism.[20]

It is in order to avoid such a false impression that we have chosen not to attempt the mammoth task of surveying the relevant writings of all the Dutch theologians of our period, since this would necessarily have meant selecting from the wide variety of such only those among them whom we considered to be of significance for our purpose. Instead, we have fixed upon two areas which, although important and substantial, are both sufficiently limited in scope to enable us to cover them comprehensively, studying everything of relevance by everyone who wrote. Granted the correctness of our choice of the areas to be examined, this method possesses the advantage that any pattern to emerge is one that can be seen to be genuinely present in the primary material and not one that has been imposed by judicious selection.

Our first concern centres upon the official formularies of Dutch Reformed orthodoxy, the Heidelberg Catechism and the Belgic Confession, dealing specifically with whatever is relevant to our concern in the documents themselves and in the Dutch commentaries upon them. The second looks to Leiden University which, on its foundation in 1575, was the first of its kind in Holland and continued throughout our period to be first in importance as the internationally acknowledged centre of Dutch learning. Here then we examine everything that bears upon our theme in the works of those who were professors of theology there, an impressive list which includes such names as Junius, Gomarus, Arminius, Vorstius, Episcopius, Walaeus and Coccejus.

It may be objected that such 'blanket' coverage runs the risk of our losing sight of the wood for the trees. We will maintain that, in the event, this

[19] *The History of Scepticism from Erasmus to Descartes*, New York, 1964.

[20] See J. Collins, *God in Modern Philosophy*, London, 1959, pp. 39-40.

is not the case and that important considerations emerge from such a study which would not otherwise do so, not least a point of considerable significance in enabling us to understand the way in which the transition from 'reformation' to 'orthodoxy' occurred in this particular sphere.

Moreover, the history of the period in Dutch theology has inclined us to consider other related issues which enable us to stand back a little from the two areas just mentioned. All save the first[21] and the last of that impressive list of Leiden professors named above were deeply embroiled in the controversies over the doctrine of Predestination which dominated the Dutch scene at this time and made it the centre of interest for all Protestantism. The division between the orthodox and the Arminian party, known in Holland as the Remonstrants, ran very deep and significant differences on questions of Natural Theology arose which repay study for the light they throw upon the underlying attitudes thus revealed.

We gave our reasons for not accepting Fatio's refusal to distinguish between 'reformed' and 'orthodox' elements in the works of the theologians in question. However, we do heartily endorse the suggestion which he then makes, with the proviso that for us the "plus ... au contraire" must be disregarded: "Il est plus utile au contraire de découvrir l'image que ces auteurs se faisent des réformateurs et de leurs autres prédécesseurs par une évaluation sérieuse des sources et des influences."[22] Throughout the course of our investigation we have paid close attention to the use which is being made of the works of other theologians; the results are often interesting and sometimes surprising. Since, in this matter of sources, the most important for the arguments for the existence of God turns out to be Melanchthon, we shall begin our study with him.

[21] Even Junius engaged in an early, albeit non-acrimonious, dispute with Arminius on this topic which was subsequently published by the latter's children after his death as the *Amica cum D. Francisco Junio de Praedestinatione per litteras habita Collatio*, Leiden, 1613.

[22] Fatio, *op. cit.*, p. XII.

CHAPTER TWO

# MELANCHTHON

As our subsequent investigations will disclose, the arguments for the existence of God which figure most frequently amongst those presented by Dutch theologians of our period stem ultimately from the list supplied by Melanchthon. The latter is a notoriously controversial figure and nowhere more so than in connection with his evaluation of the part played by natural reason in man's knowledge of God. The detailed account which follows of the evolution of his approach to this topic is undertaken with the intention of illuminating the issues which, for his Dutch successors no less than for Melanchthon, were involved when a theologian at the heart of the Reformation tradition undertook the enterprise of arguing for the existence of God.

In his early theological works, Melanchthon is prepared to go even further than Luther in emphasising the corrupt state of fallen man and the consequent impotence of his natural powers in spiritual matters. In the first edition of his *Loci Communes* (1521), Melanchthon declares, 'God's existence, His wrath and His mercy are spiritual matters which cannot therefore be known by the flesh.'[1]

In view of the importance in Melanchthon's later work of the concept of the natural law in the matter of the knowledge of God, it is interesting to note his earlier treatment of it. He begins by drawing attention to the weakness of human reason which should be at work in this field:

> 'For when natural laws are being proclaimed, it is proper that their formulas be collected by the method of human reason through the natural syllogism. I have not yet seen this done by anyone, and I do not know at all whether it can be done, since human reason is so enslaved and blinded—at least it has been up until now.'[2]

Failing reason, the natural law operates universally because, as St. Paul teaches in Romans 2, 15, God has engraved it within every man.

---

[1] 'Esse deum, dei ira, dei misericordia, spiritualia sunt, non possunt igitur a carne cognosci.' (*CR*. 21. col. 160.)

[2] 'Nam cum naturales dicantur, oportebat a rationis humanae methodo earum formulas colligi per naturalem syllogismum. Id quod nondum video a quoquam factum, et haud scio an omnino possit fieri, nempe usque adeo capta, occaecataque ratione humana.' (*Ibid.*, col. 116.)

> 'The law of nature, therefore, is a common judgment to which all men give the same consent. This law which God has engraved on the mind of each is suitable for the shaping of morals.'[3]

We shall have occasion to refer again to this important passage but for now it is sufficient to notice that this stress upon the divinely implanted source of the knowledge of the natural law is made in order to account for its operation despite reason's incapacity.

> 'When I say that the laws of nature have been impressed on our minds by God, I mean that the knowledge of these laws consists of certain so-called "concreated attitudes." This knowledge is not the product of our own mental powers, but it has been implanted in us by God.'[4]

The key to this entire discussion lies of course in the interpretation of the relevant passages in the first two chapters of the Epistle to the Romans and here we may observe that Melanchthon's consideration of them at this time confirms the low view of reason's capacity which we have noted above. One point, however, which now becomes explicit as he comments upon Chap. 1, verse 18, is his recognition that the knowledge of God's existence springs from the law of nature:

> 'God's existence is known from the law of nature. Now the first penalty of impiety is blindness and at this point those who vaunt the power of reason, whether the light of nature or the natural sharpness of the intellect, are irritated since nothing is more grievous than the surrender of our reason.'[5]

At this point it is revealing to turn to Luther's lectures on this Epistle, delivered at Wittenberg in 1515-16, which, although not actually published until 1908, provide us with the evidence for the latter's influence upon Melanchthon since the intimacy between the two was such that publication was in no way necessary to acquaint them of each other's mind on any issue. Luther's commentary upon Chapter 1, verse 19, makes that link between the content of the natural knowledge of God and the

---

[3] 'Est itaque lex naturae sententia communis, cui omnes homines pariter adsentimur, atque adeo quam deus insculpsit cuiusque animo, ad formandos mores accommodata.' (*Ibid.*, cols. 116-7.)

[4] 'Quod vero dico leges naturae a deo impressas mentibus humanis, volo earum cognitionem esse quosdam, ut isti loquuntur habitus concreatos, non inventam a nostris ingeniis sed insitam nobis a deo.' (*Ibid.*, col. 117.)

[5] 'Deinde deum esse, lege naturae cognosci. Deinde primam impietatis poenam caecitatem esse. Atque hic perstringuntur, qui vim rationis, seu lumen naturae seu acumen ingenii naturale iactant, cum non sit aliud calamitosius, quam rationi nostrae permitti.' (*Annotationes ... in Epistolas Pauli ad Romanos et Corinthios duas*, Nurenburg, 1522, no pagination.)

operation of the natural law which we have seen in Melanchthon. Of the gentiles, he writes:

> 'They knew, therefore, that it is the nature of divinity or of God to be powerful, invisible, righteous, immortal, and good, and thus they knew the invisible things of God and his eternal power and divinity. This "major" of the "practical syllogism," this basic theological "insight of the conscience," is in every mind and can never be obscured.'[6]

As an editorial footnote to the English translation explains:

> 'According to later medieval Scholasticism (Gerson, Biel, Trutvetter etc.) the "practical" syllogism (which was distinguished from the "speculative" syllogism) consisted of the following three parts; major premise, syntheresis; minor premise, ratio (iudicium); conclusion, conscientia. Synteresis ... was defined as a "natural inclination" of the soul toward the good, an inextinguishable spark (scintilla) of reason, an inborn habitus...[7]

Although Luther does not explicitly refer to the natural law here, his mention of synderesis inevitably involves it. Thus an editorial footnote to the Weimar edition of the Latin text cites the chapter on synderesis in Reisch's *Margarita* (1, xi. c. 11) 'Whence in the practical syllogism Sinderesis works out the major from the dictate of the law of nature, right reason adds the minor.'[8] Luther's influence upon Melanchthon is here unmistakable, for the latter's reference to the natural syllogism, as we saw above, indicated that it failed because of reason's weakness. The former's discussion of the practical syllogism had made exactly the same point when he went on to say,

> 'But in the "minor" they erred when they made the statement: This one here, i.e., Jupiter or someone else whom this idol represents, is of this sort, etc. Here lay the beginning of the error that led to idolatry.'[9]

---

[6] 'Cognoverant ergo, Quod divinitatis sive eius, qui est Deus, sit esse potentem, Invisibilem, Justum, immortalem, bonum; ergo cognoverunt Invisibilia Dei sempiternamque virtutem eius et divinitatem. Haec Maior syllogismi practici, haec Syntheresis theologica est inobscurabilis in omnibus.' (*WA*. 56, p. 177.)

[7] *Luther: Lectures on Romans*, trans. and ed. W. Pauck, London, 1961, p. 24.

[8] 'Unde in syllogismo practico Sinderesis maiorem ponit ex dictamine legis naturae, recta ratio minorem subsumit.' (*WA*. 56, p. 177, note 14.) The *Margarita Philosophica* of Gregory Reisch was first published at Fribourg in 1503 and went through at least eight subsequent editions between 1504 and 1535. Luther's use of the practical syllogism is illuminated by the example which Reisch gives in the immediate continuation of the passage quoted above. 'verbo gratia dicit Synderisis omne malum vitandum est. Subsumit rectae rationis ... Adulterium est malum ... infert Conscientia igitur adulterium est vitandum.' (*op. cit.*, fol. 236r.)

[9] 'Sed in minore errabant dicendo et statuendo: Hic autem i.e. Jupiter vel alius huic simulacro similis et huiusmodi etc. Hic error incepit et fecit idolatriam.' (*WA*. 56, p. 177.)

for, as we have from the editorial footnotes quoted above, the minor premise involved the use of reason and it is precisely here that the breakdown occurs.

The importance of the Romans' passage is further underlined when, in his discussion of natural law in the first edition of the *Loci Communes*, Melanchthon distinguishes three laws which fall under this heading,

> '1. God must be worshiped.
> 2. Since we are born into a life that is social, nobody must be harmed.
> 3. Human society demands that we make common use of all things.
> We get the first law, concerning the worship of God, from Rom., ch. 1. There is no doubt that in this chapter the apostle singles out this natural law when he says that God has declared his majesty to all men by founding and administering the universe.'[10]

However, despite the conviction that Paul dealt with God's existence under the laws of nature, we may note that Melanchthon's distrust of reason leads him immediately to reiterate the following caveat:

> 'But it is more characteristic of a curious than of a pious man to conclude by way of a human syllogism that God is, especially since it is not safe for human reason to argue about such great matters, as I have warned at the beginning of this compendium.'[11]

This tendency at this stage in Melanchthon's thought about the natural man's difficulty in recognizing God's existence by the use of his corrupt reason is taken still further in the 1522 revision of the *Loci Communes*. Now he expresses doubt as to whether the first of these laws, that requiring the worshipping of God, should be counted among the natural laws at all, but should rather be attributed to faith.

> 'Human reason easily infers these last two laws from arguments. So blinded is it after Adam's fall that I do not see how it can infer the first law ... In what way this latter may be numbered among the laws of nature, let others judge. For it is written that the creation is to be understood by faith (Heb. XI).'[12]

[10] '1 Deus colendus est. 11 Quia nascimur in quandam vitae societatem, nemo laedendus est. 111 Poscit humana societas, ut omnibus rebus communiter utamur. Primam legem de colendo deo accepimus ex primo cap. ad Romanos, ubi non dubium deum declarasse omnibus hominibus maiestatem suam conditione et administratione universitatis mundi.' (*CR*. 21, col. 117.)

[11] 'Sed ut possit syllogismo humano colligi esse deum, curiosi magis est quam pii disputare, maxime cum rationi humanae non sit tutum de tantis rebus argutari, ut huius compendii principio monui.' (*Ibid.*)

[12] 'Posteriores duas legas facile colligat argumentis humana ratio. Primam legem, quomodo colligere possit, non video, sic occaecata, post Adae lapsum ... Ut inter naturae leges haec numeretur aliorum esto iudicium. Nam fide intelligi creationem Heb. X1 scribitur.' (*Ibid.* 118, note 26.)

Indeed, even in the first edition, Melanchthon's concern about the effects of the Fall apparently lead him to doubt the continuing validity even of that innate knowledge of the natural law which he had expounded in the section under that heading. Thus in the following section, entitled 'The Gospel', Melanchthon says that, in addition to the natural law engraved on human minds, God also revealed further laws, as for instance that forbidding Adam to taste the fruit of the tree of the knowledge of good and evil and that forbidding Cain to be angry with his brother. He then concludes:

> 'In this way the Spirit of God was restoring the knowledge of natural law by constant proclamation. This knowledge of law was already being so darkened in human minds blinded by sin that I might almost call natural law not some innate judgment, implanted and engraved by nature on the minds of men, but simply the laws received by the fathers and handed down from time to time to posterity. Adam, for instance, taught his descendants about the creation of things, about worshiping God, and warned Cain that he should not kill his brother, etc.'[13]

The major change in Melanchthon's approach becomes evident in the first edition of his commentary on the Epistle to the Romans.[14] Commenting upon Chapter 1, verse 18, "those who hold the truth in unrighteousness," Melanchthon first identifies this truth with the knowledge of God and then asserts that men possess this knowledge, although they do not act in accordance with it. "He (Paul) calls 'the truth' the knowledge of God ... Men know that God exists, that God is angry with sinners, that God must be obeyed, and yet they neither assent nor submit to this knowledge."[15]

Moving on to verse 19, "For that which can be known of God is known to them," Melanchthon takes the important step of further identifying this natural knowledge of God with the law of nature, "Paul," he writes, "ad-

---

[13] 'In hunc modum legis naturae cognitionem instaurabat praedicatione continua spiritus dei quae iam obscurabatur excaecatis peccato mentibus humanis, ita ut mihi pene libeat vocare legem naturae non aliquod congenitum iudicium, seu insitum et insculptum natura mentibus hominum, sed leges acceptas a patribus, et quasi per manus traditas subinde posteritati, ut de creatione rerum, de colendo deo, docuit posteros Adae, sic Cainum monuit, ne fratrem occideret etc ...' (*Ibid.*, col. 140.)

[14] *Commentarii in Epistolam Pauli ad Romanos*, Wittenberg, 1532. The quotations here are cited from the *Römerbrief - Kommentar 1532*, edited G. Ebeling and R. Schafer, Gütersloh, 1965, Vol. V in *Melanchthons Werke in Auswahl*.

[15] '"Veritatem" vocat notitiam Dei ... Homines sciunt Deum esse, Deum irasci peccantibus, Deo oboediendum esse, et tamen huic notitiae neque assentiuntur neque obtemperant.' (*op. cit.*, pp. 69-70.)

duces the law of nature, namely the natural knowledge of God."[16] The hesitations on this score which we noted above have now apparently disappeared. The extent of this knowledge of God or natural law is limited and not to be confused with that revealed in the Gospel, but it is nonetheless far-reaching and includes the fundamental attributes of the divine nature.

> 'God is known to them so far as He can be known, namely that He is God, that He is good, He is just, that He demands what is fitting, that He punishes the reprobate, that He listens to and cares for those who obey the law. For men have this knowledge of God by nature, indeed it is, so to speak, a knowledge of the law not of the Gospel. For through natural reason alone men cannot establish that God is willing to forgive sins, that He wishes to be reconciled with the unworthy and unclean, that He freely reckons them as righteous although unclean. This is not natural knowledge, but it is revealed in the Gospel.'[17]

The similarity between this position and that of Luther, as expressed in what is perhaps his most explicit statement upon the relative status of the natural and revealed knowledge of God, is indeed striking:

> 'There is a twofold knowledge of God: the general and the particular. All men have the general knowledge, namely, that God is, that He has created heaven and earth, that He is just, that He punishes the wicked, etc. But what God thinks of us, what He wants to give and to do to deliver us from sin and death and to save us—which is the particular and the true knowledge of God—this men do not know.'[18]

We saw, in our survey of Melanchthon's earlier discussion of the natural law in the first edition of the *Loci Communes*, that his sense of the weakness of human reason had led him to stress that any knowledge of this law arose because God had implanted it within men's minds. In doing this, Melanchthon introduced a concept which, as we shall see, was to be of great importance in the development of his thinking on this issue:

---

[16] 'Paulus ... : allegat enim legem naturae, videlicet naturalem notitiam de Deo.' (*Ibid.*, p. 70.)

[17] 'Deus notis est eis, quatenus cognosci potest, videlicet quod sit Deus, quod sit bonus, quod sit iustus, quod requirat iusta, quod puniat impios, quod exaudiat et servet legi oboedientes. Nam hanc notitiam de Deo naturaliter habent homines, quae quidem est notitia quaedam legis non evangelii. Non enim possunt homines per solam rationem naturalem statuere, quod Deus velit remittere peccata, quod velit indignis et immundis esse placatus, quod gratis reputet iustos, quamvis immundos. Haec non est naturalis notitia, sed revelatur in evangelio.' (*Ibid.*)

[18] 'Duplex est cognitio Dei, generalis et propria. Generalem habent omnes homines, scilicet, quod Deus sit, quod creaverit coelum et terram, quod sit iustus, quod puniat impios etc. Sed quid Deus de nobis, cogitet, quid dare et facere velit, ut a peccatis et morte liberemur et salvi fiamus (quae propria et vera est cognitio Dei), homines non noverunt.' (*Commentary on Galatians* (1535). *WA*. 40. pt. 1, p. 607.)

> 'The law of nature, therefore, is a common judgement to which all men give the same consent. This law which God has engraved on the mind of each is suitable for the shaping of morals. For just as there are certain common principles in the theoretical branches of learning, in mathematics, for instance (they might be called "common thoughts" or "a priori principles," such as "The whole is greater than its parts"), so there are certain common axioms and a priori principles in the realm of morals; these constitute the ground rules for all human activity..... These rules of human activity are rightly called "laws of nature." '[19]

Again as we observed above, Melanchthon at this stage was so concerned with the effects of the fall, that even this account of the natural law was subject to severe qualification,

> 'For in general the judgment of human comprehension is fallacious because of our innate blindness, so that even if certain patterns of morals have been engraved on our minds, they can scarcely be apprehended.'[20]

In the *Commentary upon Romans*, Melanchthon has not lost sight of the effects of the Fall, but these are no longer seen as being altogether devastating:

> 'Moreover, although some knowledge of God is innate in man from the law of nature, yet this same knowledge is partly obscured by original sin'...[21]

Melanchthon now reintroduces his conception of the προληψεις in order to account for the way in which natural human reason can arrive at a knowledge of God's existence and attributes from a consideration of the wonders of creation.

[19] 'Est itaque lex naturae sententia communis, cui omnes homines pariter adsentimur, atque adeo quam deus insculpsit cuiusque animo, ad formandos mores accommodata. Nam ut sunt in disciplinis theoricis, ut mathematis, quaedam communia principia, sive κοιναι έννοαι ή προληψεις quale illud est, totum est maius partibus. Ita sunt quaedam in moralibus tum principia communia, tum conclusiones primae, ... regulae omnium humanarum functionum. Has recte vocaveris leges naturae.' (*CR*. 21, cols. 116-7.) Melanchthon is aware that the introduction of this concept, which is that of the Stoa as mediated by Cicero, does not square with the current Aristotelianism, 'Id ut conveniat cum Aristotelis philosophia non laboro. Quid enim ad me quid senserit ille rixator?' (col. 117). Nonetheless, the division between practical and theoretical principles is Aristotelian and there are scholastic formulations of it in this context which show some affinities to that of Melanchthon's. Thus Aquinas, in his discussion of Natural Law, writes, 'praecepta legis naturae hoc modo se habent ad rationem practicam sicut principia prima demonstrationum se habent ad rationem speculativam; utraque enim sunt quaedam principia per se nota'. (*ST*. 1a 2ae. 94. 2.) cf. below p. 28 for another similar resemblance to Aquinas.

[20] 'Est enim in universum fallax humani captus iudicium propter cognatam caecitatem, ita ut etiamsi sint in animos nostros insculptae quaedam formae morum, tamen eae deprehendi vix possit.' (*CR*. 21, col. 117.)

[21] 'Quamquam autem naturae hominis quaedam legis notitia de Deo insita est, tamen haec ipsa notitia peccato originis aliqua ex parte obscurata est....' (*Romans, 1532*, p. 71.)

'Yet most prudently he makes the small addition, "God has revealed it to them"; for he means that these ideas, that "God exists," "God is good," "God is righteous," "God punishes the unrighteous," are divinely implanted in human minds. For although, as he states, the intellect is able to deduce something of God from a consideration of His wonderful works in the natural universe, yet reason would not have this syllogistic faculty if God had not also put into our minds some awareness and προληψιν. And those marvellous spectacles in the natural order are signs which stir our minds so as to think about God and to arouse that προληψιν.'[22]

We shall have frequent occasion to observe that the fundamental Reformation path to the natural knowledge of God is twofold, appealing to the idea of the deity innate in man and to the providential ordering of nature and history. Here Melanchthon unites the two in such a way as to permit reason to play its part in drawing conclusions from the latter on the basis of the former.

Having thus established the way in which the mind works he proceeds as his comment upon verse 20, 'For the invisible things of Him are known from the foundation of the world', to present a brief outline of some of those arguments for God's existence and attributes which were to play such a major role in subsequent treatments of this issue within Protestant theology:

'He dwells on a description of the natural knowledge of God, from those signs and evidences from which God may be known, namely from His marvellous works in the whole natural order. For at the same time we see those sure changes of movements, the seasons, the remarkable powers of living things coming into being, the outstanding discernment of the human mind and its power of understanding, likewise also in the social order, the preservation of governments amidst the great disturbances of human affairs, the punishment of wrongdoers, the pangs of conscience. These are all witnesses that God exists, that He is good, that He is righteous, that at some time He will sit in judgement.'[23]

---

[22] 'Prudentissime autem addit particulam "Deus manifestavit eis"; significat enim has notitias "Deus est", "Deus est bonus", "Deus est iustus", "Deus punit iniustos" divinitus insitas esse mentibus humanis. Quamquam enim, ut postea dicit, mens ratiocinatur aliquid de Deo ex consideratione mirabilium eius operum in universa natura rerum, tamen hinc syllogismum ratio non haberet, nisi etiam Deus quandam notitiam και προληψιν indidisset mentibus nostris. Et illa mirabilia spectacula rerum in natura sunt signa, quae commonefaciunt mentes, ut de Deo cogitent ac illam προληψιν excitent.' (*Ibid.*, pp. 71-2.) In view of the traces of similarity to Aquinas noted above, it is interesting to read the latter's comment on this phrase, 'quia quod notum est Dei, id est, quod cognoscibile est de Deo ab lumine per rationem, manifestum est in illis, id est, manifestum est eis ex quod in illis est, id est, ex lumine intrinseco.' (*In omnes D. Pauli Apostoli Epistolas Commentarii*, Vol. 1, Liège, 1857, p. 31.)

[23] 'Commoratur in descriptione notitiae naturalis de Deo, ex quibus signis et testimoniis cognoscatur Deus, videlicet ex mirabilibus operibus in tota natura rerum, cum enim

The immediate impression made by the list as compared, for example, with Aquinas's five ways, is the overwhelming emphasis on arguments drawn from human nature and history as opposed to those from the non-human natural order. This impression is reinforced in the more expanded exposition of these same arguments which Melanchthon gives in the next paragraph but one, since there it becomes apparent that the first argument, which was the only one to appeal to the latter of the two spheres, also derives its main impulse from the existence of the human mind.

> '...because we understand that this universal cosmic order and corruptible nature has some perpetual cause, yet not an unreasoning one, since otherwise the human mind would be more perfect than the very cause itself.'[24]

Melanchthon's final comment on this section is a reiteration of the way in which original sin weakens the effect of this natural knowledge:

> 'Furthermore, this natural knowledge is to some extent obscured by original sin. For the weakness of nature is now so great that it does not assent constantly to this knowledge, but allows it to be driven out from us.'[25]

Nonetheless the preceding section which contains that fuller exposition of the arguments referred to above makes a great deal of the part played by natural reason in coming to the necessary conclusions. Thus it begins,

> 'For in some manner reason naturally understands and possesses signs and arguments collected from God's works in the whole natural order.'

Then having made the point about the existence of the human mind which we have noted, proceeds, 'Hence we infer the existence of God, by whom the natural order was founded.' Again, the pangs of conscience suffered by murderers who need fear no official punishment, provides more food for thought, 'we conclude that God inspires such terrors'. Finally, it is the judgement of reason which, in the face of the world's injustices, rightly demands that there must be reparation hereafter to reward the good and

---

videmus istas certas vices motuum, temporum, rerum nascentium mirabiles vires, humanae mentis perspicaciam et intelligendi praestantiam, item res publicas, imperiorum conservationes in tantis tumultibus rerum humanarum, poenas sceleratorum, terrores conscientiae. Haec omnia sunt testimonia, quod sit Deus, quod sit bonus, quod sit iustus, quod aliquando iudicaturus sit etc.' (*Romans*, *1532*, p. 72.)

[24] '... quia intelligimus hanc universitatem rerum et corruptibilem naturam habere aliquam perpetuam causam, et quidem non brutam, quia alioqui mens humana perfectior esset quam illa ipsa causa.' (*Ibid.*, p. 73.)

[25] 'Porro haec naturalis notitia aliqua ex parte obscurata est a peccato originis. Nunc enim tanta est imbecillitas naturae, ut non constanter assentiatur huic notitiae, sed patiatur eam nobis excuti.' (*Ibid.*, p. 74.)

punish the evil, 'Likewise reason rightly judges that good men were not formed simply for perdition'.[26]

It is true that Luther himself not only allowed that man naturally possesses the knowledge of God's existence and of many of His attributes but that he also sees this as the possession of human reason. Thus in his commentary on the Book of Jonah, first published in 1526, Luther makes this very clear, 'That is as far as the natural light of reason sheds its rays—it regards God as kind, gracious, merciful and benevolent. And that is indeed a bright light'. Yet he immediately qualifies this by indicating the fundamental incapacity of natural reason to make any proper use of this knowledge, '... Reason ... knows that there is a God, but does not know who or which is the true God,'[27] and he goes on to talk of reason playing blindman's buff with God, making every attempt to grasp him but always unsuccessfully. It is, moreover, significant that Luther never developed any arguments of the sort advanced by Melanchthon and so we may fairly conclude that, having at one time actually lagged behind his master in recognizing the part played by natural reason in the knowledge of God, Melanchthon, at this stage goes beyond him.

The second major form of the *Loci Communes* was initiated by the greatly revised and enlarged edition published at Wittenberg in 1535 and here Melanchthon employs much the same arguments for God's existence. Although, for the first time, there was a locus 'De Deo'[28] they do not appear here in the place where the schoolmen would have treated them. Indeed at this point, Melanchthon, although allowing that there are traces of the natural knowledge of God, firmly circumscribes their effectiveness.

> 'For although there are some vestiges of the deity impressed on the natural order, yet so great is the weakness of men's minds that they are not affected enough by the signs.'[29]

[26] 'Haec enim *ratio* naturaliter aliquo modo intelligit et habet signa et argumenta collecta ex operibus Dei in tota rerum natura ... Hinc *ratiocinamur* Deum esse, a quo condita rerum natura ... *ratiocinamur* Deum incutere tales terrores ... Item recte iudicat *ratio*, ... homines bonos simpliciter ad perniciem conditos esse.' (*Ibid.*, p. 73.) The emphases are ours.

[27] 'So went reicht das naturlich liecht der vernunfft, das sie Gott fur ehnen gutigen, gnedigen, barmherzigen, milden achtet, das ist ehn gross liecht ... die vernunfft ... wens das Gott ist. Aber wer odder wilcher es seh, der da recht Gott hehft, das wens sie nicht.' (*WA*. 19, p. 206.)

[28] *CR*. 21. cols. 351-2. The 1521 edition had put this topic first in the list of its principal headings (capita) of theological matters but had stated immediately thereafter, 'Mysteria divinitatis rectius adoraverimus quam vestigaverimus. Immo sine magno periculo tantari non possunt ... Proinde non est cur multum operae ponamus in locis illis supremis, de deo, de unitate, de trinitate dei, de mysterio creationis, de modo incarnationis.' (*Ibid.*, col. 84.)

[29] 'Etsi enim vestigia quaedam divinitatis impressa rerum naturae, tamen tanta est infirmitas humanarum mentium, ut non satis afficiantur illis vestigiis.' (*Ibid.*, col. 351.)

Instead the arguments are presented under another new heading, 'de Creatione,' and the manner of their presentation is equally significant. Thus they do not appear in the traditional scholastic role as the prolegomena to revelation but, on the contrary, the Christian doctrine of creation[30] is first established from Scripture and only then are the arguments appended as a 'useful and pleasant' exercise,

> After the mind has been confirmed in the true and right opinion of God and of creation by the Word of God itself, it is then both useful and pleasant to seek out also the vestiges of God in nature and to collect the arguments which testify that there is a God.[31]

Again, having given his arguments, Melanchthon further indicates their uses and we may note that all of these are explicitly directed to the faithful.

> 'Now works must be presented to the faithful, first so that they may again increase that knowledge by God's Word, and next that they may make such knowledge brighter with the added signs which are impressed on nature.'[32]

Nonetheless and although there is no doubting the fundamental importance for Melanchthon of his conclusion, 'But yet this Philosophy must be ruled by God's Word,'[33] his brief consideration of the natural philosophy of antiquity leads him to a very positive statement of the degree of the natural knowledge of God attained by those pagan philosophers, such as Xenophon, who, in contradiction to the Epicureans, reasoned aright,

---

[30] Melanchthon is very keen to emphasize that this doctrine entails the notion of God's continuing providential rule of the universe. 'However, it is necessary to warn in this section that Creation must be so understood that God does not depart from His creation in the way that a craftsman leaves a completed house or ship. But God perpetually sustains and preserves the natural order. This understanding of creation is very necessary and appropriate to the faithful. Therefore in a section about creation the perpetual sustenance and preservation of nature is always to be understood.' 'Illud autem in hoc articulo monere necesse est, quod creatio sic intelligi debeat, quod Deus non discesserit a suo opificio, sicut faber discedit a domo facta aut fabricata nave. Sed Deus perpetuo sustentat et conservat naturas rerum. Hic intellectus creationis est necessarius et proprius piorum. Itaque in articulo de creatione semper intelligatur perpetua conservatio et sustentatio rerum.' (*Ibid.*, cols. 367-8.)

[31] 'Posteaquam autem mens confirmata est vera et recta sententia de Deo, de creatione, ex ipso verbo Dei; tunc et utile et iucundum est, etiam quaerere vestigia Dei in natura, et rationes colligere, quae testantur esse Deum.' (*Ibid.*, col. 369.)

[32] 'Nunc piis danda est opera, primum ut verbo Dei iterum accendant illam notitiam, deinde etiam reddant illustriorem, adhibitis signis, quae sunt impressa naturae.' (*Ibid.*, col. 370.)

[33] 'Sed tamen haec Philosophia regenda est verbo Dei.' (*Ibid.*)

'But nature itself brought others who philosophised correctly to this light so that they both knew that there is a God and maintained that this natural order is divinely ruled and preserved.'[34]

Attempts at enumerating the arguments in these early lists are somewhat arbitrary and have led at least one distinguished commentator into confusion. Thus the editor of the modern Gütersloh edition of the 1521 and 1559 *Loci*,[35] Hans Engelland, considers that the 1535 *Loci* contain only four proofs. In this opinion he may have been guided by an early reprinting of that work—Wittenberg, 1538—which sets out the text in short paragraphs which correspond with Engelland's numbering of the arguments.[36] When, however, some years later Engelland came to write the Introduction to the English translation of Melachthon's 1555 edition of the *Loci Communes*,[37] he appears to have changed his mind for, with reference to Melanchthon's 1532 *Commentary on Romans*, he says, 'Here for the first time we meet the proofs of God, but, as in the *Loci* of 1535, only the first six.'

With the publication of the second edition of the *Commentary on Romans* in 1540, Melanchthon presents for the first time a properly itemized list of arguments, nine in all. These occupy the same position in the commentary as in the earlier edition but are now introduced by a passage similar to that employed in the 1535 *Loci Communes*:

'Nor are so many traces of God impressed on nature in vain. Through these signs God wishes us to be admonished, He wishes them to be considered and their author recognized. Therefore the studious seek these traces, but in such a way that they observe a rule, namely God's word. Afterwards indeed, for the confirmation of good opinions, it is of great advantage to hold true arguments fixed in the mind which testify that God is the creator and sustainer of the natural order.'[38]

---

[34] 'At alios qui recte philosophati sunt, natura ipsa deduxit ad hanc lucem, ut et agnoverint esse Deum, et hanc naturam regi et conservari divinitus contenderint.' (*Ibid.*, col. 370.)

[35] *Melanchthons Werke in Auswahl*, Band II, Teil 1, Gütersloh, 1952, p. 220.

[36] The 1536 (n.p.) edition has the same, much less frequent, paragraph divisions as *CR*. cols. 367-70.

[37] *Melanchthon on Christian Doctrine: Loci Communes 1555*, Trans. and ed. C. L. Manschreck, New York, 1965, p. xxvi.

[38] 'Nec frustra impressa sunt naturae tot vestigia Dei. Admoneri nos Deus vult per has notas, vult eas considerari et agnosci autorem. Ideo studiosi quaerant haec vestigia, sed ita, ut tamen regulam teneant, scilicet verbum Dei. Postea profecto ad confirmandas bonas opiniones, multum prodest tenere infixas animo veras rationes quae testantur esse Deum conditorem et conservatorem rerum.' (*CR*. 15, cols. 565-6.)

With the exception of the last two which make their first appearance here, the arguments are expanded versions of the earlier ones and it is still the case that they are drawn predominantly from the realm of human nature and history. Thus the first three are drawn from the human mind and its capacities,

> 'First ... the human mind ... Second, the distinction between good and evil known naturally to the human mind ... Third ... the knowledge innate in the human mind, both that there is a God and that He punishes evil deeds.'[39]

Even the fourth argument, 'From the order of things in the whole of nature', having referred to the various non-human phenomena which evidence this, quickly returns to man's mental ability by way of his body, 'What of the arrangement of the individual parts in the human body? What of the very recognition of number and order?'[40] Arguments five to eight all concern themselves with evidence from human history,

> 'Fifth ... Concerns the consideration of order and the consideration of political order ... Sixth. From the punishments of murderers and the preservation and destruction of empires ... Seventh. From the predictions of future events ... Eighth. Heroic activities.'[41]

When eventually at the end of the list we do, for the first time, encounter a typically scholastic physical argument,—that from causality to first cause expressed largely in terms of an appeal from motion to first mover, —Melanchthon feels obliged to put it firmly in its place in relation to the others:

> 'This argument is treated at length in Physics and is sound enough, but the previous ones are much clearer, those which are drawn from the nature of the mind, from the distinction between good and evil, and from the order in nature and society. Those indeed, which not only show that God is the creator but also the vindicator, invite us to the fear of God.'[42]

---

[39] 'Primum ... mens humana ... Secundum, Discrimen honestorum et turpium naturaliter notum est humanae menti ... Tertium ... utraque noticia insita est menti humanae, et quod sit Deus, et quod scelera puniat.' (*Ibid.*, col. 566.)

[40] 'Ab ordine rerum in tota natura ... Quid in corporum humano partium singularum distributio? Quid ipsa numeri et ordinis agnitio?' (*Ibid.*, cols. 566-7.)

[41] 'Quintum. Ad ordinis considerationem pertinet et politici ordinis consideratio ... Sextum. A poenis homicidarum et conservatione ac eversione imperiorum ... Septimum. A significationibus rerum futurarum ... Octavum. Heroici motus ...' (*Ibid.*, col. 577.)

[42] 'Hoc argumentum in physicis prolixe tractatur, et satis firmum est: sed superiora sunt magis illustria, quae a natura mentis, a discrimine honestorum et turpium, ab ordine in natura et societate sumta sunt: quae quidem testantur non solum opificem esse Deum, sed etiam vindicem, nosque ad timorem Dei invitant.' (*Ibid.*, col. 568.)

We noted in the *Loci* this concern to present God's providential ordering of the world as an essential part of His creative activity. This concern is now explicitly related to the arguments for God's existence and evidently plays a considerable part in determining what type of argument will be employed.

The third and final Latin edition of the *Loci*, now entirely rewritten and four times the size of the original work, first appeared at Wittenberg in 1543-4.[43] The article 'De Creatione' was considerably enlarged[44] and much of this expansion is accounted for by that desire of Melanchthon's to establish God's Providence which we observed in the 1535 edition. Once again he uses the simile of the ship-builder:

> 'Human weakness, even if it considers that God is the creator, yet it afterwards imagines that, just as a craftsman goes away from a completed ship and leaves it to the sailors, so God goes away from His handiwork and leaves His creatures merely to their own direction.'[45]

In particular, he mentions the doubts entertained by the Stoics and Epicureans on this score, concluding:

> 'Minds are to be strengthened against these doubts by reflection on the true article about creation, and it must be established not only that things are formed by God but also that their substances are perpetually preserved and sustained by Him.'[46]

The bulk of the case for the existence and nature of God's Providence is drawn from Scripture and Melanchthon does not stint the quotations from both Old and New Testaments. Thus he begins the article by explaining that, although he will be tracing the evidence for God to be seen in nature, yet he must first direct attention to the testimonies afforded by God's supernatural activity:

> 'However, although this contemplation of the natural universe reminds us about God, ... yet at the outset let us again direct our mind and eyes to all the testimonies in which God has revealed Himself to the church.'[47]

---

[43] The 1559 edition of this version, the last to appear in Melanchthon's lifetime, entitled, *Loci Praecipui Theologici* is given in *Melanchthons Werke in Auswahl*, Vol. II (ed. H. Engelland) Part 1, 1952, pp. 164-352 and part 2, 1953. There is no change in the nine arguments. See Pt. 1, pp. 220-3. See also *CR*. 21, cols. 602-1106.

[44] *CR. 21*, cols. 637-43.

[45] 'Infirmitas humana, etiamsi cogitat Deum esse conditorem, tamen postea imaginatur, ut faber discedit a navi extructa et relinquit eam nautis, ita Deum discedere a suo opere, et relinqui creaturas tantum propriae gubernationi.' (*Ibid.*, col. 638.)

[46] 'Adversus has dubitationes confirmandae sunt mentes cogitatione vera articuli de creatione, ac statuendum est, non solum conditas esse res a Deo, sed etiam perpetuo servari ac sustenari a Deo rerum substantias.' (*Ibid.*)

[47] 'Quanquam autem haec consideratio universae naturae admonet nos de Deo, ... tamen

The arguments for God's existence are introduced by a slightly expanded version of that section which we observed fulfilling the role in the 1535 *Loci*. Once again, no stronger motive for the exercise is given than, 'But it is useful for good minds to grasp some proofs which demonstrate that there is a God.'[48] As in the case of the 1540 *Commentary on Romans*, nine arguments are presented though they are not quite the same ones. The demonstration from the order observable in nature regains the first place which it had occupied before the latter work, whilst that from the human mind once more comes second. The ability to discern between good and evil follows next and then comes an appeal to the innate knowledge of God's existence which Melanchthon now sees as needing support from the other arguments:

> 'Fourthly: natural ideas are true: all confess naturally that there is a God, therefore this idea is true. This minor premise would be clearer if nature were not corrupt, but it must be confirmed by the other arguments which I have set out'.[49]

The pangs of conscience provide the evidence for the fifth argument whilst the sixth appeals to the preservation of civilized society in such a way as to unite arguments five and six of the earlier series. Argument seven is that from efficient causality and is set out in a more philosophically adept form than the rather muddled version encountered before.

> 'The seventh is erudite, drawn from the series of efficient causes. There is no infinite recession of efficient causes, therefore it is necessary to come to a halt at one first cause. Physics expounds the argument clearly. For if there were an infinite recession there would be no order of causes and no causes would be necessarily connected together.'[50]

For the first time, as number eight, another physical argument is employed:

> 'The eighth from final causes. In nature all things are fixed for definite uses. It is impossible that this arrangement of purposes came into being or con-

nos referamus initio mentem et oculos ad omnia testimonia, in quibus se Deus Ecclesiae patefecit ...' (*Ibid.*, col. 637.)

[48] 'Sed bonis mentibus utile est tenere aliquas demonstrationes quae ostendunt esse Deum.' (*Ibid.*, col. 641.) Cf. above p. 20.

[49] 'Quarta: Notitiae naturales sunt verae; Esse Deum naturaliter omnes fatentur; Ergo haec notitia vera est. Haec minor esset illustrior, si natura non esset corrupta, sed confirmanda est ceteris argumentis, quae recitavi.' (*Ibid.*, col. 642.)

[50] 'Septima est erudita, sumpta a serie caussarum efficientium. Non est processus in infinitum in caussis efficientibus; Ergo necesse est resistere in una prima caussa. Hanc rationem Physici dilucide explicant. Nam si esset progressus in infinitum, nullus esset ordo caussarum et nullae caussae necessario cohaererent.' (*Ibid.*, cols. 642-3.)'

tinues to exist by chance, but it must have been created by the design of an architect.'[51]

Finally the argument from the prediction of future events closes the list. One argument of the earlier series, that appealing to heroic actions, is now omitted and so the balance between the human and non-human spheres is slightly redressed, especially since the qualification about physical arguments expressed before now no longer appears.

In the 'epilogue' to the list Melanchthon again emphasizes that, 'These arguments not only testify that there is a God but are also evidences of providence,'[52] and finally directs us once more to the more powerful testimonies of scriptural revelation.

> 'Let us turn back to the first admonition, namely, that minds and eyes must continuously be alert to those special testimonies in which God has revealed Himself to the church.'[53]

Melanchthon did not suppose that his list of arguments was exhaustive but that he had chosen the most effective, 'Many others also could certainly be collected, but because they are more obscure I pass over them.'[54] His satisfaction with this choice is confirmed by their verbatim reproduction in his *Initia Doctrinae Physicae*, first published at Wittenberg in 1549. It may seem strange that a textbook on physics should begin with a 'De Deo' section but, as we noted in the 1535 edition of the *Loci*, Melanchthon was convinced of the necessary connection between good physics and the tracing of God in nature,

> 'And many traces of the deity present themselves to those who investigate and contemplate nature studiously and philosophize wisely. The Epicureans became atheists because they falsified Physics.'[55]

At first sight the inclusion of the arguments under the 'De Deo' heading might seem to indicate a reversal to their traditional scholastic setting. However, when we consider the subject matter of the work as a whole we

---

[51] 'Octava a caussis finalibus. Omnes res in natura destinatae sunt ad certas utilitates. Hanc distributionem finium impossibile est aut extitisse casu aut casu manere, sed necesse est consilio architecti factam esse.' (*Ibid.*, col. 643.)

[52] 'Haec argumenta non solum testantur esse Deum, sed etiam sunt indicia providentiae.' (*Ibid.*)

[53] 'Nos ad primam admonitionem redeamus, videlicet, Assidue mentibus atque oculis intuenda esse illa peculiaria testimonia, in quibus se Deus Ecclesiae patefecit.' (*Ibid.*)

[54] 'Possent et multa alia vere quidem colligi, sed quia sunt obscuriora, relinquo.' (*Ibid.*)

[55] 'Et plura offerent se vestigia divinitatis his, qui studiose inquirunt et considerant naturam, et prudenter philosophantur. Epicuraei facti sunt ἄθεοι, quia corruperunt Physicen.' (*Ibid.*, col. 370.)

can appreciate that for Melanchthon they remain essentially part of the topic, 'De Creatione.'

He begins by making the familiar distinction between the Law and the Gospel, emphasizing that any knowledge of God obtainable from physics comes into the former category, 'Here I warn my audience that the physical knowledge of God is knowledge of the law not of the Gospel.'[56] The predominance of the arguments' appeal to human nature and history is again forcefully underlined in this case by the maintenance of the favourable proportion of the former over against the physical even in this new context which is, on the face of it, the latter's domain. As Melanchthon himself declares, 'The whole of nature has been created to bear witness to God and especially the human race.'[57]

Again and again we have observed his concern to establish the doctrine of God's Providence and we have further noted that this has had a considerable effect upon his choice of arguments for God's existence. In this work Melanchthon follows the 'De Deo' section with a separate one, headed 'De providentia,' and here presents five of his earlier arguments to prove the existence of Providence. 'I have set out above the arguments which prove that there is a God. Many of these are also proofs of providence and demonstrate that God has a care for mankind.'[58] The first of these appeals to the order observable in nature, the second to the human mind's knowledge that God requires obedience to the moral order. The third looks to the phenomenon of the divine punishment of crimes and the fourth to that of heroic deeds, whilst the last one appeals to the prediction of future events. The status of these arguments is clearly expressed in his conclusion to them:

> 'I have recounted arguments, of which some are clearer than others, but yet some are so firm that they cannot be overthrown. Let us indeed add the surest testimonies from the Church's teaching. For without these the human assent is utterly feeble.'[59]

---

[56] 'Hinc praemoneo auditores, physicam de Deo noticiam, esse legis noticiam non Evangelii.' (*CR*. 13. col. 198.)

[57] 'Tota natura condita est ut dicat testimonium de Deo, ac praecipue genus humanum.' (*Ibid.*)

[58] 'Recitavi autem supra argumenta, quae demonstrant esse Deum. Horum pleraque etiam testimonia sunt de providentia, et ostendunt Deo curae esse humana.' (*Ibid.*, col. 204.)

[59] 'Recensui argumenta, quorum alia magis, alia minus illustria sunt, sed tamen quaedam ita firma sunt, ut labefactari non possint. Nos vero ex doctrina Ecclesiae adiungamus testimonia certissima. Nam sine his assensio humana admodum languida est.' (*Ibid.*, col. 205.)

For Melanchthon the twin issues of the existence of God and the existence of God's Providence are inextricably interwoven. Thus, although he here sets out a separate list of arguments for the latter, this brief examination of them has indicated clearly enough that they are entirely dependent upon those arguments for the former with which we have become so familiar.

What then are we to make of Melanchthon's arguments for the existence of God and how far is he guilty of the charge of having taken Reformation theology back to the Natural Theology of the Schools? When the arguments first appear in the 1532 *Commentary on Romans* they do so without any apology or explanation simply as part of the exegesis of Chapter 1, verse 20, 'The invisible things of Him are known from the foundation of the world' and as such indicate the degree and kind of knowledge of God that is within the grasp of fallen and unredeemed mankind; indeed, the ground has been prepared for their introduction by Melanchthon's treatment of the preceding verse where this knowledge is explicitly stated to be of the Law and not of the Gospel.

As we have observed above, the form and content of the arguments have largely been determined by Melanchthon's prior conviction, expressed as early as the 1522 *Annotationes*, 'That God exists is known by the law of nature' and reiterated in 1532 as a comment on verse 19, 'For he adduces the law of nature, namely the natural knowledge of God'. This overwhelming influence of the ethical strain in the arguments continues to operate even though, in conformity with their explicit connection with Romans 1, 20, they appear under the heading, 'De Creatione,' in the editions of the *Loci* from 1535 onwards. It is true that first one, then a second, purely physical argument is added to the list in 1540 and 1543 respectively, but even in their setting at the start of a text book on Physics they retain the greater part of their original complexion.

In a brief reference to Melanchthon's introduction of arguments for the existence of God, Hans Engelland confesses to being somewhat at a loss to account for their purpose:

> 'Perhaps it was a defence against the enthusiasts, with their doctrine of the Spirit apart from the word, or an ethical-pedagogical interest over against their hostility to education, or perhaps a demand for a starting point for the proclamation of the gospel or for the study of the ancient philosophers, or perhaps all these motives combined.'[60]

---

[60] C. L. Manschreck, *op. cit.*, pp. xxxvi-vii.

In view of the later use to which Melanchthon's arguments were often put, it is important to note that he himself never cast them in an apologetic role. From 1535, when they are first accorded some sort of prolegomena, they are always said to be for the confirmation of the right mind of the faithful and are never addressed to unbelievers. Nonetheless, they were always assigned to the sphere of the law and must therefore be regarded as within the scope of natural human ability in which it is evident that reason is allowed a degree of usefulness unprecedented in Reformation theology, so much so that a modern scholar can say of these arguments, 'we are still suspiciously near to Thomas Aquinas when we survey Melanchthon's catalogue of the "iudicia providentiae" in the chapter of the *Loci* "de creatione."'[61] Mention of Aquinas suggests that we compare his view of natural reason in this context with that of Melanchthon. In our account of the latter's earlier teaching on the Natural Law we noted his division between the practical and speculative principles and we referred to a similar division made in the same connection by Aquinas. Looking more closely at their handling of this point, we can see that both are concerned to show that a greater degree of certainty attaches to the theoretical, but the reason they give for this is significantly different. Thus for Aquinas the lack of certainty in practical matters is inherent and essentially due to the fact that men are here operating in the field of the contingent:

> 'Now a characteristic of reason is to proceed from common principles to particular conclusions: this is remarked in the *Physics*. However, the theoretical and the practical reason set about this somewhat differently. The business of the theoretical reason is with natural truths that cannot be otherwise, and so without mistake it finds truth in the particular conclusions it draws as in the premises it starts from. Whereas the business of the practical reason is with contingent matters which are the domain of human acts, and although there is some necessity in general principles the more we get down to particular cases the more we can be mistaken.'[62]

It is true that towards the end of this article St. Thomas does indicate that human sinfulness may have some part to play in furthering this state of affairs but its effects are by no means universal:

---

[61] F. Hildebrandt, *Melanchthon: Alien or Ally?*, Cambridge, 1946, p. 25. 'Iudicia providentiae' is surely a misprint for 'indicia'. See *CR*. 21, col. 643.

[62] 'Ad rationem autem pertinet ex communibus ad propria procedere, ut patet ex *Physic*. Aliter tamen circa hoc se habet ratio speculativa et aliter practica: quia enim ratio speculativa praecipue negotiatur circa necessaria, quae impossibile est aliter se habere, absque aliquo defectu invenitur veritas in conclusionibus propriis sicut et in principiis communibus. Sed ratio practica negotiatur circa contingentia, in quibus sunt operationes humanae; et ideo, si in communibus sit aliqua necessitas, quanto magis ad propria descenditur tanto magis invenitur defectus.' (*ST*., 1a. 2ae. 94.4.)

'To sum up: as for its first common principles, here natural law is the same for all in requiring a right attitude towards it as well as recognition. As for particular specific points, which are like conclusions drawn from common principles, here also natural law is the same for most people in their feeling for and awareness of what is right. Nevertheless in fewer cases either the desire or the information may be wanting. The desire to do right may be blocked by particular factors ... and the knowledge also of what is right may be distorted by passion or bad custom or even by racial proclivity;'[63]

If now we turn to Melanchthon's discussion under the heading 'Of the Law of Nature' in the 1544 edition of the *Loci*, we see that the practical principles are less certain than the speculative entirely owing to the Fall, apart from which they would be equally clear and evident.

'As light is set in the eyes by divine influence so are certain ideas put into human minds by which they recognize and determine most things. Philosophers call this light knowledge of the principles, "common thoughts" and "a priori principles". Moreover, a division is commonly made; on the one hand there are the speculative principles, such as the ideas of numbers, of order, of the syllogism, the principles of geometry and physics. All agree that these are most certain and are sources of the greatest usefulness in life ... On the other hand, there are the practical principles, such as the entire natural distinction between good and evil, also, that God is to be obeyed. Now these practical principles ought certainly to be as clear and as strong for us as are the ideas of numbers, however, since on account of the Fall a certain dullness has taken over, the heart has impulses contrary to the distinction between good and evil, so that men do not constantly assent to such ideas as that God should be obeyed, adultery is to be avoided, honorable agreements must be observed, in the same manner as to the knowledge that twice four is eight.'[64]

---

[63] 'Sic igitur dicendum est quod lex naturae, quantum ad prima principia communia, est eadem apud omnes et secundum rectitudinem et secundum notitiam. Sed quantum ad quaedam propria, quae sunt quasi conclusiones principiorum communium, est eadem apud omnes ut in pluribus et secundum rectitudinem et secundum notitiam. Sed ut in paucioribus potest deficere et quantum ad rectitudinem, propter aliqua particularia impedimenta ... etiam quantum ad notitiam, et hoc propter hoc qiod aliqui habent depravatam rationem ex passione, seu ex mala consuetudine, seu ex mala habitudine naturae;' (*Ibid.*)

[64] 'Ut lumen oculis divinitus inditum est; ita sunt quaedam notitiae mentibus humanis inditae, quibus agnoscunt et iudicant pleraque. Philosophi hoc lumen vocant notitiam principiorum, vocant κοιvας ἐννοιας et πρoληψεις. Ac vulgo divisio nota est, alia esse principia speculabilia, ut notitias numerorum, ordinis, syllogismi, principia Geometrica, Physica. Haec omnes fatentur esse certissima et fontes maximarum utilitatum in vita ... Alia sunt principia practica, ut totum discrimen naturale honestorum et turpium. Item, Deo est obediendum. Ac debebant quidem haec practica principia tam illustria nobis esse et firma, quam sunt notitiae numerorum; tamen quia propter labem originis accessit quaedam caligo et cor habet contrarios impetus discrimen honestorum et turpium, ideo homines non tam constanter assentiuntur his notitiis, Deo obediendum est, Adulterium est vitandum, Honesta pacta sunt servanda: sicut huic notitiae, Bis quatuor sunt octo.' (*CR*. 21, cols. 711-12.)

So far then we must say that Melanchthon's adherence to the Reformation insistence on the severity of the effects of the Fall distinguishes him from Aquinas. When, however, he proceeds straightway to assert the continuing existence of much of this natural knowledge of God in fallen man, he does not do so in order to fulfil the purpose of the typical Reformation theologian who would allow such knowledge only to ensure the inexcusability of man's sinfulness.[65] Instead Melanchthon presents the natural light struggling with errors;

> '... Notwithstanding that the true knowledge has been impressed on men that God is one, a certain eternal mind, the creator and preserver of things, wise, good, just, etc. and that this God is to be obeyed along with the distinction between good and evil, yet these true ideas ... are held captive, they are not in control but unrighteousness is in command, conflicting with these ideas, namely a turning of the will away from God ... in short, various impulses are struggling with the light divinely planted in our minds.'[66]

It would appear that the embattled natural light requires assistance in order that the practical principles regain their erstwhile parity with the theoretical and so it is that he proceeds immediately to an exhortation that it be so strengthened, presumably, though he does not say so, by resources stemming from the revealed Gospel:

> 'The divine light in our minds is not to be quenched, but is rather to be kindled and the soul strengthened so that it recognizes the practical principles, esteems them and indeed establishes them as being as certain and as strong as are the speculative, yea rather that they are as God's immutable decrees.'[67]

---

[65] Interestingly enough as early as 1525, when Melanchthon's views on the topic had yet to develop many of the more positive features to which we have drawn attention, he was attacked by Bullinger for his failure on precisely this point. Susi Hausammann upholds the validity of Bullinger's criticism, stating that Paul's intention in the Roman's passages cited in support of the existence of any natural knowledge of God was just that recognized by the Reformation insight and no more. 'Melanchthon aber hat weder in den Loci noch in den Annotationes diesen Skopus der Aussage der Apostels festgehalten. Damit redet er aber in einer Weise von Naturgesetz und natürlicher Erkenntnis Gottes, die vom Paulinischen Text her nicht gedeckt ist. Und genau, den Punkt trifft Bullinger haarscharf in seinem ersten Vorwurf ... Die Kritik ... trifft Melanchthon voll.' (S. Hausammann, *Römerbriefauslegung zwischen Humanismus und Reformation: eine Studie zu Heinrich Bullingers Römerbriefvorlesung von 1525*, Zurich, 1970, p. 254).

[66] '... etsi impressa est hominibus vera notitia, quod sit Deus una quaedam aeterna mens, conditrix et conservatrix rerum, sapiens, bona, iusta etc. et quod huic Deo obediendum sit iuxta discrimen honestorum et turpium, tamen hae verae notitiae ... capitivae tenentur, non regnant, sed regnat iniustitia pugnans cum his notitiis, scilicet aversio voluntatis a Deo ... denique varii impetus pugnantes cum lumine divinitus insito mentibus.' (*CR*. 21, col. 712.)

[67] 'Lumen divinum in mentibus non extinguendum est, sed potius excitandum, et confirmandus animus, ut agnoscat principia practica, eaque amplectatur et statuat revera tam certa et firma esse, quam sunt speculabilia, imo pariter esse decreta immutabilia Dei.' (*Ibid.*)

The very positive evaluation made here of the natural light and the fervent exhortation that it be sustained and improved indicates that, of the purposes suggested by Engelland, the ethical-pedagogical was the one which was to the forefront of Melanchthon's concern.

Clements Bauer's excellent study[68] of Melanchthon's teaching on the subject of natural law concludes:

> 'Melanchthon's development from the conception of natural law in the first version of the *Loci Communes* with its still critical and relatival character to the positive and systematic theory of natural law in the final version of the *Loci Communes* and in the *Ethicae doctrinae elementa* marks the way over a penetrating study of the works of Aristoteles and Cicero in the second and third decades of the sixteenth century. Step by step a theory of natural law is developed in the commentaries on and annotations to Aristotle's *Ethics* and *Politics* and Cicero's *Officia*—which is then connected with the further development of Melanchthon's theology with its renewed assertion of the elements of natural cognisance of the divine.'[69]

Nonetheless Bauer is well aware that, although for Melanchthon the natural law is clearly recognizable by natural reason, the effects of the Fall have weakened man's ability to assent to it.[70] In conclusion Bauer makes the important observation that Melanchthon's final system represents such an assimilation of Aristotelian thought as to mark the beginning of the second epoch of the Christianization of the Greek philosopher in the history of Western thought which, although very similar to the doctrine of High Scholasticism, is the result of Melanchthon's own intensive study of Aristotle's Ethics and Politics and their development by Cicero.[71]

As the conclusion to his presentation of the arguments for God's existence in the 'De Deo' section of his text book on Physics, Melanchthon has a paragraph which brings together much of what we have been observing about his view of the natural knowledge of God and his purpose in presenting arguments of this kind.

> 'It is useful to reflect upon these arguments often, for they confirm the worthy opinion established in good minds that there is a God and that He is not indifferent but does care for mankind. For although in the church much clearer testimonies are displayed in which God has manifestly revealed Himself, yet the consideration of these philosophical proofs is useful for they confirm good men and at the same time show up the weakness of the human mind. In other questions, such as in arithmetic or geometry, once convinced by very strong

[68] 'Melanchthons Naturrechtslehre' in *'Archiv für Reformationsgeschichte'*, Vol. 4, 1951, pp. 64-100.

[69] Bauer, *op. cit.*, p. 99.

[70] *Ibid.*, p. 98.

[71] *Ibid.*, pp. 93, 98.

> proof we give our assent. In this question about God, although we see that the proofs are true and strong, yet our assent is feeble. However, this weakness is to be deplored and is to be corrected.'[72]

How clearly does the authentic voice of the pedagogue ring out in that final phrase! However, such an emphasis upon the natural light can hardly fail to lead to a shift in the Reformation position on this issue. True, Melanchthon stresses the necessity for revelation to effect its restitution, but then no one doubted this, not even the most fervent exponent of scholastic Natural Theology, and it is the positive evaluation of the light of nature which remains as the predominant impression of his teaching.

Thus whilst we may accept C. L. Manschreck's argument that 'Melanchthon saw a redirection of reason, brought about by conversion, as the answer to the notion that reason should be abandoned,'[73] when he goes on to assert that, 'this basic orientation which centred in conversion is the clue to the "changes," the "rationalism," the "synergism," that came into the thought of Melanchthon. They were not really changes, but rather keener apprehensions of the place of reason in the Christian life,'[74] two comments are called for. First, it seems impossible to deny the term 'changes' to describe the movement of Melanchthon's thought which resulted from the 'keener apprehension of the place of reason in the Christian life.' Second, this much more positive evaluation of reason, although formally confined to its function in the Christian life, led to a much greater appreciation of the *natural* reason. Certainly for the latter to benefit properly from the arguments for the existence of God it had to be converted to the Christian Gospel but its status, quite apart from any such conversion, had evidently already been greatly exalted. If Melanchthon thus escapes the charge of rationalism he can hardly fail but be seen as one of the sources from which this soon emerged.

Another scholar[75] who defends Melanchthon against the charge of being false to his original Evangelical experience in admitting Natural Theology

[72] 'Haec argumenta saepe cogitare prodest, confirmant enim honestam sententiam in bonis mentibus statuentem et esse Deum, et non ociosum esse sed curare humanum genus. Etsi enim in Ecclesia multo illustriora testimonia proposita sunt, in quibus se Deus evidenter patefecit, tamen et harum philosophicarum demonstrationem consideratio utilis est, quae et bonos confirmat, et simul ostendit imbecillitatem humanae mentis. In alliis quaestionibus, ut in arithmetica aut geometrica convicti demonstratione firmissime adsentimur. In hac quaestione de Deo, etiamsi videmus demonstrationes veras et firmas esse, tamen languida est assensio. Deploranda est autem haec imbecillitas et corrigenda.' (*CR*. 13, col. 202.)

[73] 'Reason and Conversion in the Thought of Melanchthon' in *Reformation Studies: Essays in Honour of R. H. Bainton*, ed. F. H. Littel, Richmond, 1962, p. 169.

[74] *Op. cit.*, p. 177.

[75] F. Hübner, *Naturliche Theologie und theokratische Schwärmerei bei Melanchthon*, Gütersloh, 1936.

into the circles of Reformation thought, argues that the latter avoids this snare by maintaining a firm distinction between Law and Gospel.[76] In Hübner's view Melanchthon's proofs of God's existence and providence are not really proofs but are rather testimonies which confirm the revelation through the Word.[77] Although, as our own survey has established, we may agree that Melanchthon has indeed thus surrounded his presentation of the arguments with lengthy warnings as to the necessary limitations of the knowledge thus acquired, yet by his introduction of them he opens the door to their reproduction without the qualifications with which he hedges them about. The bulk of his arguments, with their concentration upon human nature and history, may be less prone to such revisionist treatment, but his two physical arguments are straightforward versions of scholastic proofs which, having been employed in their traditional role for centuries, stood ready to relapse to their former use with the minimum of encouragement. Hübner's own warning, at the conclusion of his work,[78] is that as soon as the 'either-or' of reason and revelation becomes a 'both,' the way to Natural Theology lies open and that even if today reason is held in check, tomorrow it may break out and take control. Melanchthon undoubtedly himself preserves the 'either-or' but, by advancing the status of reason to the degree that he does, he has helped pave the way for the rationalism that was to follow.

It would, however, be a great mistake to conclude that this was the only effect of Melanchthon's teaching on the topic. His thought embraced a wide range of elements of varying degrees of compatibility; classical and biblical humanism, Evangelical biblicism, and that distinctive blend of Ciceronian Stoicism and Aristotelianism to which Bauer has so clearly drawn our attention. Subsequent Protestant theologians were wont to take from Melanchthon whatever suited their own particular bent. Thus whilst Ursinus, who as we shall see, was the main channel for the dissemination of Melanchthon's arguments for the existence of God, marks a stage further on the road to rationalism, at the end of our period we encounter Coccejus[79] who is just as much Melanchthon's heir but who highlights other equally important elements in the latter's arguments, concentrating entirely on those which centre upon human nature and history together with an even greater emphasis upon those drawn from revelation.

---

[76] Hübner, *op. cit.*, pp. 61-3.

[77] *Ibid.*, pp. 61-3.

[78] *Ibid.*, p. 145.

[79] See below, pp.

CHAPTER THREE

# ABRIDGEMENTS OF CALVIN'S 'INSTITUTES'

Of all the influences which served to keep Reformed theology in line with the teaching of Calvin none was more direct or more powerful than that of the *Institutes* itself which appeared no less than thirteen times in three different versions of a Dutch translation between 1560 and 1650.[1] However, we have to reckon with the effect not only of the original work but also of the various abridgements of it which were early on the scene and of which some were so popular that they went through many editions and were themselves sometimes translated into the vernacular.[2] These repay study because they enable us to see how Calvin was being understood and his teaching handed on by his later followers.

In the article just cited Warfield gives details of one of the earliest of such works whose popularity in Holland carried over into the seventeenth century and indeed beyond, Guillaume Delaune's *Abridgement of the Institutes of Christian Religion composed by John Calvin. In which answers are set down to the objections of opponents.*[3] According to Warfield, Delaune, a Huguenot refugee and pastor of the French church in London, 'stood in close relations with Holland and had been vainly sought as a professor at Leiden.'[4] Hence, presumably, the Dutch translation which was published at Amsterdam in 1594 and was reprinted in 1611, 1650, 1739 and 1837.[5]

Delaune's epitome is a very competent, straightforward abridgement of the *Institutes* in which the voice of Calvin suffers no distortion. Even at the points where Delaune employs the device of an objection and an answer, the master's words are still faithfully reproduced. Thus, for example, at the conclusion of Chapter 5 of the first book:

---

[1] See B. B. Warfield - 'On The Literary History of Calvin's *Institutes*' in *Calvin and Calvinism*, pp. 373-428.

[2] For a brief but useful account of these abridgements see J. T. McNeill's Introduction to the LCC edition of the *Institutes*, pp. xlviii-l.

[3] *Institutionis Christianae Religionis a Joanne Calvino Conscriptae, Epitome. In qua adversariorum obiectionibus breviter ac solidae responsiones annotantur*. London, 1583, second edition 1584, English translation, Edinburgh, 1585, reprinted 1586 and 1587.

[4] *Op. cit.*, pp. 405-6. In the absence of any reference in support of this statement, we must assume that Warfield is dependent here, as he evidently is at several points, upon the article by C. Sepp, 'Voor de Letterkundige Geschiedenis van Calvyn's *Institutio,' Bibliographische Mededeelingen*, Leiden, 1883, pp. 88-109.

[5] *Institute ofte onderwijsinghe in de Christelijke religie, uittreksel door G. Delaunay.* Cf. A. Erichson, *Bibliographia Calviniana*, Berlin, 1900, pp. 41, 45, 52 and 55.

> 'Obiect. If we want naturall power, so that we can not clime up unto the pure and manifest knowledge of God; we shall be holden excused if we worship not God as we ought. An. All colour of excuse is cut off because the fault of so great dulnesse is within us, neither can we so pretend ignorance, but that even our verie conscience shall alwayes convince us both of sluggishness and unthankefulness.'[6]

accurately renders Calvin's opening sentence which itself effectively conveys the substance of this final section:

> 'But although we lack the natural ability to mount up unto the pure and clear knowledge of God, all excuse is cut off because the fault of dullness is within us. And, indeed, we are not allowed thus to pretend ignorance without our conscience itself always convicting us of both baseness and ingratitude.'[7]

However, as Warfield reminds us, 'Calvin intended the *Institutes* (in its later form) as a textbook in theology. It quickly took its place as such, not only among the students at Geneva, but throughout the Reformed world.'[8] Hence the rest of the abridgements we shall consider had all served as the means of a professor's course of instruction which he then published as an aid to other teachers and students. The first of these we have already mentioned, Caspar Olevianus's *Abridgement of the Institutes of Christian Religion, chosen from John Calvin's Institutes and retaining the author's arrangement and his words*, which appeared at Herborn in 1586 and, as its title proclaims, abridged Calvin in his own words. The degree of the reduction achieved may be judged when it is considered that in the first book, Chapter 3 is condensed into the space of one octavo page and Chapter 5 into that of five, which is precisely the same as in Delaune's abridgement. The established popularity of this latter was probably one reason why Olevianus's *Epitome* was not reprinted: another was surely the appearance soon afterwards at Herborn of a rather different work which had an enormous success and whose direct influence we shall have frequent cause to comment upon in our examination of subsequent Dutch works on the knowledge of God. This was Johannes Piscator's *Aphorisms of Christian Doctrine drawn for the most part from Calvin's Institutes, or Theological*

---

[6] *An Abridgement of the Institution of Christian Religion*, Edinburgh, 1585, pp. 12-13.

[7] *Institutes*, I. v. 15. *LCC*, pp. 68-9.

[8] *Op. cit.*, p. 403. Warfield goes on to mention that 'Kaspar Olevianus at Heidelberg and Herborn based his theological lectures upon it, going over one book each year and thus completing the course in four years.' In fact, we learn from Olevianus's dedicatory preface to Beza that he devoted only one term to each book, thus completing the whole each year. '... ut singulis trimestibus librum unum possem summatim interpretari: atque ita quotannis religionis Christianae summam absoluere.' *Institutionis Christianae Religionis Epitome. Ex Institutione Johannis Calvini excerpta, authoris methodo et verbis retentis*. pp. 3r-v. For Olevianus, see *PRE*, Vol. 14, 1904, pp. 358-62.

*Commonplaces set out in brief maxims* which was first published in 1589 and which had been through twelve editions by 1630.[9]

Piscator followed his friend Olevianus both in expounding the *Institutes* at Herborn on the latter's death in 1587 and in addressing his preface to Beza in which he explains the occasion and nature of this work and its relationship to that of his predecessor's.

> 'And when my Scholars desired for their furtherance in Divinitie, that I would take the paines to appoint them some Logicall disputations:[10] I soone granted their request and therefore to procede in some lawfull and good course, for their more speedie and better profite I did reduce every point of Christian doctrine, so soone as I finished any place in the Institution, into some few Aphorismes and the same I propounded unto them for disputation. And this was the first cause of writing these Aphorismes: In collecting them I have used Christian libertie, I have not followed the very wordes of the authour (for that could not well be done, the authors stile being full and large, and Aphorismes requiring brevitie) and I added some thing in the sentences, which is not in that abridgement: yet the work agreeth wel, as I thinke, and as the brethren judge, with the authors doctrine, and specially with the holy Scripture.'[11]

As Piscator himself acknowledges here, once the rendering of the *Institutes* passes beyond the stage of a mere abridgement which keeps very close to the original wording, the possibility of distortion arises. Just how far he is justified in his own claim that he has avoided this we shall shortly determine in an examination of the first set of Aphorismes which appear as Locus I, 'De Cognitione Dei'.[12] We shall undertake the survey in conjunction with a study of the one Dutch example of a similar work and so first a word or two about this and its author.

Daniel Colonius[13] was yet another member of a South Netherlands refugee family who settled in the North. He studied at Geneva under Beza and later at Leiden where in 1605 he was to be appointed the first Regent of the newly founded Walloon College in which post he continued for the

---

[9] *Aphorisimi Doctrinae Christianae maximam partem ex Institutione Calvini excerpti, sive Loci Communes Theologici, brevibus sententiis expositi.* Cf. Warfield, p. 406. Our quotations are from the third edition, Herborn, 1594. For Piscator (1546-1625), who taught at Herborn from 1584 till his death, see *PRE*, Vol. 15, 1904, pp. 414-5.

[10] The Latin reads 'disputationes Theologicas.'

[11] *Aphorismes of Christian Religion.* English translation by H. Holland, London, 1596. Facsimile edition, Amsterdam, 1973. 'The Authors Preface to Maister Beza' (no pagination).

[12] *Aphorismi*, pp. 11-13.

[13] For Colonius (1566-1635) see *BWPGN* 11, pp. 172-8; G. H. M. Posthumus Meyjes, 'Le Collège Wallon', *Leiden University in the Seventeenth Century*, Leiden, 1975, pp. 111-35; id., *Geschiedenis van het Waalse College te Leiden, 1606-1699*, Leiden, 1975, pp. 50-6.

rest of his life. The author of the article in the *Biographisch Woordenboek* describes Colonius's devotion to Calvin thus:

> 'Colonius was heart and soul a Calvinist and he never gave a better demonstration of his love for the great reformer and the high regard he felt for the *Institutes of the Christian Religion* than by his *Analysis*.'[14]

whilst Posthumus Meyjes says of him and his work,

> 'Unfortunately no-one up to now has yet made a serious study of the *Analysis*, and no more has Colonius received the attention due to him. For it must not be forgotten that this humanist Calvinist was an outstanding person to his contemporaries.'[15]

The publication which is referred to by these scholars as the *Paraphrased Analysis of John Calvin's Theological Institutes covered in 41 Disputations*,[16] was the second, posthumus, edition of 1636. The forty-one disputations held at the Walloon College under Colonius's presidency between 1623 and 1628 were first published at Leiden in the latter year as *Theological Disputations in which the Four Books of John Calvin's Institutes are paraphrastically and analytically set out for the use of studious young men.*[17] Since, as Dutch scholars have long been aware,[18] the Bodleian possesses one of the only two known copies of this first edition, our quotations are taken thence.

In assessing the influences at work upon Colonius we are further benefited by having access to a source hitherto unknown to continental scholarship, the sale catalogue of his very extensive library auctioned by Elsevir in 1636.[19] This provides confirmation, if such were needed, of Colonius's regard for Calvin who is the author of no less than twenty of the two hundred Latin theological works in folio which the former pos-

---

[14] 'Met hart en ziel was Colonius Kalvinist, en de liefde voor den grooten reformator, de hooge achting die hij voor de *Institutie Christianae religionis* gevoelde, heeft hij nooit beter kunnen toonen, dan door de *Analysis*.'[3] (*BWPGN* 11, p. 173).

[15] 'Hélas jusqu'ici personne encore n'a fait une étude sérieuse de l'Analysis', pas plus que Colonius n'a reçu l'attention qui lui reviendrait. Car il ne faut pas oublier que pour ses contemporains cet humaniste calviniste était un personnage du premier plan.' (*Le Collège Wallon*, p. 125.) Cf. *Geschiedenis van het Waalse College*, p. 56.

[16] *Analysis Paraphrastica Institutionum Theologicarum Joh. Calvini Disputationes XLI contexta.*

[17] *Disputationes Theologicae quibus Paraphrasticae et Analytice, Quatuor libri Institutionum Joh. Calvini, in usum studiosae juventutis evolvuntur.*

[18] C. Sepp, *op. cit.*, pp. 94-5.

[19] Over 2,000 volumes are listed in the *Catalogus Variorum Librorum Bibliothecae Reverendi Clarissimique Viri D. Danielis Colonii Collegii Gallo-Belg. Regentis et Ecclesiae Lug.-Batav. Pastoris. Quorum auctio habebitur In Officiana Elseviriana 23 Septemb. Stylo novo.* Leiden 1636. This is part of the Griffin Higgs' collection in Merton College library. In 1974 the present writer provided the University Library at Leiden with a xerox copy of this catalogue via Professor Posthumus Meyjes. See the latter's *Geschiedenis van het Waalse College*, note 67, p. 76.

sessed.[20] More important to us is the evidence that Colonius had studied the previous attempts at abridging the *Institutes*. Amongst the Latin theological books in octavo we encounter both the second edition of Piscator's *Aphorisms* and his later reprinting of these accompanied by his own commentary upon them,[21] and also what was probably the very first of such publications, Edmund Bunney's *Compendium of the Institutes of Christian Religion*[22] .... Colonius also possessed the Dutch translation of Delaune[23] and so the only gap in his collection is Olevianus's epitome.

The most obvious contrast between Piscator and Colonius lies in the length of their treatment. The former summarises the Locus, 'Concerning the Knowledge of God' which covers the first five chapters of the *Institutes* in eight brief aphorisms, whilst the latter devotes his first two disputations to this topic, 'First: Concerning the Innate Idea of God. From the Institutes. Book 1. Chapters 1, 2, 3, 4' (sixteen theses and three corollaries) and 'Second: From the first book of Calvin's *Institutes*, Chapter 5. Concerning the idea of God acquired from the construction and direction of the world'[24] (eighteen theses and one corollary).

Again, even granted the brevity of Piscator's treatment, what strikes us so forcefully is the very obviously methodical arrangement of the material. It comes as no surprise to learn that he was a keen advocate of the Ramist method in philosophy and of its application to theology.[25] This becomes even more evident when we look at the explanatory chart of this Locus which Piscator appends to his *Exegesis or Explanation of the Aphorisms of Christian Doctrine*.[26] Not that this was the first such means of elucidation for Delaune's work had originally included twelve pages of such charts and had increased the number to twenty-one in the second edition;[27] charts

[20] Nos. 32-46; 178-82 *op. cit.*, pp. 2, 7.

[21] '323 ... Aphorismi Piscatoris, Herbornae 1592 ... 333. Piscatoris aphorismorum exegesis, Herbornae 1622' (*op. cit.*, p. 35). For the full title of this last work, see below.

[22] *Institutionum Christianae religionis compendium simul ac methodi enarratio*. '433 Bunnii Compendium institutionum Calvini. Antw. 1582' (p. 39). This first appeared at London in 1579 and was translated into English in 1580. It was evidently eclipsed by Delaune's abridgement since its only subsequent appearance was in the Antwerp edition of which Colonius possessed a copy.

[23] 'Libri Theologici Belgici et Germanici in Octavo ... 4. De institutie van Calvin kort begrijp door Launeum overgeset uyt Latijn door Joris de Rael. Amst. 1611' (p. 45).

[24] 'Prima: De Notitia Dei Insita. Ex. Institut. Libro 1. cap. 1, 2, 3, 4.' 'Secunda. Ex. Institut. Calvini Libro primo cap. 5. De Notitia Dei acquisita ex mundi fabricatione et gubernatione.' (Colonius, *Disputationes*, no pagination.)

[25] Piscator had been Professor of philosophy at Heidelberg from 1574 until the expulsion of the Calvinists from that university in 1577.

[26] *Exegesis sive Explicatio Aphorismorum Doctrinae Christianae*. Herborn, 1622, p. 605. See below, p. 46.

[27] *Editio secunda emendatur. Tabulis etiam et Indice multo facilioribus et locupletioribus*, London, 1584.

whose predeliction for the dichotomous approach reveal their own Ramist sympathies.

The difference between Delaune and Piscator is that the former's table is subsidiary to his epitome which, as we have seen, is a faithful reproduction of the *Institutes*, whereas for the latter the dichotomous treatment has gone a long way towards dictating the construction of his aphorisms. However, we cannot quibble at the first of his divisions, 'God is known by us as Creator and as Redeemer,'[28] since it is that of Calvin himself.

> 'First, in the fashioning of the universe and in the general teaching of Scripture the Lord shows himself to be the Creator. Then in the face of Christ he shows himself to be the Redeemer; from this emerges a twofold knowledge of God.'[29]

Piscator's zest to move on to his second, apparently straightforward, dichotomy, does lead to a distortion of Calvin. For, having stated as his second aphorism, 'The knowledge of God as Creator is twofold, the one natural, the other acquired', he proceeds in his third to treat the first of this pair as the source providing the knowledge of God's attributes:

> 'The natural knowledge of God as Creator is that which appears itself by nature in adults of sound mind: so that taught thus by nobody (marginal reference: Rom. 1, vv. 18, 19 and 2, vv. 14, 15) they are persuaded that there is a God or some deity: that is, a mind, eternal, most powerful, most wise, most good: the maker and governor of the world and all things contained in it: and hence that this deity must be religiously worshipped.'[30]

However, at no point in Calvin's discussion of the innate knowledge of God in chapters three and four does he ever suggest that this goes beyond 'an awareness of divinity';[31] it is only in connection with the works of nature and providence that Calvin will allow the natural man some knowledge of God's attributes. A glance at Delaune's chart shows that he has his account of God's attributes, 'God is of this nature, 1. Goodness, 2. Excellence, 3. Righteousness, 4. Wisdom', in the correct half of the division, 'The Knowledge of God the Creator, .... 2. Provided by some other

---

[28] 'Cognoscitur a nobis Deus vel ut creator, vel ut redempter.' (*Aphorismi*, p. 11.)

[29] 'Quia ergo Dominus primum simpliciter creator tam in mundi opificio, quam in generali Scripturae doctrina, deinde in Christi facie redemptor apparet: hinc duplex emergit eius cognitio.' (*Institutes* I, ii. 1.)

[30] 'Naturalis cognitio Dei ut creatoris, est quae se in adultis sana mente praeditis sponte naturae exerit: ita ut nemine etiam docente (marginal reference: Rom. 1 v. 18, 19 et Cap. 2 v. 14, 15) persuasi sint esse deum seu numen aliquod: id est, mentem aeternam, potentissimam, sapientissimam, optimam: mundi et rerum eo contentarum conditricem atque gubernatricem: ac proinde illud numen religiose colendum esse.' (*Aphorismi*, p. 11.)

[31] *Institutes* I. iii. 1. *LCC*, p. 43.

means namely 1. The construction of the whole world which teaches. c. 5'....[32] Again, Colonius, who shows signs of being influenced by Piscator in presenting a version of the latter's second aphorism as the first half of his tenth thesis, 'The Knowledge of God can be called partly innate, partly acquired', completes this with a phrase which directly echoes that of Calvin we have just quoted, 'We call the innate that in which some awareness of divinity is inborn by nature in all men',[33] and so clearly indicates his fidelity to the reformer.

One further divergence from Calvin is to be seen in this third aphorism of Piscator's. The scriptural references given in the margin as warrant for the natural, as opposed to the acquired, knowledge of God are Romans 1, 18, 19 and 2, 14, 15, and the application of the latter verse is explained further in his *Exegesis*,

> '... Four distinctions are indicated: the first of which is taken from the subject which receives (the knowledge of God) in itself, thus "In adults of sound mind." Secondly, from the form: "It appears itself by nature." Again "Being taught by nobody" ... The second distinction deals with that spontaneous understanding of God as Creator mentioned by Paul, "the work of the Law written in men's hearts." '[34]

There is no doubt that Calvin would have applauded the use here of the verses from Romans c.l. but nowhere does he interpret those from Chapter two in this way. Both in the *Institutes* and in the Romans' commentary he restricts these latter verses to the natural law which in turn he confines to the knowledge of right and wrong. The interpretation that such is the equivalent to the natural knowledge of God, which Piscator is here applying, is that of Melanchthon whose 1532 *Commentary on Romans* succinctly states at this point, 'For they have a law, which they call the law of nature, that is, the natural knowledge divinely planted in men's souls, which judges what is right and honest and what is evil.'[35] Once again, Colonius is true to Calvin in refraining here from any mention of Romans

---

[32] See below, p. 45.

[33] 'Notitia Dei partim insita, partim acquisita vocari potest. Insitam dicimus, qua divinitatis aliquis sensus omnibus hominibus a natura est ingenitus.'

[34] '... differentiae autem indicantur quadruplices: quarum prima sumta est a subjecto recipiente in se, ibi, "In adultis sana mente praeditis." Secunda a forma ibi: "Sponte naturae se exerit." Item, "Nemine etiam docente" ... Quod ad secundam differentiam attinet, spontanea illa intellectio Dei ut creatoris a Paulo nominatur "opus legis scriptum in cordibus hominum," Romans 2, v. 15.'

[35] 'Habent enim legem, quam vocant legem naturae, h.e. notitiam naturalem divinitus insitam animis hominum, quae iudicat, quae sint recta et honesta et quae sint turpia.' (Melanchthon, *op. cit.*, p. 85.)

2, 14, 15, but he does show traces of other influences in the first Corollary appended to this disputation, 'Whether the natural knowledge of God is so called because man is furnished with the powers of understanding and willing, or whether rather because the common principle is in everyone by nature. The latter is affirmed. C.3.S.1.'[36] The point he is making is one close to Calvin's heart, that the innate idea of God forces the knowledge of His existence on everyone so that no appeal to human reason is required to establish this,[37] but Calvin himself avoids the use of the term κοιναι ἐννοιαι which had been introduced into Reformation thought in this context by Melanchthon.[38]

Aphorism five divides the acquired knowledge of God into that which is obtained from a consideration of God's works and that which is given us in Scripture, 'The knowledge of God as Creator is acquired by instruction, both human or philosophical, deduced by reasoning from a consideration of God's works, and divine, that is to say, drawn from the written Word of God.'[39] The appearance of the latter source as early as this does anticipate Calvin somewhat since the latter does not treat this until Chapter six, but its introduction here does not give rise to distortion. Both Delaune in his Chart and Colonius in the first thesis of his second disputation make precisely the same division, although the former specifically refers consideration of the scriptural source to Chapter six and the latter also excludes it from his immediate discussion:

> 'It pleased God further to set forth the knowledge of Himself in various manners and this especially in two ways, both in the works of creation and of providence, and indeed in His Word. The knowledge which arises hence can be called acquired. In these theses we will deal with the former revelation. S.1.'[40]

This same aphorism does, however, contain a serious deviation from Calvin in that the emphasis in the first of the two sources is laid entirely

---

[36] 'An naturalis notitia Dei inde dicta sit quod homo potentiis intelligendi et volendi praeditus sit, An potius quod κοινη haec ἐννοιαι omnibus a natura insit. Posterius affirm. C.3.S.1.'

[37] As we shall see, this view was resisted for precisely this reason by the leading Remonstrant theologian, Episcopius, and it may be that Colonius is here explicitly defending it against such an attack.

[38] Cf. *CR* 21, col. 711.

[39] 'Acquiritur cognitio Dei ut creatoris per institutionem tum humanam seu philosophicam, ex consideratione operum Dei ratiocinando deductum: tum divinam ex verbo scil. Dei scripto haustam.' (*Aphorismi*, p. 12.)

[40] 'Placuit Deo seipsum variis porro affectionibus cognoscendum exhibere, idque duobus praesertim modis, tum in operibus creationis et providentiae, tum vero in verbo suo. Et quae hinc oritur notitia potest acquisita dici. De priori patefactione his thesibus agemus.' S.1.

upon philosophical reasoning as the means whereby God's works deliver up the knowledge of the Creator. This emphasis is clearly underlined in Piscator's chart where this source is described as 'Human or philosophical which is acquired from the books of Philosophers.'[41] Although Calvin does make positive references to the work of natural philosophers in the second section of chapter five, the main point of his discussion there is to stress that no such expertise is required since even the most ignorant of men has the proofs of God's existence and providence thrust upon him by the creation,

> 'There are innumerable evidences both in heaven and on earth that declare His wonderful wisdom; not only those more recondite matters for the closer observation of which astronomy, medicine, and all natural science are intended, but also those which thrust themselves upon the sight of even the most untutored and ignorant persons, so that they cannot open their eyes without being compelled to witness them.'[42]

Piscator's position here opens wide the door to the use of all the a posteriori philosophical arguments for God's existence. This departure from Calvin is all the more obvious when at this point we contrast Piscator with Delaune and Colonius. The latter retains Calvin's emphasis, spelling out 'the works of creation and providence' in the course of his second disputation, whilst the former makes no mention of philosophical reasoning in his table, summarizing this source as God's creation of earthly and heavenly things and His preservation of them by His ordinary and extraordinary providence.[43]

In his last three aphorisms, six to eight, Piscator concludes by driving home the authentic message of Calvin that none of this knowledge of God as Creator has any positive effect until it is joined to that of Him as Redeemer: it serves only to render man inexcusable.[44] Colonius is equally forceful: 'In no way is man sufficiently taught by the bare witness borne to God by the creation; yet this serves to render him inexcusable. Romans 1, 19. S. 14, 15.'[45]

In conclusion, we may say that, although Colonius shows signs of having been influenced by Piscator in the traces of the dichotomous

---

[41] 'Humana seu Philosophica, quae acquiritur ex libris Philosophorum.' See below, p. 46.

[42] *LCC*, p. 53.

[43] See appended table.

[44] *Aphorismi*, p. 13.

[45] 'Nuda testificatione quae Deo redditur a creaturis, nequaquam hominem sufficienter erudiri: Ad hoc tamen eam inservire, ut reddatur inexcusabilis. Roman 1, 19. S. 14, 15.' (Thesis, XVII.)

approach which he evinces and in the vocabulary he adopts, his own much more extended treatment transmits Calvin's argument most faithfully. If then we can identify at least one area of the Dutch theological scene where the great reformer's thought on the issue of the natural knowledge of God was preserved in its integrity, our subsequent investigations will compel us to recognise that it was Piscator's version of Calvin, with the small but very significant distortions that we have noted, which exercised the greater influence throughout the period.

*Delaune's Table*

*Ex Lib. 1 de Creatione*

- Cognitio Dei* Creatoris est nobis
  - 1. Naturaliter insita: Cap. 1
    - 1. Cuius finis esse debet, Cap. 2
      - Cultus Dei recte institutus. Eius numinus reverentia cum Cap. 3
        - Timore.
        - Amore.
    - 2. Sed tale semen corrumpitur, Cap. 4
      - Inscitia: unde superstitiosus cultus, Malitia: Unde
        - Timor servilis.
        - Odium divinitatis.
  - 2. Aliunde comparata: nempe,
    - 1. Totius mundi fabrica: quae docet Cap. 5
      - 1. Qualis sit Dei
        - 1. Bonitas
        - 2. Virtus
        - 3. lustitia.
        - 4. Sapientia.
          - 1. Creando
            - 1. Coelestia.
            - 2. Terrestria.
          - 2. Conservando eadem per administrationem.
            - 1. Ordinariam
            - 2. Extraordinariam
              - In qua Providentia clarius innotescit.
      - 2. Qualis nostra sit indigentia: Ut discamus
        - 1. Nostram fiduciam collocare in eius
          - Bonitate.
          - Virtute.
          - Providentia.
        - 2. Eius obtemperare praeceptis
          - Volentes tanquam filii.
          - Non renitentes tanquam mancipia.
        - 3. Ad eum recurrere in nostris necessitatibus tanquam ad omnium bonorum fontem.
        - 4. Quas habemus dotes omnes Deo referre acceptas cum actione gratiarum.
    - 2. Scripturis, Cap. 6. Vide tabulam sequentem.

* N.B. The 'Generalis Tabula Totius Institutionibus Christianae Religionis' on the preceding page had begun by dividing 'Vera Sapientia sita est in cognitione Dei' into '1. Creatoris ex. lib. 1' and '2. Redemptoris per Filium ... ex. lib. 2.'

*Delaune's Table*

The knowledge of* God the Creator is

- 1. Engendered in us naturally Chap. 1
  - 1. The end whereof ought to be Chap. 2
    - The worship of God rightly ordered.
    - The reverence of his name with Chap. 3
      - Fear and Love
  - 2. But such seed is corrupted Chap. 4
    - Through ignorance whence cometh superstitious worship
    - Through wickedness whence cometh
      - Servile fear.
      - Hatred of the godhead.
- 2. Gotten by some other means, namely by
  - 1. The whole frame of the world: which teacheth Chap. 5
    - 1. Of what sort the
      - 1. Goodness
      - 2. Power
      - 3. Justice
      - 4. Wisdom of God are
        - 1. In creating
          - 1. Heavenly things
          - 2. Earthly things
        - 2. In preserving the same by his administration which is
          - 1. Ordinary
          - 2. Extraordinary: wherein God's providence doth more plainly appear.
    - 2. What our need is: that we may learn
      - 1. To repose our confidence in his
        - Goodness.
        - Power.
        - Providence.
      - 2. To obey his commandments
        - Willingly, as sons.
        - Not resisting, as servants.
      - 3. To run unto him in our necessity as unto the fountain of all good things.
      - 4. To acknowledge that we have received all those gifts which we have at God's hands and to thank him for them.
  - 2. By the Scriptures, Chap. 6 Read the next table.

* N.B. The 'General Table of the whole Institution of Christian Religion' on the preceding page had begun by dividing the "True wisdom placed in the knowledge of God" into that of "1. The Creator out of the first book" and that of "2. The Redeemer, by the son ... out of the second book".

*Place 1*

## OF THE KNOWLEDGE OF GOD

The Knowledge of God in which God is known by us is twofold:
Of the Creator, in which He is known by us as the Creator and Governor of all created things.

This is twofold:

- Natural, which arises from the natural working of the human mind, namely
  - 1. There is a God.
  - 2. He Himself is the Creator and Governor of the world.
  - 3. This same God must be religiously worshipped.
- Acquired, which arises from instruction either
  - Human or philosophical which is acquired from the books of Philosophers.
  - Divine which is drawn from God's word or the Holy Scriptures.

This is either

- Bare, that is lacking the disposition of piety.
- United with a disposition of piety.

Of the Redeemer, in which He is known by us as the Redeemer and Sanctifier of the redeemed.

This is either

- Bare, lacking filial trust.
- United with filial trust.

*Locus 1*

## DE COGNITIONE DEI

Cognitio Dei, qua Deus cognoscitur a nobis duplex est:
Creatoris, qua cognoscitur a nobis ut Creator et Gubernator rerum creatarum.

Eaque duplex est:

- Naturalis, quae oritur ex naturali motu mentis humanae, nempe
  - 1. Esse Deum
  - 2. Illum ipsum esse creatorem et gubernatorem mundi
  - 3. Eundem religiose colendum esse
- Acquisita, quae oritur ex institutione vel
  - Humana seu Philosophica; quae acquiritur ex libris Philosophorum
  - Divina, quae hauritur ex verbo Dei sive Sacra scriptura.

Eaque aut est

- Nuda, quae est sine affectu pietatis
- Conjuncta cum affectu pietatis.

Redemptoris, qua cognoscitur a nobis ut redemptor et sanctificator redemptorum.

Eaque est vel

- Nuda, sine fiducia filiali
- Conjuncta cum filiali fiducia.

(J. Piscator, *Exegesis sive Explicatio Aphorismorum Doctrinae Christianae*, Herborn, 1622, p. 605)

PART II

# THE ARGUMENTS FOR THE EXISTENCE OF GOD AMONG ORTHODOX DUTCH REFORMED THEOLOGIANS

CHAPTER FOUR

# COMMENTARIES UPON THE HEIDELBERG CATECHISM

Apart from the direct effect of his own works, Melanchthon's most powerful influence upon the Reformed tradition in general and the Dutch in particular was through the Heidelberg Catechism. As regards the issue of our concern, however, it is more accurate to say that it was not so much the Catechism itself as the principal commentary upon it which mediated this influence so strongly. The Catechism, drawn up at the instance of Frederick III of the Palatinate and first published in German and Latin in 1563, was the work of two Heidelberg professors, Casper Olevianus (1536-87) and Melanchthon's pupil, Zacharias Ursinus (1534-83).[1] The first Dutch translation appeared in 1566 and, as early as 1568, the Synod of Wesel had approved its use. The provincial Synod of Dort, in 1574, further recommended it and ministers were required to explain it to their congregations each Sunday in 52 lessons throughout the year.[2] Finally, at the Synod of Dort in 1619, it was solemnly adopted, along with the Belgic Confession and the Canons of the Synod, as the standard of Dutch Reformed orthodoxy.[3]

No attempt is made in the Catechism itself to argue for the existence of God or even, indeed, to raise the question. However, one of its authors, Ursinus, had lectured regularly on the Catechism both at Heidelberg and Neustadt and in 1584, a year after his death, his erstwhile pupils began publishing the notes they had taken of these lectures. The first edition appeared at Geneva with a Dedicatory Epistle dated April of that year and was immediately reprinted in Leiden.[4] In the following year a somewhat different version appeared at Neustadt with the title, *The First Part of the Exposition of the Catechism*.[5] The confusion occasioned by the appearance of these differences is well attested by the English publications of the Latin

---

[1] For Olevianus, see above, p. 35. For Ursinus see *PRE*, Vol. 20, 1908, pp. 348-53.

[2] Thus from an early stage the 129 Questions and Answers of the Catechism were divided between the 52 Sundays of the year. As regards the issue of our concern the relevant Sundays are 8, dealing with Questions 24 and 25, and 9, which treats Questions 27 and 28.

[3] See G. D. J. Schotel, *Geschiedenis van den oorsprong, invoering en lotgevallen van den Heidelbergschen Catechismus*, Amsterdam, 1863.

[4] *Doctrinae Christianae Compendium seu Commentarii Catechetici*. Cited as *Ursinus, Geneva, 1584* and *Ursinus, Leiden, 1584*.

[5] *Pars prima Explicationum Catechetricarum*. Cited as *Ursinus, Neustadt, 1585*.

edition which themselves added further complications. Thus the first, published at Cambridge in 1585, followed the Genevan version as to title and contents but, as indicated on the title page,[6] supplements Ursinus's commentary with insertions from elsewhere. As promised on the title page, the index reveals that these additions are taken from the latter's *Loci Communes* which had also appeared posthumously in 1584.[7] The appearance in London in 1586 of what must have been a pirated edition[8] brought an interesting reaction from the Cambridge printer. In 1587 he published an edition which forsook the title of the Genevan version for that of the Neustadt whilst retaining all the additions from the *Loci Communes* which he had made in his first edition. The Neustadt version was not preferred throughout but used to supplement and modify the Genevan in the interests of greater accuracy.[9]

The differences in the various publications were such that Ursinus's former pupil, David Pareus of Heidelberg (1548-1622), was charged with the task of revising them and producing a version as faithful as possible to the original lectures. The first edition published under his supervision, *Explicationes Catecheticae*, appeared at Neustadt in 1591. There were further editions in 1593, 1595, 1598, 1603, 1608, 1612, 1616, 1621 (two), 1623, 1634 and 1651.[10] A German translation, presumably of the Genevan version, had appeared at Neustadt as early as 1584 whilst the first English translation came out at Oxford in 1587 and was succeeded by at least eight further editions.[11] We shall have occasion later to detail the many editions of the Dutch translation by Festus Hommius which was first published at Leiden in 1602. Enough has been said to indicate the enormous popularity of Ursinus's Commentary and to suggest something of the influence which it might be expected to exercise.

---

[6] '... et nunc denuas non parva accessione eorum, quae in commentariis desiderabantur (quod ex indice facile apparebit) locupletati.'

[7] These had been published at Neustadt in the collection, *Volumen tractationum theologicarum*, as 'Questiones et Theses Breviter Complectentes summam Locorum aliquot Theologicorum.' The whole was reprinted, again at Neustadt, in 1587.

[8] 'Londini Excudebat Henricus Middletonus impensis Thomae Chardi.'

[9] As explained in the title page, '... a variis erratis (quae in priorem nostram additionem, partim nostro vitio irrepserat, et adhuc retinentur, multoque auctiora facta sunt in vitiosissima illa editione, quae Londini nuperrime excusa est impensis Thomas Chardi) diligenter repurgata.'

[10] The 1612 and 1616 editions were entitled, *Corpus Doctrinae Orthodoxae*, whilst those from 1621 onwards became, *Corpus Doctrinae Christianae*. Cited as *Ursinus, Frankfurt, 1621*.

[11] Despite the claim of later editions that they were 'conferred with the best and last Latine Edition of D. David Pareus', and despite the fact that they ceased to mention their 'supply of wants of out his (i.e. Ursinus's) Discourses of Divinity,' the additions from the *Loci Communes* continued unchanged throughout.

The earliest Latin edition begins the exposition of the Creed with a 'De Deo' section, 'Three commonplaces relate to this first part of the Creed and especially require to be known 1. Concerning God; 2. Concerning Creation; 3. Concerning God's Providence.'[12] The treatment is entirely Melanchthonian but, as we shall see, the arguments for God's existence are now transferred, from under the heading 'Concerning Creation' ('De Creatione'), where the latter had presented them in his *Loci Communes*, to their traditional scholastic setting in the 'Whether there is a God' section of the locus 'Concerning God.'[13] The list of eleven arguments[14] proves this fidelity to Melanchthon, for not only does it reproduce in identical order the nine which the latter gives in the 1544 edition of the *Loci Communes*[15] but adds as number ten and eleven the two, 'From heroic action' and 'From the punishments of the wicked' which appear in the slightly different set of nine arguments given in the 1540 edition of the *Commentary on Romans*.[16]

Apart from a certain measure of condensation, the reproduction is pretty faithful to its model. However, as we have mentioned, there are marked differences between some versions of the early editions of the commentary and we may note that that of Neustadt published in 1585 contains some which are of relevance to our concern. The list of arguments is the same, although the order alters with the insertion of the two additional arguments at different points, 'the punishments which are inflicted upon the wicked above and beyond the pangs of conscience' as number six and 'heroic actions' as number eight.[17] The consequent readjustment leads to the two arguments from causality, final and efficient, figuring as numbers ten and eleven respectively. The effect is to unite Melanchthon's two lists in a more logical order. Thus the two arguments concerning the divine punishment of sinners, one by conscience, the other by more drastic

---

[12] 'Ad hanc primam Symboli partem tres Loci Communes pertinent, imprimis cognitu necessarii 1. De Deo 2. De Creatione 3. De Dei providentia.' (*Ursinus, Geneva, 1584*, p. 174.)

[13] 'De Deo. Quaestiones praecipue. 1. An sit Deus.' (*Ibid.*) Cf. The position of Aquinas's five proofs in the *Summa Theologiae* la, Quaestio 2, 'de Deo, an Deus Sit,' article 3, 'an Deus sit.' It is true that Melanchthon had himself presented the nine arguments of the *Loci Communes* under the heading, 'De Deo' in his *Initia Doctriane Physicae*, Wittenberg, 1549 (*CR* 13, cols. 198-202) but, as we observed in our comments on this passage (see above, pp. 25-6), in the context of the work as a whole, they are still effectively being treated as a part of the topic 'De Creatione.'

[14] *Ursinus, Geneva, 1584*, pp. 175-7.

[15] *CR* 21, cols. 641-3. See above, pp. 24-5.

[16] *CR* 15, cols. 566-8. See above, pp. 21-2.

[17] 'Sextum sunt poenae quae sceleratis praeter conscientiae dolores infliguuntur. ... Octavum sunt motus heroici ...' (*Ursinus, Neustadt, 1585*, pp. 279-80.)

means, are brought together with the latter providing the appropriate link, 'Punishments in which entire nations and commonwealths perish,'[18] with the next argument from the ordering and preservation of political society.

The other more striking difference is the length at which the arguments are treated. Instead of the abbreviation of the Genevan version we frequently encounter an expansion of Melanchthon's treatment so that the former's three octavo pages now extend to more than five. Of much greater interest, however, is the nature of this enlargement, for, in several instances, this clearly involves the introduction of a much more decidedly scholastic manner. Thus Melanchthon's second argument, 'from the nature of the human mind,' is set out straightforwardly enough in the original,

> 'An insensible thing is not the cause of the nature of intelligence; human minds do have a cause because man does not exist by means of himself but has a beginning and emerges from elsewhere; therefore there must be some intelligent natural cause of the human mind. Therefore there must be a God.'[19]

The Genevan version is substantially the same but in that of Neustadt this becomes,

> 'Rational nature does not have the cause unless it possesses intelligence, because the cause is not inferior to its effect. But now the human mind is rational and has a cause. Therefore it possesses an Intelligence who is God.'[20]

In this way the scholastic axiom, 'Because the cause is not inferior to its effect,' which is the unexpressed foundation of Melanchthon's opening assertion, 'An insensible thing is not the cause of the nature of intelligence', is unequivocally spelled out. This explanatory process is carried still further in the paragraph of syllogistic reasoning which is added as a conclusion to this argument,

> 'The minor premise is proved. That which comes into being does so from another, since it is from another . Moreover, it cannot be from itself because nothing is its own cause. Now the mind of man comes into being. Therefore etc....'[21]

---

[18] 'Poenas quibus pereunt totae gentes et Respublicae.' (*Ibid.*)

[19] 'Bruta res non est caussa naturae intelligentis; mentes hominum habent aliquam caussam, quia homo non habet esse per sese, sed incipit et aliunde oritur; ergo necesse est aliquam intelligentem naturam caussam esse mentis humanae. Necesse est igitur esse Deum.' (*CR* 21, col. 642.)

[20] 'Rationalis natura habens causam, non nisi intelligentem habet. Quia causa non est deterior suo effectu. Atqui mens humana est rationalis, et habet causam. Ergo intelligentem habet, quae est Deus.' (*Ursinus, Neustadt, 1585*, pp. 277-8.)

[21] 'Minor probatur. Quod incipit esse, est ab alio: quia ab alio. Non autem est a se: quia nihil est sui ipsius causa. At mens hominis incipit esse. Ergo etc.'. (*Ibid.*, p. 278.)

A further example of this very scholastic treatment is appended to the third argument, from man's possession of innate notions of right and wrong, order and rationality.

> 'We frame a syllogism. The notions are not acquired nor do they exist except by an intelligent cause. For no-one creates wisdom unless he is himself wise. The notions in men are there not from experience nor are they received from men. Therefore they exist by God's agency.'[22]

A final instance of this process is to be found where the last paragraph has been added to the concluding argument in the new arrangement, that from efficient causality, in order to explain the minor premise of the syllogism used, i.e. the impossibility of an infinite series of such causes.

> 'The minor premise is proved. Infinite time is required for infinite movements. But the effect, whose causes are infinite, requires infinite movements. And therefore infinite time. This is in fact absurd: because no causes produce an established effect in this way. Therefore there is some first cause, who is called God.'[23]

It is interesting to note that Pareus's corrected editions of Ursinus's commentary, while preferring the Neustadt's version's more logical order of the arguments for God's existence,[24] remove all those peculiarly scholastic expansions which we have just noted,[25] and so reduce the length of their treatment to that of the Genevan version. The inclusion of scriptural texts in the later revisions is now the only addition. One change which Pareus does make is to incorporate the questions and answers of the Catechism in the body of the commentary in such a way as to attach the latter to particular parts of the former. In the case of the 'De Deo' section this makes for considerable incongruity. Whilst it might be considered reasonable enough to present arguments for God's existence as part of the exposition of the first article of the Creed, to do so as a commentary upon Question 25 is manifestly at odds with the latter's content.

---

[22] 'Syllogismus. Notitiae non induntur aut existunt, nisi a causa intelligente. Nemo enim sapientem facit, nisi qui ipse sapiens est. In hominibus sunt notitiae, non usu, neque ab hominibus acceptae. Ergo a Deo existunt.' (*Ibid.*)

[23] 'Minor probatur. Ad motus infinitos requiritur tempus infinitum. At effectus, quorum causae sunt infinitae, requiritur motus infinitus. Ergo et tempus infinitum. Hoc vero absurdum est: Quia eo modo causae nullae effectum institutum producerent. Ergo est aliqua prima causa, quae nominatur Deus.' (*Ibid.*, pp. 281-2.)

[24] Not surprisingly, perhaps, this order is identical with that of the same eleven arguments of the 'De Deo' section of Ursinus's *Loci Communes*, which, as we saw above, first appeared at Neustadt in 1584 (*Ursinus, Loci*, pp. 38-43.)

[25] The one small exception is the retention in the second argument of the explanatory phrase 'quia causa non est toto genere deterior suo effectu.' (*Ursinus, Frankfurt, 1621*, p. 117.)

'Since there is only one divine Being, why do you speak of three, Father, Son and Holy Spirit? Because God has so revealed Himself in His Word that these three distinct Persons are the one, true, eternal God.'[26]

The stress here is on the revealed nature of God as Holy Trinity and the fact that the bulk of the ensuing 'explicatio' is devoted to this doctrine only serves to underline the oddity of the 'Whether there is a God' ('An sit Deus?') section with which it begins.

This confusion is indicative of the tension between the essentially Reformation, revelation-orientated text of the Catechism and the commentary upon it which, as we have noted, here employs Melanchthon's arguments for God's existence, but now in the traditional scholastic role as the prolegomena to revelation. This is all the more striking when we remind ourselves that the commentator was himself co-author of the Catechism.

Furthermore, whilst, as we saw, Melanchthon was at great pains to stress that the arguments he offered were merely to confirm the faithful who themselves possessed far firmer assurance of God's existence from the testimonies of Scripture, Ursinus makes no such initial qualification but launches straight into his list of arguments with the brief introduction, 'That there is a God is proved by many arguments common to Philosophy and Theology.'[27] The treatment of the revealed doctrine of God begins immediately after the arguments have been given with Section II, entitled, 'What and of what sort is the God of the Church.' It is only now that Ursinus makes the comparison between the philosophical and theological sources of the knowledge of God:

'The philosophical description of God is that He is the eternal mind, sufficient in Himself for happiness, the greatest good and the cause of good in nature: The theological description maintained in the church is indeed fuller: that God is a spiritual being, intelligent, eternal, different from all creatures, incomprehensible, most perfect in Himself, immutable, of boundless power, wisdom and goodness, just, truthful, pure, merciful, bountiful, most free, angry with sins. This being is the eternal Father who from eternity begat the Son in His own image; and the Son, the co-eternal image of the Father, and the Holy Spirit proceeding from the Father and the Son, as it has been divinely revealed by the certain Word delivered by the prophets and apostles, and by divine testimonies, that the Father, together with the Son and the Holy Spirit, created heaven and earth and all creatures therein, and is present with all creatures to preserve and govern them by His providence and to work all

---

[26] 'Cum una tantum sit essentia divina, cur tres istos nominas, Patrem, Filium, et Spiritum sanctum? RESP. Quia Deus ita se in suo verbo patefecit, quod tres hae distinctae personae sint unus ille verus et aeternus Deus.' (*Ursinus, Frankfurt, 1621*, p. 117.)

[27] 'Esse Deum multis argumentis Philosophiae et Theologiae communibus probatur.' (*Ibid.*, p. 117.)

good things in them all; and that in mankind, created in His image, He chose and gathered to Himself an eternal church on account of and through the Son, so that by it this one and true Deity may be, according to the divine Word, acknowledged and worshipped, be celebrated in eternal life, and be the judge of the righteous and unrighteous.'[28]

In so doing he borrows an entire section from Melanchthon which the latter had used as the introduction to the presentation of his nine arguments in the 'De Deo' section of the *Initia Doctrinae Physicae*.[29]

Interestingly enough, when those responsible for translating Ursinus's commentary evidently felt the lack of these kind of qualifying remarks as to the relative status of the two sources of the knowledge of God, they did not restore such as an introduction to the arguments but instead filled out the beginning of Section II with substantial additions.[30] One such insertion made by the English translator, from the section of the locus 'De Deo' of Ursinus's *Loci Communes* entitled 'Who and of what sort is the true God,'[31] is of particular interest in shedding light on the latter's motives in presenting arguments drawn from philosophy. At the beginning the

[28] 'Quid et qualis sit Deus ecclesiae. Philosophica descriptio Dei est: quod sit mens aeterna, ad felicitatem sibi sufficiens, optima et causa boni in natura: Theologica vero et plenior descriptio habetur in ecclesia: quod Deus sit essentia spiritualis, intelligens, aeterna, alia a creaturis omnibus, incomprehensibilis, in se ipsa perfectissima, immutabilis, immensae potentiae, sapientiae et bonitatis, iusta, verax, casta, misericors, benefica, liberrima, irascens peccatis: quae est pater aeternus, qui filium ad imaginem suam ab aeterno genuit: et filius imago patris coaeterna, et Spiritus sanctus procedens a patre et filio, sicut patefacta est divinitatis certo verbo tradito per prophetas et apostolos, et testimoniis divinis, quod pater aeternus cum filio et Spiritu sancto coelum et terram, et omnes creatures in eis creaverit, et adsit omnibus creaturis, ut eas conservet ac regat sua providentia, et bona omnia in omnibus operetur, et quod in genere humano condito ad imaginem suam elegerit et colligat sibi aeternam ecclesiam propter filium et per eum, ut ab ea haec una et vera divinitas iuxta verbum divinitus agnoscatur ac colatur, et in vita aeterna celebretur, et sit iudex iustorum et iniustorum.' (*Ibid.*, p. 119.)

[29] 'Tenenda est igitur physica aliqua definitio, congruens naturali iudicio rationis et demonstrationibus. Talis est haec Platonica: Deus est mens aeterna, causa boni in natura ... Teneatur ergo definitio in Ecclesia illustrior, sumpta ex admirandis testimoniis, quibus se Deus immensa bonitate nobis patefecit. Deus est essentia spiritualis, intelligens, aeterna, verax, bona, iusta, misericors, casta, liberrima, immensae potentiae et sapientiae, Pater aeternus, qui Filium imaginem suam ab aeterno genuit, et Filius imago Patris coaerterna, et Spiritus sanctus, procedens a Patre et Filio, sicut est patefacta divinitas certo verbo, quod Pater aeternus cum Filio et Spiritu sancto condiderit et servet coelum et terram, et omnes creaturas, et in genere humano condito ad imaginem suam et certam obedientiam elegerit sibi Ecclesiam, ut ab ea haec una et vera divinitas patefacta certis testimoniis, et per verbum traditum Prophetis et Apostolis agnoscatur, invocetur et colatur, iuxta verbum illud divinitus traditum, et in vita aeterna coram conspicatur et celebretur.' (*CR* 13, cols. 199-200.)

[30] See below, p. 90, where we take note of the further brief qualification which Ursinus adds at this point.

[31] 'Quis et qualis sit verus Deus.' (*op. cit.*, pp. 46-8.)

passage parallels the one which appears in the Commentary at this point and which, as we have said, we shall examine below. However, the *Loci* version, not content with simply outlining the reasons for the insufficiency of the natural knowledge of God, adds the conventional Reformation text, 'This answer St. Paul himself expresseth, when he addeth, "That they are inexcusable, because that when they knew God, they glorified him not as God." '[32]

If, however, Ursinus apparently goes further than Melanchthon in thus underlining the essentially negative role of philosophical knowledge, when he then immediately afterwards turns to a consideration of the value of such wisdom for the unregenerate, he hints at possibilities more positive than his master had ever expressed.

> 'Now albeit philosophical wisdom cannot therefore show who is the true God, ... yet nevertheless, that voice of the nature of things concerning God ought not for these causes to be rejected as false or condemned as fruitless ... For God will also out of the Church bridle the lewd and dissolute by the testimonies which their conscience and punishments give of his will, anger and judgement, and according to them will he have the life and manners of men ruled. He will have man's corruption and his justice made more conspicuous and clear in punishing them who stubbornly withstand the known truth. He will by natural testimonies, men's consciences showing the imperfection thereof, have men stirred up to seek the true God in the Church, as it is said that men were therefore placed in the Theatre of the world, that they should seek the Lord, if so be they might have groped after him and found him.'[33]

It is this last use of 'natural testimonies' which is the most significant for it can hardly fail to carry with it the implication that the Christian should advance such testimonies to the unbeliever so that he might be 'stirred up to seek the true God in the Church'. The door is thus wide open to the apologetic use of philosophical arguments which was soon to be such a feature of Natural Theology and we may not unfairly surmise that such a motive was among those at work in Ursinus himself. Furthermore the quotation of Acts 17.27 in this context is another sign of a more positive emphasis, since it is no accident that this text was one which figured in all attempts to advance the status of the natural knowledge of God.[34]

---

[32] *The Summe of Christian Religion*, London, 1633, p. 150.

[33] *Ibid.*

[34] Thus in the controversy over the issue of the salvation of those Gentiles who had had no opportunity of knowing Christ, which we shall examine in a later chapter, De Courcelles quotes it in support of his case that such salvation is possible on the basis of natural knowledge alone. He adds the comment, 'Quid enim sibi volunt ista, nisi Deum adeo se clare universis hommibus patefecisse, ut nemo sit qui non possit eum colere, et propitium erga se experiri?' (*Opera Theologica*, Amsterdam, 1675, p. 925.)

When, at the end of Chapter two, we reviewed Melanchthon's teaching on these issues, we concluded that his position, whilst still fundamentally in keeping with that of the Reformation, was exposed to erosion by the removal of the qualifications with which he hedged it about. With Ursinus such a process is already well under way so that with him the philosophical arguments for God's existence achieve a status hitherto unknown in Reformation theology.[35]

Question 27 of the Catechism asks, 'What is the providence of God?' and replies,

> 'The omnipotent and omnipresent power of God, whereby, as it were by His hand, He upholds and governs heaven and earth with all creatures, so that those things which grow on earth, as likewise rains and drought, fertility and barrenness, health and sickness, in short, all things, happen not by chance but by His fatherly consideration and decision.'[36]

Having, in true Melanchthonian manner, established the essential link between the doctrine of Providence and that of Creation,[37] it is typical of Ursinus that before he considers the actual question posed he must first produce proofs for the existence of Providence, 'The principal questions on this topic are: I. Whether there is any Providence. II. What it is. III. How does it operate.'[38] Following Melanchthon, Ursinus indicates the philosophical objections to a proper doctrine of Providence held by the Epicureans, Stoics and Peripatetics, and proceeds to establish it from two sources, 'There are two sorts of proofs by which the existence of divine providence may be shown, the testimonies of scripture and arguments.'[39] Although his exposition of the former source concludes, 'For there is scarcely any part of heavenly teaching more frequently and more

---

[35] For Daneau, whose list of arguments were first published in 1583, see below, pp. 119-22.

[36] 'Omnipotens et ubique praesens Dei vis, qua coelum ac terram cum omnibus creaturis tanquam manu sustinet ac gubernat: ut quae terra nascuntur, pluvia item et siccitas, fertilitas, et sterilitas, bona et adversa valetudo, divitiae et paupertas, omnia denique non temere aut fortuito, sed paterno eius consilio et voluntate contingant.' (*Ursinus, Frankfurt, 1621*, pp. 142-3.)

[37] This use of his model extends to the loan of the same familiar simile, 'For the creation is not to be thought of as being like the construction of a ship which, after completion, the ship-builder hands over the direction to the ship-master.' 'Non enim fingenda est talis creatio, qualis est extructio navis, quam architectus post fabrefactionem tradit regendam nauclero.' (*Ibid.* p. 143) cf. '... imaginatur, ut faber discedit a navi extructa et relinquit eam nautis, ...' (*CR* 21 col. 638.)

[38] 'De hac praecipue quaeritur: I. An aliqua sit providentia. II. Quid sit. III. Quis eius usus.' (*Ursinus, Frankfurt, 1621*, p. 143.)

[39] 'Duo autem sunt probationum genera, quibus providentia divina esse ostenditur, testimonia scripturae et argumenta.' (*Ibid.*) cf. *CR* 21, cols. 639-41.

assiduously imparted than that of God's Providence',[40] one cannot help contrasting the single nine line paragraph he accords it with the three full pages devoted to the rational arguments. Once more the Melanchthonian balance has been tipped in the direction of a greater emphasis upon the latter approach.

As he explains, Ursinus presents two types of arguments, the *a posteriori*, drawn from God's works and the *a priori* from His nature and attributes, asserting 'Both are demonstrable and are common to philosophy and theology.'[41]

The *a posteriori* or 'arguments from effects' are given first and we see that Ursinus has expanded Melanchthon's list of five to nine[42] by including several more of those which the latter had used to prove God's existence. Indeed, Ursinus lists the same arguments in the same order, albeit now worded so as to fulfil their new purpose,[43] as he himself gave to prove the divine existence. Two items from the first list are now omitted, that appealing to the universality of the innate belief in God and that which argued from efficient causality to First Cause; both are clearly only suitable for the earlier purpose and not for the later.

The difference between the various versions of the commentary are not so numerous or so significant here as in the case of the arguments for God's existence. There, we may recall, the Neustadt edition provided expansions to the Genevan which were removed in Pareus's revision.

---

[40] 'Vix enim ulla est pars doctrinae coelestis, quae frequentius et diligentius inculcetur, quam doctrina de providentia Dei.' (*Ibid.*, p. 144.)

[41] 'Utraque sunt demonstrativa et communia philosophiae et Theologiae.' (*Ibid.*)

[42] Pareus's revision adds a tenth which is not present in the earlier versions, but this is not really an argument in itself but merely an appeal to those others which prove God's existence and His creative activity. '10. Finally it is proved by those arguments which prove that God exists, that He is the Creator and the Sustainer: except that some reach their conclusion directly, others only by consequence.' '10. Denique iisdem fere argumentis probatur quod sit Deus, quod creator, et quod conservator: nisi quod aliqua immediate, aliqua non nisi per consequens concludunt.' (*Ibid.*, p. 146.)

[43] E.g. the argument from final causality which in his earlier list appeared as, '10. The purpose and usefulness of all things does not exist by chance or by insensible nature, but by a wise and omnipotent nature, which is God. Indeed all things have been most wisely appointed to their own definite ends.' '10. Finis et utilitas omnium rerum non existit casu vel a natura bruta, sed a natura sapiente et omnipotente, quae est Deus. Omnes vero res ad suos ac certos fines ordinatae sunt sapientissime.' (*Ibid.* p. 119), becomes, '9. All things in the world are appointed for definite ends and constantly aim towards them. Therefore there is some most wise and omnipotent nature universally ordering all things by its providence and leading each of them to their appointed ends.' '9. Res omnes in mundo sunt ordinatae ad certos fines et ad eos tendunt constanter. Ergo est aliqua natura sapientissima et omnipotens sua providentia omnia universaliter sic ordinans et singula ad fines destinatos deducens.' (*Ibid.*, p. 146.)

Here the Neustadt edition again supplements that of Geneva but on this occasion Pareus preserves its additions. Thus Neustadt appends scriptural references to each argument except the last, from final causality, and supplements all, save the first and the last, with quotations from classical authors. This appeal to classical antiquity was already evident at one or two points in Melanchthon's five arguments,[44] although in his own far more extensive selection, Ursinus actually employs different quotations.

At first sight we might suppose that Ursinus was making a major innovation by his introduction of *a priori* arguments for the existence of Providence. His master Melanchthon, from whom alone he has so far drawn all his proofs, confines himself entirely to *a posteriori* arguments. What then are we to make of Ursinus's eight arguments 'from God's nature'? In fact, closer examination reveals that he has simply turned the familiar *a posteriori* arguments on their heads and, beginning with their conclusions, has deduced their premises. Thus the fifth *a posteriori* argument from rewards and punishments, '5. Rewards and punishments witness that there is some enforcer of the natural law. More peaceful are the ends of those who live moderately even outside the church. Now fearful punishments follow horrible crimes. Therefore there is a judge of the world,'[45] is reversed to become the fourth *a priori* argument from the justice of God, '4. God is utterly just and the judge of the world. Therefore He Himself rewards the good and punishes the evil.'[46] Ursinus is not therefore overthrowing Melanchthon's *a posteriori* approach but nonetheless this slightly odd supplementary treatment of it again increases the disciple's movement towards greater emphasis upon the use of rational arguments than was apparent in his master.[47]

So important was the Heidelberg Catechism in the life of the Dutch Reformed Church that it was not long before Ursinus's commentary was

[44] *CR* 13, cols. 204-5.

[45] '5. Praemia et poenae testantur esse aliquem exsecutorem legis naturae, Placidiores sunt eorum exitus, qui moderate vivunt etiam extra ecclesiam. Atrocia vero delicta sequuntur atroces poenae. Ergo est aliquis iudex mundi.' (*Ursinus, Frankfurt, 1621*, p. 145.)

[46] '4. Deus est summe iustus, et mundi iudex. Ergo ipse bonis dat praemia, malis infligit poenas.' (*Ibid.*, p. 146.)

[47] Cf. E. Bizer's examination of Ursinus's Commentary in his *Frühorthodoxie und Rationalismus*, Zurich, 1963, pp. 16-32, when he comments upon the rationalistic idea of truth which is revealed by the latter's repeated reliance upon such lists of arguments, see especially pp. 19-20. Bizer makes no mention whatsoever of Melanchthon and so never raises the question of Ursinus's dependence upon, or his exaggeration of, the rationalistic traits already apparent in his master. But See P. Althaus *Die Prinzipien der deutschen reformierten Dogmatik im Zeitalter der aristotelischen Scholastik*, Leipzig, 1914, reprinted Darmstadt, 1967; pp. 155-63.

joined by others, which were the work of Dutchmen.[48] The first of these to be written, though not to be published, is of particular interest in enabling us to begin making some assessment of the influence exerted over subsequent commentators by Ursinus's *Explicationes* since it provides us with our only example of one such work written before that influence was brought to bear. This Dutch commentary was first published at Leiden in 1598 and its title page reveals something of its history,

> *Exposition of the Catechism of the Reformed Christian Church in the Netherlands. Formerly written by E. Cornelis Corstens, in his day Minister of the Word at Delfshaven. Reviewed and adorned with many fine directions in the margins by Willem Vinck Dircxz, and now published for the first time.*[49]

Corstens himself died in July 1582[50] and so his commentary, written well before the appearance of those of Ursinus, Bastingius and Lansbergen which preceded it in terms of publication, must rank as one of the earliest such works.

In his treatment of Question 25, Corstens is entirely at one with the letter and spirit of the Catechism in confining himself to the questions of the Unity and Trinity of the Godhead and in stressing that scriptural revelation is the source of our knowledge, especially of the latter doctrine. Indeed, he begins his answer by positively labouring the point that human ingenuity is utterly unable to comprehend God, concluding with a vivid warning lest such an attempt should emulate the flight of Icarus,

> 'The Catechism informs us that we are to believe in God's being and the distinction of the persons not by human understanding but by the contents of God's Word. For were we to judge this unity of being and God's Trinitarian nature by our understanding then we would comprehend God with our understanding. And therefore this goes beyond our intellect ... and therefore we will not enquire into this high and secret thing with our understanding but with what God has revealed to us in His Word to pronounce peace. So that with ideas that range too high we should not fly with Icarus and burn and fall into the sea of God's infinity.'[51]

---

[48] The term is used in the widest sense, and thus includes natives of the Southern Netherlands, such as Bastingius and Lansbergen, who, forced by religious persecution to flee their birth-place, eventually settled in the United Provinces, and also a man like Kuchlinus who, though born and educated in Germany, nonetheless exercised the greater part of his ministry in Holland.

[49] *Wtlegghinge Des Catechismi der gereformeerde Christelicke Kercke in Neerduytslandt. Eertijts beschreven door den E. Cornelis Corstens, in sijnen tijt Dienaer des Woorts tot Delfs-haven. Ende door Willem Vinck Dircxz ... oversien en verciert met veel schoone aenwijsingen inde margien ende nu eerst in druck laten wt-gaen.*

[50] See *NNBW* VIII col. 317.

[51] ... die Catechismus te kennen gheeft datmen het wesen Gods ende het onderscheyt der persoonen niet nae vernuft des menschen maer nae het inhoudt van Godts Woort ghelooven

It is true that, when immediately afterwards Corstens turns to the issue of God's unity, he adduces the witness of the creation in language strongly reminiscent of the second Article of the Belgic Confession, 'As regards God's unity, that is well testified for us from the creation of all creatures. Because in this all visible creatures are like letters in a beautiful book to show us their creator,'[52] but the authority of Scripture is immediately invoked with the quotation of Psalms 1, 1-2, 97, 6 and Hebrews 11, 3. It is especially interesting that it is at this point that Corstens's editor, Willem Vinck Dirckz[53] feels obliged to supply what he evidently feels is lacking with an insertion in the text which reads, 'See further Ursinus in the first question, whether there is a God, in which he sets out various points and reasons from theology and philosophy on the knowledge of God and arguments for the same which they have in common.'[54] Further scriptural texts follow to prove God's unity but at the end of the section, Vinck again points the reader to Ursinus, 'See further Ursinus on the third question, that there is one God.'[55] We could hardly wish for clearer evidence of the effect that Ursinus's *Explicationes* was exercising upon subsequent commentators who, following his example, felt the necessity of concerning themselves with the issue of God's existence in their treatment of Question 25 where the text of the Catechism itself offers no warrant for so doing.

Turning to Question 27, we note that Corstens begins his treatment of Providence in the same way as Ursinus by recounting the inadequate views held on this subject by the Epicureans, Stoics and Peripatetics. Both

---

sal. Want souden wy dese eenicheyt des wesens ende die Dryevuldicheydt Gods nae onsen vernuft oordeelen soo souden wy Godt met onsen vernuft willen begrijpen: het welckeniet geschiedenen can want Godt is onbegrijpelijck. Ende daerom gaet dit onsen verstant te boven ... Ende daerom salmen dese hooge en ons verborgen dingen niet met onse vernuft ondersoecken maer met het ghene dat ons Godt in zijn Woort geopenbaert heeft te vrede wesen. Op dat wy met onse te hooge vliegende gedachten met den Icaro die vleugelen niet en verbranden ende int Meyr der ongrondelijckheyt Gods niet en versincken.' (Corstens, *op. cit.*, ff. 49$^{v}$-50$^{r}$.)

[52] 'Aengaande datter een eenich Godt is dat wort ons wel betuygt wt het scheppen van allen Creaturen. Daer in dat ons alle sienlijcke creatueren zijn als letteren in eenen schoonen Boeck om ons den werckman derselver aen te wijsen.' (*Ibid.*, fol. 50$^{r}$.) For the article of the Belgic Confession. See below, pp. 109-10.

[53] + 1614. See *NNBW* IX, col. 1211.

[54] 'Siet voort Ursinum in die eerste Vrage Offer een God is daer in dat hy verscheyden stucken ende redenen stelt die de Theologie ende Philosophie van de kennisse Godts ende argumenten der selver ghemeyn heeft.' (Corstens, *op. cit.*, fol. 50$^{r}$.) The marginal reference here, 'In compendio doctrinae Christianae, seu commentariis Catechetieis D. Ursini. Fo. 181,' directs to us the Leiden edition of 1584.

[55] 'Siet voort Ursinum opde derde Vraghe datter een Godt is.' (*Ibid.* fol. 50$^{r}$.) cf. Ursinus, 'III Unde constet unum esse Deum' (*Leiden, 1584*, pp. 186-9).

commentators, of course, are here echoing Melanchthon whose constant concern to establish God's Providence led him at times to consider these very same philosophical objections.[56] However, unlike Ursinus, Melanchthon and Bastingius who, as we shall shortly see, also includes these objections amongst those which he cites, Corstens does not resort to philosophical arguments in response. He is very ready to supply reasons in support of a fully adequate doctrine of God's Providence but the five such presented, which occupy three full octavo pages, are all rooted and grounded in Scripture. Indeed the first is headed simply, 'From the testimony of Holy Scripture', and quotes apposite sayings of Christ and the prophets, whilst the second looks to the miracles of the Old and New Testaments. Even when Corstens comes to his third reason, the succession of the different seasons of the year with all that this implies for the earth's fertility, apparently an obvious appeal to nature, he draws heavily upon scriptural quotations, concluding with a reference to the whole of the fourth chapter of the book of Amos, 'From which it is evident that all fertility and infertility does not properly speaking come from nature but from God's pronouncement.'[57] Finally for his fourth and fifth reasons, Corstens is again firmly within the sphere of relevation when he adduces first, the sense of trust in God's activity experienced by the faithful and second, the prophecies of Christ, the apostles and the prophets.

Thus in this wholly scriptural and unphilosophical way, Corstens replies to the philosophical views presented at the beginning of the Question. Perhaps the comprehensiveness of his response is the reason why Vinck does not feel it necessary to refer the reader to Ursinus for further arguments. All in all, Corstens is an impressive commentator who is faithful to the text of the Catechism. Whether others would have continued to be so had it not been for the appearance of Ursinus's *Explicationes*, the effect of whose influence we have observed in Vinck's insertions, is a question which will remain with us as we examine their works.

The first and most popular of these to be published was that of Jeremias Bastingius (1551-1595), who had studied at Heidelberg and had maintained close relations with Zanchius, Ursinus's renowned colleague there.[58] This appeared at Dordrecht, in 1588, as *An Exposition or commentary*

---

[56] Cf. The 'De providentia' section of the *Initia Doctrinae Physicae* (*CR* 13, cols. 203-6).

[57] 'Daer wt dat het dan blijckt dat alle vruchtbaerheyt en onvruchtbaerheyt niet wt die ordre der natueren maer eygentlijcken wt den zeghen Gods comen.' (Corstens, *op. cit.*, fol. 60$^{v}$.)

[58] For Bastingius see *BWPGN*, I. pp. 340-6. It is on record as early as 1581 that Bastingius had been charged by the Middleburg Synod with the task of providing exegemata on the Catechism. 'Hieremias Bastingius ende classe van Walcheren sullen maecken ex-

*on the Catechism of the Christian Religion which is taught in the churches and schools, both of the Netherlands and the Palatinate.*[59] Its popularity may be gauged by its translation into German (Neustadt, 1596), English (Cambridge, 1589), reprinted at least six times between 1592 and 1617,[60] and Dutch (Dordrecht, 1591), with seven new editions appearing between 1594 and 1762.[61]

Bastingius received his D.D. degree at Heidelberg in 1576, and so it is at least possible that he may there have attended Ursinus's lectures on the catechism. At any rate, the probability of his having read the latter's published commentary before the first publication of his own is extremely high, and we shall point to evidence which goes far towards confirming this conclusion. Bastingius's first edition of 1588, as witnessed by the English translations and by the first edition of the Dutch translation, had a plentiful supply of scriptural references in the margin and also some headings to indicate the course of the argument, but references to recent authors were, with one exception,[62] entirely confined to the sections containing erroneous views, headed 'Falsa Doctrina.'[63] The second edition, from which our Latin quotations are given, adds some forty such marginal references, the great bulk from Calvin.[64] The direct evidence for

---

egemata over den catechismum onser kercken.' See F. L. Rutgers (ed.) *Acta van de Nederlandsche Synoden der Zestiende eeuw*, Utrecht, 1889, p. 371.

[59] *In Catechesim religionis Christianae, quae in Ecclesiis et scholis, tum Belgii tum Palatinatus traditur, exegemata, sive commentarii.* This is a very rare work. According to the *Index Aureliensis* (Pt. I. T. III, 1968, pp. 336-37), there are only three copies in existence, none of which are in Dutch or English libraries. This first edition is, however, preserved in the English translation, which appeared before the second, much improved, Latin edition, and which was never revised in its subsequent reprintings. Quotations here are given from the aforementioned 'Editio altera recognita & aucta,' Heidelberg 1590. Cited as Bastingius, *Exegemata.*

[60] *Short Title Catalogue*, p. 36, Nos. 1562-1567.

[61] See C. Sepp, *Het Godgeleerd onderwijs in Nederland gedurende de 16e en 17e eeuw*, Vol. I, Leiden, 1873, p. 86.

[62] In the commentary on Question 11, there is the marginal reference, 'See Calvin lib. de praedest.' (*An Exposition or Commentairie upon the Catechisme of Christian religion*, Cambridge, 1589, p. 14.)

[63] In the opening 'Admonition to the Reader,' Bastingius tells us where he found the model for this arrangement, 'The errors contrary to the true doctrine I have set down severally without any great space between, therein following (if I be not deceived) the minister of the Italian church that is at Geneva, who in his commentary upon the Catechism of Geneva hath gone before me in this order.' (*Exposition*, fol. A2$^{r}$.) The work to which Bastingius is referring can only be *Il Catechismo di Messr. Giovan. Calvino. Con una brieve summario de quella doctrina che si crede sotto il Papato*, Geneva, 1566. No author is given on the title page, but the 'Epistola a Fedeli della Italia,' dated Geneva, 1st August, 1566, is signed 'Nicolao Balbani.' Sections headed 'Falsa dottrina' appear regularly throughout the work. For Balbani, who for a time held the post at Geneva ascribed to him by Bastingius, see *Dizionario Biografico Degli Italiani* Vol. 5, Rome, 1963, pp. 336-42.

[64] There are thirty-one references to Calvin, twenty-seven of which are to the *Institutes*,

Bastingius's knowledge of Ursinus's commentary by the time of this second edition is furnished in the most substantial marginal reference given in the entire work which, in fact, opens his treatment of Question 25, 'Vide. Cal. Inst. lib. I. ca. 13. Zanchium lib. De tribus Eloh. + Z. Ursinum in catechesi ...'[65] The text of Bastingius's commentary on this Question is the same in both editions and, in keeping with the terms of the Catechism here, he undertakes to consider the two matters of the unity of the divine substance and the distinction between the divine persons. The very fact that, entirely out of context, he feels obliged to add 'for that God is, amongst us that are Christians, needeth no proofe,'[66] indicates not only that, unlike Ursinus, he considers the proving of God's existence to be unnecessary, but also strongly suggests his knowledge of Ursinus's proofs at this point, for, let us recall, there is otherwise nothing in the text to raise this issue.

Having carried out his avowed aim on the basis of Scriptural evidence, Bastingius devotes the 'False Doctrine' section to showing that the effect of his arguments is to refute all heathen polytheism and *a forteriori* any kind of atheism. At this point, he considers it quite sufficient merely to reassert, with quotations from Cicero and John Damascene and marginal references to Romans 1, 19, 20, and Acts 14, 17 and 17, 25 and 26, that all men possess an innate knowledge of God's existence,

> 'And much more that wicked opinion of Diagoras Melius, who was surnamed Godlesse: and of Theodorus the Cyrenaicke, who both did flatlie denie that there was any God: whereas there is no nation so barbarous, no people so savage, into whome this perswasion doth not sinke, that there is a God. The knowledge of whom (that I may use Damascens words) is ingrassed and bred in us by nature, of which knowledge the Apostle disputeth in the Epistle to the Romanes, and else where against the Gentiles.'[67]

It would seem then that not only 'amongst us that are Christians', but even 'against the Gentiles', Bastingius is content to advance this single

---

eight to Beza, one to Benedictus Arelius, and one to Zanchius. Ursinus ranks third in this list for, in addition to the reference we shall be noting shortly, Bastingius refers to him in his treatment of Question 114 'Zach. Ursinum in locis pag. 258 + 295 + de lib. arbitrio.' (Bastingius, *Exegemata*, p. 514.)

[65] *Ibid.*, p. 83.

[66] Bastingius, *Exposition*, fol. 26 v, as literal a translation as one could wish for, 'nam Deum esse, apud nos qui Christiani sumus, nulla eget probatione.' (*Exegemata*, p. 84.)

[67] *Exposition*, fol. 28 r, cf. 'Et multo impia opinio Diagorae Melii, qui cognomento dictus ἄθεος itemque Theodori Cyrenaici, qui uterque simpliciter negarunt Deum esse. Quum nulla tam barbara sit natio, nulla tam gens efferata, cui non insideat haec persuasio Deum esse: utpote cuius cognito (ut Damasceni verbis utat φυσικως ἤμιν ἐγκατεσπαρτας hoc est, natura nobis sit insita atque ingenita. De qua cognitione disseri Apostolus in Epistola ad Rom. et alibi adversus gentes.' (*Exegamata*, p. 88.)

argument, merely supplementing it, in those marginal references to the New Testament passages noted above, with the argument from the natural order. In fact he is using the same pair of arguments as his avowed master, Calvin,[68] though in this instance he lays far less emphasis than does the latter on the second of the two. We must not thereby conclude that Bastingius denigrates the revelation of God open to man in the natural creation. However, he reserves his celebration of this means to the knowledge of God for a later passage, where it is unmistakably confined to the faithful.

In expounding the Catechism's answer to Question 122, on the meaning of the first petition of the Lord's Prayer, Bastingius takes his clue from the first part of the answer:

> 'Hallowed be thy name: that is allow us first of all to know thee aright, and to reverence, praise and set forth thy almighty power, wisdom, goodness, righteousness, mercy and truth which shines in all thy works.'[69]

A marginal heading clearly indicates the line of his exposition, 'God is known in two ways.'[70] The first of these is by means of Scriptural revelation,

> 'For as to the true knowledge of God, God himself hath delivered it in his word, in the writings of the prophets and apostles...'

whilst the second is set forward in a manner every bit as positive:

> 'Neither is that any other way, wherein God hath offered him selfe to be known by his workes, vertues, and properties: In the creation of heaven and earth shineth his Almightie power, that he holdeth all thinges in his hand, and maketh them to abide and continue in him: his wisdome, by the most orderlie disposing of them: his goodnesse because there was no cause why he should create all these thinges, neither can he by any other reason be moved to preserve them but for the verie same: by his righteousness in governing,

---

[68] In the opening 'Admonition to the Reader', Bastingius declared 'Moreover because I have always been delighted with reading of Calvin's Institutions and that which Fabius saith of Cicero, that I have always applied to that writer: "Let him know that he hath profited, who is very much delighted with Calvin", thereof it is, that where the matter gave leave, I expressed the meaning of our Catechist rather in his words than in mine own, partly to prick thee also forward diligently to read that book of Institutions, partly because I did see that it did not hinder but rather further my purpose.' (*Exposition*, fol. A 2$^{r}$.) We have already seen that, in the matter of the marginal references in the second edition, Bastingius gave ample proof of this predilection for Calvin's *Institutes*.

[69] 'Sanctificetur nomen tuum: hoc est da, principio ut te recte agnoscamus, et lucentum in omnibus operibus tuis omnipotentiam, sapientiam, bonitatem, iustitatiam, misericordiam, et veritatem tuam veneremur, praedicemus et celebremus...' (*Exegemata*, p. 540).

[70] 'Deum cognosci dupliciter.' (*Ibid.*, p. 542.)

> because he punisheth the offendours and delivereth the innocent: his mercie, that in so great patience he beareth with the forwardness of men: his truth, by that he is unchangeable.'[71]

The Marginal reference here is to Romans I, 20 and this interpretation of God's attributes discernible from His works in nature and in history is taken verbatim from Calvin's Commentary on the next verse of that epistle,[72] where the latter denies that fallen man can recognise them, 'Since men have not recognised these attributes in God, but here have conjured up an imaginary picture of Him as though He were an insubstantial phantom...';[73] Bastingius is thus faithful to the spirit as well as to the letter of his master. However, the application of the twofold scheme of revelation at this point in the former's commentary, where it is in no way explicit in the text of the Catechism, may be due to Ursinus. Perhaps the latter felt it necessary to introduce a reference to Scriptural revelation in order to prevent any possible misunderstanding. At any rate, not only does he do this, but so presents it as virtually to subsume that revelation through God's works which alone is mentioned in the text:

> 'However we hallow God 1/ When we acknowledge God to be such as He has revealed Himself by His word and works, that is when we know and feel the same about God's essence, about God's will and works, omnipotence, goodness, wisdom and the rest of God's attributes that God has commanded and revealed for us to know and to feel about them by His word.'[74]

Bastingius has gone some way towards restoring the emphasis of the text whilst preserving the element which Ursinus has here introduced into the

---

[71] *Exposition*, p. 176. 'Quod attinet ad veram Dei cognitionem, tradidit hanc ipsemet Deus verbo suo, scriptis Prophetarum et Apostolorum...'
'...Neque alia est ratio, qua se Deus cognoscendum praebuit per opera sua virtutes et attributa, ut in creatione coeli et terra elucet eius omnipotentia, quod tenet omnia in sua manu, facitque ut in se consistant: sapientia, ex ordinatissima dispositione: bonitas, quia nihil caussae erat, cur conderet haec omnia neque alia ratione moveri potest, ut eadem conservet, quam ob illam ipsam iustitia, in administratione, quia sontes punit, insontes vindicat: misericordia, quod tanta patientia tolerat hominium perversitatem: veritas, ex eo quod immutabilis est.' (*Exegemata*, p. 542.)

[72] *CR*. 77, col. 24. Calvin's list begins with 'aeternitas', but Bastingius omits this as it does not appear in that of the Catechism. Calvin's second attribute is actually 'potentia' but Bastingius evidently has no hesitation in treating this as 'omnipotentia.' Thereafter, he follows Calvin exactly, save that he renders the latter's 'innocentes vendicat' as 'insontes vindicat.'

[73] 'Eiusmodi virtutes quum non recognoverint homines in Deo sed somniarint tanquam inane phantasma...' (*CR*. 77, col. 24.)

[74] 'Nos autem Deum sanctificamus 1/ Quum agnoscimus Deum esse talem se patefecit verbo et operibus, id est quando eadem de essentia Dei, de Dei voluntate, atque operibus, denique omnipotentia, bonitate, sapientia, et reliquis attributis Dei cognoscimus et sentimus, quae de iis nos agnoscere, et sentire verbo suo Deus praecepit et revelavit.' (*Ursinus, Geneva, 1584*, p. 859.)

commentary and thus presenting a balanced treatment of the two-fold pattern of revelation.

When, however, we turn to Question 27 on God's Providence, we find that, although Bastingius's treatment has many individual features peculiar to himself, he has clearly deserted Calvin's pattern for that of Ursinus. The former makes no attempt to prove the existence of Providence. In his section on this topic in the *Institutes*, he will go so far as to allow that 'In general, philosophers teach, and human minds conceive that all parts of the universe are quickened by God's secret inspiration,'[75] but his chief concern is to establish, on the basis of Scripture, the absolute universality of God's particular providence rather than a mere acknowledgement of that customarily termed general. In contrast, Ursinus's three-fold division of the question, '1. Whether there is any Providence of God. 2. What is God's Providence. 3. Why knowledge of it is necessary,'[76] is closely paralleled by Bastingius, '1. To show that there is Providence in God. 2. To show out of the Scripture what Providence is, how many kinds thereof there be, and about what matters it is occupied. 3. What is the use of it.'[77]

As we saw above, Ursinus divided his proofs of Providence into the scriptural and the philosophical; the latter being subdivided into two groups, 'One containing *a posteriori* reasons, namely those drawn from the works or effects of God. The other embracing *a priori* reasons obtained indeed from God's attributes.'[78] Ursinus gave nine *a posteriori* arguments and eight *a priori*[79] Bastingius, ignoring for his part any reference to Scriptural evidence, launches immediately into his eight rational proofs for the existence of God's Providence, with only a marginal note to indicate that he is following Ursinus's subdivision, albeit in the reverse order, 'Whether there is Providence in God is proved by reasons from God's nature. 2. By

[75] I, xvi, 1. *LCC*, p. 198.

[76] '1. An sit aliqua Dei Providentia. 2. Quid sit providentia Dei. 3. Cur necessaria sit eius cognitio.' (*Ursinus, Geneva, 1584*, p. 204.)

[77] Bastingius, *Exposition*. fol. 31$^{r}$. '1. Ut demonstremus esse providentiam in Deo. 2. Ut quid sit providentia, quotuplex, et circa quae versetur, ex scripturis explicemus. 3. Quis illius usus.' (*Exegemata*, p. 97.)

[78] 'Unum continet rationes *a posteriori*: nempe sumptas ex operibus, vel effectis Dei: alterum rationes *a priori* complectitur, petitas nimirum ab attributis Dei.' (*Ursinus, Geneva, 1584*, p. 205.)

[79] The Genevan version (p. 209) adds a ninth *a priori* argument which is not properly one as it is largely concerned to explain Providence's relationship to good and evil. It is omitted in the Neustadt version and in Pareus's revisions. Oddly enough the English translation also provides nine *a priori* arguments. This it achieves by taking all eight provided by Neustadt and inserting the fifth Genevan argument as its own number five, thus giving two versions of the argument from God's goodness. (*The Summe of Christian Doctrine*, Oxford, 1587, p. 385.)

proofs from the works and effects of God.'[80] Four arguments of each sort are sufficient for Bastingius who, for the most part, avoids those used by Ursinus. Indeed, any measure of similarity between the two commentators appears to be incidental, even when they are using the same argument. Thus we may compare the two versions of the *a posteriori* appeal to man's intelligent ordering of his own affairs:

Ursinus: 'The mind and intellect in angels and men. Man, who is as it were a little world, is ruled by a mind: much more therefore is that great world, in the administration of which more wisdom is required.'[81]

Bastingius: 'If there is intelligence, understanding, reason and wisdom in mankind from where does this come upon earth if not from God? ... Hence I conclude that if man acts providently in his own matters how much more does God, from whom man received mind and reason, direct the world by providence and sure design?'[82]

Nonetheless, whatever the difference in the arguments used, the important fact is that here, in complete distinction from the question of the existence of God, Bastingius is every bit as ready as Ursinus to employ extensive arguments based wholly upon natural reason.

Why he should follow the latter's lead in the one case, having refused it in the other, is by no means clear. One possible answer emerges when we compare the 'False Doctrine' section of this Question with that of Question 25 which we considered above. This latter deals briefly with two such items, polytheism/atheism and Sabellianism. In Question 27, however, more than twice this space is accorded to the consideration of no less than five objections to the existence of Providence, all of which are philosophical.

'Setting aside Protagoras, Melius and others who either denied or at least doubted the existence of God and hence that of Providence: as also Democritus and Epicureus, who thought that everything was made and continued daily by chance and fortune, we must correct, 1. the error of those who make Providence a bare foreknowledge by which an undisturbed God beholds

[80] 'Providentia an sit in Deo probatur rationibus a natura Dei. 2. Exemplis ex operibus et effectis Dei.' (Bastingius, *Exegemata*, p. 97.)

[81] 'Mens atque intellectus in Angelis et hominibus. Homo regitur mente, qui est quasi parvus mundus: multo magis ergo magnus ille mundus, in cuius administratione plus requiritur sapientiae.' (*Ursinus, Geneva, 1584*, p. 206.)

[82] 'Quod si est in hominum genere mens, consilium, ratio, prudentia, unde haec in terras nisi a Deo defluere potuerunt? ... Hinc ita colligo: si homo provide sua agit, quanto magis Deus a quo homo mentem rationemque accepit, providentia, certoque consilio, mundum administrat?' (Bastingius, *Exegemata*, pp. 97-8.)

from heaven what is happening in the world... 2. We must also remove the raving of the Stoics who devised such a necessity from the perpetual uniting of causes and, as it were, by a natural chain linked together, that they attributed everything to secondary causes ... No less foully deceived are those who say that Providence in God extends to individual things but that man is excepted in those things which are said to be in his power ... Fourthly it is evident that those also are in no small error who have written that although God cares for other things, yet He does not concern Himself with the smallest things, as with some base living creatures and other such things ... Finally, those also among the philosophers were mistaken who thought God would not be happy if He cared for men's affairs.'[83]

Granted that these are the stock objections, three of which, as we have seen, had figured both in Ursinus's Commentary and in Corstens's as yet unpublished Dutch work, yet Bastingius clearly outdoes both these last-named in the number of such cavils raised and it may well be that, feeling something of their force, he found it necessary to meet them on their own ground by advancing philosophical arguments for the existence of Providence against them. Whether or not this provides us with a satisfactory explanation, we are nonetheless left with a clear example of a movement away from Calvin at this point in one who took such pains to declare his allegiance to the reformer.

As will emerge in our consideration of it, Bastingius's influence is very marked in the next Dutch work on the Heidelberg Catechism which appeared at Middelburg in 1594. The author was Philip Lansbergen (1561-1632), a minister who achieved fame as a mathematician and astronomer[84] and whose commentary took the form of a series of sermons, *The Catechism of the Christian Religion, which is taught in the churches of the Netherlands and the Palatinate, expounded in 52 Sermons.*[85]

[83] 'Omissis Protagoras, Melio et aliis, qui vel negabant aut saltem dubitabant esse Deum, ac proinde Providentiam: Item, Democrito et Epicureo, qui casu et fortuna putabant omnis facta esse, et fieri quotidie, corrigendus est, 1. eorum error, qui Providentiam nudam faciunt praescientiam, qua Deus otiosus e coelo speculetur quae in mundo fiunt ... 2. Etiam Stoicorum delirium tollendum, qui huiusmodi necessitatem comminiscebantur ex perpetuo caussarum nexu et implicita quadam serie quae in natura contineatur, et omnia attribuerent caussis secundis ... Nec minus turpiter hallucinati qui dixerunt de singularibus etiam esse Providentiam in Deo: sed excipi hominem in iis quae diceunter esse ἐφ' ἡμιν ... Quarto manifestum est illos etiam non parvo detineri errore qui scriptum relinquerunt etsi res aliae curentur a Deo minimas tamen ut vilia animantia atque id genus reliqua illum curare nequaquam ... Postremo errarunt quoque illi ex Philosophis qui idcirco putarunt Deum non fore beatum si curet res humanas.' (*Ibid.*, pp. 102-5.)

[84] See *BWPGN*, V, pp. 549-554, and for Lansbergen as scientist, *Dictionary of Scientific Biography*, ed. C. C. Gillispie, Vol. VIII, New York, 1973, pp. 27-28.

[85] *Catechesis Religionis Christianae quae in Belgii et Palatinatus Ecclesiis docetur, Sermonibus LII explicata.* The work was reprinted in Germany three times, Neustadt 1595, Hanover 1620 and Frankfurt 1621, and was translated into Dutch as *Den Catechismus ofte onderwysinghe in de Chr. religie in LII predicatien verklaert*, Rotterdam 1616, 3rd ed., Amsterdam 1645.

That section of Lansbergen's 8th Sermon which deals with Question 25 of the Catechism is a pretty faithful rendering, in a rearranged form, of Bastingius's treatment of the same section. Thus the former employs the same scriptural texts to establish the divine unity and then, before handling the doctrine of the Trinity in the same fashion, inserts a version of that section against atheism which, as we saw, Bastingius put at the end of his piece under the heading 'False Doctrine.' Lansbergen's rendering differs slightly but significantly from his model and thus he reverses Bastingius's order by dealing first with atheism. Again, whereas the latter's only mention of the argument from the natural order was that implicit in his marginal reference to Romans I, 20 Acts 14, 17 and 17, 25 and 26, Lansbergen explicitly states that 'Nor is this (that there is a God) demonstrated from the foregoing texts (i.e. those by which, following Bastingius, he has established God's unity) only, but also from the created order,' and then proceeds to quote the above mentioned New Testament passages in the body of his text.[86] Bastingius's emphasis on the innate idea of God is reduced to the single and now unacknowledged quotation from Cicero which the latter had earlier given 'And certainly was there ever a nation so barbarous or a people so savage that the belief that there is a God was not engraved in their mind.'[87] By such small changes Lansbergen succeeds in transforming the balance struck by Bastingius between the two traditional Reformation arguments for the existence of God.

In Sermon 10 on Question 27 concerning Providence, Lansbergen shows an even greater freedom in altering Bastingius, although he still retains the latter's framework. He reduces the points to be considered from three to two, 'However there are two which are principally demonstrated in this chapter: first that there is a providence in God, second, what is the use of this doctrine,'[88] and under the first of these headings establishes the existence of Providence from Scripture and from the attributes and works of God. Lansbergen replaces the four rather clumsy *a priori* arguments employed by Bastingius with a single more elegant one of his own which, beginning with the postulate of God's omnipotence, supreme goodness and wisdom, concludes: 'And so God is able, willing and knows how to rule this world. However, there is no doubt that God carries out that which He is willing, able and knows how to do. But God is willing, able

[86] 'Neque ex praemissis modo locis ostendere hoc promptum est, sed ex rebus quoque creatis.' (Lansbergen, *op. cit.*, p. 43.)

[87] 'Et certe, quae fuit unquam tam barbara natio, aut gens tam efferata, cuius animo non fuit insculpta haec persuasio, Deum esse.' (*Ibid.*, pp. 43-44.)

[88] 'Sunt autem duo eius capita praecipue demonstranda: Primum quid sit Providentia in Deo. Secundo, quis doctrinae huius usus.' (*Ibid.*, p. 53.)

and knows how to rule this world first created by Him: therefore He does rule it.'[89]

Again Lansbergen's use of the *a posteriori* arguments differs markedly from Bastingius's. First he considers God's works in history and then, turning to the natural order, he displays a little of his astronomical interest:

> 'Next, the consistency of the world in its nature, beauty, excellence and order, declares the providence of God most clearly. For how would such an immense construction and so many bodies dependent upon it continue to exist unless God upheld the same by His mighty word? How might those heavenly bodies complete their movements according to an unchanging law, how indeed might they reach to the opposite corners of heaven and earth journeying on to the end with all their powers, unless there was someone who ruled and supported it most efficaciously?'[90]

He concludes with his one direct borrowing from Bastingius, Chrysostom's comparison of a ship and its continuing need for guidance, with the world and the necessity for God's providence in its ordering.

In his treatment of Question 122, Lansbergen again follows Bastingius but, in so doing, greatly expands the exposition of the manifestation of the divine attributes. The revelation through God's word receives due priority:

> 'Then in order that we may know God aright, we must learn from God's word first the nature of His essence and persons, and then His attributes. The knowledge of this foundation is so necessary for us that without it we can neither know nor worship God.'[91]

Having thus underlined this point, he asserts that these attributes of God referred to in the text of the Catechism, 'shine forth clearly in all His works,' ('non obscure in omnibus ipsius operibus lucent').

---

[89] 'Potest itaque Deus, vult ac novit gubernare hunc mundum. Quod autem Deus vult, potest ac novit, non dubium est quin ad ipsum agat. Sed Deus vult, potest ac novit gubernare hunc mundum semel a se conditum: ergo etiam gubernat.' (*Ibid.*)

[90] 'Postremo, mundi consistentia in sua forma, pulchritudine, virtute, et ordine, providentiam Dei evidentissime testatur. Quomodo enim tam immensa Machina et tot corpora in eadem pendula perstarent, nisi Deus eadem sustineret verbo suo potente? Quomodo coelestia illa corpora, constante lege motus suos potente? Quomodo coelestia illa corpora, constante lege motus suos absoluerent, imo tot contraria in caelo et terra permanerent, viribusque omnibus eundem in finem contenderent, nisi quisquam esset qui potentissime haec regeret ac foveret?' (*Ibid.*, pp. 53-54.)

[91] 'Porro ut Deum rite cognoscamus; primum ex Dei verbo discere nos opportet, qualis essentia et personis sit; deinde qualis attributis ... Cuius fundamenti cognitio usque adeo nobis necessaria est, ut citra hoc nec Deum agnosci, nec a nobis celebrari possit.' (*Ibid.*, p. 296.)

Bastingius had balanced his exposition of the divine attributes known in God's works in nature and history which, as we noted above, he borrowed from Calvin, with a second piece celebrating the same attributes discernible in God's redemptive activity:

> 'God's righteousness shines and appears gloriously in the redemption of mankind, first in that He has punished sins, then in that He has exacted the obedience of the Law and forgiven sins: His goodness, in that He has done this for His own sake: His mercy, wisdom ... omnipotence ... truth ..'[92]

Lansbergen puts these two groups together, one attribute at a time. Thus God's omnipotence, as discerned in nature, gives him the opportunity once more to display something of his astronomical learning.

> 'And indeed God clearly revealed His omnipotence in heaven and earth by its creation from nothing; ... truly the same is plainly to be perceived in the preservation of the created order: ... the earth itself suspended in the air is not turned aside from its appointed place; when those higher bodies which are of immense size, move themselves by their speed and constant motion, ... when the heaven itself seems to turn full circle on its axis every 24 hours, yet is not impaired; are not these clear proofs that God upholds this frame with His powerful Word?'[93]

Examples of God's redemptive activity which display this omnipotence are Christ's death for our sins and his resurrection, and also the Old Testament type of this in the deliverance of the Israelites from Egypt. The overall impression is that Lansbergen has gone further than Bastingius in emphasising the manifestation of God in the divine works, more especially in nature, whilst never losing sight of the priority of Scriptural revelation.

The next commentary for consideration is that of Ruardus Acronius (+1611), *Catechetical Commentaries: in which the Questions and Answers of the Catechism of the Dutch and Palatinate churches are methodically, fully and clearly explained*,[94] which was published at Schiedam in 1606. After a brief introduc-

---

[92] 'In redemptione generis humani refulget et illustris apparet Dei iustitia, primo quod peccata punivit, quod legis obedientiam exegit, et peccata condonavit: bonitas, quod hoc propter se fecit: misericordia ... sapientia ... omnipotentia ... veritas ...' (Bastingius, *op. cit.*, p. 543.)

[93] 'Et omnipotentiam quidem suam Deus manifeste in coeli et terra ex nihilo creatione exeruit; ... Eadem vero perspicue in conditarum rerum conservatione cernitur: ... terra ipso in aere pendula, a statuo loco non deflectat; cum superiora illa corpora quae immensae magnitudinis sunt, ea velocitate et constantia motus suos absoluant, ... cum coelum ipsum 24 horarium spacio rotario videatur continuo in polis motu, nec tamen atteratur; an non haec manifesta documenta sunt, Deum sustinere hanc machinam verbo illo suo potente?' (Lansbergen, *op. cit.*, p. 296.)

[94] *Enarrationes catecheticae: quibus Quaestiones et Responsiones Catechismi Ecclesiarum Belgicarum et Palatinatus methodice, compendiose et dilucide, explicantur*. For Acronius, see *BWPGN*, I, pp. 29-38.

tion, Acronius begins his treatment of Question 25 by considering the issue of the natural knowledge of God and in so doing he immediately makes the classic distinction between the natural and the supernatural knowledge in a manner which calls to mind that of Luther which we noted in an earlier section, 'The knowledge of God is twofold, one universal, the other particular or special.'[95]

We noted above that Lansbergen had altered the balance struck by Bastingius between the two Reformation arguments for God's existence, favouring that from design to that from innate knowledge. In Acronius, this process is carried still further and the natural knowledge of God is drawn entirely from the order discernible in nature with no mention of any innate source. 'The universal knowledge of God can be obtained from the consideration of things and from the order in nature.' Having established this with quotations from Cicero, Romans 1, 19, 20 and references to Acts 14, 17 and 17, 26 and Psalm 19, 1, he goes on in the proper Reformation spirit to underline the limitations of this knowledge,

> 'This knowledge of God which is drawn from created things would be clearer and more perfect if human nature had remained intact: now, however, having been spoiled and corrupted by sin, it has been obliterated and made more feeble but yet not completely extinct: for a spark of this knowledge remains in human nature, showing that God exists, rendering inexcusable all who deny or doubt God's existence, or who do not seek for Him: but not showing who God is or what He is like.'[96]

Acronius then caps this passage with the anecdote of Simonides's response to King Hieron's question about the nature of God which Calvin had used in a similar context in the first book of the *Institutes*.[97]

Acronius's treatment of Question 122 is entirely in line with that of Question 25. He goes on at some length to describe the manifestation of God's attributes in the works of nature,

---

[95] 'Duplex est noticia Dei, una universalis, altera particularis seu specialis.' (*Op. cit.*, fol. 40ʳ) cf. Luther—'Duplex est cognitio Dei, generalis et propria'' (*WA* 40 pt. I, p. 607). By the time of Acronius, this had become literally a commonplace. Thus David Pareus's Locus XVII on Romans I, 19, 20, has a fourfold division which is in this respect actually twofold. 'Unde quadruplex cognitio Dei, sic cohaerens: Alia generalis, alia specialis. Generalis est omnibus hominibus sana mente praeditis communis ... specialis ... est propria Ecclesiae.' (*In divam S. Pauli ad Romanos epistolam commentarius*, Heidelberg, 1613, cols. 166-167).

[96] 'Haec Dei cognitio, quae ex rebus creatis hauritur, magis illustris et perfecta esset, si natura humana integra mansisset: nunc autem vitiata et corrupta peccato, obliterata et languidior facta est, verum non prorsus extincta: mansit enim scintilla eius noticiae in genere humano, monstrans esse Deum, reddens inexcusabiles omnes, qui Deum esse negant, sit ne Deus dubitant, aut de eo non inquirant: non ostendens, quis et qualis sit Deus.' (Acronius, *op. cit.*, fol. 40ʳ.)

[97] I, v. 12.

'For the grandeur and beauty of heaven and earth, the splendour of the heavenly bodies, the variety of created things, the wonderful order of nature, the perpetual and harmonious movement of the stars, the change of the seasons, the foundation of the earth above the waters, its most beautiful embellishment, the grandeur of the sea, the rising of springs and rivers, and in short the use and purpose to which all created things are intended, not only demonstrates the existence of God but moreover declares that the architect of so great a piece of workmanship is omnipotent, wise, good, merciful and righteous.'[98]

However, not only does he immediately add 'All these attributes of God, but especially His justice and mercy, shine forth in the work of redemption and sanctification by the Son and the Holy Spirit',[99] but he has preceded this entire passage with a clear statement of the necessity of the Scriptural revelation for any proper knowledge of God.

'For the scriptures teach that the God is one, eternal, omnipotent, immense, of infinite power, wisdom, righteousness, goodness, truth and mercy: that He is the principle and author of all things: upon whose will all things depend, and by whose holiness, the whole framework of the world is preserved and governed ... Although the whole of created nature confesses that God is powerful, wise, kind, and is loving to Man; yet the full and consolatory knowledge is not attained without this filial knowledge.'[100]

On the whole, Acronius shows a fair measure of independence of earlier commentators on the Catechism and this is underlined by the fact that, unlike them, he makes no attempt to prove the existence of God's Providence, but instead devotes his commentary upon Question 27 to expounding the answer to the Catechism's actual question 'What is God's Providence?'[101]

There are certain resemblances between Acronius and the next of the individual Dutch commentaries on the Heidelberg catechism, which we

---

[98] 'Nam amplitudo coeli et terrae, corporum coelestium splendor, varietas rerum creatarum, naturae admirabilis ordo, stellarum perpetuus et concors motus, temporum vicissitudo, terra super aquas fundata, eius ornatus pulcherrimus, maris amplitudo, fontium et fluminum ortus, denique usus et finis, adquem omnes res creatae destinatae sunt, non tantum Deum esse convincunt, sed insuper Architectum tanti opifici, omnipotentem, sapientem, bonum, misericordem et justum esse, testantur.' (Acronius, *op. cit.*, fol. 230 v.)

[99] 'Etiam in opere redemptionis et sanctificationis per Filium et Spiritum sanctum, omnia haec Dei attributa, maxime vero illius justitia et misericordia, elucent.' (*Ibid.*)

[100] 'Docet enim scriptura, unum esse Deum aeternum, omnipotentem, immensum, infinitae potentiae, sapientiae, justitiae, bonitatis, veritatis et misericordiae: principium et autorem omnium rerum: ex cuius arbitrio omnia pendent, cuiusque numine, universa mundi machina, conservatur et regitur ... Etsi tota natura condita est, ut Deum potentem, sapientem, beneficum et hominis amantem, fateatur: tamen plena et consolatoria agnitio, sine hac filii agnitione, non contingit.' (*Ibid.*)

[101] *Ibid.*, fols. 44r-47v.

shall consider, that of Sibrandus Lubbertus (1555-1625), published at Franeker in 1618.[102] The latter also here omits any proofs for the existence of Providence in his treatment of Question 27, whilst in that of Question 25 he discusses the natural knowledge of God in terms somewhat similar to those of Acronius 'The existence of God is known by nature. We cannot, however, understand what He is by the light of nature.'[103] These two points are then established each by a quotation, the first by one from Cicero on the innate knowledge of God and the second by the Simonides's anecdote quoted here from the *De natura deorum*. The use of the first of these does mark one difference for it means that Lubbertus has reinstated this source of the natural knowledge of God which Acronius had practically eliminated and, in so doing, has restored the balance between the two Reformation arguments for God's existence. Lubbertus's further comments, however, continue to be very much in the vein of the earlier commentator:

> 'The cause of this state of affairs is that man's mind is darkened and ignorance has succeeded to the place of the knowledge with which it was furnished before the fall. For this cause, before he understood rightly what, who and of what nature God is, yet now he knows that God exists but is utterly ignorant as to who God is and of what He is like.'[104]

Earlier, in his treatment of Question 25, Lubbertus does something which none of the preceding Dutch commentators had done—he borrows some of Ursinus's arguments for the existence of God. In fact, he takes over two practically verbatim, that from efficient causality and that from the order discernible in nature.[105] We saw that, in his discussion of the limitations of the natural knowledge of God, Lubbertus was content to refer only to the source of innate knowledge. It is thus small wonder that having given these two arguments from Ursinus, he continues,

---

[102] *Commentarius in Catechesin Palatino-Belgicam*. Although described by one historian of the Catechism as 'een polemisch twistschrift, vooral gerigt tegen de stelsels der arminianen' (G. D. J. Schotel, *op. cit.*, p. 168), no such characteristics are apparent in the sections relevant to our concern, an indication that these parts of the Catechism were not a matter of dispute between the Remonstrants and their opponents. For Lubbertus, Professor of Theology at Franeker for forty years from the Academy's foundation there in 1585, see C. Van der Woude, *Sibrandus Lubbertus*, Kampen, 1963.

[103] 'Esse Deum natura notum est. Quid autem ille sit? lumine naturae comprehendere non possumus.' (Lubbertus, *op. cit.*, p. 220.)

[104] 'Causa hujus rei est, quod hominis mens est obscurata, et in locum scientiae, qua ante lapsum praedita erat successit ignorantia. Hanc ob causam ante recte intelligeret, quid, quis et qualis esset Deus? nunc quidem scit esse Deum, quis vero et qualis sit? penitus ignorat.' (*Ibid.*)

[105] *Ibid.*, p. 217.

> 'Add that in all men it has been engrafted by nature that there is some holy being or divine nature which rules and governs the whole framework of things.'[106]

He then immediately links this innate knowledge with man's conscience—a theme which, with reference to Romans 2, 15, he develops as his final argument for an entire page 'From this same source is that idea among God and men which we call conscience.'[107]

It is interesting to compare this treatment of Questions 25 and 27 with that accorded them in the series of disputations on the Catechism held under Lubbertus's presidency during the years 1615-16. A number of these, including the two relevant to our concern have been preserved in a collection published in 1669.[108] In comparison with the later commentary the disputations are very slight. Thus what occupies twenty-seven solidly written octavo pages in the former's discussion of Question 25 is expressed in thirty single sentence theses in the 1615 disputation. Indeed in the earlier treatment the question of God's existence takes up only one thesis, the first, where it is dismissed as unnecessary because God has indelibly inscribed this knowledge in the souls of all men.

> 'First Thesis. Whether there is a God? The question ought not to be worth considering not only among Christians, but also not among heathen peoples, since this knowledge is engraved on the minds of all men by the very finger of God, so that although some have tried to extinguish it from their minds, yet they have striven in vain.'[109]

We see here the stress upon the innate idea of God which we noted as a feature of Lubbertus's discussion of the issue in the Commentary, and again we observe the inescapable connection, indeed the identification, of this innate knowledge with conscience and the natural law. The latter is indicated by the phrase, 'the knowledge is engraved on the minds of all men by the very finger of God', which appears to be a clear reflection of that in the second Helvetic Confession's Chapter, 'Of God's Law', where the

---

[106] 'Adde omnibus hominibus esse a natura insitum, esse aliquod numen, sive divinam naturam, quae universam rerum machinam regat et gubernat.' (*Ibid.*, pp. 217-218.)

[107] 'Ex eodem fonte est notio illa inter Deum et hominem quam conscientiam vocamus.' (*Ibid.*, p. 218.)

[108] L. Guedtman, *L. Illustrium exercitationum* which includes 'Disputatio Theologica Nona explicans 25 quaest. Catechet. De Deo uno et tribus Personis,' proponent, Bernardus Jacobaeus, Franeker, 1615 and 'Disputatio Theologica Undecimna explicans 27 et 28 quaest. Catec. De Providentia Divina,' proponent Nicolaus Olisius, Franeker, 1616.

[109] 'Thesis Prima. An sit Deus? quaestio merito non debet habere locum non solum inter Christianos, sed nec inter profanas gentes, quum eius notitia, insculpta sit ipso Dei digito omnium hominum animis, ut quamvis nonnulli eam extinguere ex animis suis sint conati; tamen frustra id sint moliti.'

natural law is contrasted with the Mosaic as 'the law ... engraved by the finger of God in men's hearts and called the law of nature.'[110] Conscience, for its part, is as clearly indicated by the final references to the unavailing attempts of some men to rid themselves of this knowledge, a topic treated at length by Calvin in the third chapter of the first book of the *Institutes*. This apart, however, the refusal to go any further into the matter must surely be seen as a conventional device by which the disputant, with only a limited time available to him, disposed of this preliminary question in the shortest possible way before moving on to deal with the other weighty matters involved in a discussion of the doctrine of God. We shall encounter several examples of precisely this treatment during the course of our examination of disputations on this theme.

Occasionally, however, a disputation selects the opening question, that of the very existence of its subject matter, for extended treatment as one of the principal themes which will occupy a large part of the entire discussion. This is the case with the 1616 Disputation, 'De Providentia', for here Lubbertus provides all the arguments for the existence of Providence which he later omitted. The first nineteen single sentence theses out of a total of thirty-seven are given over to their presentation and the task is begun with no reference to proofs from Scripture since presumably the attempt is being directed at those who would not accept scriptural authority.

> 'First thesis. However, since at the very outset, Epicurus and his followers raise objections here, denying that there is any providence for those things which exist and take place in the lower parts of the world, we must establish the contrary with demonstrative arguments.'[111]

The arguments are precisely those of Ursinus, albeit reduced to little more than headings, the nine *a posteriori* are given in theses 3 to 11 and the eight *a priori* in theses 12 to 19.

The imprint of Ursinus and, through him, of Melanchthon, should occasion no surprise. Lubbertus studied at Neustadt from 1580 to 1582, and Van der Woude describes how greatly he came under the influence of Ursinus there.[112] Later in his book, Van der Woude quotes a letter of Lubbertus's to J. J. Grynaeus of Basel,[113] in which the former expressly

---

[110] 'Legem ... digito Dei insculptam esse in corda hominum, vocarique legem naturae.' (XII, 1.) See P. Schaff, *The Creeds of the Evangelical Protestant Churches*, London, 1877, p. 259.

[111] 'Thesis Prima. Quoniam autem in primo limine hic obstrepunt Epicurus et ejus asseclae negantes ullam esse providentiam eorum quae sunt et fiunt in inferioribus partibus mundi: nos contrarium apodictis argumentis astruemus.'

[112] Van der Woude, *op. cit.*, p. 32.

[113] *Ibid.*, p. 72. The letter is dated 9th August, 1591.

acknowledges that his own theological ideas and methods have been most influenced by three men—Grynaeus, Ursinus and Sadeel. Van der Woude comments that the last-named, whom in a footnote he explains is Anthony de Chandieu (1534-1591), whose *Opera Theologica* first appeared in 1591 and were reprinted in 1593, 1599, 1615 and 1620, was the greatest of these influences. De Chandieu, as he goes on to indicate, was one of the leading exponents of Protestant neo-scholasticism and the enterprise of assimilating the matter of Scripture with Aristotelian thought forms in order to argue systematically.[114]

In considering Lubbertus's commentary on the Heidelberg Catechism, Van der Woude draws attention to the striking difference from the earlier polemical works against Bellarmine and Vorstius, where the arguments were all expressed syllogistically.[115] More than once Van der Woude mentions Ursinus as a source of Lubbertus's Aristotelianism,[116] but he apparently fails to see that the different spirit of the latter's commentary owes very much to the model of his avowed master. Although Van der Woude notes that Ursinus gave his lectures on the Catechism at Neustadt, he makes no mention of Lubbertus's having attended or having been specifically influenced by them.[117] Furthermore, he appears to have missed the fragment of a letter of Lubbertus to David Paereus, written in the same year as that to Grynaeus noted above, in which, in commending Pareus's new edition of Ursinus's commentary that corrects the distortions of a previous edition of the same, Lubbertus refers, albeit obliquely, to his own attendance at the original lectures.[118] Although we have had cause more than once to comment upon the contrast between Ursinus's commentary and the Catechism itself, here we should note that the influence of the latter's unscholastic spirit has evidently moderated the style both of its first commentator and, through him, of his Dutch pupil.

---

[114] We shall have occasion to consider De Chandieu further elsewhere. See below, pp. 107-9.

[115] Van der Woude, *op. cit.*, p. 373.

[116] *Ibid.*, pp. 32 and 374.

[117] *Ibid.*, p. 31.

[118] The entire passage is as follows:

'D. Sibrandus Lubbertus viro Clarissimo D. David Pareo. S. Veritatem dico. Magna iniuria affecit D. Ursinum, quicunque Commentarios in Catechismum sub eius nomine N. Primum dedit. Aut enim eius sententiam de Justificatione hominis ignoravit aut maligne adulteravit. Testabuntur hoc omnes illi, quicunque D. Ursinum cum aliqua attentione docentum olim audiverunt. Bene igitur et de Ecclesia, et de communis nostro Praeceptore meritus es, illustrati. xxx Vale Franeccerae. a.d. 3 Octob. Anno 1591.' This is printed amongst the prefatory pieces to Philip Pareus's edition of his father, David's final revision of Ursinus's Catechetical Lectures, *Corpus Doctrinae Christianae*, Hanover, 1634.

Another of Ursinus's pupils, Johannes Kuchlinus (1546-1606),[119] who was at Heidelberg in 1565 and again in 1572 when he was a member of the former's famous 'collegium sapientiae', was responsible for more than 140 disputations on the Heidelberg Catechism[120] given under his presidency in the States College at Leiden during his years as Regent of that institution, 1592-1606.[121] Even more than in the case of Lubbertus, Ursinus' direct influence is clearly evident, and we may remind ourselves that it was from this environment that Kuchlinus' son-in-law, Festus Hommius, emerged to undertake the Dutch translation of the *Explicationes Catecheticae*.

G. J. Vossius (1577-1649), who was to achieve international fame as a scholar,[122] was the respondent in the disputation 'On the one and triune God', on Question 25. Following Ursinus's example a list of arguments for God's existence is inserted, all of which are drawn from him. There are, however, signs that Ursinus's treatment of the Question has been developed. Thus Kuchlinus prefaces these arguments with a brief discussion of the meaning of the word 'God', whilst his approach to the presentation of the arguments themselves is more systematic. He first categorises such arguments as either natural or supernatural, and then further divides the former group into the internal and the external.

> 'However there are ... two kinds of proofs and arguments. For the one sort are sought from nature, the other are supernatural. The first kind of these are either internal or external.'[123]

[119] See *BWPGN.*, V, pp. 289-296.

[120] The precedent for disputations upon the Heidelberg Catechism had been established at Leiden as early as 1582 during Daneau's brief tenure of the chair of Theology. Just two sets of these are extant, *Theses de generali catechismi Belgicarum Ecclesiarum partitione et ordinis, qui in eo servatur, ratione Lug. Bat ... Anno 1582 Mart 3* and *Theses de prima parte catechismi Belgici; ubi de hominis miseria et eius causa agitur Lug. Bat ... Anno 1582 April 7*: (see O. Fatio, *Nihil Pulchrius Ordine*, Leiden, 1971, p. 166). Since these evidently mark the beginning of a course and since Daneau left Leiden in May, 1582, there cannot have been many in the series.

[121] 126 of these disputations, all but a few of which may be found individually in the University Library of Leiden, were published there under the title *Syntagma Thesium Catecheticarum, in Collegio Illustri D. D. Ordinum Holl. et Westphrisiae* [sic], *sub praes. D. Joh. Kuchlini, Collegii illius Regentis dignissimi* ... (n.d.). All except 4 of these were reprinted, with the addition of a further 19, at Geneva in 1612, *Ecclesiarium Hollandicarum et West Frisiacarum Catechismus* ..., the edition from which our quotations are given. (Cited as *Ecc. Holl.*) They were reprinted yet again in the following year also at Geneva, with 3 new additions, *Theologicae Disputationes de Religionis Christianae capitibus praecipuis, in Coll. Theol. D. D. Ordinum Holl. et Westfris ... habitae. Accurata perspicuaque Methodo ante aliquot annos, explicate a Rever. et Clariss. viro D. Joh. Kuchlino* ... (see L. D. Petit, *Bibliographische lijst der werken van de Leidsche hoogleeraren ... 1575-1619*, Leiden, 1894, pp. 138-140). The States College, founded in 1592 with Kuchlinus as its first Regent, played an enormously important part in the theological and philosophical instruction of those who were to become the nation's leading theologians. See P. Dibon, *op. cit.*, pp. 20-26.

[122] See C. S. M. Rademaker, *Gerardus Joannes Vossius*, Zwolle, 1967.

[123] 'Sunt autem ... indicia atque argumenta duplicia. Alia enim sunt e natura petita, alia

Under the heading of internal, Kuchlinus pretty well covers all the arguments of this sort employed by Ursinus; the existence of the human mind with its capacity for understanding, its innate possession of the grasp of basic principles and of conscience, whose inner qualms are inescapable. The effect of these is the universal consent to belief in God's existence.

> 'The internal is the human mind itself which, since it is furnished with the power of intelligence and has the indelibly engraven notions of rhetoric and of the practical principles, cannot exist in this fashion either by itself or by chance. In addition, the inner fears with which individuals are disquieted because of sins committed, even when these are not followed by any human judgement or punishment, clearly argue the same conclusion. Hence therefore (as Tully bears witness) everyone unanimously concludes with the acknowledgement that God exists.'[124]

His approach to the external arguments is less comprehensive, since he lists only four, two of which, the beautiful order in nature and the regular movement of the heavens, had been included together as part of a single argument by Ursinus,

> 'The external is, the most beautiful order in the natural universe of things, the most wise series of causes leading us to a definite end, the regular division of the heavenly movements, political society and its wonderful preservation in the human race.'[125]

Interestingly enough, the reason Kuchlinus gives for the necessity of providing such arguments for the existence of God is not the apologetic one which eventually became predominant. Indeed, he affirms that, strict-

---

vero supernaturalia. Quae prioris generis sunt, ea sunt vel interna, vel externa.' (*Ecc. Holl.*, p. 207.) As we saw above (p. 73, n. 95), Pareus's Locus XVII on Romans 1, 19, 20 classifies the natural knowledge of God as 'generalis' and the supernatural as 'specialis'. The subdivision of the former is precisely that made by Kuchlinus, 'Eaque duplex: Interno seu naturalis, et externa seu acquisita. Interna et naturalis, a natura per notitias communes insita. Externa, ex intuita operum Dei, hoc est creaturarum et eventuum in mundo omnium sensibus et mentibus sese ingenerens.' (*op. cit.*, cols. 166-167). They both go on to make a similar division of the supernatural knowledge. Pareus: 'Externa seu Ecclesiastica, toti Ecclesiae communis, foris revelata per verbum Prophetarum et Apostolorum ... Et Interno seu spiritualis, quae intus per Spiritum sanctum ex verbo Dei cordibus electorum inscribitur.' (Col. 167) Kuchlinus: 'Supernaturale itidem est vel extrinsecum, nimirum sacra Scriptura, vel intrinsecum, quod est Spiritus sanctus.' (*Ecc. Holl.*, p. 208.)

[124] 'Internum est mens ipsa humana, quae cum sit intelligendi virtute praedita, insculptasque habeat indelebiles rhetoricorum ac practicorum principiorum notitias, nec a se ipsa, nec fortuito eiusmodi existere potest. Adde quod hoc ipsum terrores interni, quibus singuli ob admissa peccata exagitantur, etiam nullo ea hominum iudicio aut poena consequente, liquide arguunt. Hinc enim est quod (teste Tullio) omnes unanimi confessione concludunt, Esse Deum.' (*Ecc. Holl.*, pp. 207-208.)

[125] 'Externum est, ordo pulcherrimus in universa rerum natura, series caussarum sapientissima ad certum nos finem ducens, motuum caelestium constans distinctio, societas politica, eiusque admirabilis in genere humano conservatio.' (*Ibid.*, p. 208.)

ly speaking, there is no need to direct arguments at unbelievers since they already possess the ineluctable testimony of their own consciences. The arguments then are to fortify the faithful in the face of sinful man's profanity.

> 'For although those who deny the existence of God are not even worthy of the common name of men, they are permitted to be more than convicted of this impiety by the feeling and assent of their own consciences: however, it is necessary that the pious continously place certain most sure proofs before their eyes with which they may both firmly refute that more than barbaric profanity and fortify themselves against all false, diabolical scoffing.'[126]

The two disputations on Providence[127] both closely follow Ursinus's treatment of Question 27. Thus they seek to prove the existence of Providence in exactly the same way as Ursinus, (a) from Scripture, (b) by use of philosophical arguments of two kinds (i) *a posteriori*, (ii) *a priori*.[128] In the first disputation Kuchlinus gives nine *a posteriori* arguments, eight of which are those of Ursinus's list of nine—the one omission being the latter's fifth argument, from rewards and punishments. These are presented in the same order as their model and their number made up by a first argument, 'From creation', drawn virtually verbatim from the opening of Ursinus's exposition of Question 27, where he argues that the world is not to be seen as a ship which, once completed, passes out of the hands of the ship-wright, but that God's continuing guidance and conserving power is a necessary part of His work as Creator. In the second disputation, Kuchlinus reverts to the nine arguments of Ursinus's list, although he presents them in his own, apparently quite arbitrary, order.

Question 122, is dealt with in a later disputation,[129] where as elsewhere, the treatment closely follows that of Ursinus, save that when we reach the

---

[126] 'Nam tametsi nec communi quidem hominum nomine digni sunt, qui Deum esse negant, licet propriarum conscientiarum sensu et consensu abunde huius impietatis convincantur: necesse tamen est pios sibi perpetuo ob oculos ponere τεκμηεια quaedam certissima; quibus fortiter tum illam plusquam Barbaricam profanitatem diluant, tum sese ipsas muniant contra fraudulentos omnes satanae insultus.' (*Ibid.*, p. 207.)

[127] 'Adsertio Divinae Providentiae Contra Epicureorum Furores, resp. Henrico Nothenio ...' (*Ibid.*, pp. 218-226) and 'De Providentia Dei Ad Quaestionem Catech. 27 + 28. Resp. Justo Bulaeo ...' (*Ibid.*, pp. 226-231).

[128] In the first disputation, in fact, the definition of the two categories of this latter subdivision, either by a printer's error or by carelessness on the part of whoever prepared the text for the press, is put the wrong way round 'rationes Philosophicae ... quarum aliae a priori h.e. ab effectis, seu operibus Dei, aliae a posteriori h.e. ab attributis, proprietatibus seu natura Dei petuntur.' (*Ibid.*, p. 221.) The correct definition duly appears in the following disputation, 'Aliae a posteriori, sive ab effectis et operibus Dei, aliae a priori, sive a natura, attributis et proprietatibus Dei.' (*Ibid.*, p. 227.)

[129] 'De Sanctificatione nominis Dei, Complectentes explicationem questionis Catecheticae 122. Resp. Joanne Martini Lydio.' (*Ibid.*, pp. 845-849.)

passage from the latter quoted above,[130] we find that Kuchlinus alters this in order so to spell out the relative status of the modes of the knowledge of God as to put the issue beyond any shadow of doubt.

> 'The method of sanctification is demonstrated in the Catechism in three ways. 1. The true knowledge of the true God which is perfectly derived from the Word of God. Also indeed from His works is drawn that knowledge which is not sufficient for salvation and which renders man inexcusable. For God is not an unknown God but is known in Israel and has been manifested in the assembly of the godly through His Word, and therefore cannot be worshipped if He is not known.'[131]

It therefore hardly seems necessary for Kuchlinus to go on to add

> 'However, we must certainly seek the true, sufficient and saving knowledge of God, not only from the works of creation ... but even from Holy Scripture.'[132]

Kuchlinus's whole approach to the issue of the natural knowledge of God with the consequences for the theological and philosophical instruction within the newly-founded States College is clearly set out in his Inaugural Oration, delivered in October, 1592 and published at Leiden in the following year.[133] The sub-title, 'An address on theological colleges' gives a fair indication of the discourse's content. It is hardly surprising that, after his long experience as a member of Ursinus's 'Collegium Sapientiae' at Heidelberg, he should seek to set out a similar pattern for the new institution committed to his charge. Against those who would dismiss all philosophy as vain speculation, Kuchlinus insists that natural wisdom does have a legitimate role to play alongside its supernatural counterpart. Of course, it has very obvious limitations and, in outlining these, Kuchlinus begins by drawing upon his master. In the Prolegomena to his commentary on the catechism Ursinus made a fundamental distinction between true philosophy and the false doctrines of the sects which could not properly be classified as philosophy. Consequently, whilst theology goes beyond philosophy, there is no conflict between the two disciplines.

> 'Therefore although true philosophy is imperfect in respect of theology and is lacking in those things which have been mentioned, yet it never conflicts with

---

[130] See above, p. 66.

[131] 'Modus sanctificationis in Catechesi triplex ostenditur. 1. Vera veri Dei cognitio, quae ex verbo Dei perfecte petitur. Ex operibus quidem ea etiam agnitio hauritur, sed ad salutem non sufficiens, et hominem ἀναπολογητον reddens. Nam Deus non est ignotus Deus, sed in Israele notus et in coetus piorum per verbum manifestatus, ideoque non agnitus non potest celebrari.' (*Ecc.Holl.*, p. 846.)

[132] 'Veram autem sufficientem et salutarem Dei agnitionem, non tantum ex operibus creationis ... Sed etiam ex Sacra Scriptura petere debemus.' (*Ibid.*)

[133] *Oratio ... Joannis Kuchlini ... electi et vocati primi Praesidis Collegii theologici, nuper ... in Academia Leydensi instituti.*

> theology. In fact, those things which are mistaken in philosophers' books ... are not philosophical, but the empty quibblings of human cleverness and ulcers of true philosophy ...'[134]

Kuchlinus draws the same distinction:

> 'Many things are conjured up from true principles and true conclusions built up from these which are not doctrines nor components, but ulcers and blemishes of true philosophy and cannot be confirmed from it with any reason.'[135]

Again the latter's two-fold limitation upon the effectiveness of philosophy as a means to the true knowledge of God:

> 'Partly because the Son of God from the secret bosom of the Father has proclaimed the new doctrine of the Gospel which the wisdom of all angels and men could not have discovered; partly because the natural knowledge of the divine law has been darkened and damaged by sin and has therefore to be explained by repetitions and declamations.'[136]

is partly then taken from the same section of Ursinus's Prolegomena:

> 'Philosophy is wholly natural ... the Gospel is above and beyond nature in so much that if the Son of God had not revealed it to us from the bosom of the father, no wisdom of men or of angels could have discovered it.'[137]

Up to this point Kuchlinus has closely followed Ursinus, but when he proceeds to expand his views on the relationship between philosophy and

[134] 'Vera igitur philosophia etsi respectu theologiae est imperfecta, et in his, quae dicta sunt, deficit: tamen cum Theologia nunquam pugnat: Quae vero in philosophorum libris erronea ... philosophica non sunt, sed inanes argutiae humani ingenii, et ulcera verae philosophiae ...' (*Ursinus, Frankfurt, 1621*, p. 5.)

[135] 'Veris principiis et inde extructis veris conclusionibus multa affinguntur, quae non dogmata vel partes, sed ulcera et naevi sunt verae Philosophiae neque ulla ratione inde confirmari possunt.' (Kuchlinus, *Oratio*, p. 19.)

[136] 'Partim quia Filius Dei protulit ex arcano sinu Patris novam doctrinam Evangelii, quae omnium Angelorum et hominum sapientia inveniri non potuisset: partim quia legis divinae notitia naturalis per peccatum est obscurata ac mutila, ac proinde repetitionibus et declamationibus fuit explicanda.' (*Ibid.*, pp. 19-20.)

[137] 'Philosophia tota est naturalis ... Evangelium, praeter et supra naturam est, adeo ut nisi filius Dei nobis e sinu patris eam revelasset, nulla neque hominum neque angelorum sapientia eam inveniri potuerit.' (Ursinus, *op. cit.*, p. 4.) Elsewhere, Ursinus makes the same twofold limitation in full, albeit in slightly different language: 'Esse quidem vera aliqua de Dei patefacta etiam extra verbum Ecclesias traditum: sed ex iis tamen, quis sit verus Deus, ostendi non posse, duplici de causa. Primum enim ipsa illa per se non sufficiunt ... Sunt autem longe plura in verbo quam in natura de ipso patefacta ... Deinde, haec ipsa etiam Vera, quae restant in mentibus et in natura de Deo testimonia, omnes qui lucem et interpretationem eorum ex verbo Dei Ecclesiae tradito petitam, in his considerandis non sequuntur, pro innata sibi caecitate ac pravitate multipliciter corrumpunt.' (*Questiones et theses breviter complectentes summam locorum aliquot theologicorum*, in *Volumen Tractionum Theologicarum*, Neustadt, 1584, p. 49.)

theology, he does so at a length and in a tone which goes well beyond that of his master. Thus he lists seven abuses of philosophy:

'(I) It is, however, a misuse of philosophy when false principles whether of theology or philosophy are framed and false doctrines are defended from these which are at odds with true philosophy and theology.
(II) When philosophy is pretended to be adequate for teaching men about God and His worship and about men's salvation.
(III) When the doctrines of the church, unknown to human reason, are drawn, not from the divine oracles, but from philosophical arguments.
(IV) When the arguments of philosophy which are rightly uttered with regard to its own subjects are extended to divine issues for which they are in no way fitted and of which philosophy is ignorant.
(V) When opinions or utterances, which are daring enough even in philosophical matters, are transferred to theological issues as uncertain, ambiguous and superfluous subtleties which then become bogged down in the conflicts of disputations.
(VI) When philosophical phrases are employed in the church's teaching with unsuitable meaning and cunningly thought out ambiguities in order to find evasions and to beguile those who do not understand the manner of speech.
(VII) Finally, when its devotees impiously claim all praise for themselves, setting up the glory of this almighty yet also human wisdom as their own.'[138]

Commenting upon this passage, Dibon[139] maintains that it is written against the rationalism of the Socinians and also against the scholastic theology of the Roman church. Certainly Kuchlinus, whilst still very much under Ursinus's influence, is evidently far more alert than the latter to the threat to the Reformed position of assigning too high a worth to natural reason in theology and it is surely significant that he feels thus

[138] '(I) Est autem abusus Philosophiae, cum praetextu sive Philosophiae sive Theologiae finguntur falsa principia et ex illis falsa dogmata defunduntur, quae cum Philosophia vera et Theologia pugnant:
(II) Cum Philosophia fingitur sufficere ad docendos homines de Deo et ejus culta et salute hominum:
(III) Cum dogmata Ecclesiae ignota rationi humanae deducuntur non ex divinis oraculis, sed ex rationibus Philosphicis:
(IV) Cum quae Philosophia de rebus sibi subjectis recte pronunciat ad res divinas extenduntur, ad quas minime congruunt, et quas Philosophia ignorat:
(V) Cum opiniones aut locutiones, quae etiam in rebus Philosophicis, usurpatae sunt, incertae ambiguae, et subtiliates otiosae transferuntur ad res Theologicas, quae illis involuntur, et in pugnas disputationum convertuntur:
(VI) Cum phrases Philosophicae alieno sensu et novis ambiguitatibus vafre excogitatis usurpantur in doctrina Ecclesiae ad quaerenda effugia, et fallendos eos, qui genus sermonis non intelligunt:
(VII) Denique cum omnipotentis et huius etiam sapientiae humanae auctoris gloria seposita, laudem omnem sibi ipsis sacrilege tribuunt.' (Kuchlinus, *Oratio.*, p. 20.) The numerals in brackets appear in the margin.

[139] *L'Enseignement*, p. 23.

obliged to devote so much of his Inaugural to this exposition of the proper relationship between philosophy and theology.[140]

Before continuing our examination of further Dutch commentaries upon the Heidelberg Catechism, it will be helpful to consider some closely related evidence from the States College. This is provided by two sets of theses for the B.D. degree defended by Caspar Barlaeus in 1605 under Kuchlinus's presidency, *Theological propositions on the Knowledge of God* and *Theological propositions on the ways of knowing God.*[141]

The first set of theses makes the standard division between the natural and supernatural means to the knowledge of God, but does so under the category of Law. 'The knowledge of God is commanded by two means. One, that of the Law of nature, the other of the written Law.'[142]. The content of the natural law is again twofold, and, in fact, although this is not made explicit here, falls into the contemplative/active division which we shall have occasion to refer to later,

> 'I call that commanded by the Law of nature, that which all men set in the theatre of the world are taught about these two chapters of the natural Law, namely, there is some God, and, secondly, He is to be worshipped.'[143]

Again, although Barlaeus does not make the internal/external division of arguments for God's existence effected in the disputation 'Concerning the one and triune God,'[144] the fact that the controlling motif is that of Natural Law means that the four arguments he gives are all of the internal sort. For the first of these arguments Barlaeus draws verbatim upon Trelcatius senior's disputation, *Concerning the natural and revealed Knowledge of God*,

---

[140] In contrast, Kuchlinus has hardly anything to say about any other aspect of the future curriculum, which he summarily treats as follows: 'hinc docti, laboriosi, et fidi paedagogiorum moderatores emergent, qui ab incunabulis doctrinam veritatis coelestis, et Latinae, et Graecae linguae, Grammatices, Dialectices, et Rhetorices rudimenta pueros docebunt.' (*Oratio*, p. 13.)

[141] *Theses Theologicae de Cognitione Dei* and *Theses Theologicae de modis cognoscendi Deum*. Both sets of theses were published at Leiden in the year of their delivery. In the case of theses for a degree ('pro gradu') much more responsibility rested with the defendant than in the case of the disputations ('exercitii causa') which formed a routine part of the course of instruction and were essentially the work of the professor who presided over them, but their content just as clearly reflected the theological position of the institution of which they were the product. For Barlaeus (1584-1648), who, as poet and philosopher, was another of the College's pupils to achieve fame, see *BWPGN*, I pp. 284-288.

[142] 'Mandatum de cognoscendo vero Deo duplex est. Unum Legis Naturae, alterum Legis scriptae.' (Thesis II.)

[143] 'Mandatum Legis Naturae voco quo omnes homines in hoc mundi theatro constituti de duobus hisce legis naturalis capitibus ex natura edocti sunt, Esse sc. aliquem Deum, secundo eum colendum esse.' (*Ibid.*)

[144] See above, p. 79.

taking his first sentence from the latter's second thesis and the remainder from the sixth.

> 'This is irresistibly proved by those common principles which God has implanted in man's nature and which remain there even though they are now greatly corrupted by sin. The Greeks called these indestructible principles common notions or καταληψεις and there is no one who does not feel them from time to time even though they earnestly combat them.'[145]

Apart from the opening section, the arguments given and the mode of their presentation owe everything to the spirit, often indeed to the letter, of Calvin. Beginning with the well-worn quotation from Cicero, which asserts that even the most barbarous of peoples believe in God's existence,[146] proceeding to the adducing of idolatry as evidence of the universality of belief, and concluding with the example of the Emperor Caligula to demonstrate the ineradicable nature of such conviction even in those who wish to repudiate it, Barlaeus draws wholesale upon Chapter 3 of the first book of the *Institutes*.

Despite this exclusive reliance upon arguments drawn from the internal source which reflects the influence of Trelcatius's disputation, there is no doubt that Barlaeus wishes to preserve the balance between the traditional Reformation pair. Thus he begins the final thesis of this first set with a brief statement of them,

> 'It is known from the beginning that God exists. This is possible ... because, to say nothing of Scripture, we have nature outside us as a teacher and mistress and within us the principles secretly recommending and assenting,'[147]

whilst his second set of theses opens with a verbatim reproduction of the third Aphorism on the innate knowledge of God from Piscator's 'Concerning the Knowledge of God' into which Barlaeus has inserted a section

---

[145] 'Evincunt hoc Primo principia illa communia, quae Deus naturae hominis insevit, atque in illa etiam per peccatum nunc corrupta grandiose deinceps conservat. Quae prinicipia irrefragabilia dixerunt Graeci κοινας ἐννοιας sive καταληψεις, quas nemo non sentit interdum, dum eas oppugnat maxime.' (Thesis III.) As we shall see, Trelcatius was one of the professors of Theology in the university until his death in 1602. For his disputation, *De Cognitione Dei Naturali et Revelata*, originally held in January, 1599 (1598 old style and so dated when published in Leiden) see below, p.

[146] It is true that Trelcatius's sixth thesis also gives this quotation but there it occurs before the passage which Barlaeus reproduces and it is introduced, 'ut expressis verbis testatur Tullius.' Barlaeus's introduction, 'Unde et Ethnicus ille ait', exactly echoes Calvin's 'ut Ethnicus ille ait'. (*Institutes* I, iii 1.)

[147] 'Principio cognoscendum est esse Deum. Hoc possibile ... quia, ut scripturam taceam, naturam extra nos habemus praeceptricem, et magistram, principiaque in nobis tacite suffragantia et consentientia.' (Thesis IX.)

extending the reference to include the external source and also indicating something more of the nature of the innate principles.

> 'I call this natural knowledge of God that which springs up of its own accord in adults of sound mind, so that being taught only by nature and the visible works of God outside us and indeed within us by the natural principles by the light of the human mind in itself, and by these both theoretical principles of true and false and the practical of good and evil, they are persuaded that there is a God, that there is one God and that He is the eternal mind, the most powerful, wisest and best creator and ruler of the world and the creatures contained therein, and furthermore that that deity is to be worshipped devoutly.'[148]

Barlaeus does not here bring forward any arguments arising from this witness of nature, but refers his readers to the commonplaces, 'Concerning God', and 'Concerning the creation', contenting himself with a lyrical outburst over the book of nature:

> 'This knowledge is indeed supplied from these reasons sought from natural theology and demonstrated in the commonplaces on God and on the Creation of heaven and earth. If anyone wishes to pursue these reasons, he must spread out and set forth the world itself which is nothing other than a book obvious and open to all in which both adults can read God and the very infants (to speak thus) can put two and two together and in which nothing is so small that it does not display God's greatness, nothing so exalted that it does not descend to instruct man in the knowledge of God.'[149]

In his second thesis Barlaeus demonstrates the truth of this natural theology from two sources, from Scripture and by reference to the four arguments given in his earlier set of theses. We would not be surprised if he now felt the need to supplement these since, as we have seen, they are all of the internal sort. The one addition which he does make, however, is a rather odd one:

> 'To which can be added an argument drawn from the nature of God Himself, who as He is the supreme good cannot be without the means of com-

[148] 'Naturalem Dei cognitionem eam voco, quae se in adultis sana mente praeditis sponte naturae exerit, ita ut docente tantum natura et operibus Dei visibilibus extra nos, in nobis vero principiis naturalibus intellectus humani lumini per se notis, iisque tum theoreticis veri et falsi, tum practicis boni et mali persuasi sint esse Deum, esse unum Deum, eumque mentem aeternam, potentissimam, sapientissimam, optimam, mundi et rerum eo contentarum creatricem atque gubernatricem, ac proinde illud numen religiose colendum esse.' (Thesis I.) For the text of Piscator's Aphorism, see above, p. 39.

[149] 'Quibus vero rationibus ex naturali Theologia petitis haec cognitio comparetur, ex loco de Deo et Creatione coeli et terrae manifestum erit. Quas etiam rationes si quis persequi velit, mundum ipsum evolvat et edisserat necesse est, qui nihil aliud est quam liber omnibus obvius et apertus, in quo et adulti Deum legere, et infantuli ipsi (ut ita loquor) combinare possunt, in quo nihil tam exiguum, quod magnitudinem Dei non repraesentet, nil tam excelsum quod ad erudiendum in cognitione Dei hominem non descendat.' (Thesis I.)

municating His hightest good to all created things according to their condition and His most bounteous mercy.'[150]

It is, in fact, Trelcatius's second argument for the existence of natural theology and has, once more, been taken almost word for word from the second thesis of the latter's disputation, on the natural and revealed knowledge of God.[151]

The traditional manner in which Barlaeus treats these arguments is confirmed when he comes to consider the purposes of the natural knowledge of God, for in allowing such knowledge no further use than that of rendering mankind inexcusable before God, he reproduces a large portion of Trelcatius' disputation which is itself at this point evidently dependent on Chapter 4 of the first book of the *Institutes*:

> 'Yet that remains to rob man of excuse and to place him without defence before God's tribunal, Rom. 1, 20. For although we all carry around that natural knowledge of God, yet some became vain in their blindness and others fall away from God with positive wickedness. Neither are to be simply excused, since they are greatly pleased with their own simplicity and stupidity. These indeed, which is worst of all, suppressing the instinct of nature and having consulted with themselves, become increasingly stupefied and transform the truth into a lie.'[152]

The clearest evidence that, within the States College, Ursinus' commentary was both used and also emended in order to remove any doubts as to the limitations of the natural knowledge of God is provided by Barlaeus's concluding discussion of the similarities and differences between the natural and supernatural means of knowing God. He begins by following Kuchlinus in using that section of Ursinus's Prolegomena to the Commentary on the Catechism which listed the differences between philosophy and the church's doctrines.

> 'First, the principles differ; for the natural is built up from principles known by nature. The other from principles which are raised up above nature ...

[150] 'Quibus addi potest ratio sumta a Natura ipsius Dei, qui ut est summe bonus ita non potest non modo summe bono sui esse κοινωνικος cum rebus creatis omnibus pro conditione ipsarum et liberrima sua misericordia.' (Thesis II.)

[151] See below pp. 123-7, where we note that Trelcatius, in his turn, derived this argument along with the great bulk of his entire disputation from Junius's *De Vera Theologia*.

[152] 'Illud tamen praestat ut homini *excusationem praecidat, eumque apud tribunal Dei sistat* ἀναπολογητον. Rom. 1, 20. Quamvis *enim Dei* illam *naturalem* cognitionem omnes *animis nostris circumferimus; alii tamen in caecitate sua evanescunt, alii vero etiam certa malitia a Deo desciscunt. Neutri tamen simpliciter excusantur, quia illi in sua sibi simplicitate ac stupore placent etiam maxime. Hi vero quod* pessim*um, suffoc*antes *naturae instinc*tum *consulto seipsos magis ac magis obstupefaciunt veritatemque in mendacium transformant.*' (Thesis IV). The material emphasized has all been taken from Trelcatius. Cf. Calvin, *Institutes* I, iv, 1, '... alii evanescant in suis superstitionibus, sive alii data opera malitiose a Deo desciscant.' I, iv. 2. '... consulto seipsos obstupefaciunt.'

> Secondly, they differ as to subject matter: the supernatural contains the whole and uncorrupt meaning of the Law and the Gospel. The natural is completely ignorant of the Gospel.'[153]

Ursinus's third and final point of difference concerned the fact that only the church's doctrine could provide us with the proper consolation in the face of sin and death. However, he immediately went on to indicate that philosophy did nonetheless provide us with some consolations in common with theology.

> 'Philosophy has indeed some consolations in common with theology such as God's providence, the necessity of obeying God, a good conscience, the worthiness of virtue and its final causes, the examples of others, the hope of reward, the comparison of events in which a lesser evil is compared with a greater and is seen to have a purpose for good.'[154]

This is an impressive list and, despite his immediate reiteration 'But the true consolations against sin and death are peculiar to the church', there is no escaping the feeling that Ursinus has a very high regard for philosophy and the knowledge it provides. In contrast, Barlaeus lists four differences, all of which serve to deflate the status of natural knowledge. Thus, for example, his last two state:

> 'The natural knowledge of God does not yield to the Creator the glory which is His due, ... no one is saved by natural knowledge, ...'

and he concludes with a final reference to the essentially negative view of it in Reformation eyes,

> 'But the natural minds of men as brutes or destitute of faith by the Spirit become inexcusable by their own faults and self-condemned.'[155]

The enormous influence exercised by Ursinus's commentary on the catechism within the milieu of the Leiden States College is underlined by the appearance of the first Dutch translation of the work in that town in

---

[153] 'Primo differunt Principia; naturalis enim ex principiis natura notis exstruitur. Altera ex principiis quae et supra naturam evecta sunt ... Secundo differunt re subjecta: Supernaturalis integram et incorruptum sententiam Legis et Euangelii continet. Naturalis Euangelium prorsus ignorat.' (Thesis XIV.) Cf. 'Primo, principiis. Philosophia tota est naturalis et e natura notis exstruitur ... Euangelium, praeter et supra naturam est ... Deinde, subiectis. Doctrina ecclesiae continet integram et incorruptum sententiam Legis et Euangelii; Philosophia Euangelium prorsus ignorat.' (*Ursinus, Frankfurt, 1621*, p. 4.)

[154] 'Habet quidem philosophia consolationes quasdam cum theologia communes ut sunt providentia Dei, necessitas obtemperandi Deo, bona conscientia, dignitas virtutis, causae finales ejusdem, exempla aliorum, spes compensationis, collatio eventuum, qua minus malum confertur cum maiori, et boni rationem habere videtur.' (Ursinus, *op. cit.*, p. 5.)

[155] 'Naturali cognitione Deo non tribuitur gloria debita creatori, ... Naturali cognitione nemo salvatur, ..., ... At naturali mentes hominum animalium seu Spiritu fidei destitutorum sua culpa ἀναπολόγητοι fiunt et αὐτοκατάκριτοι.' (Thesis XIV.)

1602, *The Treasure Book of Christian Doctrine or Exposition of the Catechism*. The translator was Festus Hommius,[156] a former pupil of the college and a son-in-law of its president, Kuchlinus. This first edition was, as its title page announced,[157] a straightforward translation of Pareus's revised edition of Ursinus's commentary. However, the second edition of 1606 saw the inclusion of passages from other commentators, Bastingius and Lansbergen, whom we have already encountered, and also two Germans, Balthasar Copius,[158] and George Spindler.[159] In his foreword to the Christian Reader, Hommius explains that these additions, which we may observe are clearly indicated by marginal references to their sources, have been made to cover those matters upon which Ursinus had not touched.

In our survey of the treatment accorded to Ursinus's commentary by Kuchlinus and his pupils in the States College, we noted signs that they were endeavouring to correct any impression the former may have conveyed of too great a stress on the natural source of the knowledge of God. As we saw in our account of Ursinus, he does devote part of the section immediately following that in which he presents the arguments for God's existence to a statement of the philosophical and theological descriptions of God which, as we observed, he had borrowed from Melanchthon.[160] To this he also adds a brief explanation:

> 'This description, which the church hands down, differs from the philosophical. In perfection, because in its description the church adds some parts of which nature is ignorant, such as concerning the three persons, the election and gathering of the church by the son, etc. and gives a clearer explanation of those known by nature. 2. In its effect or fruit, because men cannot attain to the true knowledge of God by the natural light since they cannot draw from this a true and sufficient knowledge of God neither are their minds moved to piety, that is the love and fear of God.'[161]

[156] *Het Schat-Boeck der Christelycke Leere ofte Uytlegginghe over den Catechismus*. See P. J. Wijminga, *Festus Hommius*, Leiden, 1899 and *BWPGN*, IV, pp. 198-218. For details of the editions of the *Schatboeck*, see T. D. Smid, 'Bibliographische Opmerkingen over de *Explicationes Catecheticae* van Zacharias Ursinus' in *Gereformeerd Theologisch Tijdschrift*, Vol. 41, 1940, pp. 228-43.

[157] ... *Van Doctor Zacharias Ursinus eertijts in de Universiteyt van Heydelbergh int Latijn voorgelesen: ende van Doct. David Pareus Professoor in de H. Theologie aldaer int licht uytgegeven: ende nu nieuwelijcx ten dienste der Nederlantsche Gemeynten also overgeset* ...

[158] Very little is known of Copius. Apparently he died some time shortly before 1600, having lived at Neustadt in the Palatinate (*Lexicon für Theologie und Kirche*, Vol. III, Freiburg, 1959, col. 53). A Dutch translation of his work, *Vierenvijftig Predicatien over Christelijke Catechismus*, appeared at Amsterdam in 1588 and again in 1591.

[159] For Spindler (1525-1605) see *Allgemeine Deutsche Bibliographie*, Vol. 35, Leipzig, 1893, pp. 199-200. His *Zwo und funzig Predigten über den H. Catechismus* was published at Hamburg in 1597.

[160] See above, pp. 54-5.

[161] 'Haec descriptio, quam ecclesia tradit, differt a philosophica. 1. Perfectione. quod ec-

Despite the provision of these qualifying remarks, it would appear that Hommius shared the same misgivings on this issue as his mentor and colleagues for he felt it necessary to preface Ursinus's descriptions with a substantial insertion from Spindler's work which, standing at the beginning of Section II, 'Who and what God is,'[162] spells out the relative status of the sources of the knowledge of God.

Spindler here describes a three-fold revelation, 'God reveals Himself to men in three ways.' The first, through His works, is, as the marginal reference indicates, an extended comment upon Romans 1, 19.

> 'I. By His work, by the creation and upholding of all things by which His majesty, glory, wisdom, power and goodness may be known. For when we behold the heaven, the earth and all creatures, the wonderful course of nature, this extremely beautiful ordering in which one has to serve another, the wonderful alteration and interchange of all things and how all follow their ends and are directed to what they have been created, so everything witnesses to God's presence. But although God's being is invisible, from this we can nonetheless know His wonderful goodness, wisdom, omnipotence and fatherly care.'[163]

The second, scriptural revelation, is necessary because reason in fallen man is so grossly darkened that he cannot make proper use of the first.

> 'II. But whilst human reason has been grossly darkened and cannot rightly acknowledge God's work and know who God is, so God has, on the other hand, revealed Himself by His Word.'[164]

The third, that through the Holy Spirit, provides the means whereby alone man is enabled to come to the knowledge of God mediated through the first two sources.

---

clesia in sua descriptione addit quasdam partes naturae ignotas ut de tribus personis, de electione et collectione Ecclesiae per filium, etc. et naturae notas dilucidius explicat: 2. Effectu seu fructu, quod homines luce naturali ad veram Dei cognitionem pervenire nequeunt, quandoquidem ex ea nec veram et sufficientem notitiam Dei haurire possunt, nec mentes ad pietatem, hoc est, amorem et timorem Dei permoventur.' (*Ursinus, Frankfurt, 1621*, pp. 119-20.)

[162] 'Wat ende hoedanich God zy.' (*Schat-Boeck*, 1606, fol. 81$^{r}$.)

[163] 'I. Door sijn Werck, door de Scheppinghe ende onderhoudinghe van alle dinghen waer door men sijne Majesteyt, Heerlijckheyt, wijsheyt, ghewelt ende goedicheyt kennen mach. Wand als wy aensien den Hemel, Aerde ende alle creaturen den wonderlijcken loop der nature, die overschoone ordening hoe dat eene het ander moet dienen, de wonderlijcke veranderinghe ende verwisselinghe alle dinghen ende hoe alles tot sijnen eynde loopt ende uytghericht wordt waer toe het gheschapen is: soo ghetuycht alles van Gods teghenwoordicheyt. Ende hoewel Gods wesen onsichtbaer is soo can men nochtans sijn wonderlijcke goetheyt, wijsheyt, almachticheyt ende Vaderlijcke sorghe daer uyt bekennen.' (*Ibid.*)

[164] 'II. Maer dewijle het menschelijck verstandt grouwelijck verduystert is en Godes werck niet recht bekennen can ende weten wat Godt zy, soo heeft sich Godt ten anderen gheopenbaert door sijn Woordt.' (*Ibid.*)

'III. By inspiration of the Holy Spirit ... for without the Holy Spirit's enlightenment the natural man looks at God's work with owlish eyes which cannot see the splendour of God's glory which shines in His works. Also he hears God's Word without understanding. Therefore if the Holy Spirit does not enlighten the mind and heart, man remains in blindness and darkness and can neither know God aright, nor understand His will.'[165]

Finally, a further paragraph is added to drive the message home:

'Therefore, whoever wishes to know God aright must not only regard and scan God's works, heaven and earth and all that is therein and the wonderful course of nature, but must diligently read through God's Word and believe nothing other of God than He says in His Word and must surrender his mind to the obedience of the Gospel.'[166]

Quotations, to which we shall shortly return, are then given, two from the New Testament, John 1, 18 and 1 Timothy 6, 16, and one from Hilary of Poitiers' *De Trinitate*, I, 18, and the passage concludes:

'Furthermore, we must call upon God in Christ's name that He will open our hearts with Lydia by the powerful working of His Holy Spirit and will pour out in them His Knowledge so shall we come to the right knowledge of God.'[167]

Spindler's threefold scheme of revelation is entirely in accord with Calvin's teaching as may be seen at a glance from the titles of three successive chapters of the first book of the *Institutes*; Chapter V, 'The knowledge of God shines forth in the fashioning of the universe and the continuing government of it,' Chapter VI, 'Scripture is needed as a guide and teacher for anyone who would come to God the Creator,' and Chapter VII, 'Scripture must be confirmed by the witness of the Spirit.' This dependence upon Calvin is further demonstrated by the use of two of the three quotations noted above. Thus, 1 Timothy 6, 16, 'And He alone has immortality and dwells in light unapproachable, whom no man has seen,

---

[165] 'III. Door inghevinghe des H. Gheests ... want sonder des H. Gheests verlichtinge de natuerlijcke mensche Godes werck met uylen-ooghen aensiet welcke de glants der heerlijckheydt Gods die in sijne wercken schijnt niet sien connen. Oock hoort hy Godes woordt sonder verstandt. Daerom soo de heylighe Gheest het ghemoedt ende herte niet verlicht, soo blijft de mensche in blintheyt ende duysternisse ende can Godt niet recht kennen noch sijnen wille verstaen.' (*Ibid.*)

[166] 'Daerom wie God recht kennen wil die moet niet alleen de wercken Gods, Hemel ende Aerde ende alles wat daer in is ende wonderbaerlijcken loop der nature aensien ende betrachten, maer vlijtelijck Godes woort doorsien ende van God anders niet ghelooven dan gelijck by in sijn woort segt ende moet sijn ghemoedt ghevanghen geven onder de ghehoorsaemheyt des Euangelismus.' (*Ibid.*)

[167] 'Daerbeneden moeten wy God in Christi name aenroepen dat hy met Lydia onse herten wil openen door de crachtighe werckinghe sijnes heylighen Gheests ende sijne kennisse daer in uytstorten, so sullen wy comen tot de rechte kennisse Gods.' (*Ibid.*)

nor can see,'[168] has no reference in its original context to the question at issue. Such an application is, however, clearly made by Calvin:

> 'For we should so reason that the splendour of the divine countenance, which even the apostle calls "unapproachable" (I Tim. 6:16), is for us like an inexplicable labyrinth unless we are conducted into it by the thread of the Word.'[169]

Again, the quotation from Hilary is given in such a form as to make it very unclear as to where the latter's words end and further comment begins, 'God alone is a fit witness to Himself and so we can have no knowledge of Him than from His own testimony which is His Word.'[170] In fact, the original sentence comes as the last words of chapter 18 of book 1 of the *De Trinitate*, 'For He is the fit witness to Himself who is not known except through Himself,'[171] and it is once more clearly evident that Calvin is the real source here for Spindler:

> 'For, as Hilary says, he is the one fit witness to himself, and is not known except through himself. But we shall be "leaving it to him" if we conceive him to be as he reveals himself to us, without inquiring about him elsewhere than from his Word.'[172]

Our conclusion then is that, by his inclusion of this entire passage, Hommius is repairing a lack of which he is evidently conscious and ensuring an emphasis which is essentially that of Calvin.

Interestingly enough it would appear that the English translator must have felt the same need to supplement Ursinus's commentary at precisely this point. In this case, however, the proper emphasis is restored by the insertion of a lengthy passage from the equivalent section of another work of Ursinus's, headed 'Who and what the true God is' from the 'De Deo' topic in his *Volumen tractationum theologicanum*.[173] One selection will suffice to make this clear:

> '... there are indeed some true things, concerning God, manifested otherwise also than by the word delivered to the Church, but by them notwithstanding, who is the true God cannot be shewed; and that for two causes. For first, those

---

[168] 'Ende hy heeft alleen onsterffelijckheyt, ende woont in een licht, daermen niet en can toegaen, den welcken gheen mensche ghesien en heeft, noch sien can.' (*Ibid.*)

[169] *Institutes*, I, VI, 3, *LCC*, p. 73.

[170] 'God is alleen selve een bequaem ghetuyghe van hem selven, soo en connen wy dan van hem gheen kennisse hebben dan uyt sijn eyghen ghetuyghenisse welcke is sijn woordt.' (*Schat-Boeck*, 1606, fol. 81$^{r}$.)

[171] 'Idoneus enim sibi testis est, qui nisi per se cognitus non est.' (J. P. Migne, *Patrologia Latina*, Vol. 10, col. 38.)

[172] *Institutes*, I, XIII, 21, *LCC*, p. 146.

[173] For details see above, p. 55.

things by themselves are not sufficient. For, to the knowing of the true God, it is requisite that we know and profess, not some things only, but all things which he openeth of himself, and would have known. Moreover, these self same true testimonies of God also, which remain in men's minds and in nature, all they by reason of a natural blindness in them, and pravity, do many ways corrupt, who in weighing them, follow not the light and interpretation thereof, drawn from the word of God, delivered to the Church.'[174]

Turning back to the *Schat-Boeck*, we may not that there are no significant alterations or additions to the first edition's rendering of the relevant Question 27 on God's Providence in the second or any subsequent editions, save for the considerable expansion of the scriptural citations which Pareus had appended as mere references to each Question and Answer of the Catechism. Hommius now added greatly to these, quoting them all in full under the heading, 'Testimonies of Scripture'.

The publication of the third edition at Leiden in 1617 saw a further alteration in the format of the work with the addition by Hommius of his own commentary set out in the form of tables which he inserted at the beginning of each Sunday's question.[175] For the first time then Hommius can speak to us directly, although what in fact he has to say on the issue of the natural knowledge of God comes as no surprise in the light of our discussion of the passage from Spindler which he had included in the second edition's treatment of Question 25. This latter question is now expounded in the second part of the table for the 8th Sunday under the heading, 'Exposition of the first Article' (i.e. of the Creed). The new emphasis is immediately apparent. The Catechism's Answer is given and then, before attending to the issue of God's existence which had previously followed immediately, Hommius inserts a statement on the relative status of the natural and revealed means to the knowledge of God which, for the first time introduces the typically Reformation point that the essential purpose of the former of these is to establish man's inexcusability before God.

'The knowledge of God has indeed been in some degree implanted in the hearts of men by the light of nature and can also in some measure be presented from the creatures and God's works to such an extent that man can pretend no innocence. Rom. 1, 19, 20 ... But the saving knowledge of God ... this has only been revealed to us in God's Word and must be drawn from it.'[176]

[174] *The Summe of Christian Doctrine*, Oxford, 1587, pp. 302-3.

[175] The title page announces the innovation thus, ... *Festus Hommius, die daer by ghedaen heeft voor elcke Sondagh corte Verclaringhen, bequamelick in Tafelen afghedeelt.*

[176] 'De kennisse Godts is wel eenichsins door het licht der Nature inde Herten der Menschen ingheplant ende can oock wel eenichsins wyt de Schepselen ende wercken Gods verereghen worden so verre dat de Mensche gheen onschult en hebbe voor te wenden. Rom. 1, 19, 20 ... Maer de salichmakende kennisse Godts, ... die is ons alleen in Gods woort

Coming at last to the issue of God's existence, Hommius, in complete contrast to Ursinus, points first to the wealth of Scriptural evidence before reiterating the twofold natural source, the internal and external.

> '1. That there is a God. This is not only so profusely learned in God's Word that one cannot turn up a page without finding abundant witnesses to it, but has been so implanted and known by nature in all people's hearts that there is no people or nation to be found, however barbarous or sinful they may be, which does not know that there is a God. Aristotle, lib. de coelo. text 22. Cicero, lib. 2. de Leg. and 1. Tusc. q. Seneca Epist. 21 and 118. God's works also bear witness to this both in the creation and in the maintenance and regulation of all creatures in general and especially of mankind in particular. Rom. 1. 20.'[177]

There is no mention here of any list of arguments to establish God's existence, the traditional Reformation appeal to the innate idea of God and to the order of nature and providence is deemed sufficient. Hommius thus ranges himself with the great majority of those Dutch commentators whom we have considered above. The distance between Ursinus and him is further marked by the fact that his lengthy treatment of God's Providence in the table of the 10th Sunday[178] makes no attempt to establish its existence but begins with Ursinus's second question, 'What is God's Providence.'[179] Nevertheless, whatever his reservations, Hommius was the means whereby the text of Ursinus's commentary, including the latter's extensive arguments for the existence both of God and Providence, became available to the majority of the Dutch nation.

Further evidence of the popularity of Ursinus's commentary is provided by a work which was itself the means of extending the former's influence especially among students. Indeed no less an authority than Gisbert Voetius recommended it most strongly to his own pupils.[180] This was

gheopenbaert ende moet doer uyt ghehaelt worden.' (*Schat-Boeck*, fol. 86$^{v}$.) Quotations are given from the 1638 (Leiden) reprint of the third edition. This edition was also reprinted in 1622, 1630, 1642, 1647 and 1650. See T. D. Smid *op. cit.*, p. 231.

[177] '1. Datter een Godt is. Dit wort niet alleen in Godts woort soo overvloedelijek geleert datter niet een Bladt can opgeslagen worden of men vindt daer van menichvuldighe ghetuygenissen, maer is van natueren in aller Menschen Herten soo ingheplantet ende bekent datter geen Volck ofte Natie gevonden en wort, hoe Barbarisch de selve oock sonde mogen wesen, die niet en wete datter een Godt zy. Aristoteles lib. de coelo. text. 22. Cicero lib. 2. de Leg. et 1. Tusc. q. Seneca Epist. 21 et 118. Dit ghetuyghen oock de wercken Godts soo der Scheppinghe als der Onderhoudinghe ende Regeeringe aller Schepselen int gemeyn ende voornamelijck des Menschen int bysonder. Rom. 1. 20.' (*Schat-Boeck* 1638, fol. 86$^{v}$.)

[178] *Schat-Boeck*, 1638, fols. 107$^{v}$-109$^{r}$.

[179] Cf. *Schat-Boeck*, 1606, fol. 86$^{v}$.

[180] *BWPGN*. Vol. III, p. 487. In his chapter, 'De privatis collegiis in genere, et in specie de collegiis systematicis seu locorum communium,' Voetius includes Diest's *Mellificium* alongside Ursinus's Commentary among the works there recommended. (*Exercitia et*

Henricus a Diest's *Abridgement of the Ursinus-Pareus Exposition of the Catechism*[181] which first appeared at Harderwijk in 1633. Later came a second edition with an altered title, *A Honeyed Catechism Containing the Abridgement of the Exposition of the Catechism.*[182] A third edition was published in 1648, also at Deventer and this was reprinted at least once there, in 1650.

In the Dedicatory Preface to the States of Gelderland, Diest, having incidentally made favourable mention of Hommius's translation, explains that his own work is not simply an abridged version of Ursinus's commentary but is intended also as an analysis and amplification of the latter at points where such was required:

> 'Here I offer an abridgement, yet not only an abridgement but an analysis too and indeed an amplification ... Amplification: for scriptural proofs and theological sections are added to its opinions. What were neglected or dealt with in passing there are added or inserted here, especially those issues which are widely discussed nowadays.'[183]

Turning to Question 25, we find under the heading, 'Concerning God. Does He exist?', a straightforward list of Ursinus's eleven arguments given here simply as headings with scriptural texts appended.[184] So much for the element of abridgement; that of amplification is provided by a brief introduction. Ursinus's statement, 'God's existence is proved by many arguments common to philosophy and theology'[185] is evidently felt to be inadequate, in particular it would appear to be judged so because of its lack of reference to Scripture as a source for such proofs, and so in Diest the passage becomes:

> 'Not only scripture but nature also teaches God's existence. The proofs drawn from nature (yet common to scripture) teach that God is the creator and governor of all things.'[186]

*Bibliotheca Studiosi Theologiae*, Utrecht, 1651 pp. 101-2). It had not so appeared in the 1644 edition (p. 118).

[181] *Epitome Catecheticarum Explicationum Ursino-Pareanarum*. For Diest, 1595-1673, see *BWPGN* III, pp. 486-90. Born in Germany, he studied there and in Switzerland before eventually becoming Professor of Theology at Harderwijk in 1627. From there he went in 1640 to a similar post in Deventer where he spent the rest of his life. He became known as a friend and follower of the celebrated covenant theologian, Johannes Coccejus.

[182] *Mellificium Catecheticum continens Epitomen Catecheticarum Explicationum*, Deventer, 1640.

[183] 'Hic offero Epitomen; nec epitomen modo, sed et analysin; imo et auctarium ... Auctarium: Nam et cuique sententiae suae sunt data Scripturae testimonia, et loci Theologici, ibi vel neglecti, vel obiter tractati, hic sive adjecti sive interpolati, cum primis illi, qui hodie agitantur maxime.' (Diest, *op. cit.*, *3$^{r}$.)

[184] e.g. '1. Ordo naturae pulcerrimus, Ps. 8: 19: 104: 147.4: Rom. 1, 20: Act, 14, 17: 17, 26-27.' (*Ibid.*, p. 109.)

[185] 'Esse Deum multis argumentis Philosophiae et Theologiae communibus probatur.' (*Ursinus, Frankfurt, 1621*, p. 117.)

[186] 'Esse Deum, non tantum Scriptura, sed et Natura docet. Argumenta, ex Natura petita

Further amplification follows immediately after the list of arguments and provides us with another instance of the way in which, as we have already had frequent occasion to observe, Dutch commentators from Bastingius onwards, felt obliged to rectify Ursinus's deficiency at this point by spelling out the distinction between the natural and supernatural means to the knowledge of God. Here, under the marginal heading, 'How many divisions are there to the knowledge of God?', Diest pronounces the standard Reformation verdict on the effectiveness of the former,

> 'From here derives the separation of the knowledge of God into natural and supernatural, in which the former leads to inexcusability, Rom. 1, 20; the latter to salvation, Joh. 17, 3.'[187]

Finally comes analysis in the form of a table which arranges the arguments in such a way as to explain their function.

The knowledge of God is either
- Natural (as of the creator) and this either
  - Innate, as in arguments 4 and 5
  - Acquired
    1. from the consideration of the works
       - of Creation
         1. of things themselves
            - in general, the macrocosm, arg. 1.
            - in particular, the microcosm, and of this
              1. of the mind, arg. 2
              2. the nature of the mind, as
                 - of the knowledge
                   - of the principles, arg. 3
                   - of the principle that God exists, arg. 4.
                 - of fears, arg. 5
                 - of virtues, arg. 8
         2. of the purpose of all things, arg. 10
       - of government, namely,
         - of rewards and punishments, arg. 6
         - of the political order, arg. 7
         - of prophecies, arg. 9
    2. from the investigation into the ultimate cause, arg. 11
- Supernatural (as of the Redeemer) from Scripture.[188]

---

(Scripturae tamen communia) docent Deum creatorem et gubernatorem rerum omnium.' (Diest, *op. cit.*, p. 109.)

[187] 'Cognitio Dei quotuplex? .... Hinc dependet distinctio Cognitionis Dei, in naturalem et supernaturalem: ex quibus, illa ad ἀναπολογησιν facit, Rom. 1, 20; haec ad salutem, Joh, 17, 3.' (*Ibid.*, p. 110.)

According to Diest, 'This separation, deduced from the preceeding arguments of the proofs, is set out in the following table',[189] and this table is supposed to underline the distinction between the natural and supernatural means to the knowledge of God. In fact its effect runs directly counter to the attempt to play down the significance of the former of these sources. If the only purpose of such natural knowledge is to render men inexcusable it hardly seems worthwhile providing such a thorough analysis of the philosophical arguments which stem from it. The positive effects of Diest's analysis make a deeper impression upon the reader than the qualifying tendencies of his amplifications.

Whether or not it was his intention, Diest's treatment of the proofs for the existence of Providence in Question 27 is far more effective in moderating the impression made by the philosophical arguments. After briefly mentioning the first source for such proofs, 'I. The evidence of scripture', he quite reasonably forbears to repeat the list of these arguments which Ursinus gave here as *a posteriori* for, as he says, 'You have the arguments from effects above, in the section on God, q. 1. (with the exception of the last one concerning the first cause which applies to a consequent order).'[190] He does, we may note, give the list of the *a priori*

---

[188] Cognitio Dei est, vel
- Naturalis (ut Creatoris) et haec vel
  - Insita, ut est in arg. 4 and 5
  - Acquisita
    - 1. ex contemplatione operorum
      - Creationis
        - 1. Ipsarum rerum
          - in gen. μαχροχοσμον, arg. 1
          - in spec. μιχροχοσμον, illiusque
          - 1. animae, arg. 2
          - 2. animae qualitatem, ut
            - notitiae
              - principiorum, arg. 3
              - principii, esse Deum, arg. 4
            - pavorum, arg. 5
            - virtutum, arg. 8
        - 2. finis rerum omnium, arg. 10
      - Gubernationis, puta
        - praemiorum et poenarum, arg. 6
        - ordinis politici, arg. 7
        - praedictionum, arg. 9
    - 2. ex inquisitione in causam summam, arg. 11
- Supernaturalis (ut Redemptoris etiam) ex Scriptura

(*Ibid.*, p. 111.)

[189] 'Ea distinctio, ex praecedentibus probationum argumentis deducta, sequenti tabella repraestatur.' (*Ibid.*, p. 110.)

[190] 'Argumenta ab effectis habes supra, in loc. de Deo. q. 1. (excepta postremo, de causa prima, quod pertinet ad sequentem ordinem).' (*Ibid.*, pp. 169-170.)

arguments, once again in the abbreviated form of headings and scriptural references.

We come now to one of the only two works on the Heidelberg Catechism written during our period which, at any rate on the issue of our concern, bear no signs of the influence of Ursinus's commentary. The explanation in this instance does not lie in the fact that its author, William Ames, lacked a continental background since, as we have seen, Ursinus's work was every bit as popular in England as elsewhere. We must look rather to the distinctiveness of Ames's own approach and method in theology, the influence of which we shall have occasion to refer to again in a later chapter. An English Puritan, forced to flee his native land in 1610, William Ames (1576-1633), lived the rest of his life in the Netherlands and, from 1622 until a few months before his death, held a chair of Theology at Franeker.[191] Here we will simply consider his commentary on the Heidelberg Catechism which was first published posthumously in Amsterdam in 1635.[192]

According to the anonymous editor's Preface,[193] this small work derived from instructions given privately by Ames to his students. They bear the distinctive mark of Ames's method which, according to his editor, may be summarized thus,

> 'He takes a most apposite text from God's Word, resolves and explains it most succintly, then draws out examples containing catechetical instructions and, finally, applies them to their respective uses.'[194]

The scriptural text, albeit itself selected with reference to the subject matter of the particular section of the catechism, evidently plays a large part in determining the nature of the treatment accorded to each Sunday's instruction. Thus, in the matter of our concern, Ames takes Questions 24 and 25 of the Catechism, which together provide the topic for the 8th Sunday, at their face value as being concerned with belief in God as Holy Trinity and so, taking Matthew c. 28 v. 29 as his text, he devotes his entire attention to the exposition of Trinitarian doctrine. Thus the three headings or 'Documenta' are

[191] See K. L. Sprunger, *The Learned Doctor William Ames*, Chicago, 1972.

[192] *Christianae Catecheseos Sciagraphia*. This was reprinted at Franeker in the same year and is included in the first volume of Ames' complete Latin works published at Amsterdam in 1658. An English translation, entitled, *The Substance of Christian Religion: Or a plain and easie Draught of the Christian Catechisme in LII Lectures*, appeared at London in 1659.

[193] In fact, the editor was the heir to Ames' papers, Hugh Peter. See Sprunger, *op. cit.*, p. 251.

[194] 'Textum sibi sumit ex verbo Dei maxime appositum, illum resolvit atque explicat succincte, tum Documenta elicit continentia doctrinam Catecheticam, atque ea denique ad Usus suos applicat.' (*Sciagraphia*, Franeker, 1635, pp. 3-4.)

'I. Although God is one essence, yet He is three persons, Father, Son and Holy Spirit ... II. The divine essence and all His essential attributes, and all external works belong equally to Father, Son and Holy Spirit ... III. There is a certain distinction between those three persons as to the form and mode or order of existence.'[195]

All this is entirely in keeping with the letter and spirit of the Catechism's Question and Response and the issue of God's existence is never raised.

In the matter of God's Providence, the concern of the 10th Sunday, Ames does show signs of being prepared to advance arguments for its existence. Thus, having made a number of *a priori* points to show that God's creative power is at work in the providential ordering of the world, he finally appeals to the evidence of common experience:

'IV. Common experience teaches that there is a certain wisdom present everywhere, and an effective power, by which creatures are guided in their activities: for without this the species of all things would not have been preserved and they would not have been propagated through all generations under the same shapes, forms, parts and habits. Without this creatures devoid of reason would not be led always to aim at some definite purpose and to choose the places most suitable for themselves and to seek the preservation of the whole rather than that of themselves as individuals. Without this we could not understand how certain brute beasts have such instincts as though supplied with rays of some wisdom, as is seen in ants, bees, spiders and swallows, in storks (about which scripture speaks) and many other animals which are rightly said to be born as though with law, book and lantern. With a law which they constantly follow and observe in their activities, in which a certain art and wisdom clearly appear. With a book in which they have that law inscribed since it is always present with them and is engraved in their hearts. And with a lantern since they so promptly read and understand all those things which have a bearing upon their circumstances.'[196]

---

[195] 'I. Quamvis Deus est essentia unus, tamen est persona trinus, Pater, Filius et Spiritus Sanctus. ... II. Essentia divina et omnia ejus attributa essentialia, et omnia opera ad extra conveniunt aequaliter Patri, Filio, Spiritui Sancto ... III. Inter istas tres personas distinctio quaedam est, quoad formam et modum vel ordinem subsistendi.' (*Ibid.*, pp. 44-7.)

[196] 'IV. Communis experientia docet sapientiam esse aliquam ubique praesentem, et potentem efficacem, qua creaturae in suis operationibus diriguntur: sine illa enim non conservatae fuissent omnium rerum species, et sub iisdem figuris, formis, partibus et habitibus propagatae fuissent per omnes generationes: Absque illa non dirigerentur creaturae rationis expertes ad certum aliquem finem semper tendere, et certa loca sibi commodissima capere, et conservationem universi magis quam suam propriam quaerere. Absque illa non potest intelligi, quomodo animalia quaedam bruta tales instinctus et quasi radios cujusdam sapientiae habent communicatos, ut videre est in formicis, in apibus, in araneis et hirundinibus, in ciconiis: (de his Scriptura loquitur) et multis aliis animalibus, quae recte dicuntur nasci, quasi cum lege, libro et lucerna: Cum lege, quam sequuntur et observant constanter in suis operationibus, in qua ars et sapientia quaedam manifeste apparet. Cum libro, in quo istam legem habent inscriptam, quia semper istis adest, et in ipsorum animis insculpta. Et cum lucerna, quia tam prompte legunt et percipiunt omnia illa, quae conveniunt ipsorum conditioni.' (*Ibid.*, pp. 56-7.)

The texts of Scripture here referred to are given in Section 23 of the chapter on Providence in the *Medulla Theologiae*, a work described by his modern biographer as 'the most concise and mature statement of Ames' theology.'[197] In the following section Ames makes a similar, rather more succinct statement, of the case presented above.

> '24. This government shines forth in the operation of all things, first in that they always look to some certain end, and so it is necessary that they be acted and governed by an intelligence everywhere present and omnipotent, that is, of God himself. Job. 38.27. In sending down rain to satisfy the waste places and bringing forth the bud of the tender herb. Isay. 55.10. The rain causeth that the Earth bring forth seed to the sower and bread for him that eateth. Secondly, in that the works of nature are ordained so accurately and agreeable to reason, that they cannot but proceed from highest reason. Prov. 30, 35, 36, 27, 28. Thirdly, in that besides a proper ordination already everything seeks his own perfection, they do keep as it were a common society and all do more desire the conservation of the whole than of themselves as is to be seen in heavy things which are carried upward to avoid an emptiness.'[198]

A proper estimate of Ames's position would require a much fuller discussion,[199] here it is sufficient to observe the prominence given to scriptural evidence which yet does not preclude the appeal to arguments that, in other writers, would fall within the scope of Natural Theology.

The second of the two works to bear no sign of Ursinus's influence, at least as regards the issue of our concern, was also a posthumous publication which appeared towards the end of our period.[200] The lack of such influence is, at first sight, all the more remarkable since it had originally been written at a time when its distinguished author, Hendrik Alting,[201] was a professorial colleague of Pareus's at Heidelberg. At no point in his exegesis of Questions 25 and 27 does Alting even raise the issue of the existence of God or Providence, let alone provide arguments for such.

The clue for this surprising omission is given us in the work's title and the full answer is provided in the Preface to the Reader written by Alting's sons, Menso and Jacobus, who were responsible for the publication of these writings. Apologising for the brevity of the commentary in com-

---

[197] Sprunger, *op. cit.*, p. 127, where full details are given of the many editions of this work. Our quotation is from the first English translation, *The Marrow of Sacred Divinity*, London, 1642.

[198] Ames, *Marrow*, pp. 49-50.

[199] For some comments on Ames' anti-metaphysical views, see below, pp. 174-5.

[200] *Explicatio Catecheseos Palatinae, cum vindiciis a considerationibus Novatorum et Antithesibus Socinianorum* in *Scriptorum Theologicorum Heidelbergensium*, Vol. II, Amsterdam, 1646, pp. 1-289.

[201] (1583-1644) Professor of Theology at Heidelberg, 1613-22 and at Groningen, 1627-44. See *BWPGN* I, pp. 111-19.

parison with others, they explain the circumstances of its inception. At the Synod of Dort at which their father, in company with Abraham Scultetus and Paul Tossanus, was one of the three delegates from the Palatinate, the Remonstrants, here referred to throughout as 'Innovators', ('Novatores'), had been required to present to the Synod their observations on the Belgic Confession and the Heidelberg Catechism to parts of which they had objected. John Hales preserves an account of the 39th Session of the Synod at which 'the Remonstrants were called in and willed to give up their Considerations upon the Catechism.' There follows a description of exchanges between the Remonstrants and the Synod's President, after which we read,

> 'There Scultetus stood up and, in the name of the Palatine Churches, required a Copie of these Considerations upon the Catechism. We have saith he a command from our Prince to see that nothing be done in prejudice of our Churches. The Catechism is ours known by the name of the Palatine Catechism and from us you received it. The Observations therefore upon it concern us.'[202]

These *Considerationes in Catechesin Heydelbergensem* were published by the Remonstrants in their *Acta et Scripta Synodalia Dordracena*,[203] and it is with these in mind that Alting wrote his commentary. Moreover, as the Preface tells us,[204] since he shared the orthodox view that the Remonstrants had demonstrated their affinities with the Socinians, Alting also addressed himself to the criticisms levelled against the Heidelberg Catechism by this Sect.

Since the Remonstrants had no observations to make on Question 25 and since those of the Socinians characteristically centred on criticisms of the doctrine of the Trinity, it is scarcely surprising that Alting has nothing to say on the topic of our concern. Again, the five considerations on Question 27 expressed by the Remonstrants[205] which Alting quotes in full in his reply to them,[206] are all concerned with the operation of Providence, the existence of which is here taken for granted.

---

[202] 'Mr. Hales's Letters from the Synod of Dort', p. 45, appended to *Golden Remains of the ever Memorable Mr. John Hales* ..., London, 1659.

[203] 1620, pp. 102-33.

[204] 'Praeterea, cum iis Considerationibus non obscure liqueret qualem reformationem Novatores intenderent, siquidem ex Catechismo Polonico Smalcii (Racovianus vulgo dicitur) quam plurima depromserant; non praeter institutum judicavit Parens, si ex eodam libello Antitheses Socinianas, Catechesi oppositas, prope ipsorum verbis concinnaret, suisque singulas loces confutaret.' (Alting, 'Praefatio ad Lectorem', no pagination.)

[205] *Acta et Scripta Synodalia*, p. 39.

[206] *Explicatio*, p. 84.

Such then is the explanation for the nature of Alting's treatment of these Questions, which effectively removes any suspicion that he was deliberately turning his back on Ursinus on these issues. His view of the latter may perhaps be gathered from the fact that his sons conclude their Preface by explicitly directing those who require a full discussion of the Catechism to Ursinus's Commentary as edited by their father's one time colleague.[207]

The overall impression left by our examination of these relevant sections of the Dutch commentaries on the Heidelberg Catechism can hardly fail to be that of the enormous impact upon them of Ursinus's *Explicationes*. What is so interesting is that almost all these commentators appear to have felt the necessity of correcting what they evidently sensed as the over-positive emphasis which Ursinus there lays upon the natural source of the knowledge of God. Sometimes this correction takes the form of an ignoring of Ursinus's arguments for God's existence in favour of the traditional pair of Reformation arguments, that from creation and providence and that from innate knowledge with the balance between them varying in the manner we have observed. At all times, even when Ursinus's arguments are reproduced, as in the States College disputations or in the *Schat-Boek*, considerable care is taken to reassert the deficiencies of the natural means to the knowledge of God in contrast to its supernatural counterpart.

Perhaps the greatest tribute to Ursinus's influence upon the way men approached Question 25 of the Catechism is that, since his commentary at this point raised the issue of the existence of God and the possibility of arguing for it, subsequent commentators almost invariably felt bound to consider this topic even though there was nothing in the actual text of the Catechism to suggest it. Moreover, whatever the reservations felt, Ursinus's commentary, whether in one of the constant flow of Latin editions, in Hommius's very popular translation or in a derivative work such as Diest's, continued to be the chief source whereby Melanchthon's arguments for the existence of God were available to Dutchmen. Our subsequent examination of the theologians of the period will show how much they made use of them.

---

[207] '... quae vero ad pleniorem exegesin requiruntur, ex aliorum, Ursini praesertim ac Parei, commentariis uberioribus facile supplebit.' (Alting, 'Praefatio'.)

## CHAPTER FIVE

# THE BELGIC CONFESSION

The other classic sixteenth century formulation of Christian faith for the Dutch Reformed Church was the Belgic Confession drawn up in the Walloon dialect by Guido de Brès in 1561.[1] It was revised at the Synod of Antwerp in 1566 although no changes were made in the articles relevant to our concern. In 1568 this revised Confession was adopted by the Synod of Wesel and in 1571 by that of Emden, whilst the provincial Synod of Dort in 1574 directed all ministers and school teachers to subscribe to it. Finally, as we have already observed, it was confirmed in its authoritative position by the Synod of Dort in 1618-19.

De Brès took the Gallican Confession, drawn up by the General Synod of Paris in 1559, as his model and in this connection it is interesting to consider something of the history of the Article relating to the knowledge of God. The text of the document which Calvin himself sent to the French Reformed Church to serve as the basis for this formulation of a Confession is to be found among his works in the *Corpus Reformatorum*.[2] His first article was an uncompromising statement of the sole-sufficiency of the Scriptural record for faith in God,

> 'Because, as St. Paul says, the foundation of belief is by the word of God ... we hold the books of Holy Scripture ... as the sum of the only infallible truth from God which it is not lawful to contradict, likewise because the perfect rule of all wisdom is contained there, we believe that it is not permissible to add or take away anything from it but that it must be agreed to entirely and throughout.'[3]

Only on the basis of this scriptural revelation can we proceed to the second article where, even before we consider the doctrine of the Trinity, the most basic knowledge of God's nature is clearly stated to be drawn from this

---

[1] See P. de Zeeuw J Gzn, *Guido de Brès, opsteller van de Nederlandse Geloofsbelijdenis*, The Hague, 1963.

[2] *CR*. 37, cols. 731-52.

[3] 'Pource que le fondement de croire, comme dit S. Paul, est par la parole de Dieu, ... nous tenons les livres de la saincte Escripture ... comme la somme de la seule verité infaillible procedee de Dieu, à laquelle il n'est licite de contredire. Mesmes pource que là est contenue la regle parfaicte de toute sagesse, nous croyons qu'il n'est licite d'y rien adiouster ne diminuer mais qu'il y faut acquiescer en tout et par tout.' (*Ibid.*, cols. 739-41.)

source, 'Being thus founded we believe in one eternal God, of a spiritual essence, infinite, incomprehensible and simple...'[4]

The Paris synod replaced Calvin's first two articles with no fewer than six and the nature of their changes has been thought to be significant. Thus, in the new rendering, article one begins not with Scripture but with God,

> 'We believe and confess that there is but one God, who is one sole and simple essence, spiritual, eternal, invisible, immutable, infinite, incomprehensible, ineffable, omnipotent; who is all-wise, all-good, all-just, and all-merciful.'[5]

Scriptural revelation is considered in articles two to five and the bulk of Calvin's second article now appears as number six, beginning 'This Holy Scripture teaches us that in this one sole and simple divine essence, whom we have confessed, there are three persons: the Father, the Son and the Holy Spirit.'[6] We appear to have reverted to the traditional scholastic position in which the former attributes of God are known naturally whilst the biblical record is necessary only to reveal the doctrine of the Trinity. The second article of the Gallican Confession apparently goes far to substantiate the reality of this relapse,

> 'As such this God reveals Himself to men, firstly in His works, in their creation, as well as in their preservation and control. Secondly, and more clearly, in His Word, which was in the beginning revealed through oracles, and which was afterwards committed to writing in the books which we call the Holy Scripture.'[7]

Here the traditional two stage revelation, natural and revealed, is apparently plainly stated and there are those who have seen these changes as a clear betrayal of the genuine Reformation position. Thus, in his comments on the Gallican Confession, A. C. Cochrane writes:

> 'The alteration of the first article was fraught with fateful consequences. Under the influence of the rediscovery of Stoicism in the so-called humanism

---

[4] 'Estans ainsi fondez nous croyons en un seul Dieu eternel, d'une essence spirituelle, infinie, incomprehensible et simple...' (*Ibid.*, Col. 741.)

[5] 'Nous croyons et confessons qu'il y a un seul Dieu qui est une seule et simple essence, spirituelle, éternelle, invisible, immuable, infinie, incompréhensible, ineffable, qui peut toutes choses, qui est toute sage, toute bonne, toute juste, et toute misericordieuse.' (P. Schaff, *The Creeds of the Evangelical Protestant Churches*, London, 1877, pp. 359-60.)

[6] 'Cette Ecriture sainte nous enseigne qu'en cette seule et simple essence divine, que nous avons confessée, il y a trois Personnes, le Père, Le Fils et le Saint-Esprit.' (*Ibid.*, p. 362.)

[7] 'Ce Dieu se manifeste tel aux hommes, premièrement par ces oeuvres; tant par la création que par la conservation et conduite d'icelles. Secondement et plus clairement, par sa parole, laquelle au commencement révélée par oracles, a été puis apres rédigée par écrit aux livres que nous appelons l'Ecriture sainte.' (*Ibid.*, p. 300.)

that was contemporaneous with the Reformation, natural theology here first gained an entry into Reformed Confessions.'[8]

This, of course, is the voice of Karl Barth,[9] whose criticism of the Reformed Confessions has been resisted by Pierre Courthal.[10] The latter accuses Barth of confusing a general revelation, which is indeed and very properly taught by the Reformers and the Reformed Confessions, with natural theology, which is not; pointing out that for them the effect of this general revelation was to render the natural man's impiety inexcusable. Courthal is adamant that

> 'Les confessions de foi réformées ne disent aucunement et ne laissent aucunement entendre que nous aurions déjà naturellement, une connaissance de Dieu actuelle et vraie, connaissance à laquelle viendrait s'ajouter, en complément et supplément, la connaissance de Dieu par sa Parole.'[11]

However, these are precisely the doubts which, as we saw above, are raised by the Gallican Confession and these not least because, as another French scholar has noted,[12] the second article makes no mention of inexcusability as the purpose of the natural revelation.

When, however, we look further at the Confession, the picture is by no means so clear. Thus article nine,

> 'We believe that man was created pure and perfect in the image of God, and that by his own guilt he fell from the grace which he received, and is thus alienated from God, the fountain of justice and of all good, so that his nature is totally corrupt. And being blinded in mind, and depraved in heart, he has lost all integrity, and there is no good in him. And although he can still discern good and evil, we say, notwithstanding, that the light he has becomes darkness when he seeks for God, so that he can in nowise approach Him by his intelligence and reason.'[13]

---

[8] *Reformed Confessions of the Sixteenth Century*, London, 1966, p. 138.

[9] 'Contemporaneously with the Reformation, in the so-called humanism which consisted in a rediscovery of the Stoicism of the Silver Age of Rome, natural theology was able to attain new forms and find new points of entry ... It could again recommend itself to a martyr Church—this time the French, in such a way that, in contradiction to Calvin's proposal, the mischief could be done which may now be read in article 2 of the *Confessio Gallicana* from which it quickly spread to the *Confessio Belgica* (art. 2-3).' (*Church Dogmatics*, Vol. II, 1. Edinburgh, 1957, p. 127.)

[10] 'Karl Barth et Quelques Points des Confessions de Foi Reformées.' *La Revue Reformée*, Vol. 9. 1958, pp. 1-29.

[11] Courthal. *op. cit.*, p. 7.

[12] E. G. Léonard, 'the alterations are in fact considerable in scope and theologically very serious ones', and, referring to the second article, 'For Calvin, such a statement was close to heresy, for he admitted no natural revelation but "for damnation", and here it is regarded as only slightly less evident than Scripture itself.' Léonard, *A History of Protestantism* Vol. II, London, 1967, pp. 118-9.

[13] 'Nous croyons que l'homme ayant été créé pur et entier, et conforme à l'image de

is the exact reproduction of Calvin's fifth article[14] and we could scarcely ask for a more trenchant statement of the utter inability of fallen man to obtain any positive knowledge of God. If then the alteration of the opening articles appears to offer a foothold for natural theology, the retention of this article would seem clearly to rule out such a possibility.

In fact, the significant alterations to Calvin's draft are confined to the first four of its articles and it has been suggested that any further revision may have been prevented because insufficient time was available.[15] The most obvious effect of the Parisian alterations was to enlarge Calvin's proposals from thirty-five to forty articles and it was this latter version which was published by the French Church in 1559. B. G. Armstrong[16] draws attention to the fact that this same year also saw at least two publications of the former, shorter version, neither of which giving the place of publication. This, together with the consideration that the confession of forty articles was never published in Geneva during Calvin's lifetime, whilst the thirty-five articles appeared there in 1562, leads him to surmise that the latter did not approve of the alterations made to his proposals.

There is general agreement that one of the most important influences at work in these revisions was that of Antoine de la Roche-Chandieu whom we have already encountered as an example of a Reformed scholastic.[17] Does this warrant us in drawing the apparently straightforward conclusion that the alterations are the expressions of the latter's scholasticism and that, had time been available at the Synod, these would have been more extensive, including perhaps some modification of article nine? When, seeking for confirmation of Chandieu's views on these issues, we turn to his *Opera Theologica*,[18] we find that he devotes scarcely any attention to

---

Dieu, est, par sa propre faute, déchu de la grâce qu'il avait reçue, et ainsi s'est aliéné de Dieu, qui est la fontaine de justice et de tous biens, en sorte que sa nature est du tout corrompue. Et étant aveuglé en son esprit, et dépravé en son coeur, a perdu toute intégrité sans avoir rien de reste. Et bien qu'il ait encore quelque discrétion du bien et du mal, nonobstant nous disons, que ce qu'il a de clarté, se convertit en tenébres quand il est question de chercher Dieu, tellement qu'il n'en peut nullement approcher par son intelligence et raison.' (Schaff, *op. cit.*, p. 365.)

[14] *CR*. 37, col. 743.

[15] Léonard, *op. cit.*, p. 119, 'No comparable changes were made in the rest of the text, perhaps for lack of time.'

[16] B. G. Armstrong, *Calvinism and the Amyraut Heresy*, pp. 29-30.

[17] See above, p. 78. For Chandieu, see Haag, *France Protestante*, 2nd ed. Vol. 3, cols. 327-34 and A. Bernus, 'Le ministre Antoine de Chandieu, d'après son journal autographe inédit,' *Bulletin: Société de l'Histoire du Protestantisme Française*, Vol. 37, 1888, pp. 2-13, 57-69, 124-36, 169-91, 393-415, 449-62, 561-77, 617-35.

[18] See above p. 78 for details of their publication. Our quotations are from the third edition of 1599.

them there. Thus, for example, in the matter of the natural knowledge of God, there is not a single reference in the entire 926 double-column folio pages to Romans 1, 18-21.

The great bulk of the works are directed against Roman Catholic attacks on the Reformed faith and the very fact that this last-named topic is not one of controversy between the two sides might be taken as evidence for the scholastic nature of the Reformed treatment of it. Thus in the one work[19] which, among other statements of Reformed belief, at times specifically defends the *Confessio Gallicana*, we find that article two is not apparently contested.[20]

However, a further look at this same work goes far towards reversing such a straightforward view of Chandieu's scholasticism and its effect upon his presentation of the Reformed faith. Thus, as evidence of the direction taken by the changes made in Calvin's draft in 1559, we cited article one with its setting out of the divine attributes in apparent independence of Scriptural revelation. In the *Responsio*, however, Chandieu quotes the Roman Catholic *Professio*, 'I believe that our God is omnipotent', and contrasts it unfavourably with the Reformed Confession's belief in God, which, being founded upon His Word, supplements faith in the divine omnipotence with many other attributes the knowledge of which is drawn from Scripture,

> 'First, because the object and rule of our belief is God's Word in which God has revealed Himself as far as is expedient for us: therefore we may establish our belief in that Word's teaching that God is not only omnipotent but also perfectly good, wise, true, righteous, merciful and such like: the knowledge and certainty of which things are necessary to our salvation. In the same way, when we are considering the establishment of our belief, there is no reason for us to rush headlong into the infinite abyss of God's omnipotence, but we are to remain within those bounds of knowledge which it has pleased God to set by His Word. Therefore His power as such is to be contemplated along with His will, truth, righteousness, grace and in short with all those which are declared to us by His Word.'[21]

[19] *Responsio ad fidei (quam vocant) professionem a monachis Burdegalensibus editam in Aquitania, anno 1585, ut esset verae Religionis adiurandae formula* (*Op. Theol.* pp. 395-541). For the circumstances surrounding the publication of this formula under the name of the Archbishop of Bordeaux and of Chandieu's response. See Bernus, *op. cit.*, pp. 571-3.

[20] Cf. The most popular defence of the Gallican Confession against the Roman Catholics, Pierre Du Moulin, *Bouclier de la Foy ou Defense de la Confession de Foy des Eglises Reformees du Royaume de France contre les objections du Sr. Jehan Arnoux Rionnois Jesuite*, Charenton, 1618, and with numerous editions and reprintings and translations into French and German. The first two articles appear with the comment, 'Le Sieur Arnoux ne touche point à ces deux Articles, et par consequent les approve par son silence.' (p. 2.)

[21] 'Primum, quandoquidem obiectum et regula nostrae fidei est verbum Dei, quo sese Deus patefacit, quantum nobis expedit: est quod fidem nostram in illo verbo stabiliamus,

This would certainly cover all the attributes in the second group of article one of the Gallican Confession where God is described as 'omnipotent, ... all-wise, all-good, all-just, and all-merciful'[22] and indicates the thoroughly Reformed way in which that article was regarded by at least one of its compilers.

Furthermore, the implied suggestion that further alterations in a scholastic direction might have been made to Calvin's proposals had time permitted can hardly be allowed to stand for article nine when we consider Chandieu's later defence of the seriousness of original sin. To the Roman Catholic accusation that the Reformed exaggerate the effects of this, he replies:

> 'Therefore those good defenders of sin find fault with us because we magnify original sin too much, thus they show that they have not yet learned that God is displeased with this sin which they want to speak of with only half-open mouth, in complete disagreement with Paul ... the more we magnify original sin, so much the more do we admire and praise the favour of Our Lord Jesus Christ ... "where sin abounded, there grace abounded more exceedingly."'[23]

So much then for the Gallican Confession which may reasonably be cleared of the charges brought against it by Barth and his followers. Even less justified is the former's claim that, in the words of Cochrane's echo of him, 'Having gained admission in the French Confession, the virus of natural theology quickly spread to the Belgic Confession of 1561 (Arts. II-III).'[24] The first article of the two Confessions is virtually the same, but the Belgic alters the second so as to read,

> 'We know Him by two means: first, by the creation, preservation, and government of the universe; which is before our eyes as a most elegant book, wherein all creatures, great and small, are as so many characters leading us to contemplate "the invisible things of God", namely, "His eternal power and

docente, Deum non modo esse omnipotentem, sed etiam perfecte bonum, spaientem, veracem, iustum, misericordem, et similia: quorum cognito et certitudo ad salutem nostram est necessaria. Proinde quum agitur de stabilienda fide nostra, non est quod in abyssum infinitam omnipotentiae Dei praecipites feramur: at subsistendum nobis est in iis limitibus cognitionis quos verbo suo circumscribere Deo libuit. Itaque consideranda eius potentia una cum eiusdem voluntate, veritate, iustitia, gratia, denique cum iis omnibus quue ipsius Verbo nobis declarantur.' (*Opera Theologica*, p. 412.)

[22] Schaff. *op. cit.*, pp. 359-60.

[23] 'Quod boni isti peccati patroni nos incusant, propterea quod peccatum Originale nimis exaggeremus, sic testantur se nondum didicisse quam peccatum Deo displiceat, qui de eo semiaperto tantum ore loqui velint, plurimum dissentientes a Paulo ... quo magis exaggeramus peccatum originale, eo magis admiremur et celebremus beneficium Domini nostri Jesu Christi, ... "ubi peccatum abundavit, ibi gratia superabundavit".' (*Opera Theologica*, pp. 464-5.)

[24] Cochrane, *op. cit.*, p. 139.

Godhead'', as the Apostle Paul says (Rom. 1, 20). All which things are sufficient to convince men, and leave them without excuse.
Secondly, He makes Himself more clearly and fully known to us by His holy and divine Word; that is to say, as far as is necessary for us to know in this life, to His glory and our salvation.'[25]

A cursory glance might lead us to suppose that the first means of revelation through the natural order is more positively celebrated here with the introduction of the familiar simile of the book of the creatures. In fact, of course, Calvin himself uses similar imagery but with an entirely negative intention,

> 'But upon his individual works he has engraved unmistakable marks of his glory, so clear and so prominent that even unlettered and stupid folk cannot plead the excuse of ignorance.'[26]

The Belgic Confession follows him precisely in introducing Romans 1, 20 and its conclusion.

This fidelity to the distinctive Reformation emphasis on this point is underlined still further in Article fourteen which is a version of the Gallican article nine and which, if anything, outdoes Calvin himself in its insistence on the effects of the Fall,

> 'Man ... by his sin, having corrupted his whole nature, ... he has lost all his excellent gifts which he had received from God, and only retained a few remains thereof, which, however, are sufficient to leave man without excuse; for all the light which is in us is changed into darkness.'[27]

When it comes to trying to ascertain just how Dutch theologians understood the issue of the natural knowledge of God as expressed in the Belgic Confession, we are at somewhat of a loss, since, oddly enough, although published before the Heidelberg Catechism and sharing the same

---

[25] 'Nous le connaissons par deux moyens. Premièrement: par la création, conservation et gouvernement du monde universel, d'autant que c'est devant nos yeux comme un beau livre, auquel toutes créatures, petites et grandes, servent de lettres pour nous faire contempler les choses invisibles de Dieu, savoir sa puissance éternelle et sa divinité, comme dit l'Apôtre S. Paul (Rom. 1, 20). Toutes lesquelles choses sont suffisantes pour convaincre les hommes, et les rendre inexcusables.

Secondement: il se donne à connaître à nous plus manifestement et évidemment par sa sainte et divine parole, tout autant pleinement qu'il nous est de besoin en cette vie pour sa gloire et le salut des siens.' (Schaff. *op. cit.*, p. 384.) The best means of studying the various versions of the Belgic Confession and of comparing it with the Gallican is to be found in J. N. Bakhuizen van den Brink, *De Nederlandsche Belijdenisgeschriften*, 2nd.ed. Amsterdam, 1976.

[26] *Institutes* I, v.i. *LCC*, p. 52.

[27] 'L'homme ... par son peché, ayant corrompu toute sa nature, ... a perdu tous ses excellents dons qu'il avait reçus de Dieu, et il ne lui en est demeuré de reste que des petites traces, qui sont suffisantes pour rendre l'homme inexcusable, d'autant que tout ce qui est de lumière en nous est converti en ténèbres.' (Schaff, *op. cit.*, pp. 398-9.)

position of importance as the latter as a formulation of Dutch Reformed orthodoxy, the Confession had to wait nearly a century before the publication of the first commentary upon it. The very closeness of its link with the Catechism may well be the reason for this otherwise surprising fact, since the proliferation of commentaries upon the latter work, arising out of the practical demands of the Sunday by Sunday instruction in it which the Church required, preempted any necessity for a similar treatment of the Confession. It was only as, with the heightening of the controversies over the doctrine of Predestination, men felt that orthodoxy was in danger that attention was focussed upon the Confession as its embodiment.

In the period of these controversies up to 1618 little heed was paid to the issue of our concern. However, with the publication of Festus Hominius's *Example of Dutch Controversies*,[28] the picture begins to change. This work, designed to influence the minds of the foreign delegates to the forthcoming Synod of Dort, elevated the Belgic Confession to a position of central importance since, as proclaimed in the subtitle,[29] set out article by article with extracts from the writings of the Remonstrants which deviated from it, the Confession was erected as the yard-stick of orthodoxy.

One of the chief fears which the Contra-Remonstrants entertained about their opponents centred upon the latter's alleged affinities with the teaching of the Socinians. This is immediately apparent in the *Specimen* both from Hommius's Prefatory Letter to the Reader[30] and from the passages selected by him as being contrary to the Confession. Thus as regards the second Article, 'Of the Knowledge of God', there is only one heterodox doctrine which the Remonstrants are supposed to hold in opposition to the Confession and this is one notoriously maintained by Socinus and his early followers, 'It is in no way possible to have knowledge of God without supernatural revelation.'[31] We shall consider the debate over this issue in a later chapter.[32]

[28] *Specimen Controversiarum Belgicarum*, Leiden, 1618. A Dutch translation, *Monster van de Nederlandsche Verschillen* was published at Leiden in the same year. See P. J. Wijminga, *op. cit.*, pp. 264-8.

[29] ... *Seu Confessio Ecclesiarum Reformatarum in Belgio, Cujus singularis Articulis subjuncti sunt Articuli Discrepantes, in quibus nonnulli Ecclesiarum Belgicarum doctores hodie a recepta Doctrina dissentire videntur.*

[30] '... plausibilum illam de Praedestinatione controversiam quinque illis Articulis expressam, προφασιν tantum esse, sub qua Socinianismum (aliquantulum forte interpolatum aut incrustatum) in Reformatas hasce Ecclesias introducere conentur. Idque eo magis, quod ex scriptis etiam eorum qui protestationem illam manibus suis obsignarunt, ostendere clarissime possint in multo pluribus articulis illos a recepta harum Ecclesiarum doctrina discedere, atque ad errores Socinianorum accedere.'

[31] 'Nullam omnino haberi posse notitiam de Deo, sine supernaturali revelatione.' (Hommius, *Specimen*, p. 9.)

[32] See below, pp. 211-9.

We may recall from our discussion of the matter in relation to the Heidelberg Catechism that, at the Synod of Dort, the Remonstrants presented their written considerations upon both the Catechism and the Confession. John Hales, whose account of the occasion we then quoted, had this to say about their observations on the latter,

> 'These Considerations (I speak of those on the Confession; for those others I saw not) are nothing else but Queries upon some passages of the Confession of little or no moment: so that it seems a wonder unto many how these men, which for so many years past in so many of their Books, have threatened the Churches with such wonderful discoveries of falsehood and error in their Confession and Catechism, should at last produce such poor impertinent stuff.'[33]

Indeed, it must be admitted that as regards at any rate the two articles of the Confession of concern to us, the second and the fourteenth, the few points raised are of minimal significance. The one exception is the query which the Remonstrants raise as to the purpose of the knowledge of God obtained by natural means. In connection with Article two this takes the form

> 'Whether those words, "all of which are sufficient to convict men and to render them without excuse", expressed the primary and principal purpose and effect of the knowledge, or rather the actual consequence arising from the abuse of that knowledge.'[34]

Although, in his commentary on the Romans passage,[35] Beza had expressly endorsed the more severe of the two possible ways of understanding this phrase, yet the alternative interpretation to which the Remonstrants are evidently appealing here had a very respectable lineage and had been upheld by such an impeccably orthodox Reformed exegete as Pareus of Heidelberg.

> 'But has not God revealed Himself to man for salvation? This indeed was the purpose of the revelation in itself ... and man would have attained this end before the fall. But after the fall ... neither the remaining seeds of knowledge, nor the contemplation of the world's fabric can suffice to gain that end for man, by his own fault ... Therefore the proper and salvific use of the divine

---

[33] Hales, *op. cit.*, p. 45.

[34] 'An istis verbis, "quae omnia sufficiunt ad homines convincendos et inexcusabiles reddendos", expressus sit primus et praecipuus finis et effectus cognitionis, an vero potius eventus accidentarius existens ex malo usu istius cognitionis.' (*Acta et Scripta Synodalia*, p. 88.)

[35] ' "Ad hoc ut sint, εἰς το εἶναι". Meo iudicio non tantum significat Apostolus quid illam contemplationem consequatur, sed multo magis cur Deus velit hanc lucem in tenebris lucere, nempe ut homines nihil possint praetexere. Itaque nec Veteri interpreti assentior qui convertit "Ita ut sint, ὥστε εἶναι", nec Chrysostomo qui solam consequutionem putat ita significari.' (*Annotationes Maiores in Novum ... Testamentum*, Vol. II, Geneva, 1594, p. 18.)

revelations has disappeared by man's own fault and is succeeded by the other consequent use so that, failing to respond to the persuasions of nature and the creatures, men became without excuse and self-condemned.'[36]

The Remonstrants return to this issue in their observation on Article fourteen,

'Whether that which remains behind in fallen man is correctly described. For when it is said, "nothing is left in man besides the barest sparks of the excellent gifts", of which mention had been made before, for example, goodness, righteousness and holiness. It is questioned whether some sparks of that righteousness and holiness have been left to man; and whether these words "to render men inexcusable", express the sole and proper end to which the remaining sparks can be devoted; also by what reason and with what effect are men robbed of all excuse.'[37]

At this stage, the Remonstrants are raising this question in a remarkably modest manner. As we shall see in a later chapter, when we examine the way their concern about inexcusability continued to manifest itself in the controversy with the orthodox in the period following Dort, this was not always the case. Disagreement on this issue is a constant feature of the continuing dispute and marks a fundamental difference between the two sides' whole approach to the natural knowledge of God.

Even when the Confession was treated in sermons, the emphasis appears to have remained upon its position as the touchstone of correct belief. Thus in the Dedicatory Letter to a sermon whose title claimed that it '*expressed the Confession of the true, Christian, Reformed Netherlands*'[38] the author explains that he draws upon the three formularies of orthodoxy

---

[36] 'Sed annon Deus se homini manifestavit ad salutem? Hic quidem fuit manifestationis finis per se ... fuissetque homo finem hunc assecutus ante lapsum. Sed post lapsum ... nec semina notitiarum reliqua, nec mundani opificii intuitus ad finem illum obtinendum homini sufficare potest, propria ipsius culpa ... Usus igitur proprius et salutaris patefactionum divinarum propria hominis culpa evanuit successitque alius accidentarius, ut homines non obtemperantes suasionibus naturae et creaturae fierent ἀναπολογητοι atque αὐτοκατακριτοι.' (D. Pareus, *op. cit.*, 1613, cols. 97-8.)

[37] 'An quod in lapsu homini reliquum mansit recte describatur. Nam cum dicitur, "nihil homini relictum praeter exiguas scintillas excellentium donorum", quorum ante facta erat mentio, puta bonitatis, iustitiae, et sanctitatis. Quaeritur, An hominis scintillae aliquae istius iustitiae et sanctitatis sint relictae: et an haec verba "ad inexcusabiles reddendos homines", exprimant unicum et proprium finem, cui relictae scintillae inservire possint: Item qua ratione et qua efficacia homini omnem excusationem adimant.' (*Acta et Scripta Synodalia*, p. 92.)

[38] *Predikatie vervatende de Belydenisse der ware Christelike Gereformeerde Belgie*, Amsterdam, 1625. The author, Hieronymus Vogellius ( + 1653), was one of the delegates from the province of Overijsel at the Synod of Dort and appears to have spent the rest of his ministry in that region. See A. J. Van der Aa, *Biographisch Woordenboek der Nederlanden*, Vol. 19, Haarlem, 1874, p. 311.

approved by the Synod of Dort[39] and that he appends refutations of false teaching in the margins of each section of his own work.

Article two of the Confession features in the very first of the topics with which Vogellius deals 'I. Concerning the rule of Christian belief', and it is interesting to note that he is arguing against a misunderstanding of it which is the exact opposite of that featured in Hommius's *Specimen*. Just who it was who was thus endeavouring to exalt the Book of Nature to a position of sufficiency equal to that of Scripture is not apparent but, as we shall see in a later chapter, Socinian theologians had already reversed their master's teaching on this issue. The passage begins,

> 'We believe and confess that the rule or yardstick of the Christian religion is not only the created, sustained and governed world, although we grant that the same is a large, beautiful book in which all creatures great and small are as letters which enable us to contemplate the invisible things of God, His eternal power and divinity. So also these things are more than sufficient to deprive men of all excuse if they will not acknowledge and obey this God after He has willed to reveal Himself in His Word for salvation.'[40]

The marginal refutation placed alongside declares,

> 'We here reject the errors of those who place the sufficiency of the yardstick of religion in the observation of the creatures over against the teaching of God's written word.'[41]

When at last we do come to the first published commentary on the Confession, Samuel Maresius's *Exposition of the right belief of the United Provinces or of the Confession of the Dutch churches*,[42] we can judge at a glance from its title that the concern with orthodoxy is still very much to the fore. Indeed, this is confirmed in Maresius's second Preface, addressed to the

---

[39] The third formulary was the Synod's own judgement of the Remonstrants' teaching.

[40] 'Wy gelooven ende belyden dat de Regel ofte Rightsnoer der Christelike Religie is niet sleghts de geschapene onderhoudene ende geregeerde werelt hoewel wy toestaan dat de selve een groot schoon boek is daer in alle de schepselen groote ende kleene als Letteren zijn die ons d'onsienlike dingen Godts syne eeuwige mogentheydt ende Godheydt geven te aenschouwen. So en zijn die dingen dogh maer genoegsaem om den menschen alle verontschuldinge te benemen als sy desen God niet heeft willen openbaren ter zaligheydt.' (Vogellius, *op. cit.*, p. 5.)

[41] 'Wy verwerpen hier teghen de dwalingen der genen die de genoegsaemheyd van't Rightsnoer der Religie stellen in d'aenmerkinghe der gheschapene dingen teghen de Leere van het beschreven woord Gods.' (*Ibid.*)

[42] *Foederatum Belgium Orthodoxum sive Confessionis Ecclesiarum Belgicarum Exegesis*, Groningen, 1652. In the first Preface addressed to the States General, Maresius himself comments upon the strange fact that his is the first such commentary, 'In Fatis quoque videtur fuisse ut haec vestrae Confessionis Explicatio, a nullo antea Professore Theologo, quod sciam in hoc Belgio vestro ex professo tentata, a me prodiret.' For Maresius (1599-1673), Professor of Theology at Groningen from 1642 until his death, see D. Nauta, *Samuel Maresius*, Amsterdam, 1935.

ministers of the Dutch Church, where we learn that he undertook the series of disputations at Groningen on this subject at the urging of Hendrik Alting, his senior colleague there, who had suggested this as a means of demonstrating his orthodoxy.[43] In fact, on his death in 1642, Alting himself left behind among his unpublished manuscripts an *Exegesis analytica Confessionis Belgicae* which, although later used by his son, Jacob, never saw the light and has since disappeared.[44]

Although our attention so far has been primarily focussed upon the second article of the Confession, 'Concerning the Knowledge of God', it is significant that it is not here but in his commentary upon the first article, 'Concerning God' that Maresius presents his list of arguments for the existence of God. These are given in summary fashion, beginning with two philosophical arguments,

> 'Nor will he have any doubts who attends the motion, by which the same philosopher (i.e. Aristotle) arrived at the first mover; the chain of causes which must end in a first efficient and an ultimate final cause unless there is an infinite regress.'[45]

Maresius adds a catalogue of proofs with which we have become familiar from Ursinus, 'The order of the universe ... the punishment of crimes ... heroic impulses, prophecies of the future and miracles ... the overthrowings of empires ... the pangs and urgings of conscience and the innate discernment of right and wrong.'[46] To these he appends a less familiar reference to Plutarch's assertion that some have been led to the knowledge of God by spectres and demons. Finally, we are back on well known ground with the appeal to the phenomenon of idolatry as evidence of God's existence.

As with the Heidelberg Catechism, there is nothing in the text of this first article to warrant the presentation of proofs for God's existence; we can only conclude that it is simply the pressure of scholastic usage which ensures that the article is treated as a 'De Deo' Locus. Indeed, we may observe that Maresius had set out precisely the same set of arguments in

---

[43] 'D. Altingius, solidissimus Theologus, meas tum in Facultate Collega Senior, ut pro Disputationum publicarum materia ipsam Confessionem Belgicam deligerem, quo sic publice vobis omnibus constaret nihil me alere monstri cujus gratia meae Orthodoxiae Fama apud vos debeat laborare.' (Maresius, *Exegesis* p. (**) $3^r$.)

[44] See *BWPGN*, Vol. I, p. 118.

[45] 'Nec dubitabit qui attendet ad Motum, per quem idem Philosophus ad primum motorem devenit; Causarum concatenationem, quae in prima efficiente et ultima finali ne detur progressus in infinitum, debet subsistere.' (Maresius, *Exegesis*, p. 17.)

[46] 'Ordinem Universi ... scelerum poenas ... Heroicos impulsus; Futurorum vaticinia et Miracula ... Imperiorum revolutiones ... Conscientiae synteresis et stimulos ac innatum turpis et honesti discrimen.' (*Ibid.*)

that Locus of his most popular work, the *Collegium Theologicum, sive Breve Systema Universae Theologiae.*[47]

Turning to the commentary on the second article, we note that Maresius begins in traditional fashion by making the twofold division of the natural knowledge of God, 'Indeed the natural knowledge of God is twofold, on the one hand innate and on the other acquired',[48] adding the observation, 'yet the former is less distinct than the latter and is to be perfected and completed by it.'[49] Maresius is here indicating that he has taken notice of that controversy over the status of the innate idea of God which will occupy our attention in a later chapter.[50] Strangely enough, those who opposed this latter notion did not apparently make the very obvious point that this article of the Confession is entirely silent about this means to the natural knowledge of God. Maresius acknowledges this difficulty and we may hold our breath at the manner in which he endeavours to read in such a reference here.

> 'Furthermore, although our article may at first sight seem to deal only with the acquired knowledge, yet it is also concerned with the innate, in so far as this has some bearing upon God's conservation and governance of the world. For through such knowledge of Himself implanted in every mind, the functions of conscience and the remaining seeds of honesty and justice in them, God placed those barriers to human corruption by which economic and political societies are preserved from total destruction to this day.'[51]

The only positive value for the natural knowledge of God which Maresius allows is that acceded by Calvin in the provision of that basic morality for the 'preservation of human society which otherwise would have fallen away into sheer villainy.'[52] Furthermore and again, following the reformer, although grace and revelation are entirely gratuitous and

---

[47] Locus II, 'De Dei natura et attributis,' *Collegium Theologicum*, 2nd ed. Groningen, 1649, pp. 21-2. The first edition had appeared there in 1645 and there were further reprints in 1649, 1656, 1659, 1662 and 1673.

[48] 'Cognitio vero Dei naturalis duplex est, alia insita, alia acquisita.' (Maresius, *Exegesis*, p. 48.)

[49] 'Tamen prior est minus distincta quam posterior et ab eo perficitur et completur.' (*Ibid.*, p. 49.)

[50] See below Chapter Eight.

[51] 'Porro quamvis articulus noster prima fronte videatur agere tantum de cognitione acquisita, attamen insitam quoque complectitur; quandoquidem haec non parum confert ad mundi per Deum conservationem et gubernationem: nam per insitam sui notitiam omnium mentibus, officia conscientiae et residua in illa honestatis et justitiae semina, corruptioni humanae eos obices ponit per quos hactenus ab interitu totali societates oeconomicae et politicae immunes praeservantur.' (Maresius, *Exegesis*, p. 51.)

[52] 'Conservandae humanae societati quae alias in merum latrocinium abiret.' (*Ibid.*, p. 56.) Cf. Calvin, *Institutes* II, ii, 13. *LCC*, p. 272.

undeserved, yet 'the revelation of the divine Word does not relate to beasts, but to men who assuredly use reason and possess those rough remnants of God's image once in themselves.'[53]

However, just like Calvin, Maresius reverts to the usual statement of the essentially negative effect of natural knowledge although, no doubt as the result of that controversy on the issue which we shall examine later,[54] he does not merely assert the tenet of inexcusability but presents reasons to show that fallen man has refused to avail himself of what was thus offered to him and therefore merits condemnation,

> 'Now indeed, although this natural knowledge is ineffective for fallen man and insufficient for salvation, yet it is enough to convict him and render him without excuse, as Paul teaches; because ... he does not follow that residual light but rather suppresses it of his own choice and, as the apostle says, holds down the truth of God in unrighteousness ... When an excuse is apt to be sought from invincible ignorance, in order that no one may offer this for himself, God prevents this by that natural knowledge, ensuring that each man always knows more of the good than he performs ...'[55]

Finally, Maresius presents a balanced statement of the relationship between natural knowledge and that revealed in Scripture which he had taken from Pierre Du Moulin's *De Cognitione Dei*.[56]

> 'For as the sun can be beheld only by its own light, so God cannot be known and worshipped for salvation unless He Himself leads us into all truth and makes the light of His Word shine upon us ... From the book of nature we learn that God is and from the book of Scripture we discover who He is; the former shows the power and wisdom of God, the latter discloses the rich treasures of the divine goodness and mercy in Christ: the one indiciates what is man's good, the other the way of attaining it.'[57]

---

[53] 'Nec enim Revelatio verbi Divini pertinet ad bestias, sed ad homines qui nempe et ratione utuntur et residua illa habent Imaginis in se quondam Dei rudera.' (*Ibid.*, p. 57.) Cf. Calvin, *Institutes* II, ii, 13, *LCC*, p. 270.

[54] See below pp. 192-4.

[55] 'Jam vero etsi haec notitia naturalis homini destituto, sit inefficax et insufficiens ad salutem, nihilominus tamen sufficit, ut docet Paulus, ad illum convicendum et inexcusabilem reddendum; quia ... Lucem illam residuam non sequitur sed potius ultro suffocat et ut loquitur Apostolus, veritatem Dei in injustitia detinet ... Cum excusatio soleat peti ab ignorantia invincibili, hanc ut nemo possit praetendere, Deus impedit ea notitia naturali, quatenus plus semper boni quisque scit quam facit ...' (Maresius, *Exegesis*, p. 61.)

[56] For Du Moulin (1568-1658), see below p. 182. This work was first published at Leiden in 1625, a Dutch translation, *Verhandelinghe van de Kennisse Gods* ... appeared at Rotterdam in the following year.

[57] 'Ex libro naturae cogniscitur quod sit Deus, ex libro Scripturae quis sit: ille Dei Potentiam et Sapientiam indicat, hic Divinae Bonitatis et Misericordiae in Christo reserat thesauros: ille commonstrat in genere quod nam sit hominis bonum, hic modum ejus potiundi.' (Maresius, *Exegesis*, pp. 61-2.) Cf. P. Du Moulin, *A Treatise of the Knowledge of God*, London, 1634, pp. 2, 19, 35.

All in all then, the only commentary on the Belgic Confession which dates from our period is a full and substantial statement of the standard orthodox position on the issues of our concern. The division of material between the first two articles, with the arguments for God's existence presented in connection with the first and the qualifications as to the status of such natural knowledge given in the commentary upon the second, is of considerable significance in any assessment of the way in which the two attitudes of mind represented by these respective exercises coexisted in Dutch Reformed thought. We shall have more to say on this topic.

CHAPTER SIX

# LEIDEN THEOLOGIANS

The curriculum of Leiden University, drawn up in the year of its foundation by the first professor of Theology, Guillaume Feugeray, clearly laid down the exposition of the Scriptures as the principal task of the Theology faculty:

> 'So that theology can be taught here, no torturers or insolent quibblers of the truth are proposed, but only those two heavenly and divine Testaments are expounded, the Hebrew Old and the Greek New.'[1]

However, we must recall that biblical exegesis in this period focussed very largely on problems of dogma and that the approach was dictated by the search for material for the common places ('loci communes') of systematic teaching.[2] Thus the very work which made Feugeray's name so well known throughout Protestantism and probably strongly influenced his selection for the Leiden chair, his edition of Marlorat's

> *A Treasury of the Prophetic and Apostolic, that is of the Whole divine and canonical Scriptures, arranged by alphabetical order into common places of things and doctrines, illustrated with holy examples and passages of familiar Scripture,*[3]

is, as its title clearly indicates, not simply a biblical concordance but far more the assembly of texts and references under the standard headings of the 'Loci'.

Apart from Daneau's two disputations on the Heidelberg Catechism to which we have already referred, the earliest example of teaching given in theology at Leiden, which, as it so happens includes the arguments for the existence of God, is also his handiwork, provided that it was in fact delivered there. Daneau left Leiden for Ghent in May, 1582 and the evidence to support the conclusion that his *Christianae Isagoges ad Chris-*

---

[1] 'Hic ut theologiam discere queat, non quaestionarii aut sophistae veritatis insolentes proponuntur, sed soles illi duo caelestes ac divini, alter Testamenti veteris Hebraice, alter novi Graece exponuntur.' (P. C. Molhuysen, *Bronnen tot de Geschiedenis van de Leidsche Universiteit*, Vol. I, The Hague, 1913, pp. 41-2.)

[2] See P. Fraenkel, *De l'écriture à la dispute. Le cas de l'académie de Genève sous Théodore de Bèze*, Lausanne, 1977.

[3] *Propheticae et Apostolicae, id est Totius divinae ac Canonicae Scripturae, Thesaurus, in Locos Communes Rerum, Dogmatum suis Divinis Exemplis illustratorum, et Phraeseon Scripturae familiarium, ordine Alphabetico digestus*. London, 1574, a second edition appeared at Lausanne in the following year and a third at Berne in 1601. For Feugeray, see *BWPGN*, III, pp. 49-51.

*tianorum Theologorum Locos Communes, Libri II*,[4] contains the material for his theological teaching at the former university is presented in Olivier Fatio's excellent study of Daneau's brief and stormy sojourn in the Low Countries[5] and we may confidently accept the former's conclusion that the contents of 'De Deo' and 'De Cultu Dei' were indeed taught to Dutch students. Fatio makes the further point that, since there were so few students,[6] the direct impact of Daneau's teaching would be very limited.[7] On the other hand, the immediate publication of the *Isagoges* ensured that it played its part in preparing Dutch theology for the reception of the arguments for the existence of God.

Perhaps the most immediately arresting point that strikes us at the very beginning of Daneau's third chapter, 'Whether there is a God' ('An sit Deus'), is his declared motive for undertaking the task of demonstrating the existence of God. It is necessary because there exist certain Epicureans and avowed atheists.

> 'Whether however, there is some God ... is almost superfluous to enquire, in view of the numerous and most certain proofs to demonstrate it. Yet, because there are certain Epicureans and other atheists, as Diagoras formerly wrote at the beginning of his book, "whether there are any gods at all, I do not know", we ought to assemble some arguments and commonplaces which we can use, if it should be necessary, to prove that there is some God.'[8]

This apologetic concern is absent from both Calvin and Melanchthon and is rather a feature of traditional scholasticism as exemplified by Aquinas, to whom, as we shall see Daneau refers with respect on more than one occasion.[9] The expressed desire to answer the challenge of the Epicurean and the atheist also recalls the continuing tradition of apologetic defences of the

---

[4] (Geneva), 1583. This first part appeared again at Geneva in 1588, the edition from which our quotations are taken. For full details of this publication's history, see O. Fatio, *Méthode et Théologie, Lambert Daneau et les débuts de la Scolastique reformée*, Geneva, 1976, pp. 74*-87*.

[5] *Nihil pulchrius ordine ... Lambert Daneau aux Pays-Bas* (*1581-1583*), Leiden, 1971. Fatio adds further evidence to support his contention in *Méthode et Théologie*, p. 75*.

[6] 'En 1581, sur 149 étudiants inscrits à l'Université, 18 seulement sont théologiens. En 1582, ils sonts 6 sur 68 ...', *Nihil pulchrius*, p. 95.

[7] The most famous of their number, Arminius, whom Daneau had, according to Bertius's oration at the former's funeral, singled out for praise, would almost certainly not have heard these lectures since he left Leiden for Geneva in 1581.

[8] 'An sit autem aliquis Deus ... pene superfluum est quaerere, quum tot ubique eius argumenta, eaque certissima occurrant. Quia tamen sunt quidam homines Epicurei, alii prorsus ἄθεοι et iampridem Diagoras quidam in principio sui libro scripsit "Sintne Dii omnino, an non sint, nescio", colligendae sunt aliquot rationes et loci communes, quibus uti poterimus, si erit necesse probare, quod Deus est aliquis.' (Daneau, *op. cit.*, fol. 3$^r$.)

[9] E.g. 'Melius Thomas in 1.2ae. Artic. primo', (*Ibid.*, fol. 3$^v$.)

truth of the Christian religion, the most recent of which had appeared in the Low Countries during Daneau's brief sojourn there, Philip Du Plessis-Mornay's *De la Verité de la religion Chrétienne.*[10] Thus Mornay's Preface singles out these two categories of objectors for special attention:

> 'That is the verie welspring of the Atheists, who (to speake rightlie of them) offend ... by drowning reason, or rather by bemiring it in the filthie and beastlie pleasures of the world. Othersome match their pleasures with malice ... Of such kind of stuffe are the Epicures made, who because they feele their minds guiltie of so many crimes, do thinke themselves to have escaped the Justice and providence of God by denying it.'[11]

Before presenting his arguments, Daneau refers to Aquinas's five ways and even though he evidently prefers his own which are of the more obviously Reformation sort,

> 'Thomas, in 1.2ae, Quest. 2, supplies five reasons by which God's existence is proved, the schoolmen follow them: we will here produce our own: we will leave theirs to the schoolmen,'[12]

yet for his eighth and final argument he adduces that which he explicitly recognizes as Anselm's, the appeal to the degrees of perfection:

> 'Finally, the pagan philosophers themselves prove by their natural reason that there must be some supreme Deity: because in causes and events, in which there is some order, there must eventually be a procession to some single, supreme, most perfect and motionless being, which is God. Otherwise its progression would be to infinity and there would be no order, that is nothing would be first or second. Aristotle book 12, Metaphysics, Trismegistus passim, but especially in Pimandrus and also Plato. Anselm followed this argument at length in the Monologion.'[13]

This, of course, provided Aquinas with the material for his fourth way and we may infer that Daneau had no fundamental objection to the scholastic arguments as such, merely a preference for those of his own tradition. For,

---

[10] First published at Antwerp in 1581 this work had an immediate and enormous success which continued until it was superseded nearly half a century later by Grotius's *De veritate religionis Christianae*.

[11] *A Woorke concerning the Trewnesse of the Christian Religion*, London, 1587. p. ** iii.

[12] 'Thomas in 1.2ae. Quest. 2 affert quinque rationes, quibus demonstratur Deum esse, eas Scholastici persequunter: nos nostras hinc afferemus: scholasticis suas relinquemus.' (Daneau, *op. cit.*, fol. 3$^{v}$.)

[13] 'Denique philosophi ipsi profani idipsum naturali quoque ratione probant, nimirum esse aliquem Deum et summum: quoniam in causis et rebus, in quibus est aliquis ordo, necesse sit tandem ad aliquod unum, summum, perfectissimum, et immobile deveniri, qui est Deus. Alias enim progressus fieret in infinitum, neque esset ullus ordo, id est, nihil primum, nihil secundum. Arist. lib. 12 Metaphys. ubique Trismegist. sed in Pimandro praesertim, et Plato quoque. Hoc argumentum Anselmus in Monologio fuse persecutus est.' (*Ibid.*, fol. 5$^{r}$.)

apart from this last, Daneau's arguments are a working over of the common stock of those already familiar to us in Reformation treatments of this topic. Even the addition of the scholastic argument at the end of the list reminds us of Melanchthon's similar usage and otherwise all Daneau's arguments can be found, in whole or in part, elsewhere; the creation and sustenance of the world, the universality of religious belief and the testimony of conscience. He does go beyond Melanchthon's formal list in including the evidence of scriptural wonders and an explicit appeal to the authority of the Bible as well as including a reference to the soul's immortality, this latter as part of a composite fifth argument, 'the sense of God's goodness.'[14] No attempt is made to distinguish between natural and supernatural sources for the knowledge of God's existence and Fatio's suggestion that the first three arguments appeal to external phenomena, the next three to the interior world, with Scripture and natural reason rounding off the list, seems a thoroughly plausible explanation for Daneau's arrangement.[15]

During the first decade and a half of its existence the Theological faculty at Leiden never enjoyed the services of any of its professors for longer than four and a half years and the constant change of personnel is undoubtedly one of the reasons for the low numbers of theological students attracted there.[16] A period of stability began in 1587 with the appointment of the first of three men who were to work together for eight years and between them to span twenty-four. Lucas Trelcatius (1542-1602)[17] was born in Douai and studied in Paris, Orleans and England before returning to the Southern Netherlands in 1578. He had been Walloon minister in Leiden since 1585 and continued to serve as such after he became professor.

The first piece of evidence of Trelcatius's teaching on the subject of the natural knowledge of God is to be found in a disputation, *On the Natural and Revealed Knowledge of God*, (*De Cognitione Dei Naturali et Revelata*), held in January, 1599,[18] which was subsequently published as the second item in the volume *A Collection of Theological Theses publicly propounded in order in Leiden University by Professors Franciscus Junius, Lucas Trelcatius and Franciscus*

---

[14] 'Sensus bonitatis Dei.' (*Ibid.*, fol. 4$^v$.)

[15] See Fatio, *Méthode et Théologie*, pp. 158-9.

[16] For Theology at Leiden during our period, see C. Sepp, *Het godgeleerd onderwijs in Nederland gedurende de 16$^e$ en 17$^e$ eeuw*, Leiden, 1873-4, 2 vols., and A. Eekhof, *De theologische faculteit te Leiden in de 17$^e$ eeuw*, Utrecht, 1921.

[17] For Trelcatius, see *NNBW*, X, cols. 1038-9.

[18] Old style, 1598 and so dated in the original publication at Leiden.

*Gomarus, produced from the year 1598 to the year 1605.*[19] Having distinguished between the two sorts of knowledge according to their sources and having declared them synonymous with natural and revealed theology,

> 'The same (i.e. true theology) is communicated to man by revelation which can either be according to nature, whence the knowledge of God or natural theology, or according to what they call supernatural grace whence arises the knowledge of God or revealed theology.'[20]

he proceeds to give two arguments for the former,

> 'That there is some natural Theology is proved: I. by those common principles which God first implanted in man's nature and which, though corrupt, yet He has graciously preserved ... II. The nature of God Himself who as He is the supreme good cannot be without the means of communicating His highest good to all created things according to their condition.'[21]

Here we encounter the first significant plundering of Franciscus Junius's *De Vera Theologia* which, as we shall see, is a major feature of the disputation, for Junius's second thesis had presented these same two proofs for the existence of Theology, albeit in reverse order:

> 'However, the realities themselves and the agreement of all peoples teach that theology exists. The realities, for God exists, He Himself is the principle of all good in natural things, and He both speaks and acts as God. The agreement; for all know that it is so by the light of nature.'[22]

When, in his third thesis, Trelcatius comes to define natural theology he demonstrates his complete dependence upon his Leiden colleague, for virtually every phrase has been extracted from the first section of the chapter, 'De Theologia naturali' in the latter's *De Vera Theologia*. Trelcatius's

---

[19] *Compendium Theologiae Thesibus in Academia Lugduno-Bat. ordine a DD et Professoribus Fr. Junio, Lucu Trelcatio, et Francisco Gomaro publice proposito, ab anno 1598 usque ad annum 1605 concinnatum.* Hanover, 1611, The disputation, *De Cognitione Dei Naturali et Revelata*, occupies pp. 7-13.

[20] 'Eadem communicari cum homine per revelationem, quae aut secundum naturam contingit, unde Cognitio Dei sive Theologia naturalis; aut secundum gratiam supernaturalem, unde Cognitio Dei sive Theologia revelata, quam dicunt, assurgit.' (*Ibid.*, p. 7.)

[21] 'Esse autem Theologiam aliquam naturalem demonstrant: I. principia illa communia, quae Deus primum naturae hominis insevit, atque in illa, corrupta licet gratiose, tamen deinceps servavit. ... II. Natura ipsius Dei, qui, ut est summe bonus, ita non potest non modo summe bono sui esse χοινωνιχος cum rebus creatis omnibus pro conditione ipsarum.' (*Ibid.*, pp. 7-8.)

[22] 'Esse autem Theologiam, Res ipsae et consensus omnium populorum docent: Res: nam et Deus est, et idem principium est omnis boni in rerum Natura, et loquitur, et agit ut Deus. Consensus; nam omnes ita esse agnoscunt Naturae luce.' (F. Junius, *Opera Theologica*, Geneva, 1607, Vol. I, col. 1375.) The *De Vera Theologia* was originally published at Leiden in 1594 and a second edition, 'ab ipso Autore, ante Obitum suum, recognita et emendata', appeared there in 1604. As we shall see, Junius came to Leiden as 'professor primarius' in 1592.

opening definition is Junius's Thesis XV with which he begins this tenth chapter,

> 'Natural theology is that which proceeds from principles known intuitively, by the natural light of human intelligence, in accordance with the character of human reason.'[23]

Equally the examination of the four causes of this theology is that of Junius:

> 'The efficient cause of this theology is nature itself which is the common instrument of God as man is the particular instrument of nature. The material is provided by the intuitively known principles of divine things. The formal is the outcome of those principles in accordance with the character of human reason.'[24]

the only difference being that, whilst Junius postpones consideration of the final cause: 'We have not worked out the treatment of the final cause because it is regulated by the teaching of nature and is not particularly relevant to this definition of ours.'[25] Trelcatius defines it straightway, 'The final and most important is the glory of God whom all ought to serve in their appropriate way.'[26]

This dependence continues in Trelcatius's next thesis where the distinction is drawn between fallen and unfallen nature; as borrowed from Junius, this reads

> 'However, this nature of ours is to be examined in two ways; for it may be considered simply as it was created and as it existed in its own perfection, or as when sin fell upon it when man's supernatural gifts were removed and the natural ones corrupted in innumerable ways.'[27]

---

[23] 'Theologia naturalis est, quae procedit ex principiis secundum se notis, naturali intellectus humani lumine pro ratione humanae modo.' (Junius, *Op. Theol.*, I, cols. 1390-1.) Cf. Trelcatius, 'Est autem Theologia naturalis, scientia divinarum, quae procedit ex principiis secundum se notis intellectus humani lumine pro rationis humanae modo.' (*Compendium*, p. 8.).

[24] 'Causa efficiens huius Theologiae est natura ipsa, quae instrumentum commune Dei est, ut homo instrumentum particulare naturae. Materialis, rerum divinarum principia secundum se nota. Formalis, processus ex illis principiis pro rationis humanae modo.' (*Compendium*, p. 8.) Cf. Junius, 'Nam causa efficiens huius Theologiae est natura ipsa, et lumen naturale intellectus nostri: materialis rerum diviniarum principia secundum se nota, .... Forma est, quod ex illis principiis procedit haec Theologia pro rationis humanae modo.' (*Op. Theol.*, I, col. 1391.)

[25] 'De fine adhibendo non laboravimus, quia natura docente certus est et tamen non magnopere ad definitionem hanc nostram visus est pertinere.' (*Op. Theol.*, I, col. 1391.)

[26] 'Finalis summa, Gloria Dei, cui omnia convenienter Deo ministrare debent.' (*Compendium*, p. 8.)

[27] 'Natura autem nostrae ratio duplex observanda est: nam aut secundum se consideratur simpliciterque, prout creata fuit et in suo genere perfectissima extitit; aut secundum peccatum ipsi accidens, quod dona hominis supernaturalia sustulit, naturalia infinitis modis

In fact, Trelcatius indicates that he will omit any consideration of unfallen humanity and the natural theology then obtaining,

> 'We shall say nothing about the state of that primeval nature and the relationship of theology to it according to the way in which it was instituted, since we have forfeited it by our culpable deeds and have enslaved ourselves to the worst vanity and corruption.'[28]

He thus bypasses the entire discussion which occupies Junius's seventeenth thesis, but the latter's eighteenth is incorporated as Trelcatius's fifth,

> 'After this nature had been corrupted, natural theology alas, along with all else proceeding from nature, experienced this disastrous corruption; in consequence, those common principles, or rather the vestiges and rudiments now of what previously existed, have lingered on, but in a state of extreme inner corruption, at conflict with themselves and with each other, giving rise to malice and vindictiveness; they are either so suffocated that they have almost ceased to exist, or they lose their own power with which nature endowed them.'[29]

In his sixth thesis, Trelcatius reasserts the existence of the natural knowledge of God, albeit now corrupt in our fallen state, on the basis of universal consent and of Scripture.

> 'And that this knowledge of God and divine things .... though corrupt in man's nature, yet functions as a very faint residue, we prove from the nature of each and every being among us, by the agreement of all peoples and the relevant testimony of Holy Scripture.'[30]

---

corrupit.' (*Compendium*, p. 9.) Cf. Junius, 'Naturae igitur nostrae ... ratio duplex est a nobis observanda. Nam aut secundum se consideratur natura haec, prout a Deo creata fuit, aut secundum accidens illi peccatum et corruptionem consequutam ex primorum parentum lapsu.' (*Op. Theol.* I, col. 1393.)

[28] 'De conditione autem naturae illius primigeniae, et Theologiae communicatione cum ipsa secundum modum ipsius instituta nihil dicemus, quia facto et culpa nostra ab ea excidimus, et vanitati ac corruptioni gravissimae nos mancipavimus.' (*Compendium*, p. 9.)

[29] 'Postquam igitur natura haec corrupta fuit, Theologia etiam naturalis, ut caetera omnia quae ex natura sunt, corruptionem gravissimam experta est; unde factum ut principia illa communia ac potius vestigia et rudera quaedam illius permanserint quidem, sed in sese corruptissima, inter se conturbatissime, et quae partim inscitia, partimque malitia et contumacia unius cuiusque vel suffocentur, ut parum absit quin esse desinant, vel corrumpantur adeo ut vim suam, quam natura ipsis impressit non exerant.' (*Compendium*, p. 9). Cf. Junius, 'Postquam vero natura haec corrupta fuit, illa quidem ipsa principia in singulis permanserunt, communia, obscura, atque imperfecta: sed in sese corruptissima, inter se conturbatissima, tanquam rudera naturae nostrae vitiositate nostra.' (*Op. Theol.* I, col. 1394.)

[30] 'Atque hanc conscientiam Dei rerumque divinarum ... in natura hominis etiam corrupta, aliquam tamen licet tenuissimam residuam factam esse, demonstramus a natura uniuscuiusque nostrum, consensu omnium Populorum atque adeo S. Scripturae testimonio.' (*Compendium*, p. 10.)

For his understanding of the first of these sources he returns once more to Junius, to the discussion of the latter's sixteenth thesis,

> 'And these indisputable principles called 'common notions' or καταληψεις by the Greeks, Tully interprets as ideas which no one fails to feel even while sometimes they resist them most strenuously.'[31]

Although they still contain an occasional echo of Junius,[32] Trelcatius's last two theses devoted to natural theology are concerned with fallen man's inexcusability; a theme which Junius does not touch on directly in his chapter;[33]

> 'This theology, however, occasionally less obscure in those who have studied it with diligent devotion, is yet utterly corrupt in all its modes, nor can it lead man to the supernatural goal, it only removes all excuse and causes him to appear without excuse before God's tribunal.'[34]

However, even in his handling of this topic, Trelcatius does not aspire to any originality, for his final thesis is clearly modelled on the first section of the fourth chapter of Book one of Calvin's *Institutes*,

> 'For even though by God's help we all carry with us in our minds some natural sense of religion, yet some fade away in their blindness, while others revolt from God with deliberate wickedness: yet neither one is to be simply excused since they are perfectly content in their own simplicity and stupor.'[35]

Trelcatius's disputation is remarkable for the overwhelming stress it lays upon the internal source of natural theology. The other source

---

[31] 'Atque haec principia irrefragabilia dixerunt Graeci κοινας ἐννοιας sive καταληψεις, Tullius interpretatur notiones quas nemo non sentit interdum dum eas etiam oppugnat maxime.' (*Compendium*, p. 10) cf. Junius, 'Principia itaque illi .... quemadmodum a Tullio quam plurimis locis appellantur: Graeci ἐννοιας et καταληψεις dixerunt.' (*Op. Theol.*, I col. 1392.)

[32] Thus the description of natural theology as 'Corrupta est, quia incorrupta manere non potuit in subiecto omni ex parte corrupto'. (*Compendium*, p. 10) is evidently that of Junius's, 'Theologiam vero naturalem .... fuisse corruptam. Etenim quomodo incorrupta potuisset in subiecto corrupto omni ex parte permanere?' (*Op. Theol.*, I col. 1394.)

[33] We shall see below that, elsewhere in his writings, Junius fully accepts the standard Reformation view of this topic.

[34] 'Haec tamen theologia, utcunque interdum minus obscura in iis, qui diligenti cura eam coluerunt, tamen omnibus modis corruptissima est, nec ad finem supernaturalem potest hominem perducere; tantummodo omnem excusationem ipsi praecidit, eumque apud tribunal Dei sistit ἀναπολογητον.' (*Compendium*, p. 10.)

[35] 'Etsi enim beneficio Dei omnes sensum aliquem religionis in animis nostris naturaliter circumferimus, tamen alii in caecitate sua evanescunt; alii vero etiam certa malitia a Deo desciscunt: neutri tamen simpliciter excusantur, quia illi in sua sibi simplicitate ac stupore placent etiam maxime.' (*Compendium*, p. 11.) Cf. Calvin, 'Porro sive alii evanescant in suis superstitionibus, sive alii data opera malitiose a Deo desciscant .... Quod autera error aliquos in superstitionem labi dixi, non ita accipio quasi sua eos simplicitas a crimine liberet: quia caecitas qua laborant, semper fere et superba vanitate et contumacia implicata est.'

recognized by the Reformation tradition, the external witness provided by nature and providence is totally ignored. This emphasis, along with virtually everything else in the disputation, has been taken from Junius's *De Vera Theologia* but we must not conclude from it that Trelcatius had no use for such external considerations. As we shall shortly see, he elsewhere refers to proofs of God's existence 'impressed on us both from without and within';[36] and the arguments he borrows from Ursinus for the existence of Providence are drawn from both sources.

Festus Hommius published a posthumous collection of the theological writings of the two Trelcatii, *Opuscula Theologica Omnia*,[37] and the remaining material for the elder's teaching on the natural knowledge of God is drawn thence from his extensive *Compendium Locorum Communium S. Theologiae*. In the second Locus, 'De Deo', Trelcatius disappoints our expectations by explicitly omitting the demonstration of God's existence on the grounds that this is incontestable in the face of the many witnesses to it,

> 'Since, however, the existence of God is so well known, by many and very clear evidences impressed on us both from without and within and from the assent and agreement of all peoples that it cannot be denied, we will therefore omit this first question and proceed to the definition.'[38]

Some notion of the arguments to which he would appeal can be derived from this statement and can be more fully ascertained when we come to the Locus on God's Providence, since he does supply proofs for the existence of the latter, which, as he states, are the same as those which prove God's existence.[39] As he proceeds to outline his list of arguments, we receive further confirmation of Trelcatius's lack of originality on this issue since he presents a compact version of seven of Ursinus's nine *a posteriori* arguments, omitting only those appealing to rewards and punishments and to heroic powers, together with an equally succinct summary of the latter's eight *a priori* proofs.

---

[36] 'Tum *extra* nos, tum intra nos impressis.' See below. The italics are ours.

[37] Leiden, 1614. For details of the younger Trelcatius who eventually succeeded his father to a chair of Theology at Leiden, only to die on 1607, see below p. 128.

[38] 'Quum autem et pluribus et clarionibus testimoniis constet quam ut negari possit, tum extra nos, tum intra nos impressis, assensu et consensu omnium populorum esse Deum, omissa igitur hac prima quaestione ad definitionem progrediamur.' (*Opuscula*, pp. 40-1.) As we observed in our examination of Lubbertus's 'De Deo' disputation, this summary dismissal of the task of proving God's existence was clearly the conventional device enabling the disputant to devote the bulk of his limited space to other aspects of the doctrine of God, see above p. 77.

[39] 'Ad rationes ergo quod attinet in genere notandum eas, quae probant Deum esse, probare etiam illius providentiam.' (*Ibid.*, p. 112.)

Granted Trelcatius's unoriginality, we may still ask why he feels it necessary to introduce arguments of any sort or at any rate anything beyond a simple appeal to the innate idea of God, since his earlier disputation on natural theology rules out any role for such save the strictly negative one we have noted. It is significant that, when Trelcatius does feel the necessity of outlining arguments in the Locus 'De Providentia', he does so because he recognizes that these have to be employed against those who deny the existence of such. Of course, Ursinus and Ursinus's own source, Melanchthon, had always prefaced their proofs for Providence with reference to the three classes of philosophers who held unsatisfactory views on this topic, but such were clearly the Epicureans, Stoics and Peripatetics of antiquity.[40] With Trelcatius, however, although the term Epicurean is retained, the reference is no longer to a sect of the past, but to a contemporary threat,

> '... concerning the thing itself that is the nature of His providence we will expound the definition of this in which first we show that this exists with clear and certain proofs and arguments, against the insanities of the Epicureans *which rage mightily at this time ...*'[41]

The apologetic motive is here clearly at work. Amongst the French books listed in the Sale Catalogue of the younger Trelcatius's library[42] we find 'Plessis de la verite de la Religion Christienne a Anvers 1581,' and we may wonder if this work had played a part in influencing his father in this direction.

Just how close the teaching of the younger Trelcatius[43] on the natural knowledge of God was to that of his father may be readily seen from the few pieces of evidence we possess. The first is from the very beginning of a work which enjoyed an immediate and widespread popularity.[44] Having

[40] Ursinus, 'Tres *fuerunt* sententiae de Dei providentiam: scilicet Epicureorum, Stoicorum, et Peripateticorum'. (*Doctrinae Christianae Compendium, seu Commentarii Catechetici*, Leiden 1584, p. 210.) The italics are ours.

[41] '... de re ipsa id est ipsius providentiae natura, quam definitam exponemus, ubi prius eam esse in Deo certis et claris testimoniis rationibusque contra Epicureorum furores *hodie maxime grassantes* indicaverimus ...' (*Opuscula*, p. 112.) Our italics.

[42] *Catalogus insignium librorum ex Bibliotheca ... D. Lucae Trelcatii ...* Leiden, 1607, no pagination. There are some forty French items listed of which all but a handful are theological.

[43] For L. Trelcatius, junior, (1573-1607) see *NNBW* X, cols. 1039-40. He studied at Leiden under his father from 1587, completing his education during visits to Basel, Zurich and Geneva in 1590-1. He became Professor extraordinary at Leiden in 1603 and held a chair of Theology from 1606.

[44] *Scholastica et Methodica Locorum Communi Sacrae Theologiae Institutio.* First published at Leiden in 1604, it reappeared twice in England; Oxford, 1606 and London, 1608, before receiving an English translation, *A Scholasticall and Methodicall Institution of the Common Places of Divinitie*, London, 1610. There were also two editions at Hanover, 1610 and 1621.

made the distinction, borrowed from Junius,[45] between archetypal and ectypal theology, Trelcatius confines his treatment to the latter category,

> 'By theology we mean not that archetypal ... but the ectypal expressed and depicted by revelation and gracious communication, either according to universal nature in all men or according to special grace and the measure of scripture in the church.'[46]

The introduction of the familiar twofold, Nature and Grace, schema leads Trelcatius on to provide proofs for the existence of ectypal theology which are clearly in part based upon those used by his father to demonstrate that there is a natural theology,[47] though the younger Lucas considerably expands this section,

> 'The nature of God, the light of our own natural conscience, revealed supernatural knowledge and the common experience of peoples and centuries prove the existence of such an ectypal theology.
> The nature of God, for since He is in every way infinitely good, we must not at all think that God lacks the good means to communicate good whose property it is to be a communicator of Himself or to communicate Himself to His other creatures according to their condition. (Math. 5.45.)
> The light both of our natural conscience, by which clearly shining, all men have the existence of a deity settled in their hearts, and other kinds of divine communications (Rom. 1.18, 19, 2.14, 15), as also of revealed supernatural knowledge by which we know that whole truth to be fully and plainly registered in Holy Scripture which we needed to know for our salvation.
> Common experience, for even the gentiles themselves, being strangers to God, had the oracles of the devil instead of those from God rather than that they would deny this ectypal theology or be said to lack it.'[48]

---

[45] '6. Haec (i.e. Theologia) aut est ἀρχετυπος, nimirum Dei ipsius sapientia; aut est ἐκτυπος, a Deo informata. 7. Theologia ἀρχετυπος est divinarum rerum divina sapientia. Hanc vero nos adoramus ac non investigamus. 8. Theologia ἐκτυπος .... est sapientia divinarum rerum a Deo ex archetypo ipsius informata per communicationem gratiae ad gloriam ipsius.' (Junius, *Opera Theologica*, Vol. I, cols. 1370-1.)

[46] 'Theologiam intelligimus, non illam ἀρχετυπον .... Sed ἐκτυπον ex illa priore per revelationem et gratiosam communicationem expressam et informatam; sive secundum Naturam universalem in omnibus hominibus sive secundum gratiam specialem, et modum scripturae in Ecclesia.' (*Institutio*, Leiden, 1604, p. 1.)

[47] Cf. above p. 123.

[48] 'Esse istiusmodi ἐκτυπον Theologiam, demonstrat Natura Dei: Lux tum naturalis conscientiae nostrae, tum supernaturalis scientiae revelatae: Communis gentium saeculorumque Experientia.

Natura Dei, Cum enim modis omnibus sit Infinite Bonus, nulla ratione, bono modo communicandi bonum, carere Deum existimandum est, utpote; cujus proprium sit sui esse κοινωνικον seu Seipsum communicare, cum reliquis creaturis, pro conditione ipsarum. (Math. 5.45.)

Lux, tum Naturalis Conscientiae nostrae, qua praelucente id omnes homines habent constitutum, esse divinationem, aliaque divinarum communicationum genera: (Rom. 1.18, 19,

The *Institutio* has no more to say on this issue and the only other items of relevance are contained in the opening thesis of two disputations held in 1605. The first of these, 'On God's Essence and Attributes', was reprinted in the collection published after Trelcatius's death.[49] Trelcatius gives four sources for our certainty that God exists, the Scriptures, Reason, the agreement of philosophers and experience together with the 'sensus communis',

> 'Holy Scripture confirms His existence in countless places: (Gen. 1, 2, 3, 4. Exod. 1 etc.). Reason itself strongly persuades, nay, convinces: (Rom. 1, 19, 20 etc. Plato, de ent. et uno, Ploti. 1. Enn. 1. 8 & 6 c. Iamb, de My, c. 1.3. Maxim Ty. serm. 1. Arist. 8. Phy. et 12 Meta, etc.). The assent and agreement of philosophers supports it; (Zorast. Trismegist. Socrat. Plato, Plot. Jam. Proc. M. Ty. Zono, Arist. Apul. Senec. Iam. Cic. etc.) Experience and common sense cry out.'[50]

The first and last of these had figured amongst his proofs for the existence of ectypal theology, we may note here the addition of the intervening pair and the weighty citation of pagan philosophers.[51] The effect, as Trelcatius himself goes on immediately to point out, is such that denial of God's existence is unthinkable even for those outside the Christian Church.

> 'So much so that not only is it blasphemy to deny this in God's church, but even as it is improbable, nay rather disreputable, in philosophy, so in nature that which is without substance and intelligent foundation in common sense is intolerable and requires not reasoning but reproof.'[52]

2.14, 15) tum Supernaturalis scientiae revelatae, qua scimus totam veritatem, quam scire nos ad salutem nostram interfuit, litteris sacris plene ac plane consignatam.

Communis Experientia. Nam, vel ipsae gentes a Deo alienae, oracula Diaboli pro divinis potius habuerunt quam ut ἐκτυπον hanc Theologiam negarent, eaque carerere dicerentur. (Rom. 1.21, 22, 23)' (*Institutio*, pp. 1-2.)

[49] 'De Essentia Dei et ejus attributis.' *Collegium Quartum Disputationum Theologicarum in Academia Lugduno-Batava. Francisco Gommaro, Jacobo Arminio et Luca Trelcatio Juniore Praesidibus*, 2nd ed. Rotterdam, 1615, pp. 40-57.

[50] 'Sacrae Litterae innumeris locis ΤΟ ΕΣΤΙ confirmant: (Gen. 1, 2, 3, 4. Exod. 1 etc.) Ratio ipsa firmiter suadet, imo persuadet: (Rom. 1. 19, 20 etc. Plato. de ent. et uno, Ploti. 1. Enn. 1. 8 & 6 c. 2 etc. lamb. de My. c1.3. Maxim Ty. serm. 1. Arist. 8. Phy. et 12 Meta. etc.) Philosop. assensus et consensus adstipulator: (Zorast. Trismegist. Socrat. Plato, Plot. lamb. Proc. M.Ty. Zono. Arist. Apul. Senec. Iam. Cic. etc.) Experientia et Sensus Communis acclamant.' (*Ibid.*, p. 41.)

[51] It is interesting to note how many of these are represented amongst the thirty-four items appearing under the heading 'Philosophi et Philogi' in the Sale Catalogue of Trelcatius's library. He possessed a folio edition of Plotinus's work in Greek and Latin; in quarto, Plato's *De Lege*, and a volume entitled, *Thomistii Paraph. in Arist, post et in Physicam*; in octavo, Aristotle's *Ethics* and Cicero's *de universitate* together with Strigelius's *Orationes de doctrina Aristotelis*; in decimosexto, Plato's works and Apuleius.

[52] 'Adeo ut non tantum in Ecclesia Dei hoc negare sit blasphemum: verumetiam sicut in Philosophia παραδοξον imo ἀδοξον ita in Natura, in Sensu Communi ἀνουσησια et ἀρρωσια της διανοιας est intolerabilis, quae non Λογου δεοντας sed κολασεως.' *Collegium Quartum*, p. 41.

Nonetheless, any thought that such an emphasis upon the force of the non-supernatural sources might lead to an over positive assessment of the knowledge of God available to the natural man is squashed in the first thesis of the second of the disputations dating from 1605, *Concerning the One and Triune God*.[53] Here Trelcatius follows the line his father took in the 'De Deo' Locus of the *Compendium*,[54] explicitly omitting the task of proving God's existence because it is so clearly evident. In so doing, however, the younger Trelcatius, using the familiar metaphor of the two books, divides this manifestation into the natural and supernatural and indicates the negative effect of the former,

> 'We here deliberately omit the question of existence as superfluous and beyond doubt since neither superior or inferior nature allows the natural man to miss God's existence, which natural manifestation in that vast book of nature forces the acknowledgement of God's existence sufficiently for inexcusability, nor piety and faith the Christian to whom God has revealed Himself graciously and effectively for salvation in His special Word peculiar to that book of the Church's.'[55]

As will have become apparent in the above discussion, Franciscus Junius,[56] who spent the last ten years of his life at Leiden as 'professor primarius' of theology, was a man whose teaching on the topic of our concern is of considerable interest. Junius had studied at Geneva, 1562-5, during Calvin's last years and according to Warfield, in commending the *Institutes* to his pupils at Leiden, 'used to tell them that he himself had devoted two entire years to its study.'[57] Amongst the list of his works we find mention of a *Méthode des lieux communs de la Saincte-Ecriture, disposez selon l'ordre des chapitres que Calvin a suivi en son 'Institution'*.[58] Unfortunately, a search of the Dutch libraries reveals that the work is no longer to be

---

[53] *De Deo Uno et Trino*. Leiden, 1605, no pagination.

[54] See above p. 127 cf. the remarks made there about this custom of summarily handling the issue of God's existence in the first thesis of such a disputation.

[55] 'Quaestionem An sit consulto hic ut supervacaneam et indubiam omittimus, cum, An Deus sit, quaerere nec natura sive superior sive inferior permitat homini φνχιχῳ, quem manifestatio naturalis in vasto illo naturae libro, Deum esse, sufficienter ad ἀναπολογιαν fateri cogit; nec pietas fidesve suadet Christiano, cui ipse se Deus in suo Verbo peculiari illo Ecclesiae libro gratiose et efficaciter patefecit ad salutem.' (*Ibid.*, Thesis I.)

[56] For Junius (1545-1602), see *BWPGN*, IV pp. 604-16, F. W. Cuno, *Franciscus Junius der Altere, Professor der Theologie und Pastor (1545-1602)*, Amsterdam, 1891, and C. De Jonge, *De Irenische Ecclesiologie van Franciscus Junius (1545-1602)*, Nieuwkoop, 1980.

[57] *Calvin and Calvinism*, p. 403.

[58] According to Cuno, there were two editions published at Leiden, one in 1597 and the second in 1599. (*op. cit.*, p. 245.) In a letter to J. J. Grynaeus of Basel, dated 27th December 1597, Junius Writes, 'Edidi his diebus folio uno synopsin methodicam Institutionis Calvini, quia multos magistellos video sic sapere ut etiam tanti illius viri scriptum tantum simulate vellicent.' (Cuno, *op. cit.*, Letter, 52, p. 355).

found.[59] Apparently, it only comprised a title page and five tables and we may surmise that it displayed affinities with those charts inspired by the Ramist method which we encountered in Delaune's and Piscator's abridgement of the *Institutes*. Much of Junius's ministry was spent in the Palatinate culminating in his tenure of the chair of theology at Heidelberg, 1584-92 and, as we shall see, he absorbed other influences to add to that of Calvin.

This becomes apparent when we examine the two chapters of Junius' *De Vera Theologia* of relevance to our concern, namely nine and ten which embrace theses fourteen to nineteen and which we have already had occasion to refer to in our discussion of the elder Trelcatius. The first of these theses makes the traditional distinction between natural and supernatural theology,

> 'There is therefore a twofold method of imparting theology, by nature and by grace: the former is, as it were, an internal principle of communication, the latter external. From this it follows that one type of theology is termed natural, the other supernatural;'[60]

We shall have something more to say about this internal/external distinction. Immediately following his definition, Junius makes the standard Reformation point in connection with Romans 1, 19 concerning man's inexcusability,

> 'St. Paul revealed this method of differentiating the types of communication so clearly to us when he wrote to the Romans (Ch. 1) that it cannot be denied by any intelligent man. For he declared that all men are imbued with some knowledge of God and of themselves, first by the light of nature and secondly by the authority of scripture. Of these attestations even one suffices to remove every excuse for sin from the sinner.'[61]

Chapter ten begins in theses fifteen and sixteen with a discussion of the principles innate in human beings from which natural theology proceeds. Although Junius has evidently drunk deep of the contemporary revived Stoicism as mediated to his century by Cicero,

---

[59] De Jonge, *op. cit.*, p. 263 n. 58, reports on his own unsuccessful efforts to trace this work.

[60] 'Est igitur duplex Theologiae communicandae modus, Natura et gratia; illa, velut internum principium communicationis; haec, velut principium externum illius, ex quo fit ut Theologia una dicatur naturalis, et Supernaturalis altera.' (Junius, *Opera Theologica*, 1607, Vol. I, col. 1390.)

[61] 'Hanc communicationis distinguendae viam tam aperte nobis aperuit Paulus quum ad Romanos scriberet, cap 1 ut negari a nemine sapiente possit. Nam quum omnes homines imbutos aliqua Dei et sui ipsorum cognitione pronunciat, primum quidem naturae luce, deinde vero auctoritate scripturae; ex quibus testimoniis vel unum sufficit ad praeripiendam omnem peccatoribus excusationem peccati sui.' (*Ibid.*)

> 'So we call these principles which we are discussing, 'concepts' in the way they are termed in several places by Cicero. The Greeks called them ἐννοιας and καταληψεις.',[62]

there is no escaping the strong Thomist cast of much of his thought.[63] Thus we may compare Junius's description of the part played by the principles in the process of reasoning,

> 'We call those things 'principles' which are known intuitively by the light of nature, that are known immediately and which are motionless or unchangeable, so that at length some knowledge evolves from them. The exercise of reasoning derives sure deductions from these principles as rivers derive from their sources. It compares the principles of nature with the truth of things or contrasts them with one another. It links causes with effects and from these reaches a conclusion. It defines things in general and individually. In short it so orders all things that it acquires knowledge of all those things which man's reason is able to investigate and learn.'[64]

with that of the *Summa*

> '... therefore in the order of enquiry and discovery human reasoning starts from certain truths quite simply understood, that is first principles, and then in the order of judgement by analysis returns to first principles in the light of which it studies what has been found.'[65]

In the second of the two comparisons we made in our chapter on Melanchthon between him and Aquinas, we noted that, in his discussion of natural law, the latter indicates the way in which the general principles

---

[62] 'Principia itaque illa, de quibus agimus, denotamus notionis voce; quemadmodum a Tullio quam plurimus locis appellantur: Graeci ἐννοιας et καταληψεις dixerunt.' (*Ibid.*, col. 1392.)

[63] In his one brief reference to Junius, Althaus comments upon the Thomist epistomology reflected in the *De Vera Theologia*. He considers that Junius was the first Protestant theologian to apply such a scheme. (Althaus, *op. cit.* Darmstadt, 1967, pp. 230-1). His contemporaries recognized this aspect of his learning. Thus G. J. Vossius, in a letter to Grotius, dated September 1621, in which he defends Junius's memory against the slighting remarks of Scaliger, writes of his former master, 'Quam ille sedulo Scholasticos, Thomam cum primus ... legebat?' *Briefwisseling van Hugo Grotius*, Vol. II, ed. P. C. Molhuysen, The Hague, 1936, p. 139.)

[64] 'Principia appellamus, quae per se nota sunt naturae luce, quae immediate nota sunt, et quae immota sive immutabilia, ut ex iis tandem certa scientia consequatur. Ex his principiis certos processus, tanquam ex fontibus rivos, deducit ratiocinatio, principia naturae comparat cum rerum veritate, aut ea inter se disparat; causas cum effectis iungit, atque ex iis concludit; res communes et singulares determinat; denique sic omnia ordinat, ut scientiam adipiscatur earum rerum omnium quas ratio hominis investigare et consequi potest.' (Junius, *Op. Theol.* I, col. 1391.)

[65] '... inde est quod ratiocinatio humana secundum viam inquisitionis vel inventionis procedit a quibusdam simpliciter intellectus, quae sunt prima principia; et rursus in via judicii resolvendo redit ad prima principia ad quae inventa examinat.' (*ST*, 1a.79.8.)

become increasingly indistinct as one proceeds to particulars.[66] To illustrate this he gives the example of the conclusion 'deposits are to be returned to their owners', and shows how this can be modified in practice by particular circumstances,

> 'From this principle it follows as a proper conclusion that deposits are to be returned. This is indeed true in most cases but in certain cases it can happen that it would be injurious and consequently unreasonable if deposits were returned, as for instance if someone sought to attack one's country. The more you descend into particulars the more it appears how the rule that deposits are to be returned must be handled with such caution or in such a way.'[67]

Interestingly enough when Junius wishes to illustrate the vagueness, obscurity and imperfection of the principles he picks on a very similar example, only in his case he works from the more fundamental principle of natural law, 'each should get what is due to him' ('suum cuique tribuendum'), which actually underlies the conclusion, 'deposits are to be returned',

> 'For example, it is a natural principle that each should get what is due to him. In these three respects we often fail in putting this principle into practice. For what nature decrees in general concerning each one of us, we violate in particular instances and blur those principles and general ideas by our separate conclusions through the lack of clarity in the immediate processes and the imperfection of our judgement.'[68]

Junius devotes his seventeenth thesis to discussing the state of natural theology in the unfallen Adam. Again we may note the strong impress of Thomist teaching upon his thought.

> 'For, since the nature of man has been so formed that it contains the principles within itself, it gains the increase through the exercise of reason and by study until it has arrived at correct knowledge.'[69]

---

[66] See above, p. 28.

[67] 'Ex hoc autem principio sequitur quasi conclusio propria, quod deposita sint reddenda, et hoc quidem ut in pluribus verum est; sed potest in aliquo casu contingere quod sit damnosum et per consequens irrationabile, si deposita reddantur, puta si aliquis petat ad impugnandam patriam. Et hoc tanto magis invenitur deficere quanto magis ad particularia descenditur: puta si dicatur quod deposita sunt reddenda cum tali cautione vel tali modo.' (*ST*, 1a 2ae.94.4.)

[68] 'Exempli causa, principium naturale est, ius suum cuique tribui oportere. Hic tribus modis in utendo principio hoc plerumque fallimur. Nam quod natura dictat communiter de unoquoque, nos refringimus exceptionibus, et principia illa notionesque communes singularibus nostris conclusionibus, obscuritate mediorum, et imperfectione iudicii nostri velamus.' (*Op. Theol.* I, col. 1392.)

[69] 'Nam cum natura hominis ita comparata sit, ut principia quidem in se habeat, progressum vero rationcinatione et studio assequatur, donec ad iustam scientiam pervenerit.' (*Op. Theol.* I, col. 1393). Cf. '... ordinatio interrogatio procedit ex principiis communibus per se notis ad propria. Per talem autem processum scientia causatur in anima addiscentis.' (*ST*, 1a 2ae. 84.4.)

Where, however, Junius does forsake Aquinas, and we may note that he acknowledges that he is taking his own line here, is in the limitations he attaches to Adam's knowledge of God,

> 'I am not unaware, indeed, that what I have said must seem new and strange to many: that is that unimpaired nature, as it existed in Adam from the creation, was possessed of what I may call limits to its theology and did not progress beyond them.'[70]

The constant emphasis on the position and nature of the innate principle, an emphasis which, as we shall shortly observe,[71] was absent in Aquinas, has led to Junius's departure from the latter. As Junius puts it, even unimpaired reason, whose task it was to increase man's knowledge, could only operate on the basis of the vague, obscure and indistinct principles and was thus considerably limited in what it could achieve.

> 'What follows then? Could the knowledge of divine matters be acquired in man in his unimpaired state by what I may call these instruments of nature? Not at all. For reason itself could not operate except from a position of darkness and imperfection; for he did not have means of acquiring knowledge except that which stemmed from the principles: ... From this it straightway follows that reason, even in that pure state of man's nature, could not ascend to the summit of a more extensive human knowledge than it could build up by those first principles and its own principles.'[72]

How different from St. Thomas who, although firmly denying that unfallen Adam could know God in His essence, yet allowed him a very considerable degree of knowledge by means of the created order and could say,

> 'in the state of unimpaired nature man did not need a gift of grace supplementing his natural endowment in order to love God naturally above all things, although he did need God's help moving him to do this.'[73]

Indeed, it is a remarkable feature of the entire discussion of the issue of natural theology in the *De Vera Theologia* that from its first definition on-

[70] 'Non sum quidem nescius id novum permultis et inauditum videri quod modo dicimus; naturam integram, prout in Adamo a creatione fuit, his quasi finibus Theologiae suae fuisse praeditam, nec ulterius secundum naturam processisse.' (*Op. Theol.* I, col. 1393.)

[71] See below, p. 140.

[72] 'Quid ergo? scientiane potuit rerum divinarum in homine integro perfici his naturae velut instrumentis? minime vero. Nam ratio ipsa non potuit non laborare ex obscuritate et imperfectione, cum materiam non aliunde quam ex principiis ad scientiam gignendam habuerit: ... Ex quo id continuo sequitur, non potuisse, ne in natura quidem hominis integra, rationem, ad amplius humanae scientiae fastigium ascendere, quam superstruere posset principiis, et ex principiis ipsius.' (*Op. Theol.* I, col. 1394.)

[73] 'homo in statu naturae integrae non indigebat dono gratiae superadditae naturalibus bonis ad diligendum Deum naturaliter super omnia, licet indigeret auxilio Dei ad hoc eum moventis.' (*ST*, 1a 2ae. 109.3.)

wards, Junius confines it to the internal operation of the innate principles. In so doing he turns his back here not only on Thomism but also upon the Reformation tradition which, as we have had frequent cause to observe, places as much weight upon the external witness offered to man in creation and providence as it does upon the innate source. Even when Junius does come to consider the classic Scriptural texts for such natural theology, his insistence upon the limitations arising from the state of the principles rules out any effective manifestation of God which the created order might afford. Thus of the revelation of God referred to in Acts 14, 15-17, he comments,

> 'His (i.e. Paul's) arguments show that it is unclear, for the apostle cites nothing except the testimony of nature or the things performed by God in nature, in order to assert the truth that God is supremely to be adored. But these are very weak signs of that true and living God which have not borne witness to what God has been to them from the beginning but rather state the attributes of God.'[74]

Again Junius's view of the matter leads him to put an almost contradictory gloss upon Paul's declaration in Romans 1, 20 of the clear revelation of God given in the creation,

> ' "For God has revealed it. For the invisible things of Him from the creation of the world are clearly seen, being understood by the things that are made, even His eternal power and godhead", but, without doubt, in that vague, indistinct and imperfect manner derived from the principles of nature.'[75]

If Junius has put such limitations upon natural theology in Paradise, how much more is this the case for him for fallen man and so his nineteenth thesis runs much as we might expect it,

> 'Therefore this theology is not able to lead to perfection in any way, nor does it so lead. Moreover it is not even capable of perfection which comes from outside by grace.'[76]

Junius follows Calvin in quoting the patristic adage on the effects of the Fall,

---

[74] 'Obscuram esse demonstrant argumenta illius, cum nihil Apostolus nisi naturae testimonia, aut res in natura a Deo gestas, adferat, ut declaret Dei illius summe adorandi veritatem; Haec autem tenuissima vestigia sunt duntaxat veri illius et viventis Dei, quae non id quod Deus humano generi inde a principio est, sed quod Dei est, potius testificata sunt.' (*Op. Theol.* I, col. 1392.)

[75] ' "Deus enim eum manifestum fecit. Nam invisibilia ipsius iam inde a condito mundo ex rebus factis intellecta pervidentur, aeterna videlicet eius potentia atque divinitas", nempe communi illo ex ipsis principiis naturae, et obscuro, et imperfecto modo.' (*Ibid.*, col. 1393.)

[76] 'Itaque haec Theologia nihil omnino ad perfectionem potest perducere, nec perducit unquam: ac ne perfectionis quidem est per se ipsam capax, supervenientis a gratia.' (*Ibid.*, col. 1395.)

> 'Now this is commonly known (being handed down to us first by the orthodox fathers and then by the schoolmen following them), namely that the natural gifts were corrupted and the supernatural lost.'[77]

Junius again follows Calvin in stressing the severe effects of the Fall upon man's reason, 'and indeed it was impossible that man's reason should not be brought down to a worse state and foully corrupted.'[78] As we have said, in the light of what had gone before, we can hardly be surprised at the thoroughness with which Junius dismisses natural theology in this last thesis of the chapter. He evidently again feels that he must acknowledge that he is departing from a respected tradition in stressing the latter part of his thesis; this tradition is, of course, the 'grace crowns nature' of Thomism.

> 'The third thing that we assert about this natural theology will perhaps seem rather painful to some people and hard to believe. These are the people who cannot bear that everything belonging to our nature be removed and everything belonging to God's glorious grace be adopted. For we say that this natural theology is not of itself even capable of perfection which comes from outside by grace. This means that nature has not of itself or by its own power any affinity or relationship or disposition (as they call it) by which to admit of perfection, in which it is bathed by heavenly grace.'[79]

The divorce between nature and grace could hardly be more forcefully expressed.

The twin influences of Calvinism and Thomism are nowhere more obviously apparent than in Junius's treatment of the existence of God in his disputation, 'Concerning God or that God exists' ('De Deo seu Deum

---

[77] 'Notum autem est illud in vulgo (quod optime orthodixi Patres et Scholastici vestigia illorum sequuti, tradiderunt) nempe naturalia dona corrupta esse et supernaturalia amissa.' (*Ibid.*, col. 1394.) Cf. *Institutes* II, ii, 12 *LCC*, p. 270. 'And, indeed, that common opinion which they have taken from Augustine pleases me: that the natural gifts were corrupted in man through sin, but that his supernatural gifts were stripped from him.' According to the editors of the *Opera Selecta*, Vol. III, 2nd ed. 1958, p. 245, Calvin is wrong in attributing the dictum to Augustine who can only be credited with the first half; the whole saying is that of Peter Lombard.

[78] 'Ac proinde non potuit ratio hominis in peius non ferri, et gravissime turpissimeque vitiari.' (*Op. Theol.* I, col. 1395.) Cf. *Institutes* II, ii, 12. *LCC* p. 270. 'Since reason, therefore ... is a natural gift, it could not be completely wiped out; but it was partly weakened and partly corrupted.'

[79] 'Tertius vero locus, quem de naturali hac Theologia affirmamus, fortasse nonnullis gravior et difficilior creditu esse videbitur, qui non possunt ferre, ut naturae nostrae derogentur omnia, et gloriosae Dei gratiae arrogentur. Dicimus enim naturalem hanc Theologiam per seipsam ne perfectionis quidem sibi supervenientes a gratia, capacem esse. Id est, nullam per se natura aut virtute sua affectionem, aut relationem ordinatam, aut dispositione (ut vocant) habere, qua suscipiat illam perfectionem, quae superfunditur coelesti gratia.' (*Op. Theol.* I, col. 1395.)

esse'), which is included amongst the *Theses Theologicae Heidelbergenses* in Junius's collected works.[80] The third thesis declares the thoroughly familiar twofold source of the knowledge of God's existence, 'Nature itself and scripture witness that God exists',[81] but in less familiar fashion, Junius treats the second of these sources, the supernatural, first, making it clear that a proper faith in this matter is utterly beyond the natural man,

> '7. Faith is the supernatural eye of our mind. Heb. 11, 1.
> 8. This light is affected by that and that is understood by this so that we believe God's existence.
> 9. Neither indeed can what is supernatural and spiritual be received by the natural man. 1. Cor. 2, 14.'[82]

When he does turn to the natural source, we once more encounter those 'principles' which figure so largely in the *De Vera Theologia*,

> '14. Those who are illuminated only by the light of nature, they possess certain common ideas, Rom. I (which are popularly called principles) agreeing with the supernatural light.'[83]

The effects of the Fall are such as to ensure that this knowledge has only a negative result.

> '15. Those ideas of his original nature which by His kindness God planted in men are destroyed by man and are bare and corrupt seeds. 16. From which man attains to the perception that he is to be arraigned and condemned by God and that he is rendered inexcusable by his conscience. Rom. I.19.'[84]

However, Junius does not leave the matter here but goes on to claim that the natural man can not only know of God's existence through nature, but that he can be taught by *a posteriori* proofs.[85] So far Junius is still well within the Reformation tradition. He had earlier identified the innate idea of God in man as conscience and made it the basis upon which the natural man could learn from nature.[86] This is thoroughly in accord with the

---

[80] *Opera Theologica*, Geneva 1607, Vol. I, cols. 1777-8.

[81] 'Deum autem esse, natura ipsa, et Scriptura testantur.' (*Ibid.*, col. 1777.)

[82] '7. Oculus supernaturalis mentis nostrae est fides. Hebr. 11.1. 8. Haec lux illa afficitur, et ab hac illa prehenditur, ut Deum credamus esse. 9. Neutra vero capi ab homini naturali potest, quae supernaturalis et spiritalis est.1.Cor.2.14.' (*Ibid.*)

[83] '14. Qui sola naturae luce illustrantur, ii communes quasdam notiones habent. Rom. 1. (quae principia vulgo dicuntur) convenientes cum supernaturali luce.' (*Ibid.*, col. 1777.)

[84] '15. Etenim notiones istae sunt naturae illius primigeniae, per hominem destructae, rudera, et corrupta semina, quae beneficio suo, in hominibus servavit Deus. 16. Ex quibus id homo assequitur, ut se rerum a Deo peragi damnarique sentiat et a conscientia reddi inexcusabilem, Rom.I.19.' (*Ibid.*)

[85] '19. Cognovit autem, quia id per se natura, notum est. Deum esse, Act. 14 et 17.', '20. Doceri potest, quia certae sunt a posteriori de Deo (ut vocant) demonstrationes, id est, ab operationibus et effectis eius.' (*Ibid.*, col. 1778.)

[86] '17. Est autem conscientia, haec interna lux naturae, quae assidua cuique testis est, et

position established by Melanchthon upon which we had occasion to comment in our study of the latter.[87] There we drew attention to a certain similarity which such a position shared with that of Aquinas. However, Melanchthon did not proceed to deploy St. Thomas's arguments on the basis thus established; Junius does.

> 'Thence by the creation of the world there are five of these which have been set forth for men, the nature of things, their guidedness, their motion, the nature of the efficient cause and its mode.'[88]

Just why it should be necessary to go to such trouble for the sake of the natural man for whom this knowledge, on the grounds of what has already been asserted earlier in the disputation, can have no positive effect, is nowhere stated but, undeterred, Junius devotes the remaining fifteen theses to a presentation of the 'quinque viae'. It is worth noting that he does not merely reproduce Aquinas's arguments but, either himself or perhaps following some commentator's rendering, gives them in a distinctive version, putting St. Thomas's fourth and fifth proofs before the first three as he does so. As an example of these differences we may compare the rendering of the argument from final causes:

Aquinas:

> 'The fifth way is based on the guidedness of things. For we see an orderedness of actions to an end in all natural bodies even when they lack awareness. For their behaviour scarcely ever varies and will almost always turn out well; which shows that they truly tend to a goal and do not merely attain it by chance. However, nothing which lacks awareness tends to a goal, unless under the direction of someone with awareness and understanding; for example, an arrow requires an archer. Everything in nature, therefore, is directed to its goal by someone with understanding and this we call God.'[89]

Junius:

> '25. Its guidedness and order: for whatever things are to be found in nature are directed to their goal by a certain purpose belonging either to another or to themselves.

ineluctabilis. Rom. 2.15. 18. Secundum hanc conscientiam, homo naturalis cognovit Deum esse et doceri potest.' (*Ibid.*, cols. 1777-8.)

[87] See above, p. 27.

[88] '21. Earum quinque loci, inde a creatione mundi quibusvis hominibus fuerunt expositi: natura rerum, gubernatio, motus, natura causae efficientis, et modis illius.' (*Ibid.*, col. 1778.)

[89] 'Quinta via sumitur ex gubernatione rerum. Videmus enim quod aliqua quae cognitione carent, scilicet corpora naturalia, operantur propter finem, quod apparet ex hoc quod semper aut frequentius eodem modo operantur et consequuntur id quod est optimum, unde patet quod non a casu sed ex intentione perveniunt ad finem. Ea autem quae non habent cognitionem non tendunt in finem nisi directa ab aliquo cognoscente et intelligente, sicut sagitta a sagittatore. Ergo est aliquis intelligens a quo omnes res naturales ordinantur ad finem, et hoc dicimus Deum.' (*ST*, 1a 2, 3.)

> 26. Yea, rather these are directed by a purpose not only belonging to themselves, which is changeable and deficient; but they are directed by the purpose of a principle immutable, incorrupt and necessary in itself.
> 27. Not only individuals, individually to their immediate goal, but also communally to the one goal, ultimate and common to all.
> 28. However, this purpose and direction to the right ordering cannot be brought about except by the highest intelligence, by which all things in nature are most wisely ordered to their goal: Acts 14, and this intelligence is God.'[90]

In Junius's version the end towards which creatures are directed is detailed to a far greater extent than in Aquinas, with emphasis being laid upon the interlinking of such directional tendencies into an overall design so that the intelligence at work must indeed be of the highest order. In consequence, it is scarcely surprising that the simple illustration of the archer's arrow is omitted as being inadequate to convey the complexity of the process involved.

In this disputation the disparate strands of Calvinism and Thomism are linked by the Melanchthonian device we have observed but the result is not so much a combination as a mere juxtaposition of the two ingredients. As regards the overall effect, the strongly negative stress of the first section can hardly fail to be largely stultified by the positive emphasis arising from the extended exposition of the 'five ways' which occupies the latter half of this very strange hybrid.

We may perhaps wonder that Junius himself never came to feel something of the incongruity of this juxtaposition of the two sections of the Heidelberg disputation. After all, his source for the *a posteriori* arguments had preceded the presentation of them with a denial that man possessed any clear or specific innate knowledge of God's existence, 'The awareness that God exists is not implanted in us by nature in any clear or specific way.'[91] No such reservations apparently troubled him for when next we encounter them, in a much fuller version, these two approaches to the question of God's existence are each made the subject of a separate

---

[90] '25. Gubernatio et ordo illius: nam in natura rerum quaecunque sunt ea ad suum finem diriguntur, certa intentione, aut aliena, aut sua.

26. Quin ea ipsa quae intentione sua diriguntur, non sua solum quae ipsa mutabilis est et deficiens: sed immutabilis principii atque incorrupti, et per se necessarii, intentione diriguntur.

27. Neque solum singula ad suum finem proximum singulariter, sed etiam communiter, ad unum finem summum et communem omnium.

28. Haec autem intentio ac directio ad iustum ordinem non nisi a summa intelligentia qua omnes res in natura ad finem ordinantur sapientissime, proficisci potest: Act. 14, atque haec intelligentia Deus est.' (*Op. Theol.* I, col. 1778.)

[91] 'Quod cognoscere Deum esse in aliquo communi sub quadam confusione est nobis naturaliter insertum.' (*ST*, 1a. 2, 1.)

chapter. First now come the *a posteriori* arguments under the heading, 'Of the subject of Theology, from the nature of individuals',[92] whilst the supernatural source of knowledge is also given its own chapter, the fifth, 'Of the subject of theology, from the revelation of grace.'[93]

Chapter three quickly introduces us to the familiar five proofs,[94] though we may note that they are given in yet another different sequence from that of Aquinas, on this occasion the order being, second, third, fourth, first and fifth. Furthermore, although the arguments are those of St. Thomas, their means of expression once more differs considerably from the latter's, as we can see for example from Junius's presentation of the argument from final causality,

> 'The goal of things and the direction to a goal which they also display most admirably: whether you call nature the common goal, whether the unreasoning or sensual goal which we term instinct, or whether the resolved goal apprehended by mind or conscience, the goal of all is entirely directed towards good either generally according to nature, or individually according to consciousness or with good reason according to conscience. But if they are directed to an individual good, yet that which is individual is maintained by the supreme and universal good according to that argument which we have demonstrated as our third point. Nor is it an objection that men are led astray in choosing the good and contend over the true good as conjectural; for they always seek the good according to its common reason, although a great many err in particulars. The universal goal is therefore the highest good, which good is God.'[95]

This represents a further development of Aquinas's fifth way beyond that which Junius effected in the Heidelberg disputation. Clearly the latter has

---

[92] 'De subiecto Theologiae, ex natura singulari.' Chapters three and four of Book one of *Summa Aliquot Locorum Communium SS. Theologiae*. This work appears for the first time in the second volume of the 1613 Genevan edition of Junius's *Opera Theologica* (cols. 1809-86) as one of the five works to be added there to the equivalent volume of the 1607 Genevan edition. Lacking any preface or other indication, we have only the internal evidence of its contents by which to determine its place amongst Junius's works. Cf. Cuno. *op. cit.*, p. 243.

[93] 'De subiecto Theologiae, ex revelatione gratiae.'

[94] 'Documenta naturae communis ad capita quinque referri possunt. Nam aut a causa efficiente sunt, aut a modo, aut a gradibus rerum, aut a modo, aut a gradibus rerum, aut a motu, aut denique a fine ipsarum rerum.' (*Op. Theol.* II, cols. 1812-13.)

[95] 'Finis rerum, et administratio ad finem, idem quoque testantur luculentissime: nam sive finem communem dixeris naturam, sive finem brutum vel sensualem, quem instinctum appellamus, sive finem conscitum et anima vel conscientia apprehensum, omnino finis omnium ad bonum fertur, aut universe secundum naturam, aut particulariter secundum sensum, aut cum ratione boni secundum conscientiam. Quod si ad bonum particulare feruntur, id tamen quod particulare est, continentur summo et universali bono secundum rationem illam, quam tertio loco de gradibus rerum expressimus. Nec obstat, quod falluntur homines in eligendo bono, et pro vero bono contendunt ad opinabile: semper enim bonum appetunt secundum rationem communem illius: universalis summum bonum, quod bonum Deus est.' (*Op. Theol.* II, col. 1814.)

not been content simply to reproduce stock arguments but has continued to work them over, giving them his own distinctive treatment.

Having given his five arguments, Junius shrewdly puts his finger on the axiom upon which they are founded, namely that the various chains of causality cannot be infinite.[96]

The next Chapter makes its appeal to human nature and its inherent principles of rationality,

> 'We pronounce reason unique which belongs only to man above all creatures and springs from his nature.'[97]

Once more we are introduced to the 'common ideas',[98] and we are led from the existence of man's ability to discern the true and the good to God, the supreme Truth and highest Good, from whom this faculty derives.

Both these chapters are entirely positive in their content and presentation and it is only in the fifth chapter on supernatural revelation that Junius underlines the familiar limitations of the natural means to the knowledge of God. Even here, however, the relationship of natural and supernatural is expressed in a manner which allows a positive role to the former and, perhaps, most importantly, there is no mention of inexcusability.

> 'Therefore corrupt nature teaches us according to its principles that God is one being in Himself, truly good and noble, the principle of all good ... But because nature had not been sufficiently restored to its pristine wholeness according to this means ... therefore God has tempered these same principles of nature corrupt in us, restored and renewed in the word of grace by the heavenly and supernatural means which we call the grace of God or the spirit from the use of Scripture.'[99]

---

[96] 'Atque hi omnes loci certum firmamentum habent ab uno axiomate de quo secundum naturam inter omnes convenit: nempe, Causas in infinitum dari nec debere, nec posse. Oportet igitur, ne in infinitum prolabamur, causam unam primam, et summam causarum, efficientem, necessariam, omnium formam, moventem, et finalem statuit, unde omnia illa dimanent, quae hactenus expressimus. Haec autem causa efficiens, necessaria, formalis, movens, et finalis unica universi, Deus est.' (*Ibid.*)

[97] 'Rationem singularem appellamus, quae homini tantum inest supra res creatas omnes et a natura eius profiscitur.' (*Ibid.*)

[98] 'χοιννας ἐννοιας id est communes notiones.' (*Ibid.*, col. 1815.)

[99] 'Quod ergo natura corrupta docet nos secundum principia sua, Deus esse Ens unum per se, verum bonum, nobile, principium omnis boni; ... Sed quia non satis fuerat naturam restitui pristinae integritati suae secundum modum ipsius ... propterea Deus eadem principia naturae in nobis corrupta in verbo gratiae instaurata et redintegrata, temperavit coelesti et supernaturali temperamento, quod gratiam Dei appellamus, aut Spiritum ex Scripturae usu.' (*Ibid.*, col. 1816.)

Junius, we must conclude, is a strange hybrid among natural theologians. It seems scarcely possible that the Reformed theologian who, in 1594 published the *De Vera Theologia* with its thorough-going devaluation of any natural knowledge of God, should not only have continued to present Aquinas's 'quinque viae', espoused earlier in his Heidelberg disputation, but should have gone on to improve their form and content. If pressed then the Reformed view would doubtless always be given the last word and man's natural knowledge of God assigned its official negative role. Nonetheless the impression left by such a thoughtful presentation of the Thomist arguments for God's existence could hardly fail to make a more positive effect. These proofs thus made their first appearance in the mainstream of Dutch Reformed orthodoxy; it was not long before other Leiden theologians made use of them.

If, as we have seen, Junius exercised a powerful influence over his colleague, Trelcatius Senior, we might expect to discover that this was equally so in the case of the third member of the professorial triumvirate, Franciscus Gomarus,[100] who joined the other two at Leiden in 1594; for Gomarus had studied under Junius at Neustadt during the years 1580-2 and again at Heidelberg in 1585-6. However, although the first work which we shall consider, Gomarus's disputation 'De Theologia',[101] shows signs of such influence in its early theses in, for example, the discussion of the efficient, material, formal and final causes of theology,[102] when we come to the treatment of natural theology we find that the latter develops his own position in which other influences may be traced.

His basic division of the natural/supernatural means by which theology is revealed recalls that of Pareus to which we have already had occasion to refer.[103] '... as to the means of revelation, it is both natural and general and supernatural and special.'[104] This similarity becomes more apparent as Gomarus proceeds to explain the nature of the light of reason from which the natural knowledge is drawn, for he divides the principles of

---

[100] For Gomarus (1563-1641), see G. P. Van Itterzon, *Franciscus Gomarus*, The Hague, 1929. Gomarus did not pursue his entire career at Leiden, but, following his celebrated disagreements with Arminius, resigned in 1611 when it appeared to him that the university authorities were appointing someone equally as heterodox to succeed his deceased colleague. After brief sojourns at Middelburg, 1611-15, and Saumur, 1615-18, Gomarus occupied a chair of theology at Groningen for the remaining twenty-two years of his life.

[101] This is the first item in the collection *Disputationes Theologiae. Habitae in variis Academiis* in Gomarus's *Opera Theologica*, Vol. III, Amsterdam, 1644, pp. 1-4.

[102] Theses XIX-XXII Gomarus, *Op. Theol.* III, p. 2, cf. Junius, *Op. Theol.* I, col. 1390.

[103] See above, p. 73.

[104] '... pro patefactionis modo, aut naturalis est et communis; aut supernaturalis et propria.' (Thesis XXV, Gomarus, *Op. Theol.* III, p. 2.)

theology into two categories, the theoretical and the practical, which he defines as follows,

> 'We call theoretical those the true object of whose goal is contemplation, of which the universal and primary sort are, nothing can at the same time exist and not exist etc. and the particular 1. God exists. 2. He is the Creator. 3. He is the Ruler. 4. He is the Judge. (Romans 1, 19, 30).
>
> The practical are those whose object is the carrying out of that aim by action. The universal and primary sort, proceeding indeed from the theoretical, are, good is to be done, evil is to be avoided and particularly, God is to be worshipped aright. (Rom. 1, 32 and 2, 14, 15).'[105]

This looks as though it may be a development of Pareus's comment on Romans 1, 19.

> 'For the apostle clearly talks of a twofold revelation ... One is the natural impression of the common notions about God, about good and evil, about honesty and wickedness in men's hearts in the first creation ... And these notions are partly speculative, showing that there is a God and what He is like: partly practical teaching what is pious, right, honest, and on the other hand what is impious, unjust and wicked.'[106]

What, however, is especially striking is the way in which Gomarus emphasizes the Melanchthonian view of the central importance of the innate factor in human knowledge in the face of alternatives such as those of Platononism or Aristotelianism,

> 'The first notion of these is not quickly acquired by recollection (ἀναμνησις) nor from the senses and induction (granted that it is strengthened and refined by these): but arises from the latent natural seed of reason and religion, which seed can be buried and hidden by the godless but not stifled or extinguished (Rom. 1.32) for they have a law apart from the Law; since they are a law to themselves (Rom. 2. 14). And Damascene (*Orthod. fidei*, 1, 1.C.1. etc.) rightly

[105] 'Theoretica vocamus quorum objectum est verum finis illius contemplatio, quale universale ac primum illud. Nihil potest simul esse et non esse etc. et particularia 1. Deus est. 2. Creator est. 3. Gubernator est. 4. Judex est (Romans 1, 19.30). Practica vero quorum objectum est res agenda finis ejus actio. Quale ex theoreticis fluens universale quidem ac primum illud, bonum est faciendum, malum fugiendum et particulare, Deus recte colendus est. (Rom. 1, 32 and 2, 14, 15.)' (Thesis XXVII, Gomarus, *Op. Theol.* III, p. 2.)

[106] 'Loquitur enim Apostolus distincte de manifestatione duplici ... Una est naturalis impressio notitiorum communium de Deo, de bono et malo, de honesto et turpi, in corda hominium in prima creatione ... Et sunt hae nototiae partim speculativae, ostendentes quod et qualis sit Deus: partim speculativae, ostendentes quod et qualis sit Deus: partim practicae docentes quid pium, aequum honestum sit, quid contra impium, iniquum, turpe.' (D. Pareus, *Commentarius* col. 94.) This, of course, is itself a development of Melanchthon's position 'Ut lumen oculis divinitus inditum est, ita sunt quaedam notitiae mentibus humanis inditae ... Ac vulgaris divisio nota est, alia esse principia speculabilia, ut notitias numerorum ... Alia sunt principia practica, ut totum discrimen naturale honestorum et turpium.' (*CR* 21, col. 711).

says, "for all knowledge of God's existence is naturally implanted by Him".'[107]

Further signs that Pareus may be an influence emerge in Gomarus's next thesis where he divides natural theology as follows. 'However, this natural theology in man ... is either immediate and inborn, or mediated and acquired.'[108] However, as he elucidates his meaning, Gomarus gives further evidence of the importance he attaches to the natural light, thus he stresses its role in the acquisition of the second type of natural theology, 'Mediated theology is that which, in adults of sound mind, is communicated by the object arousing the sense of natural things and by the natural potentiality of the soul and the active light.'[109] Great as is his emphasis on the innate source of natural theology, Gomarus does not neglect the other traditional means, the book of nature,

> 'Wherefore this world is in the place not only of a master, a witness, a public crier (Job 12, 7, 8, 9. Ps. 19, 1, 2, 3, Acts 14, 17), but also of a book, a glass, a theatre in which is displayed for reading His favours towards us and our duty towards Him which are to be contemplated as if indeed by touching. (Rom. 1, 14, 20, Matt. 6, 26. Prov. 6, 6. I Cor. 1, 21. Acts 17, 27.)'[110]

The next thesis, in outlining the way in which reason operates, yet again underlines the importance of the natural light,

---

[107] 'Quorum prima notitia, non ex ἀναμνησει recordatione: nec ex sensu et inductione (licet hisce confirmetur et expoliatur) raptim acquisita: sed ex latente rationis et religionis semine naturali enata; quod semen ab impiis premi potest et obscurari; sed non opprimi nec extingui (Rom. 1, 32) habent enim legem sine lege: quoniam sibi ipsis sunt lex (Rom. 2, 14). Recteque Damasenus (Orthod. fidei, 1.1.C.1. etc.) πασι γαρ ἡ γνωσις του εἶναι θεου ὑπ αὑτου φυσιχος ἐγχατεσπαρτας.' (Thesis XXIX, Gomarus, *Op. Theol.* III, p. 2.)

[108] 'Haec autem naturalis theologia in homine ... vel immediata et congenita est, vel mediata et acquisita.' (Thesis XXX, Gomarus, *Op. Theol.* III, p. 2.) Pareus's arrangement of the natural knowledge of God, we may recall, ran thus, 'Generalis est omnibus hominibus sana mente praeditis communis. Eaque duplex: Interno seu naturalis, et externa seu acquisita. Interna et naturalis, a natura per notitias communes insita. Externa, ex intuita operum Dei, hoc est creaturarum et eventuum in mundo omnium sensibus et mentibus sese ingenerens.' (*Commentarius*, cols. 166-7). It seems more than likely that Pareus, in his turn, was drawing upon that much used locus, 'De Cognitione Dei' of Piscator (see above p. 39.) 'Cognitio Dei ... duplex est; una naturalis, altera acquisita. Naturalis cognitio Dei ... est quae se in adultis sana mente praeditis sponte naturae exerit ... Talem Dei notitiam hominum mentibus a natura esse insitam ...' etc. (Piscator, *Aphorismi*, p. 11.)

[109] 'Mediata theologia est, quae in adultis sana mente praeditis naturalium rerum objecto sensum excitante et naturali animae potentia ac lumine agente communicata est.' (Thesis XXXIII, Gomarus, *Op. Theol.* III, p. 2.)

[110] 'Unde mundus hic instar non solum magistri, testis, praeconis (Job 12, 7, 8, 9. Ps. 19, 1, 2, 3, Acts 14, 17.), sed etiam libri, speculi, theatri in quo suam cum Deitatem, tum erga nos beneficia et nostrum erga ipsum officium legendae praebet et contemplanda, imo quasi palpanda. (Rom. 1, 14, 20, Matt. 6, 26. Prov. 6, 6. I Cor. 1, 21. Acts 17, 27.)' (Thesis XXXV, Gomarus, *Op. Theol.* III, p. 2.)

> 'Indeed, implanted reason aroused to true attention through the senses and the propensity of the will, is by its own light like a natural eye for reading and contemplation (Rom. 1, 20), for the understanding of simple matters, for addition and division, for reasoning and setting in order, by which things mediated theology is established, as are the rest of the sciences.'[111]

Finally, Gomarus shows his fidelity to the traditional Reformed views as to the purpose of natural theology in fallen man,

> 'Since it was left behind by God both as an incentive to the fear of God (Jer. 5, 22, 24. Acts 17, 27) and from this the basis of political and economic order and the good of human society (Rom. 2, 14, 15) and a matter to convict ungrateful impiety and to add to the glory of God the creator and judge. (Rom. 1, 20, 32. Acts 12, 48.)'[112]

Gomarus' commentary on Romans 1, 20 also contains a lengthy endorsement of the familiar position and one of the appended 'logical conclusions' ('Consectaria') succintly states, 'The natural knowledge of God which is supplied from the contemplation of created things can remove the pretext of ignorance from wicked doers.'[113] Furthermore, on Romans 2, 14, 15, Gomarus takes his stand, not with Melanchthon, but with Calvin,

> '... its purpose is against the gentiles who could have alleged ignorance of the law as an excuse. For he teaches that since they did not have the law of Moses yet they have the law of nature ... And so in this way the apostle proves that all gentiles are sinners and liable to condemnation.'[114]

Gomarus does not furnish us with any list of arguments for the existence of God among his extant works and so we have to ascertain what these would be by looking at those he presents for the existence of Providence. This is a justifiable expedient because, as he says himself in the second

---

[111] 'Ratio vero insita per sensum et voluntatis ad verum observandum, propensionem excitata, naturali sua luce instar est oculi legentis ac contemplantis (Rom. 1, 20), apprehensione simplicium, compositione et divisione, ratiocinatione et ordinatione quibus, ut reliquae scientiae, sic theologia mediata constituitur.' (Thesis XXXVI, Gomarus, *Op. Theol.*, III, p. 2.)

[112] 'Quoniam divinitus relicta est, cum in timoris Dei stimulum (Jer. 5, 22, 24. Acts 17, 27) et ex eo ordinis politici et Oeconomici fulcrum et societatis humanae bonum, (Rom. 2, 14, 15) tum in convincendae ingratae impietatis argumentum et augmentum (Rom. 1, 20, 32. Acts 12, 48) ad Dei creatoris ac judicis gloriam.' (Thesis XLI, Gomarus, *Op. Theol.* III, p. 3.)

[113] 'Cognitio Dei naturalis quae ex rerum creatarum contemplatione comparatur, sceleribus ignorantiae praetextum eripere potest.' (*Analysis et Explicatio Epistolae ad Romanos*, Gomarus, *Op. Theol.* II, p. 10.)

[114] '... contra gentiles occupatio est qui legis ignorantiam praetendere potuissent. Docet enim quamvis legem Mosis non habuerint, habere tamen legem naturae ... Atque hoc modo hactenus probavit Apostolus, omnes gentiles esse peccatores et damnationi obnoxios.' (*Ibid.*, p. 11.)

thesis of a rare disputation on the latter topic,[115] the same arguments are applicable in both cases,

> 'On its nature it is asked in general whether it exists and in particular what it is. The first question is open and clear by the light of nature and can be proved by the same arguments as those for the deity.'[116]

Turning then to Gomarus's more extended treatment of the subject, *A Summary of the Orthodox Doctrine of God's Providence*,[117] we find that he devotes the whole of the second chapter to such a list. He begins by repeating that the same arguments prove the existence of Providence as that of God, a statement made here as a quotation from the first chapter of Nystenus's *De Providentia*. Since, therefore, all men possess an innate conviction of the latter truth, only the Epicureans can deny the former.[118] The argument from the nature of God is driven home with quotations from the Book of Isaiah, from Nystenius again, but most succinctly from Lactantius.[119] We may note that this corresponds to Ursinus's first argument, 'from the nature of God. 1. There is a God: therefore there is a providence.'[120]

For the remainder of his list Gomarus turns to *a posteriori* arguments,[121] which, although he presents them in his own formulations, are all, save one, to be found amongst those of Ursinus. They comprise appeals to the following familiar phenomena,

> (i) 'to ... the most excellent workmanship of the world ...' (ii) 'And not only the world as a whole, but also the constitution and direction of man (for which he is spoken of as the microcosm and "the summary of the greater world" ', (iv) 'something religious as it were a seed inserted most deeply in the breasts of all human beings.' (v) 'the most obvious and abundant examples of divinity in the punishments of wicked doers and kindness towards the virtuous', (vi)

---

[115] *De Providentia Dei*, Leiden, 1601, no pagination. According to Petit *op. cit.*, p. 77, this is not reprinted anywhere else.

[116] 'De natura quaeritur generatim An sit et nominatim Quid sit. Prior quaestio aperta et naturae luce perspicua est iisdem n. argumentis quibus divinitas demonstrari potest.' (Gomarus, *De Providentia Dei*.)

[117] *Conciliatio Doctrinae Orthodoxae de Providentia Dei*. Leiden, 1597. A Dutch translation, *Accort van de recht-sinnige leere der voorsienicheyt Gods*, appeared in 1613. Our quotations are from the collected works, Gomarus, *Op. Theol.* III, pp. 157-76.

[118] 'Nam quum omnibus mortalibus innatum et eorum animis quasi insculptum sit aliquem esse Deum, adeo ut ne ipsi quidem Epicuraei id negaverint quis providentiam illius inficietur.' (*Ibid.*, p. 158.)

[119] ' "Etenim si Deus est" inquit Lactantius De ira Dei c.9. "utique providens est".' (*Ibid.*)

[120] 'a natura Dei. 1. Deus est: igitur est providentia.' (*Ursinus, Leiden, 1584*, p. 214.)

[121] 'Verum, ut ab illa sublimi Dei natura, ad opera illius ...' (Gomarus, *Op. Theol.* III, p. 158.)

'conscience', (vii) 'miracles', (viii) 'the most true and clear predictions of events still many centuries in the future.'[122]

The one exception is Gomarus's third argument which points to the universality of man's religious belief and practices and includes the well worn quotation from Cicero. Both Calvin and Daneau had appealed to this phenomenon, the former to establish the innate idea of God in man, the latter to argue for God's existence.

What strikes us most about Gomarus's choice of arguments is that they all fall within the more traditional Reformation sphere of the appeal to nature and history, not least to sacred history, even to the extent of his omission of those few scholastic arguments employed by Melanchthon, Ursinus and Daneau. If, taking him at his word, we are to accept that these are also substantially the arguments that Gomarus would have put forward for the existence of God, then we must acknowledge his fidelity to the Reformation tradition and also note that he is here quite untouched by Junius's rendition of the 'quinque viae'.

Trelcatius Senior and Franciscus Junius died within a few months of each other in the plague of 1602 and the following year saw the appointment of Arminius.[123] We shall here pass over the controversies[124] which were to make the latter the most famous of all Leiden's theologians and in this chapter concentrate upon his use of the arguments for the existence of God which are contained in his private disputation, 'On the Object of the Christian Religion; and first about God its primary object and God's existence.'[125]

The sale catalogue of Arminius's library reveals[126] that he owned many

---

[122] (i) 'ad ... illustrissimam mundi fabricam ...' (ii) 'Nec mundus solum universalis, sed hominis etiam constitutio et regimen (unde μικροκοσμος et ''mundi majoris breviarium'' dicitur)', (iv) 'religionis quoddam quasi semen omnium mortalium pectoribus insitum penitissime'. (v) '... apertissima copiosaque divinae in sceleratos vindictae et erga probos benignitatis exempla', (vi) 'conscientia', (vii) 'de miraculis', (viii) '... rerum etiam multis post seculis futurarum praedictiones verissimae et clarissimae.' (Gomarus, *Op. Theol.* III, pp. 158-9.)

[123] For Arminius (1560-1609) see C. Bangs, *Arminius, a study in the Dutch* Reformation, Nashville, 1971.

[124] For a discussion of Arminius's part in one such controversy which is relevant to our topic, see below pp. 179-81.

[125] 'De Objecto Christianae Religionis, et primo de Deo primario ejus objecto, et quod Deus sit.' Disputation XIV in *Disputationes magnam partem S. Theologiae complectentes Publicae et Privitae*, Leiden, 1610, pp. 23-25, 2nd edition, Leiden, 1614. Reprinted in Arminius's *Opera Theologica*, Leiden, 1629, pp. 350-352.

[126] *Catalogus Librorum Clarissimi Viri D. D. Iacobi Arminii quondam in Academia Lugdunensi Theolog. professoris*, Leiden 1610, p. 8. 'Loci Communes Trelcatii ... Lansbergius in Catechism Heidelb ... Bastingius in Catechesin Palatinam'; p. 11. 'Junius de Vera Theologia'; p. 12. 'Danaei Isagoge Christianae II volumnibus'; p. 13. 'Gomarus de Providentia'; p. 18. 'Catechesis Ursini'.

of the works which we have already encountered and it also refers to that from which he took the model for this disputation, 'Conr. Vorstii Tractatus de Deo.'[127] In commenting upon an earlier draft of this study, Hoenderdaal[128] has pointed out that Arminius could not have used the 1606 edition of Vorstius' work as his own private disputation was composed in 1604. Although Hoenderdaal recognizes that, since Vorstius' disputation was originally held at Steinfurt in March, 1598, Arminius could readily enough have had a copy,[129] he nonetheless allows himself to speculate on the possibility that the similarities between the two works can be accounted for by the common tradition which they shared. However the detailed comparison between Arminius's set of theses and the first item in Vorstius's book, 'The first theological disputation about God, namely on God's existence, in which God's existence is proved against the atheists',[130] which we shall now undertake, establishes beyond any reasonable doubt that Arminius has here used Vorstius as his starting-point.

Although Arminius's piece is very much shorter than Vorstius's,[131] the similarities become apparent as early as their second and third theses. Thus, Vorstius:

> '2. First, however, comes the doctrine of faith, as it were a foundation of the other part, since he who approaches God must hold firmly to these two truths, that God exists and that those who worship Him are rewarded (Heb. 11, 6). Nor is it possible for correct and serious worship to be offered to God by one who is ignorant of His nature, will and works ... 3 ... Undoubtedly for a correct understanding of this doctrine of the nature of God, being the noblest and most wholesome of all, we must before all else keep in our minds that axiom of faith, that God exists.'[132]

---

[127] *Ibid.*, p. 8. *Tractatus Theologicus De Deo sive de Natura et Attributis Dei*, Steinfurt, 1606; a second edition appeared there in 1610. This, of course, was the book which achieved such notoriety for its author and led to the storm of controversy over his appointment to Leiden as Arminius's successor in 1610. For Vorstius (1569-1622), see *Biographisch Lexicon voor de Geschiedenis van het Nederlandse Protestantisme*, Vol. I, Kampen, 1978, pp. 407-10. See also below pp. 204-13.

[128] G. J. Hoenderdaal, *NAK*, 60, 1980, p. 212.

[129] Another possibility, which Hoenderdaal does not mention, is the 1602 edition of the *Tractatus De Deo*, now no longer extant, to which Petit, *op. cit.*, p. 93, draws attention.

[130] 'Disputatio prima theologica De Deo Nempe de Existentia Dei: In qua demonstratur contra Atheos, Deum Esse.' (Vorstius, *De Deo*, pp. 1-9.)

[131] Arminius's presents fourteen brief theses and one corollary occupying three octavo pages, Vorstius, twenty-two longer theses and an appendix covering nine quarto pages.

[132] '2. Praecedit autem doctrina Fidei, tanquam fundamentum alterius partis: quia accendentem ad Deum oportet haec duo arcte tenere, Deum esse, et cultores suos remunerari: Heb. 11, 6. Neque enim fieri potest, ut recta et serio Deum colat, qui istius Naturam, Voluntatem et Opera ignorat ... 3 ... Verum ad hanc doctrinam de Natura Dei, omnium certe nobilissiman ac saluberrimam, recte percipiendam, oportet ante omnia constitutum in animis nostris habeamus primum illus Fidei axioma Deum esse.' (*De Deo*, pp. 1-2.)

Arminius:

> 'II. In God, who is the primary object of the Christian religion, three things must be considered in order. First, the nature of God, of which the excellence and goodness is such that religion can honourably and usefully be performed to it. Secondly, the acts of God, on account of which religion ought to be performed to Him. Thirdly, the will of God, by which He wills religion to be performed to Himself and that he who performs it be rewarded and, on the contrary, he who neglects it be punished.
> III. Every treatise on the nature of God, must be prefixed by this primary and chief axiom of all religion; God exists, without which every inquiry into God's nature is vain; for, if the divine nature had no existence, religion would be a mere phantasm of human conception.'[133]

Each man sets out ten arguments and, although he is by no means a slavish imitator, Arminius evidently draws all save one of his list from that of Vorstius. The latter in his turn has borrowed extensively and has moved on a stage further than Junius in conflating the scholastic and Reformation arguments by putting together most of Aquinas's five ways with the bulk of Ursinus's list. Vorstius's first argument, 'From the succession of those things which move and are moved',[134] is a pretty faithful rendering of St. Thomas's first way; Arminius omits it altogether, for reasons which we shall consider later. From the marginal heading of Vorstius's second proof, 'From the succession of efficient causes' ('A serie causarum efficientium'), we might expect a version of Aquinas's second way but, although it does indeed contain elements of this, e.g. 'However, nothing can be from itself, for then indeed it would be at once the cause and effect of itself',[135] it takes as its starting point the axiom 'Nothing naturally comes into being from nothing' ('naturaliter Nihil ex nihilo fieri'), and draws almost as much from the latter's third proof which is actually making a different point. As if this was not sufficient a hotch-potch, Vorstius concludes his thesis with a sentence from Ursinus's version of the argu-

---

133 'II. In Deo primario Christianae Religionis objecto tria ordine consideranda. Primo, Natura Dei, cujus ea est excellentia et bonitas, ut Religio illi honeste et utiliter praestari possit. Secundo, Actiones Dei propter quas illi Religio praestari debeat. Tertio, Voluntas Dei, qua vult sibi praestari Religionem et praestantem ipse remunerari, contraque negligentem punire.
III. Tractatui de natura Dei praemitti oportet Religionis omnis primum et summum axioma, Deum esse: sine quo inane est quicquid de natura Dei inquiritur, utpote quae nullam existentiam habens purum putum phantasma sit futura conceptus humani.' (Arminius, *Disputationes*, pp. 23-4.)

134 'A serie eorum quae movent ac moventur.' (Vorstius, *De Deo*, p. 3.)

135 'Nihil autem fieri potest a seipso, denique simul esse caussa et effectum suipsius.' (*Ibid.*, p. 4.) Cf. '... nec tamen invenitur nec est possibile quod aliquod sit causa efficens, sui ipsius, quia sic esset prius seipso quod est impossibile.' (*ST.*, 1a, 2, 3.)

ment, 'The succession of causes and effects', 'Therefore there is some first cause upon which all the rest actually depend.'[136] Arminius unscrambles this mixture, dropping the Ursinus passage and taking the materials provided in Vorstius's version of St. Thomas second and third ways for his own first and second axioms.

> 'The first axiom is, nothing is or can be from itself. For thus it would at one and the same time, be and not be, it would be both before and after itself, and would be both the cause and effect of itself. Therefore, some one being must necessarily be pre-existent, from whom, as from the primary and supreme cause, all other things derive their origin. But this being is God ... The third axiom is, no finite force can make something out of nothing, and the first nature has been made out of nothing. For, if it were otherwise, it neither could nor ought to be changed by an efficient or a former: and thus nothing could be made from it. From this it follows, either that all things which exist have been from eternity and are primary being, or that there is one primary being. That this being is God.'[137]

For his third argument Vorstius deserts Aquinas for Ursinus.

> 'The third is drawn from what is known of reason which forces us to admit that man is endowed with a certain faculty of mind, dependent itself on some other cause. Now no cause can be in any way inferior to its own effect, since no one could confer on another what he entirely lacks himself. From which it results that there is some supreme and most wise mind which bestows intelligence and the common ideas on men: these do not exist by chance nor can they spring from the mere potency of matter. But this mind is God.'[138]

This Arminius uses as his second axiom,

> 'Every efficient primary cause is better or more excellent than its effect. From this it follows that, as all created minds are in the order of effects, some one

[136] 'Series causarum et effectuum', 'Est igitur aliqua Caussa prima a qua reliquae omnes vel immediate pendent.' (Vorstius, *De Deo*, p. 4.) Cf. Ursinus *Corpus Doctrinae*, p. 119.

[137] 'Primum axioma est. Nihil esse aut esse posse a se ipso; sic enim esset simul et non esset, seipso prius et posterius esset, suique ipsius causa et effectus esset. Ergo oportet unum aliquod ens esse necessario prae existens, unde ut a causa prima et suprema ortum ducunt omnia reliqua. At hoc est Deus ... Tertium axioma est, ullum vim finitam aliquid facere ex nihilo, et naturam primam esse ex nihilo factam: secus enim ab efficiente mutari neque potuit neque debuit. Et sic ex illa nihil fieri potuit. Unde sequitur aut omnia quae sunt esse ab aeterno et entia prima, aut unum esse ens primum; et hoc est Deus.' (Arminius, *Disputationes*, p. 24.)

[138] 'Tertia ducitur ab evidente Ratione: qua fateri cogit hominem esse mentem quadam praeditum, quae ab aliqua caussa pendeat; et nullam caussam toto genere esse deteriorem suo effectu, quum nemo alteri id conferre possit, quod ipse nullo modo habet. Unde efficitur esse aliquam Mentem supremam et sapientissimam, quae hominibus intelligentiam et notitias communes indidit: quippe quae nec casu existunt, nec a materiae potentia oriri possunt. Haec at mens est Deus.' (Vorstius, *De Deo*, p. 4.) Cf. 'Rationalis natura habens causam, non nisi ab intelligente natura existere potest: quia causa non est toto genere deterior suo effecto. Mens humana est natura rationalis et habet aliquam causam. Ergo a natura intelligente exsistit, quae est Deus.' (Ursinus, *Corpus Doctrinae*, pp. 117-8.)

mind is supreme and most wise, from which the rest have their origin. But this mind is God.'[139]

Vorstius returns to fairly straightforward versions of Aquinas's fifth and fourth ways for his own fourth and fifth arguments 'from the ordering of things to a purpose' ('a rerum ordinatione ad finem') and 'from the degrees and differences of similar things,' ('a gradibus et differentia rerum congenerum'). Of these Arminius uses a version of the former for his sixth argument '... from the order which there is in things, and from the ordered arrangement and direction of all things for a purpose ...',[140] but he ignores the latter, preferring as his own fifth argument an appeal to the harmony and variety of created beings,

> 'The magnitude, perfection, multitude, variety and harmony of all things that exist, supply us with the fifth argument, which loudly proclaims that all these things proceed from one and the same being and not from many beings. But this being is God.[141]

Having thus employed at least some portion of each of St. Thomas's proofs, Vorstius now works through most of the remainder of Ursinus's list. Thus his sixth reason, 'from the witness of conscience' ('a testimonio conscientiae') incorporates not only Ursinus's argument of that heading but also part of the latter's next one, 'the rewards of the good and the punishments of sinners', ('Praemia bonorum et poenae sceleratorum').

> 'Conscience, which declares to each person from within that God exists. For this, after the commission of sins which, though perhaps unknown to other people, does not cease to accuse a person and to torture him with unknown torments; conversely, when a thing has been well done, even in the face of the mendacity and calumny of others, it is apt to excuse us and fill us with a particular kind of joy (Rom. 2, 15). Yet this could not be so unless some higher judge is acknowledged who thus decrees punishments for crimes and rewards for good deeds.... Furthermore, this supreme judge is God.'[142]

---

[139] 'Omnem causam efficientem primariam suo effecto praestantiorem esse. Unde sequitur, quum et mentes omnes creatae sint in ordine effectuum, unam aliquam esse supremam et sapientissimam mentem a qua originem habent. At haec est Deus.' (Arminius, *Disputationes*, p. 24.)

[140] '... ab ordine qui in rebus est, et ab ordinata omnium ad finem dispositione et directione ...' (*Ibid.*, p. 25.)

[141] 'Quintum argumentum nobis suppeditat ipsa rerum existentium magnitudo, perfectio, multitudo, varietas, concordia: quae clamat ab aliquo et ab uno esse omnia ista, non autem a multis. At hic est Deus.' (*Ibid.*)

[142] 'Conscientia, quae unicuique intus dictat Esse Deum. Haec enim post admissa peccata, licet aliis hominibus incognita non cessat hominem accusare, et coecis termentis excruciare: contra in negotio bene gesto, etiam adversus aliorum mendacia et calumnias, excusare nos et gaudio quodam perfundere solet, sicut videre est Rom. 2, 15. Quod non faceret, nisi aliquem superiorem Judicem agnosceret qui ut sceleratis poenas, ita probis praemia constituit .... Porro hic supremus judex Deus est.' (Vorstius, *De Deo*, p. 5.)

Arminius uses this as his fourth axiom but again removes the element which Vorstius had added,

> 'The same is proved by the practical axiom or conscience which is in all rational creatures. It excuses and exhilarates a man in good deeds; and, in those which are evil, it accuses and torments, even in those things which have not come, and which never will come, to the knowledge of any creature. This is an obvious indication that there is some supreme judge, who will institute a strict inquiry and will pass judgement. But this judge is God.'[143]

He does precisely the same with Vorstius's next reason, 'from providence surrounding the human race', ('7. a providentia circa genus humanum'), which puts together Ursinus's seventh and eighth arguments, 'political society' and 'heroic impulses'; in Arminius's seventh argument, this reverts to 'the preservation of political, ecclesiastical and economic society among men ...'[144]

Ursinus's ninth argument, from predictions of the future, gives Vorstius his eighth reason, which Arminius in turn uses as his ninth. However, for his penultimate argument, Vorstius goes beyond Ursinus in an appeal to the miracles of the Old and New Testaments which differs from that made by Daneau,[145] and, with its reference to the wonderful effect that these had in the rapid spread of the Gospel, appears to draw much more directly than the latter upon the apologetic tradition to which we have already had occasion to refer.[146]

> '... from the almost countless miracles very well known even among nations outside the people of God, by which true religion has been attested through many centuries. These indeed are almost beyond belief, which God ordained through Moses and His other servants; yet even greater are those miracles which Jesus Christ, Son of God, firstly by his own direct action and then indirectly through his disciples, after his resurrection from the dead and ascension into heaven, wrought with such mighty power that within a few years he set almost the whole world alight .... it is the property of God alone to produce miracles: which indeed exceed the powers of the whole of created nature, such as when something is produced from nothing, or when one substance is suddenly changed into something else.'[147]

[143] 'Probat idem axioma practicum seu conscientia quae omnibus creaturis rationalibus in est, in benefactis excusat et exhilarat, in malefactis accusat et cruciat, etiam in iis quae in nullius creaturae notitiam venerunt aut venient unquam; quod manifesto indicio est aliquem judicem supremum qui requiret et judicabit. At ille est Deus. (Arminius, *Disputationes*, p. 24.)

[144] 'Societatis politicae, Ecclesiasticae et oeconomicae inter homines conservatio ...' (*Ibid.*, p. 25.)

[145] See above, p. 122.

[146] See above, pp. 120-1.

[147] '... ab infinitis pene miraculis apud alias etiam gentes extra populum Dei notissimis quibus religio vera multis seculis confirmata fuit. Ubi tametsi stupenda sunt illa quae Deus

In view of the explicitly apologetic concern of this disputation such an affinity is scarcely surprising; Arminius, who evinces no such motive, uses this as his eighth argument but omits that part to which we have drawn attention,

> 'We take our eighth argument from the miracles which we believe to have been done, and which we perceive to be done, the magnitude of which is so great as to cause these far to exceed the entire force and power of the created universe. Therefore a cause must exist which transcends the universe and its power or capability. But this cause is God.'[148]

Finally, both Vorstius and Arminius conclude with the argument from universal consent which had appeared fifth in Ursinus's list. In this instance Arminius's contents himself with just the first sentence of his source's paragraph: 'To these proofs may be added the universal and continued agreement of all peoples, which is to be considered as the law of nature...', becoming for him, 'Finally, there is added the continual and universal agreement of all peoples which is to be held as a law, indeed as a divine oracle.'[149]

Arminius appends a Corollary which, when taken in conjunction with some further observations added by Vorstius,[150] explains why the former omits the latter's argument from motion. Vorstius tells us that the famous Julius Caesar Scaliger[151] had objected to this on the grounds that the cause of physical motion need not be God Himself but some lesser mover. In fact, it is clear from a closer look at the passage cited from Scaliger's *Exer-*

---

per Mosem aliosque servos suos designavit: excellunt tamen imprimis ea quae Filius Dei Jesus Christus tum immediate per se, tum mediate per suos discipulos, postquam ipse ex mortuis excitatus in coelum ascendit, tanta potentia patravit ut paucis annis totum pene orbem terrarum incredibili religionis studio inflammaverit .... solius Dei est vera miracula edere: quippe quae vires totius creatae naturae excedunt, videlicet, cum aliquid ex nihilo creatur, vel cum substantia alicujus rei subito in aliam rem immutatur.' (Vorstius, *De Deo*, p. 6.)

[148] 'Octavum argumentum sumimus a miraculis quae et facta esse credimus et fieri videmus, quorum ea est magnitudo ut totam creati universi vim et potentiam, longissime excedant. Ergo necesse est causam esse quae ipsum universum eiusque potentiam superet. At ista est Deus.' (Arminius *Disputationes*, p. 25.)

[149] 'His demonstrationibus accedit universalis ac perpetuus omnium populorum consensus, qui instar legis naturae putandus est ....' (Vorstius, *De Deo*, p. 6.) 'Accedit denique perpetuus et universalis omnium populorum consensus qui instar legis, imo oraculi divini habendus est.' (Arminius, *Disputationes*, p. 25.)

[150] In 1606, Vorstius added a lengthy series of 'Notae' to the first of his original disputations (pp. 121-49). We shall have occasion to comment more fully on these in a later chapter. See below pp. 204-7.

[151] Vorstius *De Deo*, pp. 130-1. For J. C. Scaliger (1484-1558). See below p. 208. The *Exercitationes Exotericae de Subtilitate* first appeared at Paris in 1557. Our quotations are from the Frankfurt edition of 1582.

*citationes Exotericae* that the latter is taking Duns Scotus's position. Thus, Scaliger's judgement,

> 'From this it is agreed that Avicenna's opinion is preferable to that of Avenroes. For Avenroes was not right in writing that metaphysics receives from nature this knowledge that God exists.'[152]

is taken directly from Scotus's *Opus Oxoniense*[153] as is the consequence,

> 'For since also God is not that first intelligence moving the first sphere, but something other beyond and outside all motion, even if, by natural process I arrive at the first answer. I will not yet understand by motion that God exists.'[154]

As we shall observe in a later chapter,[155] the famous *Disputationes Metaphysicae* of Franciscus Suarez also rejected the argument from motion on essentially the same Scotist grounds and Arminius's Leiden colleague, the Scots professor of philosophy, Gilbert Jacchaeus reproduced the Suarez discussion in the chapter, 'On the infinite being or God' ('De Ente infinito seu Deo'), in his own *Institutiones Metaphysicae* which, although not first published until 1616, was no doubt the subject of Jacchaeus's philosophical teaching in Arminius's day. In the light of this we can now well appreciate the latter's omission of the argument from motion and his corollary,

> 'On account of the differences of very learned men, we allow it to be open to discussion whether, from the motion which is apparent in the world, and from the fact that whatever is moved is moved by something else, it can be concluded that God exists.'[156]

Our further comment must be that the use of scholastic arguments for the existence of God has reached a remarkably high level of sophistication within Dutch Reformed circles for such a discussion to be encouraged among his students by a professor of theology.

The overall impression left by the fore-going comparison of Vorstius's and Arminius's list of arguments for God's existence is not so much the

---

[152] 'Ex hisce constat esse Avicennae quam Avenrois sententiam potiorem. Avenrois enim non recte scripsit accipere a naturali primum Philosophum cognitionem hanc: Deus est.' (Scaliger, *op. cit.*, p. 27.)

[153] Prologue, I, q.3.a.1.n.3.

[154] 'Etenim cum Deus non sit intelligentia illa prima, primum orbem movens, sed aliud quiddam supra et extra omnem motum, etiam si naturali indagatione devenero ad motorem primum, nondum intelligam per motum Deum esse.' (Scaliger, *op. cit.*, p. 27.)

[155] For all details about Suarez, Jacchaeus and the works mentioned, see below pp. 229-30.

[156] 'An ex motu qui in mundo apparet et ex eo quicquid movetur ab alio movetur, concludi possit Deum esse, propter virorum doctissimorum dissessiones, disquiri permittimus.' (Arminius, *Disputationes*, p. 25.)

fact that the latter has used the former, interesting though this discovery certainly is, but rather the manner in which Arminius has thoroughly reorganized his model's material. Indeed, for the first time in our survey of such lists of proofs we encounter a genuine attempt at a systematic approach.[157] Arminius divides his catalogue into a group of four axioms, three of which are theoretical and one practical, and supplements this by a second, comprising six arguments. The basis for this and the greater degree of certainty which, it is implied, attaches to the first category stems from Melanchthon's theory of knowledge, according to which the ultimate pre-suppositions of knowledge, the 'ideas born with us' ('notitiae nobiscum nascentes'), are such that we concur immediately we grasp them.[158] Melanchthon further divided these into the 'speculative principles' ('principia specubilia'), such as, 'the whole is greater than the part', and the 'practical principles' ('principia practica') of ethics. Engelland has asserted, at least by implication, that Melanchthon set out his list of arguments for God's existence according to this scheme,

> 'By virtue of the ''principia specubilia'' it is possible to reason a posteriori from perceptible effects to God as the cause, and by virtue of the ''principia practica'' to take for granted an immediate consciousness of God, which consists in the natural faculty to distinguish between good and evil and in a consciousness that we should obey God and be punished for disobedience.'[159]

Of course, we may accept that Melanchthon's arguments will, on analysis, fall into one or other of these two categories, but a study of the latter's lists such as we undertook in Chapter Two reveals no such scheme in their presentation which appears to be largely haphazard. Arminius, on the other hand, does apply the distinction between the theoretical and practical principles which he refers to as axioms,

> 'God's existence ... can be demonstrated by various arguments. First by certain theoretical axioms, and because when the terms in which these are expressed have once been understood, they are known to be true, they deserve to be called implanted ideas.'[160]

From the material available in Vorstius's version of three of Aquinas's arguments, he selects three such scholastic axioms, whilst the phenomenon of conscience provides him with his practical axiom.

---

[157] This is perhaps a little unfair to Daneau whose list of arguments (see above, pp. 120-2) does show some regard to an ordering principle and may itself have played a part in influencing the arrangement of Arminius' second group of 'argumenta'.

[158] Cf. *CR* 13, cols. 647 sq.

[159] C. L. Manschreck, *op. cit.*, p. xxix.

[160] 'Deum esse .... argumentis variis demonstrari potest, et primo ab axiomatis nonnullis theoreticis quae propterea quod terminis tantum intellectis vera esse cognoscuntur, notionum insitarum nomine appellari merentur.' (Arminius, *Disputationes*, p. 24.)

Even Arminius's second group of arguments shows signs of an ordering principle.[161] Thus, five and six appeal to the order of the natural world, seven to that of human affairs, eight and nine to evidence from supernatural sources whilst ten rounds off the list by indicating the overall effect in the universality of religious belief. We may, of course, take exception to Arminius's choice of theoretical axioms and feel that his selection is somewhat arbitrary. Thus, why should Aquinas's fifth way, with its appeal to final causality in nature, be relegated to the status of an argument, when it could surely be upgraded by choosing as an appropriate axiom let us say, 'All natural beings act for a purpose' ('Omnia entia naturalia finis gratia agunt')?[162] Nonetheless, when compared to the somewhat incongruous juxtapositioning of scholastic arguments and those of a more traditional Reformation hue such as we have encountered hitherto, Arminius's disputation stands out as a genuine attempt at welding together the two types of arguments into a coherent order.

The effects of Arminius's synthesis may be discerned in the scheme of arguments for the existence of God presented by Gomarus's successor, Polyander,[163] who devotes nearly two-thirds of an early disputation to this topic.[164] He quickly introduces the familiar twofold, natural/supernatural means to the knowledge of God and then proceeds to an interesting subdivision of the former of these,

> 'There are two means of this knowledge: nature and revelation. Nature because it supplies us with consciousness and experience. Consciousness is either of knowledge or of deeds.'[165]

Although, as we shall see, Polyander differs from Arminius in very many ways, here he is setting out a framework for the arguments for God's existence which, in its essentials, follows that of the latter. Thus Arminius's major division between axioms and arguments is reflected in Polyander's division between consciousness ('conscientia') and

---

[161] See above, p. 156, for the suggestion that Daneau may have prompted Arminius here.

[162] As we shall see, Arminius's disciple, Episcopius, treats the argument from final causality under this heading which he refers to as one of the 'principia' in nature from which we may argue to the existence of God. See below pp. 231-3.

[163] Johannes Polyander a Kerckhoven (1568-1646) had been minister of the Walloon church at Dordrecht. His thirty-five years' tenure of the chair is a record for the Leiden of our period. See *NNBW*, IX, cols. 815-6 and the forthcoming study by A. J. Lamping.

[164] *Theses Theologicae de Deo*, Leiden, 1613, no pagination, reprinted as the seventh item (pp. 37-43) in the collection, *Disputationes Theologicae de Praecipius Christianae religionis capitabus*, appended to Polyander's *Syntagma Exercitationum Theologicarum*, Leiden, 1627.

[165] 'Huius cognitionis sunt duo intrumenta: natura et revelatio. Natura siquidem conscientiam nobis suppeditat et experientiam. Conscientia aut est scientiae aut facti.' (Polyander, *De Deo*, Theses III-V.)

experience, ('experientia'), whilst the former's distinction between the theoretical and practical axioms becomes the latter's 'Consciousness either of knowledge or deeds' ('conscientia scientiae aut facti'). Arminius gave three theoretical axioms based on the relationship between finite causes and beings and the First, Supreme and Necessary Cause and Being. Polyander contents himself with the presentation of a single thesis which incorporates much of what his predecessor had to say,

> 'Knowledge reveals itself in that reason, which is God's gift to man, perceives that the secondary causes of things subordinate in themselves cannot go on infinitely, since this would be mere confusion; but that there is one first and supreme cause of them all which indeed moves and limits other things but which is by its nature and power unmoved and infinite, and this is God.'[166]

Again, whereas Arminius had preceded this with his remarks about the nature of the theoretical axioms, referring to them as 'innate ideas', ('notiones insitares'), Polyander follows his example with an explanation which identifies his 'knowledge' with the common notions, (κοιναι ἐννοιαι),

> 'Some call this knowledge the innate and common idea of God, because God has inserted it in man's mind and because it proceeds from certain natural principles and the remains of the divine image which philosophers call the common notions; such as, that God exists, that He is one, that He is good, that He is to be worshipped, that He is the creator of the world, etc.'[167]

Arminius's one practical axiom was that of conscience, and, although Polyander does not use the word itself since he has already employed 'conscientia' in a different sense, he also cites this phenomenon as the only example of the consciousness of deeds,

> 'By the term "deeds" we understand every act of man both internal and external. In both sorts of act our thoughts within our minds either accuse and torment or excuse and exhilerate us.'[168]

Finally, Arminius added six further arguments without explanation; Polyander gives another seven which he introduces thus,

[166] 'Scientia in eo se patefacit, quod ratio homini divinitus concessa perspiciat causas rerum secundas sibi subordinatas non posse in infinitum procedere, quoniam haec mera esset confusio: sed earum omnium unam esse causam primam et supremam res alias quidem moventem et finientem; sed sua natura et virtute immobilem et infinitam, quae sit Deus.' (*Ibid.*, Thesis VI.)

[167] 'Hanc scientiam nonnulli insitam ac communem de Deo notitiam appellant, propterea quod Deus illam hominis menti indiderit atque ex quibusdam profluat principiis naturalibus et reliquiis divinae imaginis quas Philosophi vocant κοινας ἐννοιας; cuiusmodi sunt, quod sit Deus, quod unus, quod bonus, quod adorandus, quod mundi conditor, etc.' (*Ibid.*, Thesis VII.)

[168] 'Facti nomine hic omnem hominis internam aut externam actionem intelligimus. In utraque actione cogitationes nostrae nos intus in animis nostris vel accusant et excruciant, vel excusant et exhilarant.' (*Ibid.*, Theses IX-X.)

'Experience abounds in various signs of the divine holiness and in certain ideas which theologians call "acquired" because it is acquired from the contemplation of these signs by the power of natural understanding.'[169]

Arminius had used Vorstius as his model; Polyander draws upon a work of the latter's Steinfurt colleague, Clemens Timpler.[170] Indeed, the *Metaphysicae systema methodicum* was, as we shall see, instrumental in effecting an important change in Vorstius's view of the innate idea of God.[171] Timpler gives nine arguments for the existence of God, the first six of which are philosophical and differ markedly from those of Vorstius's, reflecting the influence of Franciscus Suarez's *Disputationes Metaphysicae*.[172] In the three remaining, non-philosophical, arguments there are traces of Timpler's theological colleague's influence which shows clearly enough in the eighth,

'The eighth proof is drawn from the evidence of world history. For that testifies through every century that the political, ecclesiastical and economic order has been wonderfully preserved and that those who violate it have suffered severe punishments.'[173]

Timpler's final proof appeals to the phenomena of conscience; it is drawn from Vorstius's and is, in turn, adopted virtually verbatim by Polyander.[174]

Polyander, indeed, has taken the bulk of his arguments from Timpler, though without any regard for the latter's order of presentation. Thus the section which we quoted above as the former's equivalent to Arminius's

---

[169] 'Experientia nititur variis divini numinis indiciis atque a quibusdam Theologis vocatur notitia acquisita; eo quod ex istorum indiciorum consideratione vi naturalis διανοιας acquiratur.' (*Ibid.*, Thesis XI.)

[170] For Timpler (1567-1624), Professor of Philosophy at Steinfurt from 1595, See M. Wundt *Die Deutsche Schulmetaphysik des 17 Jahrhunderts*, Tübingen, 1939, pp. 72-8. The *Metaphysicae*, first published at Steinfurt in 1604, was his most important work. Apart from pirated editions it was reprinted no less than four times, the last in 1616. Some idea of its popularity in Holland may be gathered from the fact that, as the sale catalogues of their libraries show, both Trelcatius junior and Colonius possessed copies and also that Hugo Grotius recommended it in his suggested scheme of study for the French ambassador, du Maurier, (Grotius to Du Maurier, 13th May, 1615, *Briefwisseling van Hugo Grotius*, Vol. I, p. 385.)

[171] See below, pp. 208-11.

[172] First published in Spain in 1597, the first German edition appeared at Mainz in 1600. See below p. 229.

[173] 'Octavo demonstratio sumitur a testimonio historiae mundanae. Illa enim testatur omnibus seculis ordinem politicum, ecclesiasticum et Oeconomicum mirabiliter esse conservatum et illius violatores atrocibus poenis fuisse affectos.' (Timpler, *op. cit.*, p. 392.) Cf. Vorstius, *De Deo*, pp. 5-6. See above, p. 153.

[174] Timpler, *Metaphysicae*, p. 392. Cf. Vorstius, *De Deo*, p. 5 and Polyander, *De Deo*, Thesis X.

theoretical axioms is drawn from Timpler's third proof, 'from the necessary dependence of second causes upon a first cause.'[175] When we come to consider Polyander's seven arguments or 'indicia' based on experience, we find that Timpler provides him with three, the wise ordering of nature (Polyander's second; Timpler's sixth) from the degrees of goodness in created beings (Polyander's sixth; Timpler's fifth), and that from universal consent which is the seventh argument for both. There are also points of similarity in the first argument which they both employ, that from the existence of the world to its necessary First Cause, but Polyander waxes eloquent over 'this created order' ('hanc machinam'), in a manner quite unlike that of Timpler.[176] The clearest evidence that the former is drawing upon another source comes in his fourth argument which is virtually a doublet of his second which he took from Timpler, 'the most beautiful order of countless brute creatures...'[177] This unknown work was also probably the source of the version of Polyander's fifth argument appealing to 'heroic activities and powers exceeding the capacity of ordinary nature,'[178] since the same verbosity is apparent, in marked contrast to the versions we have encountered in Melanchthon and Ursinus.

All in all, Polyander presents us in this section with something of a rag-bag of arguments which appear to have been put together from their different sources without regard to method or order. However, his effort at organizing an overall scheme for the presentation of the arguments becomes apparent again when he moves on to consider those which stem from revelation whether internal or external, for the latter category comprises the record of secular as well as scriptural history and accordingly includes Timpler's eighth argument.

> 'Revelation from which it is resolved that God exists is both internal and external ... the external is either from histories both profane and sacred, or from God's word ... Because histories both profane and sacred bear witness to the political, ecclesiastical and economic order.'[179]

There is a case to be made either way for which category this latter argument falls into, depending upon whether it is the preservation of the

---

[175] 'A necessaria dependentia causae secundae a prima.' (Timpler, *Metaphysicae*, p. 391.)

[176] Polyander, *De Deo*, Thesis XII.

[177] 'Ordo pulcherrimus innumerarum creaturarum brutarum...' (*Ibid.*, Thesis XX.)

[178] 'Motus heroici ac virtutes communem naturae captum superantes.' (*Ibid.*, Thesis XXI.)

[179] 'Revelatio ex qua Deum esse constat, aut est interna, aut externa ... Externa, aut sit per historias tam profanas quam Ecclesiasticas: aut per Dei verbum .... Historiae siquidem tam profanae quam Ecclesiasticae attestantur ordinem politicum Ecclesiasticum et Oeconomicum...' (*Ibid.*, Theses XXIV, XXVI, XXXVII.)

church or political society, which is stressed. When, however, we come to the next transfer which Polyander makes, there can be no doubt that logic is on his side. Under the list of considerations among the 'revelation of the divine word' ('verbi divini revelatio') which is 'far more certain than the others', ('caeteris longe certior'), he refers briefly to two arguments which Arminius, following Vorstius, had included alongside the others, 'from the most certain miracles and the predictions of future events.'[180] In this respect, at any rate, Polyander has gone beyond Arminius in organizing the arguments for God's existence into a more coherent pattern. We may also note that, like the latter, he makes no mention of inexcusability as the purpose of the natural knowledge of God which is the more surprising since in his case the framework of his presentation invites such a comment as a part of the comparison to be made between the relative effectiveness of the two means to the knowledge of God.

Vorstius, although officially appointed a professor of theology, was never permitted to teach at Leiden and, whilst he stayed in Gouda engaged in writing replies to the numerous criticisms levelled at him, the young Remonstrant minister, Simon Episcopius was chosen as Polyander's colleague. We shall return to Episcopius in a later chapter, pausing here only to mention that the one piece of relevant evidence from his Leiden professorate, the disputation, 'On the Knowledge of God', ('De Cognitione Dei') which we shall have cause to examine closely,[181] is modelled upon that of his former master, Arminius, which we have already studied.

Following the Synod of Dort in 1619, both Episcopius and Vorstius were dismissed and exiled and their places taken by Walaeus and Thysius, who were joined in the following year by André Rivet from France. In company with Polyander they presided together over Leiden's theology for another twelve years and, so great was their concern to prevent the discord that had previously prevailed in the faculty, they determined to present a united front by publishing their disputations jointly. The result was that celebrated embodiment of Dutch Reformed orthodoxy, the *Synopsis Purioris Theologiae*, a collection of fifty-two such sets of theses which first appeared at Leiden in 1625.[182]

---

[180] 'Certissimis rerum futurarum praedictionibus, miraculis.' (*Ibid.*, Thesis XXVIII.)

[181] See below, pp. 216-8.

[182] Subsequent editions appeared at Leiden in 1632, 1642, and 1658. Our quotations are from the first edition. See G. P. Van Itterzon, 'De "Synopsis Purioris Theologiae." Gereformeerd Leerboek der 17de Eeuw', *NAK*, Vol. 23, 1930, pp. 161-213, 225-59.

Antonius Thysius,[183] was responsible for the issue of our concern to which he devoted seven theses of the sixth disputation, 'On the nature of God and the divine attributes', ('De Natura Dei et divinis Attributis'). He prefaces his treatment of the arguments for God's existence with a declaration of his motive in presenting them; it is the apologetic one of refuting the blasphemies of the atheists,

> 'However, although the existence of God is not a matter for questioning in theology since as a science presupposes its subject matter so theology presupposes this as clear by its own light and not to be disputed by the faithful; yet because of certain insane and more than diabolical blasphemies of atheists (James 2, 19. Psalm 10, 4, 14, 1 and 53, 2 (although more by straining than by sense) we will prove this by the twofold evidence of nature and reason.'[184]

The appeal to nature and reason is interesting, especially when we see how this is carried through. The first category contains just one argument, that from the innate idea of God,

> 'Indeed it is the nature of man that this notion is written in the human mind as a first truth and primary principle, (Rom. 2, 15) and it has such and so great an inclination and propensity to this as may be shown and proved (Rom. 1, 19. Acts 17, 27, 28). And so sense and the common agreement of all men argues for God's existence.'[185]

Then comes an appeal to the design of the greater and lesser worlds which is seen having a foot in both camps, nature and reason,

> 'Indeed nature itself and reason, that is, the whole world, by its workmanship, order, arrangement, embellishment and various use, and most of all, man, the microcosm, yea the image of God by which he expresses God more accurately, displays to us the wisest, most beneficent and most powerful artificer and architect...'[186]

---

[183] (1565-1640). Born at Antwerp, he studied at Leiden and at various other European universities, including Geneva and Heidelberg. From 1601-19 he served as the first Professor of Theology at the newly founded 'Illustre' School at Harderwijk. See *NNBW*, V, cols. 923-4.

[184] 'Quamvis autem quaerendum in Theologia non sit, An Deus sit, cum ut scientia suum subjectum, ita hoc ipsum Theologia praesupponat, quodque id, ut sua luce clarum, a piis disputari fas non sit; tamen propter insanam et plus quam Diabolicam Atheorum quorundam blasphemiam Deum negantium, Jac. 2, 19. Ps. 10, 4. 14, 1 et 53, 2 (quamvis conatu potius, quam sensu) duplici indicio, Naturae et Rationis id demonstrabimus.' (Thesis III, *Synopsis*, p. 63.)

[185] 'Naturae hominis quidem, quod haec notio, ut prima veritas et primum principium humanae menti sit inscripta, Rom. 2, 15 et ad eam inclinationem et propensionem habeat talem et tantam, ut indicasse sit evicesse, Rom. 1, 19. Act 17, 27, 28. Atque ita sensus et consensus communis omnium, Deum esse arguit.' (Thesis IV, *Ibid.*, p. 63.)

[186] 'Quin natura ipsa ratioque, id est, universus mundus, fabrica, ordine, dispositione, ornatu suo ac vario usu, maxime homo μιχροχοσμος imo imago Dei qua pressius Deum exprimit, sapientissimum, beneficentissimum et potentissimum artificem et architectum nobis exhibit....' (Thesis V, *Ibid.*, p. 63.)

There follows a sixth thesis which lumps together a further six arguments the bulk of which certainly do fall under the heading of reason,

> 'Other weighty and various arguments are added to this; namely from the world and most of all from the constancy and orderly motion of the heavens to the first mover and author of motion who exists by act, (Aristotle, Metaphysics Bk. 12, cp. 6); from the order of efficient causes to the first efficient cause in which they are grounded and on which the rest depend; from limits to the ultimate limit and limiter; from good and the perfection of being to the first essence, the highest good and most perfect nature; from the fear of conscience after sin committed as though fearing a supreme judge; from the severe punishments with which God punishes contempt of Himself and horrible sin, etc. (Cicero, On the Nature of the Gods).'[187]

In some respects then Thysius has retained the framework employed by Arminius and Polyander, presenting a pair of arguments and then backing them with a further list, but he has dropped their choice of the theoretical and practical axioms in favour of a reversal to the traditional Reformation appeal to the innate idea and to the order of nature. To some extent, this marks a return to Junius's scheme, although Thysius does not merely append a block of scholastic arguments but follows the example of his immediate predecessors in putting in two Ursinus-type arguments to complete the list. No particular source is apparent for this collection, although it may be noted that all of these proofs appear amongst those assembled by Timpler.

Thysius then follows Polyander in proceeding to the evidence from revelation and in including miracles and prophecies in this category.

> 'But much firmer is that held by the faithful from God's witness and the light of faith.... The proofs are in open oracles, various works ... outstanding miracles... Prophecies of the future and their occurrences...'[188]

Finally, he adds a thesis which goes far to repair the omission we noted in Polyander in emphasizing the relative effectiveness of the two means of knowledge, though even here the theme of inexcusability is not expressed.

---

[187] 'Cui accedunt et aliae rationes, eaeque graves et variae; nempe a mundo et maxime constanti et ordinatio coelestium motu ad primum motorem motusque auctorem qui actu sit, Arist. Lib. Metaphys. 12, c. 6; ab ordine causarum efficientium ad primam efficientem in qua consistatur et a qua reliquae dependeant; a finibus ad extremum finem et finitorem; ab esse bono et perfectione ad primam essentiam, summum bonum et perfectissimam naturam; a conscientiae metu post admissa peccata, tamquam metuentis supremum judicem; a poenis atrocibus, quibus Deus contemptum sui et atrocia peccata punit, etc. Cic. de Natur. Deor.' (Thesis VI, *Ibid.*, pp. 63-4.)

[188] 'Sed multo firmius id tenetur a fidelibus testiomonio Dei et fidei lumine ... Testimontia autem sunt in apertis oraculis, operibus variis ... miraculis illustribus ... Propheticis vaticiniis et eorum eventis....' (Theses VII-VIII, *Ibid.*, p. 64.)

'Therefore God exists and the knowledge of Him which is available is therefore said by the apostle be to the knowledge of God, (Rom. 1, 19) However, it is available from natural revelation, (Ps. 19, 12. Acts 14, 15, 17 and 17, 24, 1 Cor. 1, 21) which in nature is partly corrupt, unstable and insufficient for salvation (Rom. 1, 20) then there is the supernatural which is whole, certain and is in the elect with saving effect (Ps. 19, 18, 1 Cor. 1, 21).'[189]

Not that this means that Thysius did not hold fast to this fundamental Reformation tenet. Indeed, in the course of his Leiden Inaugural oration,[190] he had devoted a passage to the consideration of natural theology which concluded,

'This then is that natural theology which is considered corrupt in nature and is neither sufficient, nor constant so that it does not everywhere and always explain the universal truth and, unless the Law lays down the way first, it does not attain legal perfection. And so it is neither salvific nor capable of effecting salvation in that it can never exceed the limits even of its own law; and so it can go no further than to convict man and render him inexcusable.'[191]

When, however, we recall that, although in his later 'De Deo' disputation the testimonies of revelation are declared to be so much more certain than those provided by nature and reason, we can scarcely fail to notice that they occupy less space and it is therefore not surprising that the extremely negative account of natural theology's role which Thysius had expressed in his Inaugural is here considerably modified.

Antonius Walaeus[192] had come to Leiden from Middelburg where he had been professor at the newly founded 'Illustre' School. His collected works were published posthumously[193] and are of particular interest since they contain two versions of a 'De Deo' Locus which each provide a different set of arguments for God's existence. The explanation for the

---

[189] 'Est igitur Deus, ejusque notitia habetur, quare et γνωστον του θεου Apostolo dicitur Rom. 1, 19. Habetur autem patefactione cum Naturali, Ps. 19, 12. Act. 14, 15, 17 et 17, 24. 1 Corint. 1, 21. quae in natura corrupta ex parte, inconstans, et ad salutem inefficax est, Rom. 1, 20 tum Supernaturali quae integra, certa, atque in electis cum effectu salutari est, Ps. 19, 18. 1 Cor. 1, 21.' (Thesis IX, *Ibid.*, p. 64.)

[190] 'Oratio de SS. Theologia Eiusque studio capescendo.' Delivered in December, 1619, this was published in the collection, *Orationes Inaugurales A. S.S. Theologiae Professoribus et Collegi Illust. Ordinum Hollandiae et West Frisiae Moderationibus habitae*, Leiden, 1620.

[191] 'Haec ergo est illa Theologia Naturalis quae in natura corrupta considerata neque sufficiens, neque constans est ut quae neque veritatem universam ubique et semper explicat et non nisi praevia Lege ad perfectionem legalem assurgit; adeoque nec salutaris, nec ad salutem efficax est ut quae efficacia sua legem non excedat; ideoque ulterius non subvehit quam ad hominem convincendum et inexcusabilem reddendum.' (*Op. cit.*, p. 17.)

[192] For Walaeus (1573-1635), see *NNBW* II cols. 1513-17.

[193] *Opera Omnia*, 2 vols., Leiden 1643. A second edition from which our quotations are given, appeared there in 1647.

difference is probably sufficiently accounted for in the Dedicatory Preface which Antonius's son, Johannes, furnished for the first volume of his father's *Opera*, where he explains the nature of the two collections of the Loci which it contains.

> 'Thus to those entering upon the sacred ministry he gave the *Handbook of Reformed Religion* with which to smooth the way and to open the doorway of theology for them. The initiated he admitted more thoroughly and revealed everything in his *Commonplaces and Counsels in Sacred Theology*.'[194]

The section of the *Enchiridion* dealing with God's Existence ('Quod Deus Sit') opens with a statement as to why it is necessary to undertake the task of proving this,

> 'It would be entirely superfluous to prove God's existence were it not that there are men to be found who are so impious and who "say in their hearts there is no God", ....Since, however, atheistic men have been found in every century, it will therefore not be without use to strengthen belief against them and to confirm this also with invincible arguments.'[195]

The motive then is the same as that expressed by Thysius in his 'De Deo' disputation.

In the *Enchiridion*, Walaeus presents arguments from two sources, nature and Scripture,[196] but in this work, the first category ignores any philosophical arguments and presents the bulk of Ursinus's list, the appeals to conscience, universal belief, the wonderful order of the great and little worlds, the fulfilment of prophecies and the rewards and punishments meted out to men according to their deserts.

The conclusion is that, 'These arguments invincibly prove God's existence'[197] and the appeal to Scripture is limited to a brief paragraph since that source has far more important things to tell us about God than the fact that He exists,

> 'Indeed, Holy Scripture from beginning to end was instituted not only to prove to us that God exists, but also to engender in us the perfect knowledge of Him and His will.'[198]

---

[194] 'Ita sacro Ministerio initiandis *Enchiridion Religionis Reformatae* dedit, quo iis applanaretur via, et Theologiae vestibulum aperiretur. Initiatos, *Locis Communibus Sacrae Theologiae et Consiliis* penitius admisit et omnia revelavit.' (Walaeus *Opera Omnia* I, p. A* 3$^{r}$.)

[195] 'Quod sit Deus probare esset plane supervacuum nisi homines tam impii reperirentur qui 'in corde suo dicunt non est Deus', ... Quia tamen omnibus seculis homines Athei reperti sunt, ideo ad fidem adversus eos firmandam non inutile fuerit id etiam argumentis invictis confirmare.' (*Ibid.*, p. 25.)

[196] 'Argumenta autem peti possunt; vel ex natura, vel ex Scriptura.' (*Ibid.*)

[197] 'Haec argumenta invicte demonstrant Deum esse.' (*Ibid.*)

[198] 'Scriptura vero Sacra ab initio usque ad finem ad id instituta est non tantum ut nobis Deum demonstret; sed etiam ut perfectam ejus et voluntatis illius notitiam nobis ingeneret.' (*Ibid.*)

Turning now to the Locus 'De Deo' in the work designed for those of greater maturity, Walaeus's opening statement here looks more closely at the nature of the arguments to be advanced against such monsters as require them and he gives his reason for choosing the *a posteriori*,

> 'However, against such monsters of men as these *a priori* arguments will not be adequate because nothing is prior to God, but *a posteriori* arguments, that is from effects, proofs and absurdities in the same manner as it is customary for principles to be demonstrated.'[199]

His first set of arguments come then under the heading, 'From absurdities', ('Ab absurdis'), but once the first of these is disposed of,

> 'It would follow that this visible world exists and is governed by no cause; no rewards are laid up for the righteous after this life; no punishments for the wicked. But not only all men's consciences, but reason also, teaches that this is absurd.'[200]

Walaeus has recourse to philosophical arguments which bear the mark of Suarez's *Disputationes Metaphysicae*.[201]

> '2. Because the so admirable beauty, variety, order and constancy of things is not possible on its own account: for then there must exist a prior being, since every cause is prior to its effect.... 3. Because all things share in wisdom and goodness, therefore there is some being good, righteous and wise in itself, otherwise there would be an infinite regress. 4. Everything acts for some purpose; therefore there is some ultimate purpose and an intelligent cause of purpose which guides all things to this purpose.'[202]

This dependence upon Suarez is the more apparent when Walaeus considers the objection, 'But nature is the cause of all things' ('At natura est omnium rerum causa'). As we shall see when we come to study Episcopius's more extended treatment of these arguments and the replies to objections to them,[203] Suarez had dealt with them at some length.

---

[199] 'Adversus tamen ejusmodi hominum monstra haec argumenta sufficiunt quae non a priori petuntur, quia Deo nihil est prius, sed a posteriori, effectis scilicet, testimoniis et absurdis, quemadmodum principia tantum demonstrari solent.' (*Ibid.*, p. 151.)

[200] 'Sequeretur mundum hunc adspectabilem a nulla causa esse aut regi: nulla praemia esse reposita justis post hanc vitam; nullas peonas secleratis. At haec absurda esse, non tantum conscientia omnes homines docet, sed etiam ratio.' (*Ibid.*)

[201] For Suarez, see below, pp. 229-31.

[202] '2. Quia tam admirabilis decor, varietas, ordo et constantia rerum non potest esse a se ipso: tum enim se ipso prior exsisteret, quia omnis causa est prior suo effectu .... 3. Quia omnia habent participatam sapientiam, bonitatem; ergo datur aliquid per se bonum, justum, sapiens: alioqui daretur progressus in infinitum. 4. Omnia agunt propter aliquem finem: ergo datur finis aliquis extremus et datur causa finium intelligens quae omnia ad hunc finem dirigit.' (Walaeus, *Opera Omnia,* I p. 151.)

[203] See below, pp. 229-31.

Walaeus makes three such responses to this query that nature is itself the cause of the ordered phenomenon it contains,

> 'This is false: because nature does not produce new kinds of things ... but only reproduces the old, ...'

Secondly against the possibility that nature is eternal,

> '... this is refuted for the reason that it is not possible for eternal and infinite causes, movements and natural ends ever to attain the status of present causes since in infinity there is no end, neither before or after.'

Finally, still in connection with this possibility,

> '3. Lastly, if it was eternal therefore it either shared in order and reason or else was devoid of them. If it shared in order and mind then we have God. If they say eternal nature was and is a mindless thing then how did it produce the mind and reason which it does not itself possess? ...'[204]

Walaeus's second set of arguments 'From God's effects', ('Ab effectis Dei'), return to the familiar catalogue, 'The predictions of future events .... Miracles .... Heroic impulses .... the often unexpected punishments of the wicked and acquittals of the righteous,'[205] whilst his third heading concludes the matter by appealing, 'From the witnesses of all nations.'[206]

The contrast between the two presentations of the arguments is evident enough as is the far greater sophistication of that aimed at the more advanced audience. In this way we can perhaps appreciate why theologians such as Walaeus felt themselves obliged to resort to the kind of philosophical arguments here presented. At the lower level it might be sufficient to appeal to the order and beauty of nature, but it does not require too much growth in perception for such questions to arise as those which he is constrained to handle about the possibility of nature itself being the cause of its own characteristics.

We shall have occasion to notice the similarities between the second of Walaeus's treatments of the arguments and that accorded to them by Episcopius in his posthumous, *Institutiones Theologiae*.[207] Such likenesses

[204] 'Id falsum: quia natura non producit nova rerum genera ... sed veteres tantum re producit ... refutatur ex eo, quod ab aeternis et infinitis causis, motibus, finibus naturalibus nunquam potuisset perveniri ad statum et caussas praesentes, cum infiniti nullus sit terminus nec retro nec ante. 3. Deinde si fuit aeterna; ergo aut ordinis et rationis particeps aut expers. Si particeps ordinis et mentis habemus Deum. Si dicant, aternam naturam fuisse et esse rem brutam, quomodo illa mentem et rationem produxit quae ipsa non habuit? ...' (Walaeus, *Opera Omnia,* I p. 151.)

[205] 'Praedictiones rerum futurarum .... Miracula .... Heroici motus .... poenae saepe inexpectatae sceleratorum et liberationes justorum.' (*Ibid.*, pp. 151-2.)

[206] 'A Testimoniis omnium gentium.' (*Ibid.*, p. 152.)

[207] See below pp. 229-37.

must be accounted for by their use of their common source, Suarez, since Episcopius died in 1647 and neither of Walaeus's two works which we have considered were published before then. Nonetheless, although not apparent from the 'De Deo', Loci, when we turn to the first item in the latter's *Loci Communes*, 'De Theologia' we find him applying many of the customary limitations to the status of natural theology.

Walaeus there gives three means by which natural revelation is effected. The first of these 'From the engraving of the common notions' ('Inscriptione notionium communium'), he defends against Socinus's objection by adducing the phenomena of conscience and universal consent. Although he does not here name the intermediate position of those like Vorstius and Episcopius[208] who rejected the first means but held to a revelation through the book of nature, his continuing defence appears to be directed against it.

> 'Certainly this is indeed true of everyone and furthermore this sense is innate in everyone as the mental pangs of the ungodly and tyrants prove which could not arise from a consideration of the creatures and belong also to those who have no judge to fear in the world.'[209]

For his second and third means, Walaeus sub-divides the second of the traditional Reformation pair, the appeal to nature and to providence into its constituent parts, '2. From the consideration of the creatures' and '3. From the ordering of things.'[210]

When Walaeus turns to the question of the purpose of the natural knowledge of God's he does so in explicit opposition to the views of the Remonstrants, though we must remember that those of Episcopius were as yet largely unpublished,

> 'What is the use of this natural knowledge of God and divine things and can man be saved by it? The Remonstrants affirm this together with the Pelagians of old.'[211]

Although, as we would expect, the uses of the natural knowledge of God fall far short of opening the way to salvation, yet they do extend beyond the mere establishment of fallen man's inexcusability. Thus the first of the

---

[208] See below pp. 205-28.

[209] 'Certe hoc de omnibus omnino verum est, ac proinde hic sensus omnibus innatus quod et angores impiorum ac Tyrannorum quoque evincunt, qui ex rerum creatarum contemplatione nasci non possunt et eorum quoque est qui nullum judicem quem metuant in mundo habent.' (Walaeus *Opera Omnia* I, p. 115.)

[210] '2. Contemplatione rerum creatarum' ... '3. Gubernationisque rerum.' (*Ibid.*)

[211] 'Quis sit usus hujus naturalis de Deo et rebus divinis scientiae: et an homo per eam servari possit? Id asserunt Remonstrantes cum Pelagianis veteribus.' (*Ibid.*, p. 116.)

four purposes is that of providing the necessary minimum of decent behaviour for the continuation of man's communal life,

> 'And first indeed that by the guidance of these (i.e. remaining traces of the divine image in man) men preserved life in society from savages and brigands and set up an honest and civic order amongst themselves.'

The second has the less positive aim of bringing home to man the greatness of his loss,

> 'Secondly, because God wishes in some way to show from these remains how great was the dignity and excellence of that image of God which man lost by sinning.'

The third is the familiar

> 'so that all pretext is taken from man in his just condemnation.'[212]

which shortly afterwards Walaeus, bearing in mind the Remonstrants' criticisms on this topic, defends against the twofold charge of injustice,

> 'The excuse of ignorance is taken from him because God revealed Himself to everyone in and through nature ... The excuse of impotence is taken from man because man does not even do what he is by nature able to but holds this down in unrighteousness ... because sometimes he perceives in himself his impotence and depravity not so as to deplore it or to entreat God's help and thus to dispose himself as he ought, but rather he is pleased with this depravity and impotence.'[213]

Walaeus's fourth and final item is the most positive of all,

> 'Finally ... that God wishes these remains to survive because He wants to use them to restore man. For although He can make sons of Abraham out of stones, yet He normally gathers His church from men endowed with reason. Just as where the remains of some notable house survive the house can be most easily restored to its old from.'[214]

---

[212] 'Et primo quidem quod harum ductu homines a feris et latronum societate vitam agant alienam et inter se instituant externum ordinem honestum et civilem.' 'Secundo quia Deus ex reliquiis illis aliquo modo voluit ostendere quanta fuerit dignitas et praestantia ipsius imaginis Dei quam homo peccando amisit.' 'ut omnis praetextus homini in justa ejus condemnatione adimatur.' (*Ibid.*)

[213] 'Praetextus ignorantiae tollitur eo quod Deus se ipsum omnibus in natura et per naturam manifestet ... Praetextus impotentiae hominum tollitur quia ea saltem quae per naturam potest homo non facit sed ea in injustitia detinet ... quod impotentiam suam et pravitatem quam in se nonnunquam sentiscit non ita deploret, nec ad auxilium Dei postulandum ita se componit et debet, sed potius in ea pravitate et impotentia sibi placet.' (*Ibid.*, p. 118.)

[214] 'Denique ... quod Deus voluerit has reliquias superesse quia iis uti voluit ad hominem restaurandum. Etsi enim ex lapidibus filios. Abrahae possit facere, tamen non nisi ex hominibus ratione praeditis Ecclesiam suam solet colligere. Quemadmodum ubi reliquiae alicujus egregriae domus adhuc supersunt commodissime forma antiqua ejus domus potest renovari.' (*Ibid.*, p. 116.)

Even though he proceeds immediately to counter any suggestion that proper observance of the natural law can bring about this restoration, 'Not, however, that the restoration of the image of God in man depends upon good use of the natural law',[215] yet we are left with a sense that there is some positive value in man's natural knowledge of God. When this impression is added to that derived from the 'De Deo' Loci, we must conclude that Walaeus, who on any reading is the most impressive of the Leiden theologians of his day, occupies a position which, though consciously faithful to the Reformed tradition, has in fact moved some way and under the same neo-scholastic influences in the same direction as that of the Remonstrants.

The fourth member of the Leiden quartet which acted together for so long in the promulgation of orthodox Reformed Theology, André Rivet,[216] was the first to go, leaving in 1632 to become tutor to the Stadtholder's son. Since, however, the three large folio volumes of his collected works[217] contain nothing of relevance to our concern, we may turn immediately to his successor.

Jacobus Trigland[218] gave the bulk of his attention to recent Dutch church history, producing his celebrated *Kerkelijke Geschiedenissen* in 1650. The one work which touches on matters of interest to us arises out of Trigland's concern, amply demonstrated in his history's account of the controversies leading to the Synod, with the refutation of the Remonstrants' errors. His *Antiapology or examination and refutation of the whole Apology of the Remonstrants* (*Antapologia sive Examen atque Refutatio Totius Apologiae Remonstrantium*) was published posthumously in 1664 and its appearance gives the lie to E. G. Léonard's contention that 'The Arminian affair was so dead that a confirmed Contra-Remonstrant, Jacobus Trigland ... already regarded it as belonging to the past.'[219] In the course of his first chapter, 'On man's communion with God and God's revelation through nature' ('De Communione hominis cum Deo et Dei Manifestatione per Naturam'), Trigland advances the traditional Reformation pair of arguments, the appeal to the natural order and to the innate idea and,

[215] 'Non tamen ex bono usu legis naturae pendet imaginis Dei in homine restauratio.' (*Ibid.*)

[216] For Rivet (1572-1651), see H. J. Honders *Andreas Rivetus*, The Hague, 1930.

[217] *Opera Theologica*, Rotterdam, 1651-60.

[218] Trigland (1583-1654), was born and raised a Roman Catholic and attended Louvain University before embracing the Reformed faith as a youth. See *NNBW* VI, cols. 1282-4.

[219] Léonard, *op. cit.*, p. 258. Leonard evidently assumes this because Trigland made this the subject of his *Kerkelijke Geschiedenis* but the appearance of this work indicates precisely the opposite conclusion since it was the orthodox rejoinder to Uytenbogaert's *Kerkelijke Historie* (1647) which had presented the Remonstrants' account of these events.

in connection with the first, quotes the second article of the Belgic Confession. To this he adds a line or two justifying the business of proving God's existence in terms which recall those of Melanchthon in their lack of concern for the apologetic motive.

> 'Therefore although the existence of God is not questioned in theology but God's existence is there presupposed, yet for the sake of encouraging and exciting piety the truth of that presupposition is also proved from nature itself.'[220]

When we consider Trigland's criticism of the second section of the Remonstrants' *Confession* and their subsequent *Apology* for it,[221] we find that he picks out the statement from the latter which says of arguments for God's existence,

> '*because arguments drawn from nature, in comparison with these which are taken from God's revelation through His Word*, ought to be considered weak and uncertain, in any event more laboured and burdened with many controversies.'[222]

In fact only the second part of this 'quotation' is to be found in the text of the Apologia, the first part which we have underlined is Trigland's own concoction. By this device, and by the ignoring of a further statement in the latter work, he is endeavouring to show that the Remonstrants are rejecting the traditional pair of natural arguments which, as we have seen, he has himself just put forward. Since these are, as he claims, very far from being attended by the kind of disadvantages alleged by Episcopius,

> 'rather a certain Deity can evidently be demonstrated from them and men's minds can be firmly convinced about this. For everywhere in the world, above and below, on right and left, they show themselves to all men, and make their impressions on eyes, ears, hands and minds',[223]

Trigland goes on, the Remonstrants' appeal for arguments that make a straightforward impression is clearly satisfied.

However, Trigland has been misrepresenting his opponents' position since the *Apologia* is not concerned with the kind of natural argument for

---

[220] 'Quamvis ergo in Theologia non quaeratur an sit Deus sed ibi praesupponatur esse Deum, fidei tamen confirmandae pietatisque excitandae et acuendae gratia, praesuppositi istius veritas rite demonstratur etiam ex ipsa natura.' Trigland, *op. cit.*, p. 34.

[221] For the details of these works, both written by Episcopius, see below pp. 219-21.

[222] '*Quod argumenta e natura desumta, prae iis quae sumuntur ex manifestatione Dei per verbum suum*, infirma atque incerta, saltem operosiora et controversiis pluribus impedita censeri debeant.' Trigland, *op. cit.*, p. 35; *Apologia*, fol. 25v. The emphasis is ours.

[223] 'Quin ex illis certa Deitas demonstrari evidenter animique hominum de ea solide convici queant. Nam ubique terrarum, supra infra, a dextris et sinistris, omnibus hominibus sese exhibent atque in oculos, aures, ora, manus, animosque eorum sese ingerunt.' (Trigland, *op. cit.*, p. 36.)

which he is contending but with philosophical arguments; hence the concern for the unlearned,

> 'The others, which are deduced from philosophical principles, are worked out so laboriously, obscured by so many exceptions, so many distinctions, hypotheses and intricate postulates, that the unlearned person is often not able to follow them and all the most learned not rarely find that they are lost in them.'[224]

We may reasonably conclude that Trigland is deliberately ignoring the issue of such philosophical arguments and that it may be that he does so because he himself prefers rather to employ the traditional Reformation pair. As such, he represents a more conservative attitude and provides us with a contrast to the more sophisticated approach which we observed in Walaeus.

From the one scrap of evidence left us it would appear that Trigland's colleague for seven years, Frederick Spanheim[225] was also inclined to be conservative on the issue of our concern. Just one thesis at the beginning of the 'De Deo' disputation in the posthumously published collection[226] considers the question of the proof of God's existence and Spanheim dismisses it in the conventional fashion.

> 'The question, whether God exists, which it is sometimes customary to bring up here, we pass over as impious or at any rate as unnecessary and we judge that this principle of God's existence ought not to be proved among Christians but supposed.'[227]

However, he is not content simply to leave the matter there and continues with a defence against the Socinian attack which indicates that he himself would rely upon the traditional Reformation pair,

> 'certainly that is so deeply impressed in consciences that it cannot be removed and in whose demonstration the light of the mind subjectively and the light of being objectively equally agree. Therefore the Anti-trinitarians, who deny the innate knowledge of God and merely take account of the acquired knowledge, seriously err.'[228]

---

[224] 'Caetera, quae ex principiis Philosophicis deducuntur, tam operose sunt elaborata, tot exceptionibus involuta, tot distinctionibus, hypothesibus, postulatis intricata ut indoctus ea saepe adsequi non possit et doctissimi quique non raro reperiant quod in iis desiderant.' (*Apologia*, fol. 25v.)

[225] Spanheim (1600-49) was Professor of Philosophy at Geneva from 1626 to 1630 when he was appointed to the Chair of Theology there. He came to Leiden in 1642. See *NNBW* X cols. 953-5.

[226] *Disputationes Theologicae Miscelleneae*, Geneva, 1652.

[227] 'Quaestionem, An sit Deus quae hic quandoque moveri solet, velut profanam, vel ut non necessarium saltem amolimur et principium istud esse Deum non probandum inter Christianos sed supponendum censemus.' (Spanheim *op. cit.*, p. 38.)

[228] 'quippe quod altius impressum conscientiis, quam ut revelli possit, et in quo

Constantine L'Empereur[229] was professor of theology for only two years before his death in 1648. Prior to that he had held the chair of Hebrew since 1627 and, as one would gather from this fact, his interests lay in the field of philology and textual criticism. With the appointment of Abraham Heidanus[230] in 1648 we move beyond our period into one in which the impact of Descartes was increasingly felt as a positive force in Dutch theology. None of Heidanuš's publications before the turn of the half-century contain anything of relevance to us and we shall accordingly omit him from our survey.

The last Leiden theologian for our consideration then is the celebrated Johannes Coccejus[231] who was appointed in 1650 after fourteen years as a professor at Franeker during which time he had published his most famous work, *A Summary of the doctrine of God's Covenant and Testament.*[232]

In a disputation, 'On Theology and its principles,[233] Coccejus presents the traditional Reformation line on natural theology,

> 'Natural theology is that which is known without God's Word and without the revelation of the Word ... The means of natural knowledge is reason and the notions engraved for it, the judgement of conscience, the works of God and the contemplation arising from their movement. That which must necessarily be known about God, namely His eternal power and divinity, that is His existence, omnipotence and divine perfections are known naturally (Rom I: 19, 20) and understood well enought to convince man of the obligation of glorifying God and giving Him thanks (Rom, 1, 21).'[234]

When we turn to the 'De Deo' disputation in the same series we find Coccejus, whilst admitting that the knowledge of God's existence is

---

demonstrando lux mentis aeque subjective concurrit ac lumen entis objective. Peccant itaque graviter Antitrinitarii qui notitiam Dei innatam negant et eam acquisitam duntaxat censent.' (Spanheim, *op. cit.*, p. 38.)

[229] See *BWPGN* II, pp. 727-35.

[230] For Heidanus (1597-1678), see *BWPGN*, IV, pp. 2-9.

[231] Coccejus (1603-69), had been the pupil of Martinius at Bremen and of William Ames at Franeker. Before his appointment to the latter university he had held a chair at Bremen from 1630. See *BWPGN* II, pp. 123-48. For Coccejus' federal theology, see G. Schrenk, *Gottesreich und Bund im älteren Protestantismus vornehmlich bei Johannes Coccejus*, Gütersloh, 1923.

[232] *Summa doctrinae de foedere et testamento Dei*. Leiden, 1648, 2nd Edition 1653.

[233] 'De Theologia et principiis ejus'. The first in the collection *Aphorismi per Universam Theologiam Breviores, Opera Omnia*, Vol. VII, Amsterdam, 1701, p. 3.

[234] 'Theologia est naturalis quae etiam sine verbo Dei et quae duntaxat verbi revelatione innotescit .... Medium notificationis naturalis est Ratio et ei insculptae notitiae, Judicium conscientiae, Opera Dei et illorum animadversio gignens discursum .... Quod de Deo necessario cognoscendum est, ipsius scilicet aeterna potentia et divinitas, h.e. existentia, omnipotentia et divinae perfectiones naturaliter cognoscuntur (Rom. 1: 19, 20) intellige quantum satis est ad hominem convincendum de obligatione glorificandi Deum et ei gratias agendi, Rom. 1: 21 ...' (*Op. cit.*, p. 3.)

available to all by nature, passes over this means in favour of the scriptural revelation,

> 'And all these are known in some measure naturally, yet God's name is revealed more fully in the Scriptures for its perfection of natural knowledge. The greatest argument for God's existence is that He revealed Himself from heaven at one time when He gave the Law, then when the son of God took flesh and suffered in it, arose and was taken up into heaven.'[235]

The equivalent disputation in the following collection, 'Fuller Aphorisms throughout the whole of Theology' ('Aphorisimi per Universam Theologiam Prolixiores'), actually provides us with a list of arguments for God's existence,

> 'We know that God exists, at once from the natural deeds of God, then from conscience discerning good from evil and partly cultivating, partly fearing judgement, then from judgements and the ordering of the nations of the world, then from His extraordinary revelation, the divinity and divine name revealed to conscience from the diffusing Word, from wonderful works, particularly from the pouring out of the Holy Spirit, and the fulfilment of prophesies, also from the spirit of evil which rivals and attacks God, from the witness of the Spirit to conscience whose power we feel in us correcting and consoling.'[236]

Whilst a slightly larger place is here accorded to arguments of a natural origin yet once more the emphasis is overwhelmingly in favour of those stemming from scriptural revelation and the life of the faithful Christian. As for philosophical arguments, there is no mention of them; they would be quite out of place.

In Coccejus we can discern the combination of two influences in particular, that of Melanchthon, mediated through Martinius of Bremen, and especially that of William Ames upon whose distinctive approach to theology we have had cause to remark before.[237] In a well known disputation, *Against Metaphysics*,[238] Ames had attacked the metaphysicians'

[235] 'Et haec omnia naturaliter aliquomodo noscuntur plenius tamen et ad naturalis cognitionis perfectionem nomen Dei revelatur in Scripturis. Maximum argumentum, quod sit Deus, est quod se revelavit ex coelo tum quando legem dedit, tum quando carnem assumsit filius Dei et in ea passus, resurrexit et in coelum sublatus est.' (*Opera Omnia* VII, p. 4.)

[236] 'Deum esse, scimus tum ex factis Dei naturalibus, tum ex conscientia bonum a malo discernente et judicium partim exercente partim metuente, tum ex judiciis, et coercitione gentium mundi, tum ex manifestatione sui extraordinaria, tum ex verbo divinitatem redolente et divinum nomen ad conscientiam patefaciente, tum ex operibus mirabilibus, nominatim effusione Spiritus sancti, et implementis prophetiarum, tum ex spiritus maligni quo ut Deum aemulatur et impugnat, tum ex testimonio Spiritus ad conscientiam, cujus efficaciam in nobis et emendandis et consolandis sentimus.' (*Ibid.*, p. 18.)

[237] See above, p. 101.

[238] *Adversus Metaphysicam*, Franeker, 1629: a second edition, from which our quotations are given, appeared at Leiden in 1632. It was included in Ames's *Philosophemata*, published at Leiden in 1643 and in the fifth volume of his collected Latin works, Amsterdam, 1651.

—several times refering specifically to Suarez—presumption that they could provide a natural theology different from the revelation of Scripture,

> 'There is, however, a certain presumption of almost all metaphysicians that they offer to their readers some natural theology entirely other than that which we have presented by supernatural revelation in Holy Scripture; this is not to be wondered at in heathen philosophers, but it ought not to be carried on at all among Christians who know the perfect theology transmitted in every part of their scriptures.'[239]

In particular Ames took exception to the claim,

> 'They say that metaphysics deals with God and divine things as far as they can be known by the natural light;'[240]

Against this he had insisted that there was no truth about God that was not available from Scriptural revelation and hence there was no need to erect a separate discipline for the handling of it,

> 'There is nothing true or certain about God and divine things known by the natural light which is not also known from divine revelation and ought to be treated by that name in sacred theology ... therefore no necessity compels that they be dealt with as some sort of divinity in another discipline.'[241]

The importance of such views for Coccejus's biblical theology in general and for his attitude towards the question of the proof of the existence of God in particular is evident enough. The natural knowledge of God is duly recognized, because Scripture itself witnesses to it, but no arguments are presented which stem from the independent discipline of philosophy and, as quickly as possible, he moves on to the really significant proofs which shine out from the greater light of God's own revelation.

If, with this last Leiden professor, we have returned to a very conservative 'Reformation', approach to the arguments for God's existence, we are nonetheless bound to observe that the chief impression left by the investigation conducted in this chapter is that of the establishment at the heart of Dutch theology not merely of the sort of proofs favoured by

---

[239] 'Certa tamen praesumptio omnium fere Metaphysicorum est quod polliceantur suis lectoribus naturalem quandam Theologiam aliam plane ab illa quam supernaturali revelatione traditam habemus in sacra Scriptura: quod in Ethnicis philosophis non est mirandum, sed neu tiquam ferendum inter Christianos qui Theologiam in Scripturis traditam suis omnibus partibus consummatam agnoscunt.' (Ames, *Adversus Metaphysicam*, p. 4.)

[240] 'Metaphysicam de Deo et rebus divinis tractare dicunt quatenus possunt cognosci lumine naturali.' (*Ibid.*, p. 7.)

[241] 'Nihil est veri et certi de Deo et rebus divinis lumine naturali notum quod non cognoscatur etiam ex divina revelatione et eo nomine tractari debeat in Theologia sacra ... nulla igitur necessitas adigit ut quaedam divinam in alia disciplina tractentur ...' (*Ibid.*, p. 9.)

Melanchthon and Ursinus and familiar to us from our study of commentaries upon the formularies, but of the out and out scholastic kind, stemming first from the medieval schoolmen and later from the neo-Thomism of Suarez.

This is not to say that use of the schoolmen's arguments meant the unqualified acceptance of their standpoint on natural theology, but it cannot be without significance that Leiden theologians only presented such arguments in the 'De Deo' Locus and sometimes did so without the standard reformed qualification that the natural knowledge of God serves solely to render man inexcusable; a caveat which was invariably uttered when the issue was raised in the Loci, 'De Cognitione Dei' and 'De Theologia'.

We may remind ourselves that we are dealing here with theology in its university setting in which philosophy was also being taught and debated. The moment that theologians introduced arguments involving the application of reason to physical phenomena then they had moved into the philosophers' territory and it is scarcely surprising that the professors of theology who did so were influenced by their philosophical colleagues and sometimes showed signs of the kind of increasing organisation and sophistication that we noted in Arminius and Walaeus.

Not that the picture is one of straightforward development; the example of Coccejus alone would be enough to prevent this being the case. Some theologians had less predeliction for philosophical arguments than others and there were a few who evidently preferred to stay within the tradition which we have characterised as that of the 'Reformation'. It would be reasonable to suppose that any threat to the Reformation position of the sort posed by the controversies over Predestination would serve to sharpen the focus on certain of the issues of our concern. Thus we turn next to see how such were treated in those disputes between Remonstrants and Contra-Remonstrants which bulked so large on the Dutch theological scene during our period.

# PART III

# NATURAL THEOLOGY IN THE CONTROVERSIES BETWEEN REMONSTRANTS AND CONTRA-REMONSTRANTS

## CHAPTER SEVEN

# NATURE, GRACE AND INEXCUSABILITY

For much of our period the Dutch theological scene was dominated by the controversies between Arminius and his followers and their opponents over the doctrine of Predestination which, although reaching a climax in the triumph of the more rigidly orthodox form of Calvinism at the Synod of Dort (1618-19), continued to occupy men's minds for a long time thereafter. Whilst questions of Natural Theology were not to the fore in these disputes, issues centering upon the relationship between Nature and Grace were raised and sometimes in a form well worth examining for the light they throw upon certain fundamental differences of attitude underlying the approach of the two sides to the use of the arguments for God's existence.

One such issue turned upon the capacity of fallen man for the knowledge of God and came in time to concern itself with the question of the possibility of the salvation of those who had never heard the Christian Gospel. One very important strand in this debate concerns the status of the knowledge of God which can be derived from a consideration of the natural creation and focuses upon the two New Testament passages which, as we have had frequent cause to observe, are most cited in this connection: Romans, cap. 1, verses 19 following, and Acts, cap. 14, verse 17.

Throughout our investigation we have had frequent cause to observe the importance of the theme of inexcusability as the sole effect of man's natural knowledge of God. That this may fairly claim to be a touchstone in assessing the fidelity of a theologian to the Reformed tradition will emerge clearly enough as we follow the course of the controversies outlined in this chapter.

From the outset the orthodox opponents of Arminius accused him of Pelagianism and sought to put this interpretation upon any of his utterances which might even remotely bear it. In this endeavour they were not above manufacturing and attributing to him statements which they considered in keeping with their view of his position. One collection of such concoctions, *31 Theological Articles*, provoked an Apology from Arminius.[1] The topic of our concern is clearly presented in Article XV, 'If

[1] *The Works of James Arminius*, translated by J. Nichols, 2 vols, London, 1822, 1828, *Apology against 31 Theological Articles*, Vol. I, pp. 669-706, Vol. II, pp. 1-79.

the heathen, and those who are strangers to the true knowledge of God, do those things which by the power of nature they are enabled to do, God will not condemn them, but will reward these their works by a more enlarged knowledge by which they may be brought to salvation.'[2] In response, Arminius first denies ever having made any such statement, 'For,' as he says, 'what man is there who as "a stranger to the true knowledge of God", will do a thing that can in any way be acceptable to God?' Then comes the introduction of one of the crucial scriptural passages, '... therefore, it is needful for him to have a true knowledge of God, which the Apostle attributes even to the Gentiles (Rom. I, 18-21, 25, 28, II, 14, 15).'[3]

Arminius's interpretation of the status of this true knowledge as it emerges from his consideration of Romans I, 18-21 is very significant.

> 'Is "nature",' he asks,
> '...when entirely destitute of grace and of the Spirit of God, furnished with the knowledge of that truth which is said to be "held in unrighteousness", by the knowledge of "that which may be known of God, even His eternal power and Godhead", which may instigate man to glorify God, and which deprives him of all excuse, if he does not glorify God as he knows Him? I do not think, that such properties as these can, without falsehood and injury to divine grace, be ascribed to "nature" which, when destitute of grace and the Spirit of God, tends directly downward to those things that are earthly.'[4]

In this way, Arminius takes the important step of assigning the knowledge of God obtainable from the natural order to the realm, not of nature, but of grace.[5] His reason for so doing is apparent from his own remark '... if our brethren really think that man can do some portion of good "by the

---

[2] Arminius, *op. cit.*, p. 14.
[3] *Ibid.*, p. 15.
[4] *Ibid.*
[5] Arminius was, of course, endorsing a viewpoint which had a long history. Thus a contemporary English commentator on Romans I, 19, "For God hath showed it unto them", writes '... 3. Some understand it of the natural infusion of those principles and notions of God imprinted in the mind, Martyr, Pareus. But these seem to be two distinct things, to be manifest in them, and God hath manifested to them. 4. Therefore hereby the Apostle signifieth thus much: that beside the natural instinct and light of the mind, God did concur withall: as Augustine saith, not only natural reason did hereunto profit, sed Deus continuo adiuvit, ne sola natura sufficere videretur: but God did also continually help, that nature alone should not seem to be sufficient: ex glos. ord. so they had divinum concursum mediante lumine naturali, they had concurring the divine help together with the natural light ... This then is added, least any man should solis rationis viribus, to the strength only of reason ascribe whatsoever knowledge of God, Gualter.' (A. Willet, *Hexapla, that is A Six-fold Commentarie upon the most Divine Epistle of the Holy Apostle S. Paul to the Romans*, London, 1611, p. 60).

powers of nature''; they are themselves not far from the Pelagianism, which yet they are solicitous to fasten on others ...'[6]

The Remonstrants took their name from the Remonstrance, a declaration by forty-four of Arminius's followers, drawn up after his death by his friend Uytenbogaert and presented to the States of Holland in 1610. The declaration contains five articles which briefly summarize this party's doctrine on the points at issue and that of our concern is covered by article three:

> 'That man has not saving grace of himself, nor of the energy of his free will, inasmuch as he in the state of apostasy and sin, can of and by himself neither think, will, nor do any thing that is truly good (such as saving faith eminently is); but that it is needful that he be born again of God in Christ, through his Holy Spirit, and renewed in understanding, inclination, or will, and all his powers, in order that he may rightly understand, think, will, and effect what is truly good, according to the Word of Christ, John 15, 5: ''Without me you can do nothing.'' '[7]

As it stands this declaration, which the Remonstrants duly endorsed at the Synod of Dort in 1618, is so utterly orthodox that it seems astonishing that it could have provoked that Synod's condemnation.[8] This, however, came about because the body ignored this official statement and settled upon such extracts from the various writings of the Remonstrants which would bear the kind of Pelagian interpretation to which we have seen that Arminius had objected. Thus among the errors rejected under this heading, they condemn those

> 'Who teach that ''Corrupt and brute man is so able to use common grace, which is to them the natural light or the gifts remaining after the fall, that by

---

[6] Arminius, *op. cit.* p. 15. For an interesting discussion of Arminius's disagreement with the English Puritan, William Perkins, as it relates to this issue, see C. Bangs, *Arminius, A study in the Dutch Reformation*, Nashville, 1971, pp. 212-16, 'Perkins had charged this position with being Pelagianism, Arminius replies ''The Pelagians attributed the faculty of well-doing to nature wholly, or only in part to grace, but this doctrine attributes it entirely to grace''.' (*op. cit.*, p. 216).

[7] 'Homo salvificam fidem non habet a se, neque ex liberi arbitrii sui viribus, quandoquidem in statu apostasiae et peccati nihil boni (quod quidem vere bonum sit, cujusmodi in primis est fides salvifica) ex se et a se potest cogitare, velle aut facere; sed necessarium est ut a Deo, in Christo, per Spiritum ipsius Sanctum regeneretur atque renovetur, intellectu, affectibus seu voluntate, omnibusque viribus, ut vere bonum recti possit intelligere, meditari, velle atque proficere sicut scriptum est, Joh. XV, 5, ''sine me nihil potestis facere''.' (Schaff, *op. cit.*, pp. 546-7.)

[8] In fact, as Hoenderdaal has pointed out, there was no disagreement over this article which only came into disrepute because the Remonstrants joined it to the fourth which declared that grace was not irresistible. (See G. J. Hoenderdaal, 'Arminius en Episcopius', *NAK*, 40, 1980, p. 206.)

that good use he can gradually obtain the greater grace that is the evangelical or salvific and salvation itself.'' '[9]

We may note here how, despite all Arminius's protestations to the contrary, the orthodox party have identified his 'common grace', with the 'natural light'.

The French Reformed Churches had chosen their delegation to the Synod but their King forbade its attendance. To compensate for his enforced absence, one of the best known of their number, Pierre Du Moulin,[10] published his own exposé of the Remonstrant position in anticipation of the Synod's verdict. His *The Anatomy of Arminianism or explanation of the controversies which are raised in Belgium over the doctrine of providence, predestination, the death of Christ, nature and grace* was published at Leiden in 1619.[11] Before turning to his treatment of the passage in question, we may note Du Moulin's unequivocal statement of the orthodox Calvinist position on the relative validity of the two sources of the knowledge of God.

'Although the works of God, which are everywhere before our eyes, do abundantly testify and even against men's wills do show the infinite power, goodness and wisdom of God: yet this light is but dim and nearer darkness in comparison of the light of the word of God, whereby he doth not only give us assurance of his omnipotency, majesty and providence, but also reveal to us his will. For surely the contemplation of the creatures doth not touch men with the sense of sin nor doth show to a man the way of salvation and reconciliation with God: yea and there can be no profitable and saving contemplation of nature unless those things which in a doubtful light and in worn-out letters are hardly read to by the word of God, as it were through spectacles, appear plain and distinct to us ... Furthermore, although the knowledge of the

[9] 'Qui docent: ''Hominem corruptum et animalem gratia communi, quae ipsis est lumen naturale, sive donis post lapsum relictis, tam recte uti posse, ut bono isto usu majorem gratiam, puta evangelicam, sive saluturem, et salutem ipsam gradatim obtinere possit.'' ' (Schaff, *op. cit.*, p. 569.)

[10] For Du Moulin (1568-1658) see L. Rimbault, *Pierre Du Moulin*, Paris, 1966. Quite apart from the centrality of his *Anatome* to the continuing debate, the justification for including this Frenchman in our discussion lies in the fact that he had close connections with Dutch theology. Indeed he spent the period 1592-8 in Leiden for the last five years of which he was professor of philosophy. On no less than three occasions, in 1611, 1619, and finally in 1641, the authorities unsuccessfully invited him to return to Leiden, as professor of Theology. See P. C. Molhuysen (ed.), *Bronnen tot de Geschiedenis der Leidsche Universiteit, 1610-47*, The Hague, 1916, pp. 20, 85, 91 and 257.

[11] *Anatome Arminianismi, seu Enucleatio controversiarum quae in Belgio agitantur super doctrina de providentia, de praedestinatione, de morte Christi, de natura et gratia*. Subsequent editions appeared at Leiden in 1620 and 1621 and there was a Dutch translation, *Anatome Arminianismi: Dat is, ontledinghe van de bedriechijcke Arminaensche leere*, Amsterdam, 1620. The English translation, from which our quotations are given, was published at London in 1620 under the title, *The anatomy of Arminianism: or, The opening of the controversies lately handled in the Low-countryes, concerning the doctrine of providence*; it was reprinted in 1626.

creatures doth not suffice to salvation, yet the Gentiles who were instructed by no other teacher than nature, are therefore inexcusable because they did not use these (although small) helps to a good purpose as they might: and because they endeavour to choke or deprave those natural good notions and sparks of goodness which are put into them by nature. Therefore they alone do profit in piety by the teaching of the creatures and are by the pricks of conscience stirred up to the fear of God, to whom God hath vouchsafed the prerogative of his Word.'[12]

We may compare the Statement with Article four of the Synod of Dort's official statement of the doctrine 'De Hominis Corruptione'.

'There remain, however, in man since the fall the glimmerings of natural light, whereby he retains some knowledge of God, of natural things, and of the difference between good and evil, and discovers some regard for virtue, good order in society and for maintaining an orderly external deportment. But so far is this light of nature from being sufficient to bring him to a saving knowledge of God and to true conversion, that he is incapable of using it aright even in things natural and civil. Nay farther, this light, such as it is, man in various ways renders wholly polluted and holds it in unrighteousness; by doing which he becomes inexcusable before God.'[13]

On Romans I, 18-21, Du Moulin will have no truck with Arminius's interpretation; but at least he does argue against genuine views of the latter.

'Surely here is no mention of sufficient grace which the Arminians think to be supernatural. For here the Apostle speaketh of the light of nature, and of any sort of the knowledge of God by the creatures which may be had without supernatural grace, by which the Apostle doth not say that man hath power of believing in Christ or that he can dispose or prepare himself to regeneration but he only saith that the power and that the deity of God was seen of them by the creatures that they might be inexcusable. And they are inexcusable not because they have abused that grace which was mediately or immediately sufficient to salvation, but because they have not used the light of nature as far as they might and have endeavoured to choke the light engrafted in them.'[14]

He similarly refutes the attempt of Arminius's followers to put the same interpretation on Acts 14, verse 17:

' "Nevertheless he left not himself without witness." They do falsely think that this witness was some sufficient saving and supernatural grace and the

[12] *Anatome*, pp. 145-6.

[13] 'Residuum quidem est post lapsum in homine lumen aliquod naturae, cujus beneficio ille notitias quasdam de Deo, de rebus naturalibus, de discrimine honestorum et turpium retinet, et aliquod virtutis ac disciplinae externae studium ostendit: sed tantum abest, ut hoc naturae lumine ad salutarem Dei cognitionem pervenire, et ad eum se convertere possit, ut ne quidem eo in naturalibus ac civilibus recte utatur, quinimo qualecumque id demum sit, id totum variis modis contaminet, atque in injustitia detineat, quod dum facit, coram Deo inexcusabilis redditur.' (Schaff, *op. cit.*, p. 565, I. 588.) Cf. Calvin, *Institutes*, I. vi. 1.

[14] *Anatome*, p. 418.

> law naturally engraven in their hearts which should be a schoolmaster to Christ. For the Apostle in the following works doth explain what manner of testimony this is, saying that God gave them rain from heaven, and fruitful seasons and filled their hearts with food and gladness; no mention of supernatural grace ...'[15]

Du Moulin's work provoked a weighty rejoinder from the Remonstrant, J. A. Corvinus,[16] in which all the former's arguments are subjected to a detailed examination and refutation. Corvinus is prepared to accept Du Moulin's traditional statement on the relative status of the two modes of the knowledge of God, provided certain considerations are borne in mind. Thus, while he agrees that the true and saving knowledge of God can only be learned from His Word, yet he is concerned to establish that the knowledge obtainable from a contemplation of the created order is such as may stir men to realise that God is to be worshipped and even to stimulate them to undertake that worship as far as they are able.

> 'Although the true way of worshipping God is to be learned from the Word of God; yet the knowledge of the invisible God which is discerned by the understanding from created things also implants in minds that God is to be worshipped and creatures are stimulated through it so that they worship God according to that knowledge.'[17]

Indeed he will go so far as to say that this natural knowledge may itself be said to be saving in so far as it precedes the fuller knowledge of God's Word. For both modes of knowledge have the same purpose which is that man should seek, worship and glorify God.

> 'Although the knowledge of God which is drawn from created things is not in itself sufficient for salvation and in that sense it cannot be said to be salvific: yet that same knowledge can be said to be salvific to the extent that it is itself led to salvation and immediately precedes the knowledge conducive to salvation... However, both forms of revelation, whether the more obscure and imperfect or the clearer and more perfect have the end that we seek, worship and glorify God.'[18]

---

[15] *Anatome*, p. 419.

[16] *Petri Molinaei novi anatomici mala encheiresis, seu Censura Anatomes Arminianismi*, Frankfurt, 1622. Corvinus (+ 1650), a pupil of Arminius's at Leiden was a signatory of the Remonstrance and one of that party to appear before the Synod of Dort. See *BWPGN*. II, pp. 275-9.

[17] 'Quamvis vera ratio Deum colendi discatur ex Dei verbo: tamen cognitionem invisibilium Dei quae ex rebus factis intellecta pervidentur, mentibus etiam ingenere quod Deus colendus sit, et creaturas per eam instigari, ut Deum secundum istam cognitionem colant.' (Corvinus, *op. cit.*, p. 589.)

[18] 'Quamvis cognitio Dei quae ex rebus creatis hauritur per se non sufficit ad salutem, et eo sensu negari possit eam esse salutarem: eandem tamen cognitionem eatenus dici posse salutarem, quatenus ipsa etiam dirigitur ad salutem, et praecedit cognitionem immediate ad salutem conducentem. ... Utraque autem ista revelatio sive obscurior sit et imperfectior,

So far Corvinus has conducted the argument within the terms of the traditional grace—nature dichotomy to which he began by saying that he had no objection. However, when he comes to considering Du Moulin's attack on Arminius's interpretation of Romans I, 18-21, he follows the latter's view exactly and for the same reason. The Arminian position may fairly be summarized thus:

> It is evident that the good pagan does obtain sufficient knowledge of God to enable him to believe in the Deity as Creator of the world and to worship Him accordingly. Furthermore, we may trust that God in His justice and mercy will in some way crown this with greater grace sufficient for salvation. However, to say that such knowledge is purely natural is to leave oneself open to the ever present threat of the charge of Pelagianism. Hence such effective knowledge must itself be the result of grace.

Thus to Du Moulin's objection that the knowledge obtainable from the creatures is of nature and not of grace, Corvinus replies:

> 'We deny that nature furnished by that knowledge is entirely devoid of grace and the Spirit of God, ... The reason is because when that knowledge avails for anything that would thus have all to be ascribed to nature: which is Pelagian. Therefore, we attribute that knowledge also to the action of grace.'[19]

Corvinus also takes issue with the traditional Calvinist interpretation of the Romans passage which sees the purpose of the natural revelation as being only to render all mankind inexcusable in their failure to serve and worship God.[20] Indeed he uses the charge of inexcusability as one of the bases for his claim that the knowledge obtained from the creatures is of grace.

> 'Inexcusability, which is here presented as the purpose of that knowledge. For they cannot be rendered inexcusable unless a certain measure of grace has been accorded to them. Indeed they cannnot be rendered inexcusable except for abuse of that grace. Whence, on the other hand, they render themselves excusable by the use of the same and consequently inexcusability is not the first purpose of the grace accorded, but its first purpose is that men should use

---

sive clarior et perfectior, cum habet finem ut Deum quaeramus, colamus, glorificemus.' (*Ibid.*, pp. 589-90.)

[19] 'Nos naturam ista cognitione instructam gratia et spiritu Dei prorsus destitui negamus, ... Ratio est, quia cum ista cognitio ad aliquid valeat, id omne tum erit quoque naturae adscribendum; quod Pelagianum est. Quare istam etiam cognitionem merito tribuimus gratiae.' (*Ibid.*, p. 632.)

[20] As we saw above, (pp. 112-3), at the Synod of Dort the Remonstrants had included an objection to this understanding of the matter in their *Considerations* upon the second article of the Belgic Confession.

> it rightly and by that right use they are either gracious or accepted or at least excusable before God.'[21]

According to Corvinus, the purpose of the New Testament passages which have traditionally been seen as setting forward the natural knowledge of God is that, by the contemplation of the benefits of nature, men may be stirred up to seek and worship their Author. For this to happen, however, the action of grace must be posited. Thus, of the benefits of nature referred to in Acts, 14, 17, he writes:

> '... that they witness to the goodness of God and indeed (just as Rom. 1 and Acts 17 agree) so that the gentiles by feeling seek God; it is apparent that the internal aid of grace was present with them, by which, through the contemplation of those benefits their minds were stirred up to seek God and through the contemplation of those benefits they were moved to worship the author of the same.'[22]

In 1638 at Amsterdam and without the knowledge or consent of the author appeared another work of Du Moulin's relevant to this discussion, *An Examination of the Doctrine of Messrs. Amyrault and Testard ... concerning Predestination and the points which stem from it.*[23] To this small work, the anonymous editor added his own somewhat lengthier and highly critical, *The Advice of a disinterested person on the said Examination.*[24] Although neither the Bibliothèque Nationale, the British Library, nor the Bodleian have recognized the fact in their catalogues, the author of this latter work, who was responsible for the publication of the whole, was the Remonstrant minister, Etienne de Courcelles.[25] As he explained in a letter of 6th February, 1638 to Uytenbogaert accompanying a copy of the book,

[21] 'Item inexcusabilitas, quae hic posita est pro fine istius cognitionis. Nam inexcusabilitas reddi non possunt, nisi quibus aliqua mensura gratiae collata est. Illi vero non possunt reddi inexcusabiles, nisi per gratiae istius abusum. Unde sit per eiusdem usum e contrario eos reddi excusabiles; et per consequens, inexcusabilitatem non esse primum finem collatae gratiae; sed primum eius finem esse, ut homines ea recte utantur, et per istum rectum usum vel grati et accepti vel saltem excusabiles apud Deum sint.' (Corvinus, *op. cit.* p. 632.)

[22] '... ut testarentur de bonitate Dei, et quidem (quemadmodum ex Rom. 1 et Act. 17 constat) ut gentes vel palpando Deum quaererent; manifestum esse, ipsis adfuisse internum gratiae auxilium, quo mentes per istorum beneficorum considerationem ad Deum quaerendum excitarentur, et per contemplationem istorum beneficiorum ad eorundem authorem colendum moverentur.' (*Ibid.*, p. 633.)

[23] *Examen de la Doctrine de Messieurs Amyrault et Testard ... touchant la Predestination et les points qui en dependent.*

[24] *Advis d'un personnage désinteressé sur ledit Examen.*

[25] Etienne de Courcelles, or Stephen Curcellaeus (1586-1659), born and educated at Geneva, became a minister of the French Reformed Church in 1614. By 1626 his sympathy for the Arminian position had driven him from that church into that of the Remonstrants at Amsterdam. On Episcopius's death in 1643 he succeeded to the latter's post as Professor of Theology at the newly founded Remonstrant seminary in that city. See *BWPGN* II, pp. 337-40.

'... I beg you not to publicize the confession that I here make to you in secret of having laboured at this work. For I am especially desirous that Mr. Du Moulin should not know where it comes from ...'[26]

It will not be necessary to our purpose to examine in detail the teaching of Amyraut[27] and Testard which provoked Du Moulin's anger because of its affinities with Arminianism. For one thing this would take us outside our area into that of French theology and for another, as we shall have occasion briefly to note, at the Synod of Alençon in 1637 the two men retracted all the statements to which Du Moulin had taken exception. Our concern rather is to see whether there has been any development (a) in Du Moulin's position in the period since the publication of his *Anatome Arminanismi*, (b) in that of the Remonstrants, as presented now by De Courcelles, who was soon to become the leading theologian of that party.

As regards the former De Courcelles himself claimed that there had in fact been no change at all. Thus, when explaining the occasion and purpose of his own *Advis*, he writes:

'My purpose is not to amuse myself in the refutation of all the errors and impertinences in which Mr. du Moulin's little book abounds. For having done almost nothing except copy and reproduce in brief what he treated at greater length in his Anatomy of Arminianism, there is no need of any other reply to those points than that which Mr. Corvinus delivered against it fifteen years' ago and to which he has up to now made no response ...'[28]

In the 'Fifth Controversy'[29] Du Moulin deals with the now familiar topic, 'Concerning salvation without Jesus Christ'. Having outlined the

---

[26] '... je vous prie de ne publier point la confession que je vous fais ici à l'oreille d'avoir travaillé à cet ouvrage. Car je désirerois surtout que monsieur Du Moulin ne senst point d'où il vient ...' (*Briefwisseling van Hugo Grotius*, Vol. 9, ed. B. L. Meulenbroek, The Hague, 1973, p. 789.) Cf. *ibid.*, p. 320 for Grotius's letter of 28th May, 1638, thanking De Courcelles for the gift of the same book.

[27] Amyraut's thought is the subject of B. G. Armstrong's excellent study *Calvinism and the Amyraut Heresy*, Madison, 1969. For Armstrong's review of this particular controversy with Du Moulin, see pp. 84-96.

[28] 'Mon dessein n'est pas de m'amuser à la refutation de toutes les faussetez et impertinences, dont le livret du sieur du Moulin fourmille. Car n'y ayant fait presque autre chose que copier et reduire en abbregé ce qu'il avoit traitté plus au long en son Anatamie de l'Arminianisme, il n'est point besoin d'autre response à ces endroits là, que de celle que le sieur Corvinus passé quinze ans y a opposé, et à laquelle jusqu' à present il n'a rien repliqué ...' (*Advis.*, p. 2.) Such a rejoinder to Corvinus's work had been undertaken by Antonius Walaeus, the Calvinist successor to Episcopius's chair at Leiden. His *Responsio ... ad Censuram Joannis Arnoldi Corvini, in Cl. Viri D. Petri Molinaei Anatomei Arminianismi*, Leiden 1625, however, does not touch in any detail upon the particular points which we have been considering.

[29] *Examen*, pp. 71-83.

passages in his opponents' works which he sees as arguing for this Arminian proposition, he objects:

> 'I say then that this doctrine which wishes that men can be saved without knowing Jesus Christ, is a new Gospel... By this doctrine the sun and the rains become evangelists, and this without being able to produce a single example of a man who has been saved by this means.'[30]

Du Moulin then proceeds to a powerful piece of dysteleology which underlines the essential limitations of what men can achieve by the contemplation of the natural order.

> 'It is unimaginable how a man can have saving faith in Jesus Christ by contemplation of the creatures, by the sun, the moon, the rains, etc. For by these things a man will never learn what God in His counsel has provided for the expiation of our sins by the death of a Redeemer. On the contrary, every man who is led by natural reason alone, seeing the lightnings, the hailstorms, the earthquakes, the floods, plagues, droughts etc., becomes afraid of it, considering all nature armed against man, and all the creatures conspiring to his ruin, without perceiving there any means of peace and reconciliation with God. Nevertheless, all peoples, including the greatest philosophers, who have had no other instruction than that of nature, have never by the least suspicion or conjecture thought of the doctrine of our redemption.'[31]

If, in this last passage, Du Moulin has carried his attack forward from the *Anatome*, when he comes to consider Romans I, 18-21 he has nothing new to add to what he argued in his earlier work:

> '... they suppose something which is not the case, namely that St. Paul means that by the contemplation of these works God has given sufficient means and instruments to the gentiles for obtaining salvation if they use them well; and that the covenant of grace is preached by the sun, rains, fertile seasons, etc. This is not found in Calvin nor in any of the orthodox but indeed in the writings of the Arminians who also use this passage for their universal grace. The apostle does indeed say that the power and divinity of God are to be seen

---

[30] 'Je dis donc que cette doctrine qui veut que les hommes puissent estre sauvez sans cognoistre Jesus Christ, est un nouvel Evangile ... Par cette doctrine le Soleil et les pluyes deviennent Evangelistes, et ce sans pouvoir produire un seul exemple d'un homme qui ait esté sauvé par ce moyen.' (*Examen*, p. 77.)

[31] 'Est chose inimaginable comment par la contemplation des creatures un homme peut avoir une foy salutaire en Jesus Christ, par le Soleil, la Lune, les pluyes, etc. Car par ces choses un homme n'apprendra jamais que Dieu en son conseil ait pourveu à l'expiation de nos pechez par la mort d'un Redempteur. Au contraire tout homme qui se conduit par la seule raison naturelle, voyant les foudres, les gresles, les tromblemens de terre, les inondations, pestes, sterilitez, etc., en concevra une frayeur, considerant toute la nature armée contre l'homme, et toutes les creatures conspirantes à sa ruine, sans y appercevoir aucun moyen de paix et de reconciliation avec Dieu. Pourtant toutes les nations, voire les plus grandes Philosophes, qui n'ont eu autre instruction que celle de la nature, n'ont jamais rien conceu par le moindre soupcon ou conjecture de la doctrine de nostre redemption.' (*Ibid.*, p. 78.)

from the works of creation, but not the doctrine of our redemption. He condemns the gentiles for having resisted the witness of nature and the voice of the creatures, and what they have of light and the natural impressions, of honesty and the knowledge of God, and of not having used these aids as much as they could, but he does not accuse them of having mistaken the doctrine of our redemption preached by the creatures.'[32]

Again, so far from showing any signs of taking the points made against him earlier by Corvinus, Du Moulin merely underlines, with quotations from Beza and Calvin, the traditional view that the purpose of the natural knowledge of God given is to render mankind inexcusable.

> 'Beza ... in these notes on this passage, "In my view the Apostle means not only what follows from that contemplation, but rather why God wishes this light to shine in the darkness, namely that men cannot put forward the pretext of any ignorance" ... and ... There is (says Calvin) a great difference between this knowledge which serves *only* to remove any excuse, and the other which avails for salvation, of which Christ makes mention. John 17, verse 3.'[33]

Just how fair a representation Du Moulin has given of his opponents' teaching is not to our purpose to enquire. However, it is worth noting that, at the Synod of Alençon at which their views were subjected to intensive scrutiny and where Du Moulin pressed hard for their condemnation, they made the following statements:

> 'Monsieur Testard and Amyraud declared further, that although the Doctrines obvious to us in the Works of Creation and Providence do teach and preach repentance, and invite us to seek the Lord, who would be found of us; yet nevertheless, by reason of the horrible blindness of our nature and its universal corruption, no man was ever this way converted; yea and it is utterly impossible that any one should be converted but by the hearing of the Word of God ... And forasmuch as the Word of God hath always revealed the knowledge of the Lord our Redeemer ... they hold it as an undoubted truth

[32] '... ils supposent une chose qui n'est pas à savoir que S. Paul entend que Dieu par la contemplation de ses ouvrages ait donné aux Gentiles des moyens et instruments suffisantes pour parvenir au salut, s'ils s'en fusent bien servis; et que l'alliance de grace leur est preschee par le Soleil, pluyes, saisons fertiles, etc. C'est ce qui ne trouvera point en Calvin, ny en aucune Orthodoxe, mais bien és escrits des Arminiens, lesquels aussi employent ce passage pour leur grace universelle. L'Apostre dit bien que la puissance et divinité de Dieu paroissent és oeuvres de la creation, mais non pas la doctrine, de nostre redemption. Il condamme les Gentiles pour avoir resisté au tesmoignage de la nature et à la voix des creatures, et à ce qu'ils avoient de lumiere et d'impressions naturelles, d'honnesteté et de cognoissance de Dieu, et ne s'estre servis de ces aides jusqu' où ils pouvoient, mais ne les accuse pas d'avoir mesprisé la doctrine de nostre redemption preschée par les creatures.' (*Ibid.*, p. 81.)

[33] 'Beze ... en ces notes sur ce passage, "Meo judicio non tantum significat Apostolus quid illam contemplationem consequatur, sed multo magis cur Deus velit hanc lucem lucere in tenebris, nempe ut homines non possint ullam ignorantiam praetexere" ... et ... Il y a (dit Calvin) grande difference entre cette cognoissance qui sert *seulement* pour oster toute excuse, et l'autre qui sert a salut, de laquelle Christ fait mention. Jean 17, vers. 3.' (*Ibid.*, pp. 81-2.)

that now under the New Covenant the distinct knowledge of Christ is absolutely necessary for all persons who are come unto years of discretion in order to their obtaining of eternal salvation ...'

Finally and most interestingly, since this is precisely one of the cardinal points that has been at issue throughout between the Arminians and their opponents:

'And whereas divers persons were much offended at the Professor Amyraud for calling that knowledge of God which men might gain from the consideration of his works and providence (unless their corruption were extreme) by the name of faith. The said Professor declared that he did it because he reckoned that that persuasion which some have, that there is a God, and that he is a Rewarder may bear that name, he owning however that St. Paul did simply and plainly style it the knowledge of God, 1 Cor. 1. 21. The Assembly enjoined him not to give the name of faith to any other knowledge of God, but unto that which is engendered in us by the Holy Spirit, and by the preaching of his word, according as the Scripture useth it ...'[34]

In view of the unimpeachable orthodoxy of these declarations it is hardly surprising that:

'... Testard and Amyraud having acquiesced in all, as above declared, and having sworn and subscribed to it, the Assembly gave them the right hand of fellowship by the hand of their moderator and they were honourably dismissed to the exercise of their respective charges.'[35]

De Courcelles devotes Chapter 13 his *Advis* to the consideration of Du Moulin's 'Fifth Controversy'. He is most effective in his attack on the orthodox understanding of inexcusability in the Romans passage:

'For how is it, I ask you, that they have been inexcusable before God, if He has not given them sufficient knowledge which they needed to have to avoid damnation? ... it is absurd, and contrary to God's goodness, to say that He has given them insufficient knowledge to render them inexcusable. Absurd, I say, because an insufficient knowledge cannot deprive them of every legitimate excuse; on the contrary, it leaves them a very fair subject for complaint at His rigour that He demands of them something which surpasses the powers which He has given them. It is contrary also to His goodness, because in manifesting Himself in this way to them He would propose not their salvation but their ruin, which is Calvin's barbarous opinion.'[36]

---

[34] J. Quick, *Synodicon in Gallia Reformata*, London, 1692, Vol. II, p. 356.

[35] Quick, *op. cit.*, p. 357.

[36] 'Car comment est-ce, je vous prie, qu'ils ont esté inexcusables devant Dieu, s'il ne leur avoit point donne une suffisante cognoissance de ce qu'ils avoient besoin de scavoir pour eviter la damnation? ... c'est une chose absurde, et contraire à la bonté de Dieu, de dire qu'il leur a donne une cognoissance insuffisante pour les rendre inexcusables. Absurde, dis-je, pource qu'une cognoissance insuffisante ne leur pouvoit oster toute legitume excuse, au contraire elle leur laissoit un très juste subjet de se plaindre de sa rigeur, de ce qu'il exigeoit d'eux une chose qui surpassoit les forces qu'il leur avoit donnees. Contraire aussi à sa bonté,

However, at no point in this attack on inexcusability, does De Courcelles follow Corvinus in using any such considerations to further arguments for claiming that the knowledge obtained from the creatures is of grace rather than of nature. Indeed, a very significant fact to note throughout De Courcelles's entire discussion is his reticence on this issue which had previously marked such a clear disagreement between the two parties. He is careful not to claim too much for this form of knowledge:

> '... the instructions which God gives to men in His works cannot in truth be called sufficient to lead to salvation in the way which is declared to us in the Gospel by faith in Jesus Christ, but only so far that God has given indications that He is willing extraordinarily to be content with this degree of piety that such instructions can produce in those who were destitute of all other means of knowing Him, of whom His justice does not allow him to demand more than they have received.'[37]

Later he gives further indications of his recognition of the limitations attaching to the extent of the knowledge of God obtainable from a consideration of the natural order and supplements this with evidence from the action of God's providence in human affairs.

> 'The sun and the rains with the other wonders that we perceive in nature indeed serve to lead us to some degree to the knowledge of God, as St. Paul says, Acts 14, 17 ... But yet they are not sufficient alone for saving knowledge. They must be supplemented by the examples of His providence in the punishment of the wicked and the reward of the good. For it is principally by this that those who take notice of it are induced to fear and to serve Him ...'[38]

Although the great bulk of the *Advis* is devoted to challenging Du Moulin's arguments, De Courcelles does not hesitate to disagree with

---

pource qu'en se manifestant ainsi à eux, il se seroit proposé non point leur salut mais leur ruine, qui est la barbare opinion de Calvin.' (*Advis*, p. 117.) Cf. p. 121. 'Car nul n'est inexcusable pour avoir manqué à faire une chose impossible.'

[37] '... les instructions que Dieu donne aux hommes en ses oeuvres ne peuvent à la verité estre appellées suffisantes pour amener à salut en la maniere qui nous est declarée en l'Evangile par la foy en Jesus Christ, mais seulement entant que Dieu a donné des indices qu'il se vouloit extraordinairement contenter de ce degré de pieté, que telles instructions pourroient produire en ceux qui ont esté destituez de tout autre moyen de le cognoistre, ausquels son equité ne luy permet point de demander plus qu'ils n'ont receu ...' (*Ibid.*, p. 121.)

[38] 'Le Soleil et les pluyes avec les autres merveilles que nous appercevons en la nature servent bien de degrez pour nous amener à la cognoissance de Dieu, suivant ce que S. Paul dit Act. 14, 17 ... Mais toutesfois ils ne suffisent pas seuls pour le cognoistre à salut. Il y faut conjoindre les exemples de sa providence en la punition des mechans et remuneration des bons. Car c'est par là principalement que ceux qui y prennent garde peuvent estre induit à le craindre et servir ...' (*Ibid.*, p. 125.) Although we would not gather this from Du Moulin's criticism of them, we may note that, in the report of their declarations at the Synod of Alencon, both Testard and Amyraut were at pains to refer to the 'Works of Creation and Providence.' See above, p. 190.

Amyraut and Testard when he feels it to be necessary. In so doing on one occasion he makes an important point which serves to clarify the whole issue under discussion. He begins by agreeing with the reasons given by Du Moulin to show that one cannot believe in Jesus Christ without knowing him and he proceeds to attack Amyraut and Testard for suggesting that this might in some way be possible. He explains:

> 'The source of their error is that they did not distinguish as they should between the faith which one can in some sort have by contemplation of His works, and faith in Jesus Christ for which a particular revelation is required. Faith in God is absolutely necessary for salvation and there is no difficulty in pronouncing that without it no one can have eternal life. It is this which the apostle discusses, Hebrew 11, and which he proves by a multitude of examples from the Old Testament ... But faith in Jesus Christ as mediator between God and men and who by his death has ransomed us from perdition, is not necessary until it is announced and one has the means of knowing him ...'[39]

Much of the force of Du Moulin's arguments was, as we have seen, directed against the absurdity of the preaching of the Gospel by means of the creatures, 'The sun and the stars are not preachers of the Gospel'.[40] Thus in making this distinction between faith in God and faith in Jesus Christ, De Courcelles effectively guards his position from any such accusation. It should, however, be noted that such a distinction would not make the slightest difference to Calvin's view on the validity of the natural knowledge of God, for this is concerned precisely with that knowledge of Him as Creator—'it is needful that another and better help be added to direct us aright to the very Creator of the universe.'[41]

A brief rejoinder to De Courcelles from the orthodox Reformed quarter came from another Frenchman who was to spend the rest of his days in Holland, Samuel Maresius,[42] Professor at Groningen. In the course of 'On Justification', one of the controversies handled in a huge two volume

---

[39] 'La source de leur erreur est qu'ils n'ont pas sceu distinguer comme ils appartient entre la foy qu'on peut en quelque sorte avoir par la contemplation de ses oeuvres, et la foy en Jesus Christ, à laquelle est requise une revelation particuliere. La foy en Dieu est absolument necessaire à salut, et ne fay point de difficulté de prononcer que sans icelle nul n'aura la vie eternelle. C'est ce que traitte l'Apostre, Hebr. 11, et qu'il prouve par une multitude d'exemples de l'ancien Testament ... Mais la foy en Jesus Christ, comme Mediateur entre Dieu et les hommes, et qui par sa mort nous a racheté de perdition, n'est necessaire que lors qu'il est annoncé, et qu'on a le moyen de le cognoistre ...' (*Ibid.*, pp. 126-7.)

[40] 'Le Soleil et les Astres ne sont point predicateurs de l'Evangile.' (*Examen*, p. 79.)

[41] *Institutes* I, vi. i. *LCC* p. 69. Cf. also the title of Book I, 'The Knowledge of God the Creator.'

[42] See above, pp. 114-8.

series directed against the Jesuit, Jacobus Tirinus,[43] he turns aside to refute the 13th Chapter of the *Advis d'un personnage desinteressé*.

Some allowance must be made for the necessary and self-confessed brevity of Maresius's treatment, but even so his handling of Romans 1, 18-21 can scarcely be considered adequate. In the face of De Courcelles's arguments he merely devotes a sentence to the reiteration of the orthodox position,

> 'God has manifested Himself sufficiently through the works of creation to the gentiles for their inexcusability so that they cannot use ignorance as a pretext, yet not sufficiently for salvation.'[44]

Equally inadequate is his dismissal of De Courcelles's important distinction between faith in God and faith in Jesus Christ,

> 'But this is useless; because Christ expressly demands faith in God and in Himself, John 14, 1, nor is it possible to conceive how there can be faith in God from the works of nature, but from the revelation of grace ...'[45]

Maresius's shrewdest criticism is levelled against De Courcelles's contention that, for faith to be aroused apart from the preaching of the Gospel, the contemplation of the natural order must be supplemented by the consideration of Providence's punishing of sinners and rewarding of the virtuous. Maresius objects:

> 'But when he has confessed that the works of nature are insufficient for this, I do not know by what means he wishes to distinguish the course of ordinary providence from these: and from the example of Asaph, Psalm 73, it is well known that despair rather than faith is born in righteous men from what happens in the world to the good and the evil, until they come into the sanctuary of God, where, as it says in verse 17, they learn from the oracles of God about the end and fate of the evil.'[46]

With the above exception, Maresius's brief criticisms are not in themselves of any great interest. Their real importance lies in the fact that, unnoticed by their object for ten years, they eventually provoked a

[43] *Theologiae Elenchticae Nova Synopsis*. Groningen, 1646-1648.

[44] 'Sufficienter Deus se manifestavit etiam Ethnicis per opera creationis ad eorum in excusabilitatem, ut non potuerint ignorantiae causam praetexere, non tamen sufficienter ad salutem.' (Maresius, *op. cit.*, Vol. II, p. 282.)

[45] 'Sed id frustra; quia Christus fidem in Deum et in se ex asse exigit Joh: XIV, 1, nec fides in Deum ex operibus naturae uti fingit potest haberi, sed ex revelatione gratiae ...' (*Ibid.*, p. 284.)

[46] 'Sed cum ipso fatente opera naturae sint insufficientia ad id, nescio qua ratione Providentiae ordinariae cursum ab illis velit distinguere: et Asaphi exemplo, Psal. LXXIII per totum constat ex iis quae in hoc mundo eveniunt bonis et malis, potius desperationem nasci probis quam fidem, donec veniant in Sancturia Dei, ut ibid loquitur vers. 17 et ex Dei oraculis de malorum fine et exitu edoceantur.' (*Ibid.*, p. 283.)

response from De Courcelles written at the very end of his life, 'On the necessity of the knowledge of Christ', which appears as the third item in *Four theological dissertations against Samuel Maresius*.[47]

Before examining the New Testament texts upon which he bases his case, De Courcelles makes a clear statement of his position on the issue in general:

> 'God does not allow those to whom the Gospel has never been announced to be entirely destitute of those means by which they can believe in Him and by faith show obedience and subjection to Him ... For it would be absurd to think that those who truly believe in God the Lord of the world should undergo that dreadful penalty because they did not believe in Christ; granted that they did not refrain from doing this, nor were they able to because it was not revealed to them.'[48]

We may note that De Courcelles is here employing the distinction which he drew earlier in the *Advis* between faith in God, here described as 'in God the Lord of the world', and faith in Jesus Christ.

On Romans 1, 19-21 De Courcelles quotes Maresius's reiteration of the orthodox view that the purpose of such natural knowledge was to render all mankind inexcusable and counters it with a further, devastatingly succinct demolition of such a concept of inexcusability:

> 'Indeed, God's gracious revelation renders no one inexcusable in itself or by its nature, but only to the extent that it is despised or rejected. For he is inexcusable who can produce no just excuse why he has not done God's will. Therefore it does not apply to those to whom God has indeed revealed His will but to whom He has necessarily denied the requisite powers to obey Him. For no more legitimate excuse can be given than that which results from impotence: since, as nature teaches and all men agree, no one is obliged to do the impossible.'[49]

[47] 'De necessitate cognitionis Christi', ... *Quaternio dissertationum theologicarum adversus Sam. Maresium*, Amsterdam, 1659, reprinted in Van Limborch's edition of De Courcelles's *Opera Theologica*, Amsterdam, 1675, in which this 'Tertia Dissertatio' occupies pp. 919-32. This is turn drew a reply from Maresius, *Defensio fidei Catholicae et orthodoxae ... opposita quaternioni Steph. Curcellaei*, Groningen, 1662, which we shall not pursue since it adds nothing of significance to his earlier arguments.

[48] 'Deus illos quibus Evangelium non est annuntiatum nunquam permisit esse omnino destitutos iis mediis, quibus in se credere, et ex fide sibi obedientiam et subjectionem exhibere possent ... Absurdum enim foret existimare eos qui vere in Deum mundi Dominum credunt, horrendam istam poenam propterea subituros, quod in Christum non crediderint; licet id nec facere tenerentur, nec possent, cum sibi revelatus non esset.' (Curcellaeus, *op. cit.*, p. 925.)

[49] 'Verum gratiosa Dei manifestatio neminem per se, seu ex natura sua reddit inexcusabilem, sed tantum quatenus contemnitur aut rejicitur ... Inexcusabilis enim ille demum est, qui nullam justam affere potest excusationem cur Dei voluntatem non fecerit. Quod in eos non quadrat, quibus Deus manifestavit quidem suam voluntatem, sed vires ad ei obtemperandum necessario requisitas denegavit. Nulla enim magis legitima excusatio dari

At one point in his exposition of this passage De Courcelles refers to the effect of this natural revelation as being that of grace.

> 'From this it is apparent that those to whom God has not revealed Himself by the word of the law or the Gospel are not destitute of the capacity for all knowledge of God and of obtaining salvation, if only they do not abandon the grace offered to them ...'[50]

Are we to conclude from this that, despite the reticence earlier shown in the *Advis*, De Courcelles now wishes to assume the position of the earlier Arminians on this issue? Any such queries are effectively answered in his exposition of the other relevant New Testament passage, Acts 14, 17. Of this he says,

> 'For the works which God produces through His ordinary servant nature and which strike our senses at every moment, afford the fullest evidence of the divine omnipotence, goodness and wisdom: therefore they who have them have been furnished with sufficient means by which they can believe in God and worship Him.'[51]

Whatever may be the 'gracious' effects of this mode of the knowledge of God there is not the slightest doubt that the means of its revelation are wholly natural—'through His ordinary servant nature.' Furthermore, he proceeds immediately to consider the possible objection that such contemplation of the works of God in nature is insufficient to show men how He is to be worshipped:

> 'Perhaps you will say that rains, fruitful season and food which alone the apostle mentions, do not teach how God is to be worshipped. I reply. These are offered as examples among the many others which we have, and are alone sufficient with careful consideration to persuade that there is a God and that He ought to be loved, feared and worshipped. Once this is established, it is obvious that reason, with which all are equipped, sufficiently indicates that the finest worship of God is a pious and honest life by which He is better pleased than by any gifts.'[52]

---

potest, quam ea quae ab impotentia proficiscitur: cum ad impossibile, ut natura docet, et omnes homines consentiunt, nemo obligatus sit.' (*Ibid.*, p. 926.)

[50] 'Ex quo apparet eos quibus Deus verbo legis aut Evangelii se non patefecit, destitutos non esse omni Deum cognoscendi et ad salutem perveniendi facultate; si modo gratiae sibi oblatae non desint ...' (*Ibid.*)

[51] 'Opera enim quae Deus per naturam ministram suam ordinariam efficit, et singulis momentis sensus nostros feriunt, amplissimum praebent testimonium omnipotentiae, bonitatis et sapientiae divinae: quod qui habent, sufficientibus instructi sunt mediis, quibus ad credendum in Deum et ipsum colendum adduci possint.' (*Ibid.*, p. 925.)

[52] 'Dices forte pluvias, tempora fructifera, et cibos, quorum solorum Apostolus meminit, non docere quomodo Deus sit colendus. Resp. Ista exempli gratia, inter plurima alia quae habemus allata fuisse, et vel sola attente considerantibus sufficere ad persuadendum Deum esse, et oportere ipsum amare, timere, colere. Quo pacto vero in eo se gerere conveniat,

What is so significant here is that De Courcelles clearly indentifies the means by which the natural man is able to make use of the revelation made to him by God in nature as 'reason with which all are equipped'. Thus, for the first time in the course of this protracted controversy reason is given an essential role in a sphere which the earlier Arminians felt obliged to assign to the operation of grace.

If we seek the cause for this development in De Courcelles's views during the twenty or so years between the appearance of the *Advis* and that of the *Quaternio*, then we need look no further than Episcopius[53] whose *Institutiones* De Courcelles had published in 1650.

Episcopius does not himself directly engage in the controversy which we have been following, but he does have much to say of relevance in the course of Chapter VIII[54] of the first book of the *Institutiones Theologicarum*, a chapter devoted to a description of natural religion. The title clearly indicates Episcopius's approach to the topic, 'Concerning Natural Religion and its first act which is the discerning of good from evil.'[55] The starting point for religion is thus seen to lie in moral obligation and the essential means by which this is discharged is immediately declared in the opening sentence, 'And this natural religion is wholly religion which has right reason alone as a rule and measure, whose first act is ...'[56]

The fundamental objection to such an approach and one which would be raised against it by all orthodox Calvinists is that natural reason in fallen man is too corrupt to play the role here assigned to it. During the course of his discussion Episcopius briefly notes and dismisses this.

> 'For although some assert and contend that natural reason is so corrupt that there are scarcely any fragments of it remaining, this seems to me to entirely alien to the truth, if attention is paid to those principles which we have mentioned. For there is no man to be found, provided only that his reason is intact; who will not agreeably assent to and approve those same things, supposing only that he acknowledges God and confesses himself a man.'[57]

---

ratio qua omnes praediti sunt, satis indicat, nempe praestantissimum Dei cultum esse piam et honestam vitam, qua magis delectatur quam ullis donariis.' (*Ibid.*, p. 925.)

[53] For Episcopius, the leading Remonstrant theologian at Dort and until his death in 1643, see below pp. 213-38.

[54] *Opera Omnia*, Amsterdam, 1650, Part I, pp. 17-20.

[55] 'De Religione naturali, ejusque primo actu, qui est honestum a turpi discernere.' (Episcopius, *op. cit.*, I, p. 17.)

[56] 'Atque haec religio naturalis plane religio est, quae rectam solam rationem pro regula ac mensura habet, cujus actus primus est ...' (*Ibid.*)

[57] 'Quod enim quidam asserunt et contendunt, rationem naturalem adeo corruptam esse, ut pene nulla ejus rudera reliqua sint, id mihi plane alienum videtur a vero, si ad illa quae diximus principia attendatur. Nullus enim homo, si modo rationis compos sit, reperietur, qui istis non lubens adsentietur et suffragabitur, supposito quod Deum tantum agnoscat, et

He does admit that in many men reason is seriously darkened by the effects of sin and error, but nonetheless affirms that such never lose that remnant of the natural law which can serve as the basis for their improvement and even indeed for their capacity to become Christians.

> 'I admit, however, that reason is seriously darkened in many by false ideas or by an evil manner of living ... yet always there remains in them a remnant of the natural law, as far as the common precepts, with the help of which they can be freed from errors to return to better virtue and to be taught and instructed in the knowledge of the most holy religion.'[58]

After a survey of pre-Mosaic Israelite religion, Episcopius adduces Romans I, 18-32 to clinch his argument. His exposition of this passage is not intentionally directed to the points at issue in the foregoing debate between Remonstrants and Calvinists, but his treatment of it is nonetheless very significant. His first concern is to establish from these verses the fundamental elements of natural religion.

> 'For in that chapter it is attributed to the peoples to whom the knowledge of the Mosaic Law and the Gospel had not reached. First, that they know a fourfold truth. 1. There is a God and He is to be worshipped and glorified. 2. Corruptible and created idols are not to be worshipped in place of the incorruptible God and creator ... 3. One must abstain from all the impurities which are recounted in verses 29, 30 and 31. 4. Those who do not abstain from them are worthy of death and this is the judgement of God Himself.'[59]

Episcopius does, however, immediately make clear his recognition of man's failure to sustain such knowledge effectively, 'Secondly, it is affirmed of those that not only did they not follow the whole of this truth, but also that they held it down in unrighteousness.'[60]

---

se hominem fateatur.' (*Ibid.*, p. 18.) The orthodox response to this may be seen in a work to which we shall shortly refer to more fully, Leonard van Rijssen, *De vuile en zielverdervende leer der Nieuwe Remonstranten*, Schoonhaven, 1662, p. 6, where the first half of this passage is quoted in translation with the comment, 'There is no spiritual good remaining nor capacity for belief and therefore he must be born again. John 4.5, Rom. 7.18.' 'Daar is geen geestelijk goet overgebleven, noch bequaamheyt om te geloven, ende waarom hy ook wedergeboren moet worden. Joh. 4.5. Rom. 7.18.' For van Rijssen see *NNBW* IV col. 1190.

[58] 'Interim fateor, in multis per falsas opiniones aut pravam vivendi consuetudinem, rationem non leviter obscuratam esse ... manente tamen semper in illis reliqua lege naturali, quoad communia praecepta, cujus beneficio liberari possunt ab erroribus, ad meliorem frugem redire, et sanctissimae Religionis scientia erudiri atque instrui.' (Episcopius, *op. cit.*, I, p. 18.)

[59] 'Nam in isto capite gentibus tribuitur, ad quas legis Mosaicae et Evangelicae cognitio non pervenerat. Primo, quod veritatem cognoverint quadruplicem. 1. Deum esse eumque colendum ac glorificandum esse. 2. Non esse colendas imagines corruptibiles et creatas, praeterito incorruptibili Deo et creatore ... 3. Ab impuritatibus omnibus quae vers. 29, 30, 31, recensentur, abstinendum esse. 4. Eos qui ab iis non abstinent dignos morte esse, idque jus Dei ipsius esse.' (*Ibid.*, p. 19.)

[60] 'Secundo, de iis affirmatur quod veritatem hanc totam non modo non sint secutae, sed eam etiam in injustitia detinuerint.' (*Ibid.*)

Having made a more detailed analysis of the features of natural religion, Episcopius returns to a closer examination of the Romans passage. He devotes a lengthy section to establishing that Paul is here referring to all men, both Jews and Gentiles, to whom the Gospel has never been proclaimed. He does not name the proponents of the opposing view against which he is arguing,

> 'To these some are wont to object that the apostle in this chapter is only speaking of people who have already been called by the Gospel and have been provided with the knowledge of the true God and the divine will.'[61]

In fact this is an example of Episcopius's courteous but resolute rejection of the position of Socinus. 'I reply: although there are some who make this plausible argument, yet the contrary reasons seem to me to outweigh them.'[62] An unusual exegesis of Romans I, 20 was fundamental to this latter view and Socinus had duly provided one such in several places,[63] but perhaps most succinctly in the Racovian Catechism[64] where this verse was cited to prove that 'man by nature hath nothing common with immortality' and 'could not by himself know the way leading thereunto.' Socinus's interpretation ran thus:

> '... the apostle affirmeth those things which God hath by the Gospel discovered to men to be such as were invisible from the very creation of the world. So that they could by no means be traced out by men. For the very matter which the Apostle in this place proposeth to be handled intimateth that those works whereby the invisible things of God were known are to be understood of the works done under the Gospel.'

To the query, 'But that place is commonly interpreted in another sense', Socinus replied that this was due to a misunderstanding of St. Paul's meaning:

---

[61] 'Hisce opponi a quibusdam solet, Apostolum in hoc capite non loqui nisi de gentibus jam per Evangelium vocatis, et cognitione veri Dei et divinae voluntatis instructis.' (*Ibid.*)

[62] 'Respondeo: Etsi nonnulla sint quae verisimilem hanc opinionem faciunt, tamen contrariae rationes mihi videntur praeponderare.' (*Ibid.*) cf. *Institutiones* Book I cp. III where, after briefly reviewing Socinus's arguments against the existence in man of any natural knowledge of God, Episcopius responds in the same manner, 'Rationes hae etsi speciem quandam veri habeant, tanti tamen mihi non videntur ponderis ...' p. 7. For our discussion of Socinus's position and Episcopius's relationship to it. See below pp. 202-29.

[63] *Praelectiones Theologicae*, Racow, 1609, p. 5 (see below, p. 204), cf. *Responsio ad libellum Jacobi Wuieki*, in, *Operum Tomus Alter continens ... Scripta Polemica*, Amsterdam, 1656, p. 592.

[64] *Catechesis Ecclesiorum quae in Regno Poloniae* ..., Racow, 1609, cp. I, pp. 21-24. The quotations are given from the English translation, *The Racovian Catechism*, Amsterdam, 1652, pp. 12-13. For a full and interesting criticism of this exegesis from the orthodox Calvinist standpoint, see S. Maresius, *Foederatum Belgium orthodoxum* ..., Groningen, 1652, pp. 53-4, 'Rom. I, 19.20 quam perperam Socinus et ex illo Ostorodius et Catechesis Racoviensis ita detorquent ...'

'For whereas the Apostle wrote, From the creation of the world, they read, By the creation of the world. Again they join the same words not with the clause going before (an example of which joining you have in the 13 of Mat. ver. 35. I will open my mouth in parables, I will disclose things hidden from the foundation of the world) but with the clause coming after, as if the Apostle meant that the invisibles of God were seen by the creation of the world.'

Having thus established the fact that the Romans passage applies to all mankind prior to the Gospel revelation, Episcopius proceeds to a more detailed analysis. It is interesting to see the way in which his very insistence on the role of right reason in natural religion enables him to by-pass the whole controversy over inexcusability which we have outlined above. As we noted earlier he clearly recognizes men's universal failure to carry out the precepts of natural religion. With the aid of reason these latter were readily to be deduced by them from the ποιηματα ('created things', verse 20) which Episcopius interprets not, with the great majority of commentators, as 'the works made at the creation',[65] nor, following Socinus, as 'the miracles or signs performed by Christ and the apostles',[66] but as

'... all examples both of goodness or grace and of severity or the temporary divine anger, which have ever been done or set forth by God before the Gospel revelation.'[67]

and 'νουμενα' ('understood') Episcopius interprets as

'the inference which was made by reasoning or the acute mind from those signs and indications of the divine grace and punishment.'[68]

Episcopius has no qualms about accepting that the purpose of all this divine disclosure is that sinful men may be rendered inexcusable because

---

[65] 'Opera per creationem facta.' (Episcopius, *op. cit.* I, p. 20), cf. e.g. D. Pareus, *In divam S. Pauli ad Romanas epistolam commentarius*, Heidelberg, 1613, col. 97, 'ποιηματα vocat res conditas.' This interpretation was also shared by the later Socinians who, as we shall see (see below, p. 232), reversed their master's position on the natural knowledge of God. Thus in his commentary on Romans, first published at Racow in 1636, Crellius writes, 'vox ποιηματων, seu operum, non actiones aliquas, quas vox operum apud Latinos nonnunquam significat: ... sed opera per actionem affecta, et post eam relicta denotat, qualia sunt res a Deo conditae, et in oculos nostros indurrentes: de quibus loquitur David, cum ait: "coeli enarrant gloriam Dei" ...' (J. Crellius, *Opera Omnia Exegetica*, Vol. I, Amsterdam, 1656, p. 79.)

[66] 'Miracula aut signa per Christum Apostolos edita.' (Episcopius, *op. cit.* I, p. 20), cf. '... per opera, hoc est per mirabiles ipsius Dei et divinorum hominum, praesertim vero Christi et Apostolorum ejus operationes', (*Praelectiones Theologicae*, p. 5), cf. ... *ad ... Wuieki*, in *Operum Tomas Alter continens ... scripta polemica*, p. 592.

[67] '... omnia tum bonitatis sive gratiae, tum severitatis sive irae divinae temporalis documenta, quae unquam ante Euangelium revelatum facta aut edita a Deo sunt.' (Episcopius, *op. cit.* I, p. 20.)

[68] 'Collectionem quae ratiocinatione sive ingeniosa mente facta fuit ex istis signis atque indiciis gratiae atque ultionis divinae.' (*Ibid.*)

they failed to use the gift of right reason which would have enabled them to know and obey God. However, unlike the orthodox Calvinists, the implication for him is that they could quite readily have made proper use of their rationality in this respect.

> 'To what end indeed? So that in this way they might be inexcusable, ... because when they had known God or known with the benefit of right reason the other favours of God (for neither, as in Acts 14, 17 had He left Himself without a witness, giving them gifts and rains and fruitful seasons suitable for filling their hearts with food and gladness; indeed, as it is said in Chapter 17 verse 26, by making the whole human race of one blood ... so that they might seek the Lord if perhaps by feeling they might find Him, etc.) they were easily able and ought with good right to have done, yet they did not glorify God neither did they give Him thanks, but on the contrary, as though abandoning all human wisdom and the universal dictate of right reason, defiled themselves with the most abominable idolatries and the wickedest lusts.'[69]

The natural man's inexcusable culpability before God is thus the more forcibly underlined as the status of his rationality and consequent moral potentiality is exalted. There is no question of God's having required of men anything they were not able to give Him which, as we have seen, was the aspect of the Calvinists' understanding of man's inexcusability before God that the Remonstrants found so objectionable. Such a reliance upon right reason as the means whereby fallen man can appropriate the knowledge of God in this fashion marks a major and most significant shift in the Remonstrants' position on this issue.[70] Thus Dort's Condemnation,

---

[69] 'Quorsum vero? ut hac ratione reddantur ἀναπολογητοι, ... propterea quod cum Deum cognovissent, aut cognoscere beneficio rectae rationis aliorumque Dei beneficiorum (neque enim, uti est Act. 14, 17 ἀμαρτυρον εἀυτον ἀφηκεν, dona iis tribuendo, et pluvias temporaque fructibus edendis apta largiendo et implendo cibo ac laetitia corda eorum; imo uti cap. 17 vers. 26 dicitur, faciendo ex uno sanguine totam gentem humanam ... ut quaererent Dominum, si forte palpando eum invenirent, etc.) facile potuissent ac jure meritoque debuissent, tamen ut Deum non glorificarunt, neque ei gratias egerunt, sed contra veluti omnem humanam sapientiam et universum dictamen naturalis rationis abdicantes, foedissima idololatria et turpissimis libidinibus se coinquinarunt.' (*Ibid.*)

[70] That their opponents were well aware of the important differences between the teaching of the later Remonstrants and that of Arminius on this, among other topics, is clearly apparent from van Rijssen's work which draws attention to the distinction in its very title, ... *Nieuwe Remonstranten*. (See above, p. 197.) In it this champion of Voetian orthodoxy sets out such passages as that of Episcopius's referred to above and appends selections from Arminius and his contemporaries which underline the changes that have taken place. The first chapter (pp. 1-13) is headed 'Van de Religie en natuurlijke Theologie' and not surprisingly amongst the quotations designed to show up the infidelity of the later Remonstrants is that one from Arminius *Apology against 31 Theological Articles* with which we began the section. (Van Rijssen, *op. cit.*, pp. 10-11. See above, p. 180.)

which, as we saw, was originally pronounced upon a travesty of the doctrine represented by Article three of the Remonstrance, proved subsequently to be appropriate enough when applied to the views which the leading Remonstrants eventually came to hold. The next chapter will provide us with further evidence of Episcopius' emphasis upon the natural man's responsible rationality.

## CHAPTER EIGHT

# THE INNATE IDEA OF GOD

At the beginning of the seventeenth century the most dangerous external challenge to Dutch Reformed orthodoxy, apart from the old enemy of Rome, would almost certainly have been seen as Socinianism which early in the century reached the zenith of its power in Poland and whose influence was beginning to be felt throughout Protestantism.[1] The leader of the movement, Faustus Socinus[2] himself, had launched an attack upon the whole enterprise of man's having or obtaining any knowledge of God apart from revelation and the reverberations of this brief chapter of his *Praelectiones Theologicae*[3] continued to echo through discussions of the topic for the next half century.

Socinus denied both of the sources of the natural knowledge of God to which, as we have frequent occasion to observe, Reformed Theology appealed. He began by rejecting the first of these, the innate idea of God, for which, in a manner somewhat akin to the early Melanchthon's attempt to account for the universality of the natural law,[4] he substituted an original and continuing divine revelation:

> 'It is quite an accepted opinion nowadays that by nature there is in man an implanted idea of some divinity ... We judge this to be a false opinion which seems to have arisen only from this, that all men appear to be imbued with that idea of some divinity. Really it was to be observed that from the very beginning when man was created, God revealed Himself to him. This first man, since he lived for nine hundred and thirty years was easily able to imbue his descendants with the idea of divinity. Nevertheless it was not necessary in this case since God Himself revealed Himself by various means not only to the first man but repeatedly to others born of him, in a manner clearly apparent from the sacred histories.'[5]

---

[1] See E. M. Wilbur, *A History of Unitarianism: Socinianism and its Antecedents*, Cambridge, Mass., 1946, and for Socinianism in relation to Dutch theology, W. J. Kühler, *Het Socinianisme in Nederland*, Leiden, 1912, and J. C. Van Slee, *De Geschiedenis van het Socinianisme in de Nederland*, Haarlem, 1914.

[2] For Socinus (1539-1604) see M. Martini, *Fausto Socino et La Pensée Socinienne*, Paris, 1967.

[3] Racow, 1609, pp. 3-7.

[4] The section from the first edition of the *Loci Communes* reads thus: 'ita ut mihi pene libeat vocare legem naturae non aliquod congenitum iudicium, seu insitum et insculptum natura mentibus hominum, sed leges acceptas a patribus, et quasi per manus traditas subinde posteritati, ut de creatione rerum, de colendo deo, docuit posteros Adae, sic Cainum monuit, ne fratrem occideret etc...' (*CR* 21, col. 140). See above p. 14.

[5] 'Receptior hodie sententia est, homini naturaliter ejusque animo insitam esse

The most powerful of the objections which he advances against the innate idea is that based on the phenomenon of individuals and peoples who possess no belief in a deity:

> 'Not only individual men, but entire peoples are found today who have no inward sense or notion of any deity. These are in the new western world in the province of Brazil ... But such people are also to be found elsewhere, a recent history of India attests.'[6]

Against the second argument of the traditional pair, the appeal to the natural order, Socinus objects that philosophers have held varying views as to what can be deduced in this respect from a consideration of the world and that, in the case of Aristotle in particular, these had led to a very inadequate understanding of God's providence and to the denial that He was the world's Creator.

> 'But there are those who say that at all events it cannot be denied that, from the arrangement alone of this world, if anyone directs their attention then anyone you like can clearly know not only that there is a God but may even perceive that He watches over human affairs ... That opinion ... is convicted of falsity because there were certain outstanding philosophers, chief among whom, as it may be believed, is Aristotle, ... who did not regard this arrangement of the world in this way ... they were not able to get as far as conjecturing that God cares for these lower individuals nor even did they think that He has care for individual men. Rather they could not even grasp that the world has been created by God, indeed they clearly denied this.'[7]

Socinus then backed his case by refuting the orthodox interpretation of some of the chief scriptural texts on which the upholders of the traditional

---

Divinitatis alicujus opinionem ... Haec sententia, quam nos falsam esse arbitramur, non aliunde potius orta fuisse videtur, quam ex eo, quod videantur omnes homines opinione ista Divinitatis alicujus imbuti esse. Verum animadvertendum erat, ab ipso initio cum homo creatus fuit, Deum se illi patefecisse, qui primus homo cum nongentis triginta annis vixerit, posteros suos facile Divinitatis opinione imbuere potuit. Quamquam hac re opus non erat, cum ipse Deus, non primo homini tantum, sed aliis subinde ex eo natis, sese variis rationibus patefecerit, quemadmodum ex Sacra historia clare liquet.' (*Praelectiones Theologicae*, p. 3.)

[6] 'Non singuli tantum aliqui homines, sed integri populi hodie inveniuntur, qui nullum penitus sensum aut suspicionem Divinitatis alicujus habent. Hi sunt in novo occidentali orbe in Bresilia provincia ... Sed et alibi quoque ejusmodi gentes repiriri, Indiae recens historia testatur.' (*Ibid.*, p. 4.)

[7] 'At sunt qui dicant, id saltem negari non posse, ex sola hujus mundi machina, si quis animum advertat, posse quemlibet, non solum Deum esse, manifeste cognoscere, verum etium rebus humanis eum prospicere, plane percipere ... Sententia ista ... ex eo falsitatis convincitur, quod praestantissimi quidam Philosophi inter quos maxime, ut creditur, Aristoteles, ... qui hanc mundi machinam non aspexerint modo ... huc pervenire non potuerunt, ut Deum inferiora haec singula curare suspicarentur, vel hominum saltem singulorum eum curam habere intelligerent. Quinetiam ne creatum quidem a Deo mundum fuisse assequi potuerunt, imo id plane negarunt.' (*Ibid.*)

view were wont to base their case, i.e. Psalm 19 v. 1, Romans 1 v. 20 and Acts 17 vv. 26-27. Just how far he was prepared to go in his exegesis may be seen from his treatment of the Romans passage:

> 'But it must be known that the words, "from the creation of the world", ought to be joined with the words "the invisible things" and have the same meaning as Matthew 13.35. "Things hidden from the foundation of the world". And many interpreters have changed the preposition "ex" into "a" contrary to the credibility of the Greek codices themselves which do not have ἐκ κιτισεως but ἀπο κιτισεως. Therefore the apostle speaks in this place of God's eternal divinity, that is, that which God perpetually wishes to show us in His eternity and power (for "divinity" also has this same meaning elsewhere, as is declared elsewhere in his writings, Col. 2. 9.), that is, the promises which never fail (in which sense he had said a little earlier, the Gospel is the power of God). These, I say, which never after the world had been created, had been seen by men, that is, had not been known to them, were perceived through the works, that is, through the miracles of God Himself and of holy men especially indeed through the actions of Christ and his apostles.'[8]

In our examination of Arminius's use of the arguments for the existence of God we discovered that he had used those of Conrad Vorstius's disputation of 1598.[9] When the latter published his collection of ten 'De Deo' disputations in 1606 some eight years after this date, he added a series of notes which in fact far exceeded the original disputation in length.[10]

In the original disputation Vorstius had prefaced his presentation of the arguments by referring to a threefold scheme whereby God reveals himself to men:

> 'The first is set forth to all men and is in a certain manner natural which spontaneously arises in all adults endowed with a sound mind. For these understand that there is a God by reasoning partly from the common principles implanted in them and partly from the visible works of God, Psalm 19, 1, 2. Rom. 1, 20, 21. Another means by which God makes Himself a little clearer

[8] 'Sed sciendum est verba, "a creatione mundi", debere conjungi cum verbo "invisibilia", eundemque sensum esse qui est Matth. 13. 35. "Abscondita a constitutione mundi." Plerique interpretes ex praepositione "a", "ex" fecerunt, contra ipsorum Graecorum codicum fidem qui non ἐκ κιτισεως, sed ἀπο κιτισεως habent. Ait igitur eo in loco Apostolus, aeternam divinitatem Dei, id est, quod nos Deus perpetuo facere vult (Divinitas enim hoc sensu alibi quoque apud ipsum enuntiatur, ut Col. 2. 9.) aternamque potentiam, id est, promissiones quae numquam intercident (quo sensu paulo superius dixerat Evangelium esse potentiam Dei) haec, inquam, quae nunquam, postquam mundus creatus fuerat, ab hominibus visa fuerant, id est, non fuerant eis cognita, per opera, hoc est per mirabiles ipsius Dei et divinorum hominum, praesertim vero Christi et Apostolorum ejus operationes, conspecta fuisse.' (*Ibid.*, p. 5.) For another version of the same exegesis, see above, p. 198.

[9] See above, pp. 149-56.

[10] As an 'Admonitiuncula ad Lectorem' explains, the 1606 edition only contains the additional notes to the first of the ten disputations (pp. 121-149). The 1610 edition supplied the remaining notes and increased the work to 466 pages.

> to us to be seen in a particular expression, i.e. Holy Scripture. Psalm 147, 19, 20. Heb. 1, 1. Finally there is that by which He has clearly specially adopted those whom He has already drawn more closely to Himself to whom He has truly revealed Himself by the Holy Spirit, so that a most certain fullness of awareness fills their minds. 2 Cor. 1, 21. 22. 1 John 2, 20.'[11]

In this he has clearly drawn upon that Locus, 'Concerning the Knowledge of God', of his former master, Piscator, which we studied in an earlier chapter,[12] although he has adopted it to suit his own framework.

Thus Vortius has joined together Piscator's 'Natural knowledge of God ... which rises spontaneously in adults endowed with a sound mind'[13] with the first part of that knowledge of God which the latter distinguished as 'acquired ... drawn from instruction whether human or philosophical from the consideration of God's works',[14] under the heading of 'Natural'. The second part of Piscator's 'acquired' knowledge, 'the divine namely that drawn from the written word of God',[15] provides Vorstius with the second element in his scheme, whilst the last is evidently suggested by part of the former's final aphorism, 'It is necessary, however, that this knowledge of God as redeemer be added to an allied filial trust.'[16]

When we come to Vorstius's later notes on this seventh thesis we shall see that Piscator continues to provide him with material, but first we must note a new influence, since Vorstius has evidently imbided Socinus's exegesis of Romans 1, 20-21 and so can no longer apply this text to the natural means of the knowledge of God:

> 'The first of these is the external operation, for example the creation of heaven and earth, etc. From which His power and divinity can to some degree be perceived: as the two primary passages of scripture attest. But, however, the latter of these (Rom. 1, 20, 21) has been applied by some only to the glorious

---

[11] 'Prima omnibus hominibus exposita est et quodammodo Naturalis quae se sponte exerit in omnibus adultis sana mente praeditis. Hi enim partim ex communibus principiis sibi inditis, partim ex visibilibus Dei operibus rationcinando colligunt, Deum esse, Psalm 19, 1, 2. Rom. 1. 20, 21. Altera eorum quibus Deus se paulo familiarius exponit propria est quam in verbo ipsius, h.e. S. Scriptura, expressam videmus. Psalm 147., 19, 20. Heb. 1, 1. Postremo plane singularis est qua solos eos dignatur quos jam propius sibi conjunxit quibus nimirum per Spiritum sanctum se revelat, ita ut mentes eorum certissima quadam plerophoria compleat. 2 Cor. 1, 21. 22. 1 John 2, 20.' (Vorstius, *De Deo*, p. 3.)

[12] See above, pp. 35-43.

[13] 'Naturalis cognitio Dei ... quae se in adultis sana mente praeditis sponte naturae exerit.' (Piscator, *Aphorismi*, p. 11.)

[14] 'Acquisita ... per institutionem tum humanam seu philosophicam, ex consideratione operum Dei ratiocinando deductam.' (*Ibid.*, p. 12.)

[15] 'Divinam ex verbo scilicet Dei scripto haustam.' (*Ibid.*)

[16] 'Necesse est autem accedere ex verbo cognitionem Dei ut redemptoris eamque cum filiali fiducia conjuctam.' (*Ibid.*, p. 13.)

deeds of Christ and the apostles by which the Gospel teaching was confirmed; not as customarily referring to the universal works of the first creation.'[17]

As indicated, Vorstius continues to draw from Piscator's *Aphorisms*, but with important modifications. Thus of the first means of the knowledge of God he writes:

> 'That is either clearly philosophical which can be called in some way natural, drawn indeed from the principles known by nature, through the discursive mental faculties, by the diligent contemplation of the works of God, and this way is rough, dark and narrow: or truly theological, that is perceived from God's word. Then this again is either bare and merely historical, ... or salvific and joined with the feeling of piety ... and this finally deserves to be called the true and solid knowledge of God in this age.'[18]

Vorstius returns to Socinus's arguments a little later in support of a major change which has taken place since the delivery of his original disputation:

> 'We do not consider that there is any innate knowledge of God in us: since, strictly speaking, no awareness of any matter appears to be inborn in man; ... For in other passages a sure idea of the deity is attributed to faith, not to nature, Heb. 11, 6. And Holy Scripture attests elsewhere that there are those who deny that there is a God, Psalm 10, 4 and 14, 1 ... and again entire nations are to be found who appear to have no notion of the deity, as writers on the affairs of the Indies openly attest about the Brazilians and other peoples of the new world. Indeed things which are simply natural ought to be necessary and the same for all men. It is very far from being the case that the knowledge of divine providence in relation to the world and the human race in particular is innate by human nature, indeed both Epicurus and Aristotle and other outstanding philosophers clearly lacked it.'[19]

---

[17] 'Horum primum est operatio externa, puta creatio coeli et terra, etc. Unde potentia et divinitas ipsius aliquo modo perspici possunt: quemadmodum duo prima Scripturae loca testantur, Sed tamen horum posterior (Rom. 1, 20, 21) a nonnulis ad gloriosa tantum Christi et Apostolorum facta, quibus Euangelii doctrina confirmata fuit; non ad universa opera primae creationis, referri solet.' (Vorstius, *De Deo*, pp. 126-7.) Cf. Vorstius's formal commentary on this passage, 'τοις ποιημασι. Intelligit omnia ea, quae tum a Christo, tum ab Apostolis facta fuerunt ad Evangelii confirmationem.' (*Commentarius in omnes Epistolas Apostolicas*, 1631, p. 6.)

[18] 'Illa vel plane philosophica est, quae et Naturalis aliquo modo dici potest, hausta nimirum ex principiis Natura notis, per discursum mentis opera Dei studiose contemplantis, eaque valde rudis, obscura et angusta est: vel vere Theologica, nempe ex Dei verbo percepta. Tum haec rursus vel nuda et mere historica est, ... vel salvifica et cum pietatis affectu conjuncta ... At que haec demum vera et solida Dei cognitio in hoc seculo dici meretur.' (Vorstius, *De Deo*, pp. 127-8.) Cf. Piscator, 'VII. Iam notitia Dei creatoris quae acquiritur ex verbo Dei, aut nuda est, aut cum affectu pietatis. VIII ... Atque haec demum vera et salutaris cognitio Dei dici meretur, qua scilicet Deus a nobis et ut creator, et ut redemptor cognitus recte a nobis colitur.' (*Aphorismi*, pp. 12-13.)

[19] 'Non existimamus innatam esse nobis aliquem Dei notitiam: quum proprie loquendo nullius rei cognitio homini videatur innasci; ... Nam alioqui firma divinitatis opinio fidei

However, we must note that Vorstius only includes this last objection amongst those to be directed against the innate idea, whilst Socinus had used it to deny that any knowledge of God can be derived from a consideration of the natural order. For Vorstius only goes halfway with Socinus and wishes to retain this latter means:

> 'It remains, therefore, that this knowledge is termed natural to this extent that man has natural means of assistance within and around him by which if he uses these aright and can rise to them by reasoning, he can prove sufficiently well for himself and for others that there is a God.'[20]

From this it appears that, although Vorstius is content to make use of Socinus's exegesis and arguments to back his position, the real motive for his rejection of the innate idea is not theological as it was for the latter, but philosophical. Indeed, Vorstius indicates as much in the defence of his *De Deo* which he published soon after his arrival in Holland, where his first chapter entitled, 'Whether and to what extent any natural knowledge of God is given',[21] concludes thus,

> 'And this is enough about the first article which ought soberly to be seen as philosophical rather than theological since it treats not unintelligibly of the very principles of human nature and the natural order and of the means of knowing God from the very foundations of physics.'[22]

and ends with a quotation from J. C. Scaliger's *Exercitationes Exotericae De Subtiltate* and a reference to the second chapter of the fourth book of Timpler's *Metaphysics*.[23]

---

tribuitur, non naturae, Heb. 11, 6. Et alibi S. littera testantur, quosdam esse qui Deum esse negent, Psal. 10, 4 et 14, 1. ... et etiamnum integras nationes inveniri quae nullam divinitatis opinionem habere videntur sicut de Brasilianis et quibusdam aliis novi orbis populis, scriptores rerum Indicarum aperte testantur. Quae vero simpliciter naturalia sunt, etiam necessaria et apud omnes aequalia esse oportet. Tantum abest, ut cognitio divinae providentiae circa mundum et praecipue circa genus humanum per naturam homini sit innata quippe qua et Epicurus et Aristoteles et alii praestantes philosophi plane caruerint.' (Vorstius, *De Deo*, pp. 128-9.)

[20] 'Restat igitur, ut eatenus tantum Naturalis haec cognitio dicatur, quatenus homo naturalia in se et circum se praesidia habet quibus si recte utatur, eousque ratiocinando assurgere potest, ut Deum esse et sibi ipsi et aliis quantum satis est demonstrare, possit.' (*Ibid.*, p. 129.)

[21] 'An et quatenus aliqua detur naturalis Dei cognitio.' *Apologetica Exegesis sive Plenior Declaratio Locorum aliquot ex libro ejusdem de Deo ... excerpta, eique pro erroneis imposita*, Leiden, 1611, pp. 1-6.

[22] 'Atque haec de primo Articulo sufficiant: qui sane philosophicus potius quam theologicus videri debet: quum de ipsis Naturae humanae principiis deque naturali ordine et modo Deum cognoscendi ex ipsis Physicae fundamentis non obscure disserat.' (*Ibid.*, p. 5.)

[23] 'Qui plura hic desiderat, adeat. Metaphys. M. Timpleri lib. 4. cap. 2. quaest. 3.' (*Ibid.*, p. 6.)

In our discussion of Melanchthon we noted that a synthesis between Ciceronian Stoicism and Aristotelianism provided the basis for his approach to the question of the natural knowledge of God and the enterprise of constructing arguments for His existence.[24] However, Melanchthon's Aristotelianism was not that of Aristotle himself and when, under the pressure generated by the humanist concern to return 'ad fontes', philosophers increasingly turned away from the various compendia hitherto in use to the original works,[25] the former's interpretation was bound to be challenged.

> 'A salient aspect of Melanchthon's teaching was his doctrine of innate principles, particularly moral principles, and of the innate character of the idea of God, both of which are intuited by means of the "lumen naturale". This doctrine was opposed to the Aristotelian view of the mind as a "tabula rasa".

So writes F. C. Copleston[26] and we can scarcely be surprised to discover philosophers reasserting Peripatetic anti-innatism. Thus Vorstius's Steinfurt colleague Clemens Timpler, whom we have already encountered as the source of many of the arguments for God's existence employed by Polyander,[27] following no doubt the lead of J. C. Scaliger,[28] answers the question, 'whether the knowledge of God's existence is innate in man', in the negative with a direct appeal to the authority of Aristotle:

> 'The negative of that thesis is true. For the action which makes something 'innate' in man is the moment of a man's conception in his mother's womb. Yet already he is so very far from being a man, whether as an infant hitherto enclosed in his mother's womb or delivered into the light, that, through the weakness of his reason, he understands nothing even of the name by which God is called in his mother tongue until with progress in age the use of reason is yielded through nature itself. Moreover, all human reasoning and knowledge proceeds naturally from its first origin in the senses, as Aristotle proves elsewhere and in the last chapter of book 2 of the Posterior Analytic.'[29]

---

[24] See above pp. 31-3.

[25] An example of this attitude is provided by the incident at Leiden in 1582 when six students complained to the Senate about the use of such handbooks in the teaching of physics and logic. 'Nam inter compendiarios istos, ante paucissimos, aut nullos, qui non ab Aristotelis mente, adeoque ab ipsa veritate deflexerint, alii quidem magis alii minus.' The Senate responded by endorsing the students' plea for the study of the authentic Aristotle. (See Dibon, *op. cit.*, pp. 12-14.)

[26] F. C. Copleston, *A History of Philosophy*, Vol. III, London, 1953, p. 227.

[27] See above, pp. 159-60.

[28] Julius Caesar Scaliger (1484-1558). See, W. Hall Jr. 'The Life of Julius Caesar Scaliger (1484-1558)', *Transactions of the American Philosophical Society*, N.S. 40, 1950, pp. 85-170. Scaliger's *Exercitationes Exotericae de subtilitate*, first published at Paris in 1557, continued to be widely read throughout the seventeenth century. There were at least eleven reprints of the work between 1576 and 1665.

[29] 'Thesis illius negativa est vera. Id enim proprie dicitur actu innatum esse homini quod

Timpler evidently realized that he was here challenging Melanchthon for the first objection he considers against his rejection of the innate idea is the very point which lay at the heart of the latter's innatism, his understanding of the natural law,

> 'We know the dictates of the natural law as innate knowledge. And the law of nature reiterates that there is a God. Therefore its knowledge is innate in us. The reason for the proposition is because, as Paul teaches in Romans 2, 15 the natural law is inscribed on the hearts of all peoples. The assumption is proved because this firm opinion is agreed among all peoples that there is a God. In every thing, however, the agreement of all peoples must be considered as the natural law, as M. Brutus says, book 1, Tuscul, question 2.'[30]

In response Timpler advances the claims of right reason as the essential factor in the operation of the natural law in terms reminiscent of the Thomist tradition which Suarez was so shortly to re-emphasize in his own fashion in the *De Legibus ac Deo Legislatore* (1612):

> 'To objection 1 I reply by denying the proposition: for the law of nature is nothing other than right reason, or at least the command of right reason. Right reason, however, has no place in children who are not yet able to grasp and understand what right reason dictates. Therefore the knowledge of what the natural law dictates is not innate in infants.'[31]

Interestingly enough Timpler defends his position not only against the upholders of the innate idea but also, on the other hand, against those who denied the possibility of any natural knowledge of God. Thus the last two objections he considers are essentially those of Socinus which were evidently current before their publication in the latter's *Praelectiones*:

---

simul ac homo in utero matris est genitus, cepit ipsi in esse. Iam autem tantum abest ut homo infans sive in utero matris adjuc conclusus; sive in lucem editus, statim actu cognoscat Deum esse, ut neque vocabulum ipsum quo Deus in sua lingua materna nominatur ob rationis infirmitatem intelligat donec progressu aetatis usus rationis per naturam ipsi concedatur. Praeterea omnis intellectio et cognitio humana naturaliter primam suam originem ducit a sensu: quemadmodum id Aristoteles tum alibi, tum lib. 2 poster. analyt. cap. ultimo demonstrat.' (*Metaphysicae Systema Methodicum*, Steinfurt, 1604, p. 389.)

[30] 'Quod lex naturae dictitat eius cognitio nobis est innata. Atqui Deum esse lex naturae dictitat. Ergo eius cognitio nobis est innata. Propositionis ratio est quia ut Paulus docet 2. capite Rom. v. 15. lex naturae omnium gentium cordibus est inscripta. Assumptio probatur, quia inter omnes gentes firma constat haec sententia, esse Deum. Omni autem in re omnium gentium consensio lex naturae est putanda, ut ait M. Brutus lib. 1. Tuscul. quaest. 2.' (*Ibid.*, pp. 392-3.)

[31] 'Ad 1. objectionem respondeo per inficiationem propositionis: lex enim naturae nihil aliud est quam recta ratio, aut jussum saltem rectae rationis. Recta autem ratio non habet locum in infantibus, quippe qui nondum capere ac intelligere possunt quid recta ratio dictitet. Propterea neque cognitio eius quam lex naturae dictitat in infantibus est innata.' (*Ibid.*, p. 393.)

> '4. No dogma of faith is known to man from natural principles. That there is a God is certainly a dogma of faith. Therefore it is not known to man from natural principles. 5. If it were known to man from natural principles that there is a God, no man would be found who, using reason aright, could either deny that there is a God or at least doubt it. But in times' past there have been several who have been atheists enough to deny or doubt that there is a God, e.g. Pythagoras, Melius the Poet, Theodorus Cyrenaicus and others, as Cicero records in the opening part of book 1 on the Nature of the Gods. Therefore, that there is a God is not known to man from natural principles.'[32]

Timpler's reply to the first of these indicates an openly Thomistic view of the relation of nature and grace:

> 'I reply to 4 by denying the proposition. For it can happen that there can be one and the same dogma both of faith and of nature, which is consequently also known naturally. Nor is there any disharmony between the book of nature and of scripture, but rather the highest agreement. From this it is rightly said that the book of nature leads man to the book of scripture. And Thomas in the Summa Theologiae, question 2, article 2, says; faith presupposes natural knowledge, as grace does nature.'[33]

Here, of course, we encounter a longstanding identity of view with his theological colleague Vorstius whose appendix to the original disputation on the existence of God, headed, 'On the use of human reason in theological matters', stated as its first point:

> 'The doctrines of the Christian faith are not contrary to right reason: there is no reason for any of them to be outside the scope of natural comprehension. For grace does not destroy nature, but perfects and presupposes it; nor does divine revelation extinguish the light of reason, but enlightens it and leads it from darkness and weakness to clarity and greatness.'[34]

---

[32] '4. Nullum dogma fidei ex naturalibus principiis non est homini notum. At qui esse Deum est dogma fidei. Ergo ex naturalibus principiis non est homini notum. 5. Si ex naturalibus principiis homini esset notum Deum esse nullius hominum ratione recte utentium reperiretatur qui Deum esse aut negaret aut saltem dubitaret. Sed fuerunt olim nonnulli qui ita fuerunt ἄθεοι ut Deum esse vel negaverint vel dubitarint, v.g. Pythagoras, Melius Poeta, Theodorus Cyrenaicus et alii, quemadmodum Cicero horum mentionem facit in principio lib. 1. de natura Deorum. Ergo ex naturalibus principiis homini notum non est, esse Deum.' (*Ibid.*)

[33] 'Ad 4 respondeo per inficiationem propositionis. Fieri enim potest ut unum et idem sit dogma fidei et dogma naturae et per consequens etiam naturaliter notam. Neque dissensio est inter librum naturae et scripturae, sed potius summa consensio. Hinc recte dicitur librum naturae deducere hominem ad librum scripturae. Et Thomas in summa Theolog. quaest. 2 art. 2 ait; fidem praesupponere cognitionem naturalem sicut gratia naturam.' (*Ibid.*, p. 394.)

[34] 'De Usu Rationis humanae in rebus Theologicis', 'Dogmata Christianae fidei Rectae Rationi contraria non sunt: licet illorum nonnulla captum istius naturalem excedant. Non enim Gratia Naturam destruit sed perficit ac praesupponit: nec divina revelatio lumen rationis extinguit, sed illustrat atque ex obscuro et exiguo clarum magnumque efficit.' (Vorstius, *De Deo*, pp. 8-9.)

In view of the common ground shared by the two Steinfurt professors it is hardly surprising that the theologian's reaction to Socinus should have taken the form that it did.

However, once the spotlight of suspicious orthodoxy was turned upon Vorstius when the issue of his appointment to Leiden as Arminius's successor arose,[35] sufficient affinities to Socinus were obvious as to bring about a growing storm of protest. We have already referred to Vorstius's response to this criticism, his *Apologetica Exegesis*. Just how justified is his contention therein expressed that the question of the innate idea was really philosophical is amply borne out by his explanation of his own view:

> 'However, no act of that kind which involves the use of reason or functions actively (as is the case with the one with which we are dealing here), for example understanding or intellectual activity (or again no moral act) is, properly speaking, innate in us. Nevertheless the faculties for these acts, together with their organs and certain other adjuncts, are innate in us from the outset. Indeed, these acts necessarily require, from the outset, not only appropriate sense organs, but also a rational exercise of them, as can be seen both from the very constitution of human nature and continuing general experience and also from the received teaching of Aristotle, book 2, Posteria Analytic final chapter, where he teaches that all knowledge arises from the senses.'[36]

Earlier in this same first chapter, Vorstius had stressed that he was not denying the existence of a natural knowledge of God in man, but merely trying to define it with proper regard for philosophical realities:

> 'Wherefore there can be no just cause for reproof, especially since I do not simply deny that there is some natural knowledge of God in us; but this should be understood as a more indirect and implicit consequence for the sake of specific terminology, if only the reader will understand it in the same sense as I describe it.'[37]

One reader who was in no way prepared to understand Vorstius in anything but the most unfavourable light was Festus Hommius, whose

---

[35] See A. W. Harrison, *The Beginnings of Arminianism to the Synod of Dort*, London, 1926, pp. 165-89.

[36] 'Nullus autem actus ejusmodi qui usum rationis includit aut praeexigit (qualis hic ipse est de quo nunc agimus) puta intellectio, sive actus intellectualis (nullus item actus moralis) proprie loquendo nobis innascitur: tametsi facultates horum actuum, una cum suis organis et aliis quibusdam adminiculis, inde ab initio nobis innatae sunt. Equidem actus isti non modo expedita sensuum organa sed et rationale eorundem exercitium necessario praerequirunt: uti notum est, tum ex ipsa humanae naturae constitutione ac generali perpetuaque experientia, tum ex doctrina Aristotelis, hactenus ubique recepta, lib. 2. Poster. Analyt. cap. ult. ubi cognitionem omnem a sensu oriri docet.' (Vorstius, *Apologetica Exegesis*, p. 2.)

[37] 'Quare nec jure hic quidquam reprehendi potest: praesertim quum non simpliciter a me negetur quandam in nobis esse naturalem Dei cognitionem: sed haec potius et quo ad vocabulum et quo ad rem ipsam, ultro concedatur: si modo talis a lectoribus intelligitur qualis hoc ipso loco a me describitur.' (*Ibid.*, pp. 1-2.)

*Specimen Controversiarium Belgicarum*, as we saw in our study of the Belgic Confession, ignored all the former's qualifications of his view and roundly identified it with that of Socinus on the issue of the natural knowledge of God, declaring in connection with the second article of the formulary, 'It seems to be taught against this article that there cannot be any knowledge of God at all without supernatural revelation.'[38]

Hommius's selections from Vorstius are predictable enough and include the latter's denial of the innate idea of God from his notes to the *De Deo* disputation and also his wholesale adoption of the Socinian exegesis of Romans 1, 20 as it appeared from his comments on the passage which much later appeared in the posthumously published commentary on that epistle.[39] In his reply to the *Specimen*, Vorstius, understandably complains at what is evidently Hommius's willful overlooking of his support for the acquired natural knowledge of God. When, however, he takes up the matter of the exegesis, his defence is less convincing since there is no disputing the identity of view with Socinus here and, in the instance of his strained exegesis[40] in particular, his appeal to the adage, 'attention ought to be paid not to who said anything but to what is said',[41] will scarcely suffice.

In defending his rejection of the innate idea of God it is interesting that Vorstius makes no attempt to urge in his own favour the fact that the actual text of the second article of the Belgic Confession has itself nothing to say about this means to the natural knowledge of God, contenting itself with that obtainable from a consideration of the creation and governance of the world. We have noted the desperately contrived manner in which Maresius in his commentary on the Confession seeks to read in such a reference to the innate idea at this point.[42] Perhaps it is a mark of the confidence with which Reformed orthodoxy held this doctrine that Hommius

---

[38] 'Contra hunc Articulum doceri videtur. Nullam omnino haberi posse notitiam de Deo sine supernaturali revelatione.' (Hommius, *op. cit.*, Leiden, 1618, p. 9.) See above, p. 111.

[39] *Commentarius in Omnes Epistolas Apostolicas ... olim in Gymnasi Steinfurtensi publicis Praelectionis propositus*, 1631.

[40] One example given by Hommius is enough to establish both the dependence upon Socinus and the oddity of the interpretation. 'Schol. ad Romans I, 20', runs thus, 'τα γαρ ἀορατα.) Haec verba prolepsin continent, quae Apostolus concedit hactenus quodammodo invisibilia et occulta fuisse, quae nunc in Evangelio clare revelata sunt. Itaque comma ponendum est post nomen κοσμος, et prima ista verba sic interpretanda sunt. Quae enim ipsius invisibilia fuerunt inde a creatione mundi. Phrasin prorsus similem Matth. 13.35.' (*Specimen*, p. 10, Vorstius, *Commentarius*, p. 6.)

[41] 'Non quis discat, sed quid dicatur, attendendum esse.' (*Apologetica Responsio ad ea Omnia quae Festus Hommius nominatim ipsi nuper impegit in eo libro, cui titulum fecit, Specimen Controversiarum Belgicarum*, n.p., 1618, p. 19.)

[42] See above, p. 116.

could so unblushingly condemn Vorstius's rejection of it as being contrary to an article of the Confession which makes no mention of it.

Hommius adds just one more brief extract from another suspect source.

> 'From Simon Episcopius, A Private Disputation concerning the Knowledge of God, corollary 2, 3. Whether the knowledge of God is natural? We make a distinction. Whether the knowledge of God which is obtained from natural is natural? We deny.'[43]

To this Episcopius[44] immediately responded with the ironically entitled, *Optima Fides Festi Hommii*,[45] in which, by placing the relevant passages in parallel columns with their genuine versions, he showed how Hommius had misquoted him on four occasions. The first of these is the Corollary 3 quoted above where for 'natural' ('naturalis') we should read 'saving' ('salutaris'). In a brief note Episcopius points out that Hommius's version is evidently stupid and that a study of the theses to which it was attached would have made its proper sense unmistakable.

Hommius had obtained his version of Episcopius's private disputations from copies taken down by the latter's pupils. He published the full text of some thirty-three of these in the same year as his *Specimen*,[46] and in a Preface defended himself against Episcopius's rejoinder. He acknowledged that in the context of the Corollary 'salutaris' would make more sense than 'naturalis' but nonetheless insists that Episcopius must have meant the latter.[47] Of the four reasons he gives for this insistence the chief is the third in which he first objects that to the corollary 'Whether the knowledge of God is natural: Episcopius does not reply affirmatively, as do all the

---

[43] 'Sim. Episcopio, Disp. priv. de cognit. Dei, corol. 2.3. An Cognitio Dei sit naturalis? Distinguimus. An cognitio Dei, quae ex natura habetur, sit *naturalis*? *Negamus*.' *Specimen*, pp. 10-11.

[44] (1583-1643). Professor of Theology at Leiden from 1612 and chief spokesman of the Remonstrants at the Synod of Dort, Episcopius was dismissed from his chair and exiled in consequence of that Synod's decision. He was one of the leaders of the group which set up the Remonstrant Brotherhood in 1619 and the author of their *Confessio* published in 1622. After several years' exile in France, Episcopius returned to Holland and eventually became the first Professor of Theology at the Remonstrant Seminary founded in Amsterdam in 1634, a position which he held until his death. (see *BWPGN* II, pp. 749-64.) The bulk of the works published during Episcopius's life-time are devoted to the exposition and defence of the Remonstrant position in the face of continuous and often virulent attack. His greatest and most influential writings only appeared posthumously in the two volumes of his *Opera Theologica*, the first of which edited by De Courcelles, was published at Amsterdam in 1650, and the second, edited by Philip Van Limborch and Arnold Poelenburg, at Rotterdam in 1665.

[45] See *Op. Theol.* Pars Altera, II, pp. 461-62.

[46] *Collegium Disputationum Theologicarum in Academia Leydensi privatim institutarum a M. Simone Episcopio.*, Dordrecht, 1618.

[47] *Collegium*, p. *3$^{r}$.

orthodox, but by a distinction.'[48] As Hommius then indicates we must refer to the theses themselves to see what is meant by this distinction and so he quotes the relevant passage which is, in fact, Thesis VII.[49] He grants that Episcopius does indeed allow for some natural knowledge of God:

> 'There are indeed in man "common ideas known by nature and various arguments taken from natural means" which are the principles from which the knowledge of God can be derived,'[50]

but he notes that Episcopius evidently feels obliged to add supernatural sources of revelation, 'but "supernatural and divine revelations or their continual transmission by perpetual succession" must be added to these to produce the knowledge of God.'[51] In this event, argues Hommius, it is no longer nugatory to pose his version of Corollary 3, 'Whether the knowledge of God which is from nature is natural?' since the disctinction just drawn by Episcopius makes this a fair question. Furthermore, because the latter has felt it necessary to bring in supernatural sources of revelation, it is evident that for him our knowledge of God is not natural. Hommius concludes that Episcopius's answer to this corollary indicates his true position, 'and so he thus replies to it with the view of Vorstius and the Socinians, "We deny." '[52]

Episcopius replied immediately in his *Brevis Responsio*.[53] To Hommius's main argument on this issue he first points out that to make a distinction is not the same as a denial and he goes on to defend his use of the former. For he says, if we are to refute the plausible arguments of the Socinians we must explain what we mean by calling the knowledge of God 'natural' since it is evident that many men, including not a few philosophers, deny not only knowledge of God but even His very existence.[54] We shall return

---

[48] 'An sit cognitio Dei naturalis?' Episcopius 'non respondet Affirmative, uti omnes orthodoxi, sed per distinctionem.' (*Ibid.*, p. *3$^v$.)

[49] Episcopius's Disputation 'De Cognitione Dei' was not actually published until 1646 when it appeared as the 3rd Disputation in the 2nd Part (pp. 151-153) of his *Disputationes Theologicae Tripartitae*. It is reprinted in *Op. Theol.* Pars Altera, II, pp. 412-413, whence we learn that this series of private disputations was originally delivered between November, 1612 and December, 1615 (*Ibid.*, p. 411.)

[50] 'Esse quidem in homine "notiones communes natura notas, et argumenta varia ex media natura petita" quae principia sint ex quibus cognitio Dei derivari possit.' (*Collegium*, p. *3$^v$.)

[51] 'Sed ad ingenerandam Dei cognitionem iis accedere debere "supernaturales et Divinas revelationes, aut earum perpetuo successu continuatas traditiones." ' (*Collegium*, p. *3$^v$.)

[52] 'Atque ita ex Vorstii et Socinianorum sententia ei respondetur, "Negamus." ' (*Ibid.*)

[53] *Brevis Responsio ad Praefationem, quam edito a se Disputationum privatarum M. Simonis Episcopii Collegio praefixit, et in qua optimam suam fidem adstruere conatur Festus Hommius*, (*Op. Theol.* Pars Altera, II, pp. 463-66.)

[54] *Brevis Responsio, op. cit.*, p. 464.

to this argument. Furthermore, he refers to Thesis VI of his Disputation where

> 'Episcopius clearly says that with Scripture he presupposes the knowledge of God, namely as something learned beforehand, outside and before all scripture and further outside even of supernatural revelation; yea rather it can and should be derived from indubitable principles.'[55]

There was no further published response from Hommius and, although, as we shall see, the accusation continued to be levelled at the Remonstrants, this is a good point at which to make a preliminary assessment. First, on the specific point at issue, there can be no doubt that Hommius's version misquoted Episcopius and that 'salutaris' and not 'naturalis' is the original reading. Furthermore there must be the strongest suspicion that Hommius was fully aware of this. However, it must still be asked, granted that the latter and all such opponents of the Remonstrants were determined thus to scent out Socinianism, does Episcopius here give them any grounds for this charge?

The argument from silence must always be used with care but one can hardly help noting with another celebrated Contra-Remonstrant[56] that Episcopius, at any rate at this stage, appears to have nothing to say about Natural Theology. The Disputation On the Knowledge of God is the only clue to his thinking on this subject and we may fairly note that at crucial points it is open to the kind of misunderstanding displayed by Hommius. Thus, in defending himself against the latter, Episcopius, as we saw above, claimed that the statement in his sixth thesis that the knowledge of God's existence 'is presupposed by us in Scripture and can be derived from indubitable principles'[57] established the natural knowledge of God beyond question. However, when in the following thesis he sets out these principles it immediately appears that they are only partly natural and evidently comprise supernatural revelations as well.

> 'Moreover, these principles are partly certain axioms and common ideas known by nature itself, and at the same time the conclusions involved in them; partly supernatural and divine revelations and their continued

[55] 'Diserte dicat Episcopius, a se cognitionem Dei cum Scriptura praesupponi, tanquam scilicet aliquid praecognitum, citra et ante Scripturam omnem; ac proinde citra supernaturalem etiam revelationem; quin imo, ex principiis indubitatis etiam derivari posse ac derivandam esse.' (*Ibid.*)

[56] Gisbertus Voetius *Selectorum Disputationum Theologicarum*, I, Utrecht, 1648, p. 171, '... Episcopii Theses (ubi nihil de Theologia Naturalis).'

[57] 'A nobis cum Scriptura praesupponi, et ex principiis indubitatis derivari posse.' (*Op. Theol.*, Pars Alt. II, p. 413.)

> transmission by perpetual succession, partly various argument drawn both from natural means and from actions far surpassing the power of nature.'[58]

Thus despite Episcopius's subsequent defence that the knowledge of God's existence presupposed by Scripture is 'outside supernatural revelation', Hommius had been able to interpret the matter otherwise on the basis of the phraseology of thesis VII with its reference to supernatural revelations. No doubt there was a strong element of a wilfulness to understand his opponent thus, but Episcopius cannot be absolved from a certain ambiguity of expression at this point.

Our understanding of Episcopius's meaining here is aided by the recognition that this disputation, 'On the Knowledge of God', is largely based on that Private Disputation of his late master Arminius, 'On the Object of the Christian Religion; and, first, about God, the primary object and what God is', which we examined in our study of the latter's use of the arguments for God's existence.[59] Episcopius takes the three points of his third thesis from Arminius's second thesis. Thus the latter's

> 'In God, who is the primary object of the Christian religion, three things have to be considered in order. First, the nature of God, of which the excellence and goodness is such that religion can honourably and usefully be performed to it. Secondly, God's actions, on account of which religion ought to be performed to it. Thirdly, God's will, by which He wills religion to be performed to Himself and that he who performs it be rewarded; and, on the contrary, that he who neglects it be punished.'[60]

becomes in the former,

> 'The knowledge of God as the primary object is to be divided (1) into the knowledge of the divine nature, (2) into the knowledge of the divine works, (3) into the knowledge of the divine will.'[61]

---

[58] 'Principia autem illa, partim sunt axiomata quaedam, communesque notiones natura ipsa notae, simul atque termini earum attenduntur; partim supernaturales divinaeque revelationes, et earum perpetua successione continuatae traditiones; partim argumenta varia ex media tum natura, tum actionibus longe naturae vim excedentibus, petita.' (*Ibid.*)

[59] 'De Objecto Christianae Religionis, et primo de Deo primario ejus objecto, et quod Deus sit.' (Arminius, *Disputationes*, pp. 23-6.) See above, pp. 149-57.

[60] 'In Deo primario Christianae Religionis objecto tria ordine consideranda. Primo, Natura Dei, cujus ea est excellentia et bonitas, ut Religio illi honeste et utiliter praestari possit. Secundo, Actiones Dei propter quas illi Religio praestari debeat. Tertio, Voluntas Dei, qua vult sibi praestari Religionem, et praestantem ipse remunerari, contraque negligentem punire.' (Arminius, *Disputationes*, p. 23.) Episcopius repeated this formulation at the beginning of the 'De Deo' section of the *Institutiones Theologicae*, Book IV, Section II, cp. I, 'De cognitione Dei in genere'. (*Op. Theol.*, Vol. I, Pt. I, p. 280.)

[61] 'Cognitio Dei ut primarii objecti consistit intribui: 1. in notitia naturae divinae, 2. in notitia operum divinorum, 3. in notitia divinae voluntatis ...' (Episcopius, *Op. Theol.* 'Pars Altera', II, p. 412.)

In this third thesis Arminius moves on immediately to raise the question of God's existence:

> 'To every treatise on the nature of God, must be prefixed this primary and chief axiom of all religion; there is a God: without this every enquiry into God's nature is vain, for, if it had no existence, religion would be a mere phantasm of human conception.'[62]

This prefaces the demonstration of the divine existence which he gives in the remaining eleven theses of the disputation. Episcopius takes up this preface in his own thesis VI, 'However, it is useless to know of what sort the divine nature is unless it is first of all certain that there is some divine nature';[63] whilst the contentious thesis VII, as we will now show, represents a compressed summary of Arminius's proofs of God's existence.

The first of these are certain theoretical axioms,

> 'That there is a God ... can be demonstrated by various arguments; and first by certain theoretical axioms which, because when the terms in which they are expressed have once been understood, they are known to be true, deserve to be called implanted ideas.'[64]

Arminius's theses V to VII, as we saw in our earlier chapter, give three such scholastic axioms, each of which provides the basis for a proof for God's existence, whilst the fourth axiom, supplied in thesis VIII, is the practical one, man's conscience, which leads him to conclude the existence of a supreme Judge of his actions. In Episcopius's summary all this becomes 'There are partly certain axioms and common ideas known by nature itself, and at the same time the terms involved in them.'[65]

Having presented his axioms, Arminius proceeds in the remainder of the disputation to outline six arguments ('argumenta') which we may fairly conclude Episcopius refers to as 'and finally various arguments' ('partim denique argumenta varia'), for the first two, the magnitude and order of nature (theses IX and X) are indeed 'drawn ... from natural means',

---

[62] 'Tractatui de natura Dei praemitti oportet Religionis omnis primum et summum axioma, Deum esse: sine quo inane est quicquid de natura Dei inquiritur, utpote quae nullam existentiam habens purum putum phantasma sit futura conceptus humani.' (Arminius, *Disputationes*, pp. 23-24.)

[63] 'Qualis autem natura divina sit cum frustra cognoscatur nisi primo certum sit esse aliquam naturam divinam.' (Episcopius, *Op. Theol.*, Pars Altera II, p. 413.)

[64] 'Deum esse ... tamen argumentis variis demonstrari potest; et primo ab axiomatis nonnullis theoreticis, quae propterea quod terminis tantum intellectis vera esse cognoscuntur, notionum insitarum nomine appellari merentur.' (Arminius, *Disputationes*, p. 24.)

[65] 'Partim sunt axiomata quaedam, communesque notiones natura ipsa notae, simul atque termini earum attenduntur.' (Episcopius, *Op. Theol.*, Pars Altera II, p. 413.)

('ex media...natura...petita'), whilst arguments seven to nine (theses XI-XIII) come under the category 'drawn from ... actions far surpassing the power of nature'; ('ex ... actionibus longe naturae vim excedentibus, petita'); a point which is expressly made by Arminius in relation to argument eight (thesis XII), 'from miracles ... the magnitude of which is so great as to cause them far to surpass the entire force and power of the created universe.'[66] In a sense, of course, arguments eight and nine, miracles and the fulfilment of 'the predictions of future and contingent things' ('praedictiones rerum futurarum et contingentium'), might be considered to be of supernatural rather than natural origin and, as we saw in our earlier chapter were so reclassified by Polyander in his 'De Deo' disputation.[67]

However, it is not to this reference that Hommius objects and even if he had realised that Arminius had provided the model for Episcopius's disputation it is doubtful that he would have cavilled at its orthodoxy had the latter contented himself with such a summary.[68] No, as we saw above, the phrase on which Hommius picked was the only one in Episcopius's thesis which does not summarize Arminius's arguments, 'partly supernatural and divine revelations and their continued transmission by perpetual succession.'[69] Moreover, it does not require an overly sensitive nose for heretical sources to note a distinct affinity here with the infamous Socinus. For we may recall that, in the already cited second chapter of his *Praelectiones Theologicae*, the latter had argued that the explanation for the widespread belief in God was not to be derived from Nature but from revelation and its continuing tradition.[70]

In the added light shed by our discovery of Arminius's disputation as Episcopius's model, we may conclude that whilst, on the one hand, the in-

---

[66] 'A miraculis ... quorum ea est magnitudo ut totam creati universi vim et potentiam longissime excedant.' (Arminius, *Disputationes*, p. 25.)

[67] See above, p. 161.

[68] In the very place in which he is objecting to that part of Episcopius's *Apologia* which pointed out the drawbacks of arguments for God's existence 'ex principiis Philosophicis deducuntur' (see above, p. 215). Gisbert Voetius expresses the orthodox approval of the earlier disputation, '... et Praeceptorem suum Arminium Disp. privat. 14, a th. 4 usque ad finem.' (*Selectones Disputationes Theologicae*, I, p. 170.)

[69] 'Partim supernaturales divinaeque revelationes, et earum perpetua successione continuatae traditiones.' (Episcopius, *Op. Theol.* Pars Altera II, p. 413. *Praelectiones Theologicae*, p. 3.) In fact, the immediate source of Episcopius's phrase may well be Vorstius's revised views on the 'Consensus omnium gentium' where, having rejected the innate idea of God, he writes that religious belief originates '... neque ex solis Naturae principiis; sed potius ex aliqua Dei patefactione inter homines inde ab initio mundi celebrata, et per traditionem continuam conservata.' (*De Deo*, p. 139.)

[70] See above, p. 202.

clusion of a new element in the form of the reference to supernatural revelation confirms Hommius's ability to sniff out the traces of Socinian affinities, yet, on the other, the fact that Episcopius has based himself on such an orthodox presentation of the arguments for God's existence indicates that even at this period, when he makes little or no direct reference to the topic, he is maintaining an essential hold on the validity of the natural knowledge of God.

Episcopius was the author of the Remonstrants' official confession[71] in which, strictly speaking, no attempt is made to demonstrate the existence of God. The first chapter is headed 'On Holy Scripture, and its authority, perfection and clarity' and only its first two sections are relevant to the former issue.

> '1. Whoever wishes to worship God aright and certainly and undoubtedly to obtain eternal salvation, must of necessity first of all believe that there is a God, and that He bounteously rewards those who seek Him (Heb. 11 v. 6).'[72]

Opponents were not slow to point out the kinship with Socinianism which the particular use of this text portrayed. Thus Nicolaus Bodecherus, himself a deserter from the Remonstrant cause, used this sentence to begin his *Sociniano-Remonstrantismus*,[73] a work in which he sought to demonstrate the affinities between the two heterodoxies by setting out their teaching in parallel columns. By the side of this opening of the Remonstrant Confession he placed a quotation from the first chapter of the Racovian Catechism, 'On the Knowledge of God',

> 'Who does not see that it is necessary for salvation to believe that there is a God? Since unless we believe that there is a God we cannot even believe that this way was handed on by Him. Hence the author to the Hebrews says: He who comes to God must believe that there is a God.'[74]

---

[71] *Confessio sive Declaratio Sententiae Pastorum, qui in foederato Belgio Remonstrantes vocantur, super praecipuis articulis Religionis Christianae*, 1622. The Dutch translation, *Verklaringhe van 't ghevoelen der Leeraren, die in de Gheunieerde Nederlanden Remonstranten worden ghenaemt, over de voornaemste Articulen der Christelyke Religie*, actually appeared in 1621 before the original Latin version.

[72] '1. Quisquis Deum rite colere, et aeternam salutatem certe atque indubie consequi vult, ante omnia ei necessum est, ut credat "Deum esse et praemia largiri quaerentibus ipsum" (Heb. 11 v. 6).' (*Confessio*, p. 1.)

[73] ... *Hoc est: Evidens demonstratio Remonstrantium in pluribus Confessionis partibus cum Socinianis sive reipsa, sive verbis, sive etiam Methodo consensus*, Leiden, 1624.

[74] 'Quis non videt, ad salutem esse necessarium credere Deum esse? Cum nisi crederemus Deum esse, ne viam quidem hanc ab eo esse traditam, credere possemus. Hinc etiam author ad Hebr. ait: Accedentem ad Deum credere opportet quod Deus sit.' (Bodecherus, *op. cit.*, p. 1.)

In his brief rejoinder to this work, *Bodecherus Ineptiens* (1624),[75] Episcopius does not deign to deal with this passage and his general defence is that, of course, there are many points on which the Remonstrants are in agreement with the Socinians but that this is equally true of the Contra-Remonstrants.

In 1626 the four professors of Theology at Leiden[76] published their *Censura* of the Remonstrants' Confession. They took note of the second section of Chapter I where it was stated:

> 'That there is a God and that He has at various times and in different ways spoken in past times to the fathers by the prophets, and that He has at last in latter times most fully declared and manifested His final will by His only begotten son, has been confirmed by so many great and mighty proofs, signs, wonders, mighty deeds or works, gifts or distributions of the Holy Spirit, and other wonderful effects, and certain events of several prophecies and testimonies of men worthy of belief, that anything more certain, more substantial and more complete to establish belief in it and to remove any just doubt cannot be given or justly required.'[77]

Their comment on this passage makes two points of relevance to our concern. The first:

> 'In this section the Remonstrants appear to confuse the question, "whether there is a God", with another, "Who and what He is". For the texts of Holy Scripture which they use here only indirectly prove "that there is a God ..."[78]

They then proceed to make the direct charge that by their silence on this issue the Remonstrants are effectively Socinian in their failure to assert the natural knowledge of God.

> 'Meanwhile, the other scriptural sayings, which Socinus in his *Praelectiones*, Ostorodius in his *Institutes*, and the other Socinians indiscriminately reject so as to remove man's natural knowledge of God, the Remonstrants here also by their silence cunningly ignore, namely those which expressly and directly show that there is a God: such as Psalm 19, Acts 14, Acts 17, and Romans 1

---

[75] *Op. Theol.*, Pars Alt. II, pp. 48-58.

[76] Johannes Polyander, André Rivet, Antonius Walaeus, Antonius Thysius. *Censura in Confessionem sive Declarationem Sententiae eorum qui in foederato Belgio Remonstrantes vocantur* ...

[77] 'Deum esse eumque multis vicibus, multisque modis, olim Patribus per Prophetas locutum esse; tandem vero postremis temporibus per unigenitum filium suum nobis ultimam voluntatem suam plenissime declarasse ac manifestasse ...; tot tantisque argumentis, signis, prodigiis, virtutibus, spiritus S. distributionibus, ac testimoniis hominum fide dignorum comprobatum est, ut ad fidem ei rei faciendam, et dubitationem omnem justam eximendam, certiora, solidiora, et perfectiora ulla dari, aut requiri jure nequeant.' (*Confessio*, p. 1.)

[78] 'In hac sectione Remonstrantes questionem, "An sit Deus", cum altera, "Quis et qualis sit", confundere videntur. Nam loca S. Scripturae, quibus hic utuntur tantummodo indirecte probant, "Quod sit Deus" ...' (*Censura*, p. 11.)

which are revealed from the works of creation and providence. From which all men furnished with a sound mind know that there is a God and that He is to be worshipped ...'[79]

In 1630 Episcopius replied in his *Apology for the Confession ... against the Censure of the Four Leiden Professors*.[80] He briefly dismisses the first of these objections as entirely missing the point.

> 'Indeed those texts are not adduced in order to prove either directly or indirectly that there is a God; not at all ... for they relate to the subject of the question not to the accepted presupposition ...'[81]

The second objection he deals with at greater length. First he explains that it was not the Remonstrants' intention in this section simply to prove that there is a God but also to show that He has revealed His will so that men may worship Him as He wishes. In fact they set out only to prove the latter directly for once this is done the former is thereby established. 'For when this has been demonstrated and proved, the former is at the same time proved and demonstrated'.[82] Episcopius then proceeds to argue that proofs of God's existence from natural principles are, so far as the matter is presented in the Confession, 'not only unnecessary, but even superfluous ...'[83] God's revelation of Himself in the Old and New Testaments is sufficient to prove His existence to all who are of sound mind. In comparison the other arguments are obscure and contentious, 'all others ... are weak and uncertain, at all events more laboured and beset with many controversies ...'.[84] In conclusion he indicates that the question of God's existence is held by the Confession to be among the 'praecognita' and he finishes by quoting one of the Censors, Thysius, who had expressed a similar sentiment in the *Synopsis purioris Theologiae*. In fact, a glance at the wider context of this quotation removes much of its force in

---

[79] 'Alia interim Scripturae dicta, quae Socinus in suis praelectionibus, Ostorodius in sua insitutione, aliique Sociani ad naturalem Dei cognitionem homini detrahendam passim rejiciunt, Remonstrantes hic quoque silentio suo astute dissimulant, ea, scilicet, quae Deum esse proprie ac directe ostendunt: cuismodi sunt, quae Psal. 19. Act 14. Act 17. et Rom. 1. ex operibus Creationis ac Providentiae producuntur. Unde omnes homines sana mente praediti intelligunt esse Deum, eumque colendum esse ...' (*Censura*, p. 11.)

[80] *'Apologia pro Confessione ... contra Censuram quatuor professorum Leidensium.'* (*Op. Theol.*, Pars Altera II, pp. 95-283.)

[81] 'Atqui loca ista non allegantur, ad probandum seu directe, seu indirecte, quod sit Deus; nihil minus; ... pertinent enim ad subjectum quaestionis, non ad praedicatum ...' (*Apologia*, fol. 25$^r$.)

[82] 'Hoc enim evicto ac probato, prius istud simul probatum atque evictum est.' (*Ibid.*)

[83] 'Non modo non necessarium, sed superfluum etiam ...' (*Ibid.*, fol. 25$^v$.)

[84] '... caetera omnia ... infirma atque incerta, saltem operosiora, et controversiis pluribus impedita ...' (*Ibid.*)

Episcopius's argument. For, having indeed said that the existence of God is not to be questioned in Theology since as a science it presupposes this as its subject, Thysius immediately goes on, at the very point at which Episcopius ceases to quote him, to say,

> 'yet on account of certain insane and more than diabolical blasphemies of the atheists who deny God ... we will demonstrate this by the two-fold evidence of nature and reason,'[85]

before devoting the next three paragraphs to that presentation of the traditional proofs for God's existence which we examined in chapter six.[86]

The conclusion at this stage must be that Episcopius has not succeeded in clearing himself of the charge that his lack of enthusiasm for the proofs of God's existence from natural sources appears to bring him into line with the similar views of Socinus. Thus, when the next work to set Remonstrant and Socinian teaching in parallel columns, thereby endeavouring to show their affinities, appeared,[87] it is hardly surprising that the very first heading under which it couples them together is 'On the Knowledge of God through nature. Argument: From the light of nature no one can know that there is a God.'[88] As the Remonstrant contribution here Peltius perpetuates Hommius's false version of Episcopius's corollary to his Private Disputation 'De Cognitione Dei'—the history of which we have already followed. The Socinian extracts are those to which, again we have seen, the four Leiden professors drew attention in their *Censura*, that is, Ostorodius's *Institutes*, cap. 1 and Socinus's *Praelectiones*, cap. 2. The debate appears to have reached a point at which it is merely repeating itself.[89] The impression must be that, although his opponents are doubtless misunderstanding, indeed at times, deliberately misrepresenting him, Episcopius has failed satisfactorily to clarify his position on this issue.

Episcopius's presentation of the arguments for the existence of God in Book I of his *Institutiones Theologicae* are best viewed against the background of the protracted controversy which we have just outlined. He begins this exercise in Chapter III and it is soon evident that the misunderstandings

---

[85] 'Tamen propter insanam et plus quam Diabolicam Atheorum quorundam blasphemiam Deum negantium ... duplici indicio, Naturae et Rationis, id demonstrabimus.' (*Synopsis*, p. 63.)

[86] See above, pp. 162-4.

[87] Johannes Peltius, *Harmonia Remonstrantium et Socinianorum*, Leiden, 1633.

[88] 'De Cognitione Dei per Naturam. Argumentum: Neminem ex luce naturae cognoscere posse, esse Deum.' (Peltius, *op. cit.*, p. 1.)

[89] In the Leiden professors' brief response to Episcopius's *Apologia, Specimen Calumniarum atque heterodoxarum opiniorum ex Remonstrantium Apologia excerptarum*, Leiden, 1630, the issue of the natural knowledge of God is passed over in silence.

which have hitherto prevailed are going to be removed. Thus, he acknowledges the objection that God's existence cannot be questioned since it is the very presupposition of all theology—a position which, as we saw above, he himself appeared to be arguing in the *Apologia*. Now, however, he proceeds to set this aside for precisely the same reason as did Thysius in that section of the *Synopsis* of which, as we noted, Episcopius had previously quoted only the first part; 'But, however, since we see that there are certain mortals so mad or impious that they not only doubt whether there is a God but dare openly and publicly to deny that there is a God ....'[90] In order to confute the atheists on the issue of God's existence Thysius as we saw, had outlined his intention, '... we will demonstrate this by the twofold evidence of nature and reason.'[91] Episcopius indicates, a significantly different method in which reason is to play the supreme role:

> '... I show by that method not only the defences that may be placed against so deadly an error, but even by which powerful arguments they may be convicted and brought back to a healthier mind, if only they are willing to be led by right reason and at the same time they do not obstinately refuse to listen.'[92]

Years earlier, in the *Apologia*,[93] in a passage the brevity of which made its relevance to his argument unclear, Episcopius had accused his critics of failing to distinguish accurately between the two questions;

> ' "Whether the idea of any deity is implanted or innate in man"; and "whether man can know that there is a God from what is called the book of nature or from natural principles." '[94]

These two questions are those of Clemens Timpler from that second chapter of the fourth book of his *Metaphysics* which we have already encountered more than once. In the latter's version they read, 'Whether the knowledge of the existence of God is innate ... whether it is known to

---

[90] 'Sed tamen quia videmus esse mortales quosdam adeo aut vecordes aut profanos, ut non dubitare modo am Deus sit, sed aperte ac palam negare audeant Deum esse ...' (*Op. Theol.*, I, p. 6.)

[91] '... duplici indicio, Naturae et Rationis, id demonstrabimus.' (*Synopsis*, p. 63.)

[92] '... ostendam, qua ratione non tantum muniti esse possitis contra tam capitalem errorem, sed etiam quibus argumentis eos convincere valeatis et ad saniorem mentem reducere, si ullo modo ratione recta duci velint, et animum simul ac frontem non obstinent.' (*Op. Theol. I*, p. 6.)

[93] Cf. also the point which we noted earlier in the *Brevis Responsio* where Episcopius contended that in order to refute the plausible Socinian arguments we must explain what we mean by calling the knowledge of God 'natural'. See above, p. 214.

[94] ' "An homini naturaliter insita seu innata sit divinitatis alicujus opinio"; Et, "An ex libro Naturae, qui vocatur, sive ex naturalibus principiis homo possit cognoscere Deum esse." ' (*Apologia*, fols. 25$^{r-v}$.)

man from natural principles that there is a God.'[95] Episcopius now presents them thus:

> 'However, two questions are possible when it is disputed whether there is a God. I. Whether there is naturally in man and his mind an implanted or innate idea of the deity? II. Whether there are certain principles in nature from which man, with the help of right and natural reason, is able to deduce this conclusion, that there is a God.'?[96]

He rejects the first of these for the same reason as Timpler:

> 'It hardly seems true to me. Since I believe that it is the condition of the human mind that not only may no idea be naturally impressed upon it but even that no use of reason can have a place in it except by word and instruction: to the extent that the mind of man deprived of those aids would remain simply as a bare writing tablet, and if not guided, would follow nature in the fashion of a beast.'[97]

However, it is evident that Episcopius has learned the lesson of the long series of misunderstandings to which this refusal had given rise, for, in firmly assenting to the second of the questions proposed, he immediately defends this affirmation against the objections of Socinus whose position his opponents had constantly asserted that he shared. 'As far as the second question is concerned, I see that there are those who deny this and claim that we can and ought to have that knowledge from revelation or tradition.'[98] Episcopius does not identify these objectors to Natural Theology[99] explicitly but their four reasons which he presents are the same four, set down virtually verbatim, advanced by Socinus in that second

---

[95] 'Utrum cognitio de Dei existentia homini sit innata ... utrum homini ex naturalibus principiis notum sit Deum esse.' (Timpler, *op. cit.*, p. 389.)

[96] 'Duo autem quaeri possunt, cum disputatur an sit Deus. I. Utrum homini ejusque animo naturaliter insita sive innata sit deitatis opinio? II. Utrum principia quaedam in natura sint, ex quibus homo rationis rectae et naturalis auxilio, conclusionem hanc deducere possit, quod sit Deus?' (*Op. Theol.*, I, p. 6.)

[97] 'Mihi id vix verisimile videtur. Quia credo istam esse conditionem animae humanae, ut non modo nulla ei notio naturalitur impressa sit, sed ut nullus etiam rationis usus in ea locum habere possit nisi per sermonem et institutionem: adeo ut hominis anima illis adminiculis destituta, veluti tabula rasa mansura sit, et non nisi sectura ductum naturae, bruti instar.' (*Ibid.*)

[98] 'Quod ad secundum quaesitum attinet, video esse quosdam qui id negant, et ex sola revelatione sive traditione scientiam istam haberi posse ac debere asserunt.' (*Ibid.*, p. 7.)

[99] This omission has confused at least one modern scholar, A. H. Haentjens, who, having noted Episcopius's rejection of the innate idea of God and contrasted this with Calvin's position, proceeds to identify the anonymous exponents of the view that the knowledge of God must be from revelation alone, against whom the former argues, not with Socinus but with the orthodox Calvinists. 'Het Calvinism dat Episcopius bestrijdt wil alleen van een geopenbaard Godsbegrip weten in afwijking van de *Institutio* zelve, die spreekt van een natuurlijke "notio Dei." ' (*Remonstrantsche en Calvinistische Dogmatiek*, Leiden, 1913, p. 15.)

chapter of his *Praelectiones Theologicae* to which we have already had frequent occasion to refer. At this point Episcopius merely says that he believes that these reasons are insufficient to undermine the validity of Natural Theology's proofs of God's existence and he promises to reply to them after his own presentation of these latter.

In fact Episcopius devotes a short chapter (VI) to the promised task which he heads, 'A reply to the argument of those who think that the existence of some God cannot be known except by faith.'[100] In the course of this chapter we clearly see that Episcopius is arguing for the same position as Timpler and Vorstius which is distinct in this respect from that of traditional Reformed theology on the one hand and of Socinus on the other. He evidently sympathizes with the latter whose rejection of the natural knowledge of God he sees as stemming from the Calvinist view that such must be ineradicably and irresistibly engraved in the human mind,

> '... because they wish that knowledge of God to be a natural idea impressed on the mind which therefore cannot fail to be naturally present and to inhere in the mind.'[101]

For if the knowledge of God is thus so clearly present in men's minds by nature, what then is the point of any additional revelation? In contrast Episcopius claims that the willing use of right reason is necessary before the principles given in nature can yield knowledge of God:

> 'It is necessary to look for another response: namely that the knowledge of God is not so natural that by necessity it entirely inheres in man as flowing from the principles of nature, but is natural only in this way, *that if a man is willing only to use reason* he can find certain principles in nature through which, with the help of that right reason, he may arrive at the knowledge of God.'[102]

and the virtue for Episcopius of such a view is that it allows a part for revelation to play in counteracting any weakness arising from defects in the necessary use of right reason.

> 'For even though it is possible, with the help of right reason, to attain to the knowledge of God, yet it can happen that a man is either so negligent and

---

[100] 'Respondetur ad argumentum eorum qui Deum aliquem esse nonnisi fide cognosci posse putant.' (*Op. Theol.*, I. p. 16.)

[101] '... quia cognitionem illam Dei, volunt esse notionem naturalem, animo impressam, proinde, quae non potest non naturaliter inesse, atque inhaerere animo.' (*Ibid.*)

[102] 'Quare alia responsione opus est: videlicet cognitionem Dei, non esse sic naturalem, ut necessario omnimo homini insit, eique non possit non inesse, tanquam ex naturae principiis fluens, sed sic tantum naturalem, *ut si homo velit ratione tantum uti*, principia quaedam reperire possit in natura, auxilio rationis istius rectae, per quae deveniat in Dei cognitionem.' (*Ibid.*) My emphasis.

slothful as not to care about knowing God, or he does not apply his mind and right reason with judgement, ... Hence revelation is useful, which strengthens a man, and faith is necessary which comes to the aid of that weakness and counteracts those faults.'[103]

In setting forth such views Episcopius is manifestly turning his back on the whole Reformed tradition which would argue that, since the chief purpose of the innate idea of God was to ensure fallen man's inexcusability, revelation thus becomes the most urgent of necessities. Unlike Vorstius then, the heart of Episcopius's objection to the doctrine of the innate idea is not philosophical but theological. For him man, even fallen man, must be in a position in which he is free to use his right reason and so, if he will, 'so that if man is willing only to use reason',[104] make his approach to God. Thus his very approach to the task of presenting arguments for God's existence to atheists is founded upon his assurance that they have the capacity to respond to such, 'if they are willing to be led in any way by right reason.'[105] This is a view which is not only totally at odds with that of Calvin but also goes far beyond that of Arminius in its assertion of human freedom.[106]

This emphasis of Episcopius's is especially apparent in his presentation of that argument for God's existence to which those who upheld the innate idea of God customarily appealed, 'that from universal consent.' Indeed we may reasonably suppose that this latter fact occasioned Episcopius's particular emphasis upon the role of reason and the will at this point. This is his fourth argument and for the first time in his presentation of them he draws directly and extensively from the famous work of his fellow Remonstrant, Hugo Grotius, incorporating verbatim many passages of the relevant section of the *De Veritate religionis Christianae*. Although in this work the latter does not explicitly reject the innate idea of God, at least he never alludes to it[107] and instead advances two possible causes of the universal belief in a God:

---

[103] 'Nam etiamsi auxilio rationis rectae, ad cognitionem Dei perveniri potest, tamen fieri etiam potest, ut homo vel adeo socors et segnis sit, ut de cognoscendo Deo non laboret, sive animum et rectam rationem in consilium non adhibeat, ... Hinc patefactio utilis, quae hominem fulciat, et fides necessaria, quae infirmitati isti succurrat, et vitiis istis occurrat.' (*Ibid.*)

[104] 'ut si homo velit ratione tantum uti.' (*Ibid.*)

[105] 'si ullo modo ratione recta duci velint.' (*Ibid.*, p. 6.)

[106] Cf. the latter's Public Disputation XI, 'De Libero hominis Arbitrio ejusque viribus' with its description of the condition of the mind and the will in fallen man in Theses VII-X. (Arminius, *Opera Theologica*, 1629, pp. 263-4).

[107] However, there are grounds for concluding from additions made to later editions of Grotius's *De Jure Belli ac Paris* (1631 and 1642) that he was moving towards some recognition of the innate idea.

'No other cause at all can be given which extends to all the human race: which cannot be anything else than the oracle of God Himself or tradition ...'[108]

Episcopius adds to these in a way which significantly underlines that necessary use of reason and the will to which we have already referred.

'No other cause for the agreement can be given other than either the oracle of God Himself, or tradition or of the matter itself, or this evidence of reason and principles known from them; to the extent that these are like first notions which compel the mind to assent, *if anyone is willing to be led in any way by reason.*'[109]

Although from the quotation just given Grotius appears to follow the standard view that belief in God is universal, his earlier statement, 'that there is some deity is assumed from the most obvious agreement of all peoples', is immediately qualified by the phrase, 'with whom reason and good custom have not been completely extinguished and induced to savagery.'[110] Episcopius's position does, of course, permit him to allow of exceptions to belief and he later takes up the suggestion of Grotius as to the nature of any such to enable him to admit of them in accordance with his already noted rejection of any naturally innate idea of God.

'But let it be, granted even that some such peoples are to be found, yet nothing is proved other than that the idea of a deity is not naturally impressed on the minds of all, which we do not wish to deny. For thus that idea could not be extinguished or suffocated at all. But it can happen that men degenerate so far in this that they do not employ reason to help but carry on by the instinct of nature alone like the beasts and *they wish for insensibility* ...'[111]

Again we may note Episcopius's stress on the role of human free will in determining the matter of belief. Moreover, even in the extreme cases of nations, 'who have been reared in the midst of barbarity and only accustomed to brutish senses', his faith in their essential rationality is not

---

108 'Omnino causam eius aliquam dari convenit, quae se ad omne genus humanum extendat: quae alia esse non potest, quam aut oraculum dei ipsius, aut traditio ...' (*De Veritate*, Leiden, 1627, p. 5.)

109 'Causa hujus tanti consensus alia dari non potest, quam aut oraculum Dei ipsius, aut traditio, aut rei ipsius, sive rationum et principiorum ex quibus id intelligitur evidentia; quatenus illa veluti primae notiones sunt, quae mentem cogunt assentiri; *si quis ulla modo ratione duci velit.*' (*Op. Theol.*, I, p. 9.) My emphasis.

110 'Numen esse aliquod sumitur a manifestissimo consensu omnium gentium' ... 'apud quas ratio et boni mores non plane extincta sunt inducta feritate.' (*De Veritate*, p. 5.)

111 'Sed, esto: detur etiam nationes aliquas tales repiriri, nihil aliud tamen evincetur, quam notionem illam divinitatis non esse naturaliter impressam animis omnium; quod negare nos nolumus. Sic enim nullo modo extingui posset notio ista, nec suffocari. At fieri posse ut homines eo usque degenerent, ut rationem in consilium non adhibeant, sed solo naturae instinctu Brutorum instar ferantur, ac *ferri velint*, ...' (*Op. Theol.*, I, p. 10.) My emphasis.

overthrown, for, 'they are accustomed with those who lead them back to reason and those principles to assent to them with little difficulty as if by this they were awakened from a deep sleep by the stimulus of nature.'[112] The issue of various peoples alleged to have no belief in God was one of the objections to the existence of any natural knowledge of God raised by Socinus and Episcopius is here explicitly answering it: 'This is one of those arguments which we said is used by certain people to prove that all knowledge of God is from faith alone ...'[113] It is interesting to note that in disputing Socinus's claim that there are nations devoid of any belief in God, Episcopius has no qualms in taking over here an entire section of a very orthodox Dutch refutation of the former's *Praelectiones*[114] which drew upon a series of recent accounts of the New World in order to demonstrate that all peoples yet discovered possessed at least some religious ideas.

In his reply to Socinus's objection that certain philosopohers had held atheistic views, Episcopius first draws on the response which Timpler made to this.[115]

> 'Thus once there was Diagoras Melius the poet, Theodorus Cyrenaeus, of whom the name atheist was used, Euhemerus Tegeates and others. I reply; 1. Philip Mornay in cap. 1 of the Truth of the Christian Religion amply proves with arguments which are not to be dismissed that those philosophers denied the gentile gods and their idols and superstitious worship rather than God.'[116]

For his second answer Episcopius turns once more to Grotius from whom he incorporates large sections of which the chief tenor is that such inadequate philosophical views are essentially due to the wilful perversity of their upholders:

> 'This is most certain and beyond all doubt that in every age and century the more honest a man the more diligently did he keep this knowledge in himself

[112] 'Quae in media barbarie educatae et solis tantum sensibus brutorum instar adsuefactae' ... 'cum iis qui ad rationem et principiis ista eos reducunt, haud gravate iis adsentiuntur, naturae quasi stimulo veluti ex profundo somno expergefacti.' (*Ibid.*, p. 10.)

[113] 'Hoc argumentum unum ex istis est, quibus dicebamus quosdam uti, ad probandum cognitionem omnem Dei ex sola fide ...' (*Ibid.*)

[114] J. Junius, *Refutatio Praelectionum Theologicaram Fausti Socini Senensis*, Amsterdam, 1633, pp. 36-7. For Junius (+ 1635) see *BWPGN* IV, pp. 621-2.

[115] See above, p. 210.

[116] 'Ita olim repertus Diagoras Melius Poeta, Theodorus Cyrenaeus, cognomento idcirco vocatus ἄθεος, Euhemerus Tegeates et alii. Resp. 1. Philosophos istos, gentilitios potius Deos, eorumque idola et superstitiosum cultum quam Deum negasse, prolixe probat Philippus Mornaeus in cap. 1 de veritate Religionis Christianae.' (*Op. Theol.*, I, p. 10.) Cf. Timpler: 'Quod vero ad Meliam poetam et Theodorum Cyrenaicum attinet, qui vulgo dicuntur Deum negasse, illi non tamen verum Deum quam idola et gentilitios Deos negasse putamus, quemadmodum Mornaeus docet capite 1. de veritate relig. Christianae.' (*Metaphysicae*, p. 394.)

about God, so that it is altogether necessary that this departure from that common and universal opinion of notions about the deity received from all past generations has taken place from the corrupt disposition of those whom it would most benefit if there were no God whom it is necessary to worship and to reverence with a pure mind and life in so far as He is the arbiter and judge of all human deeds.'[117]

Provided only that philosophers determine to use their faculties correctly then Episcopius confidently asserts:

'With the help of right reason the great majority of philosophers know that there is a God and reject the arguments of the few who think the contrary; therefore it is possible to attain to this knowledge with the help of right reason.'[118]

So much then for Episcopius's fourth argument. In all he presents five, each of which is treated at some lenght. The first appeals to the scholastic principle 'Everything that is comes from something else' ('Omne quod fit ab alio fit') and is evidently based on Suarez's formulation of the argument in the 29th disputation of the celebrated *Disputationes Metaphysicae* which exercised such an enormous influence upon Dutch philosophy and natural theology in this period.[119] According to Dibon and Robbers the first obvious signs of this in Holland are to be found in the work of the Scots professor of philosophy at Leiden, Gilbert Jacchaeus,[120] in particular

[117] 'Hoc certissimum est et extra omne dubium, omni aetate et seculo quo quisque fuit probior eo diligentius ab ipso custoditam de Deo notitiam ut omnino necesse sit a pravo eorum ingenio quorum interest ne Deus sit quem colere ac revereri pura mente ac vita necesse sit, quique adeo actionum omnium humanarum arbiter ac judex sit, istam a communi et ubique gentium recepta ab omni retro aevo de divinitate sententia discessionem profectam esse.' (*Op. Theol.*, I, p. 10.) Cf. Grotius, *De Veritate*, p. 7.

[118] 'Plerique omnes philosphi, rationis rectae ope Deum esse intellexerunt et rationes paucorum contra sententium rejecerunt: ergo rectae rationis ope ad istam cognitionem perveniri potest.' (*Op. Theol.*, I, p. 10.)

[119] The *Disputationes Metaphysicae* of Franciscus Suarez (1548-1617) was first published in 1597 in Spain. Some idea of its popularity may be judged from a glance at the subsequent editions: Mainz, 1600, 1605, 1614, and 1630; Cologne, 1608 and 1614; Lyons 1614; Paris, 1619. Both H. Robbers ('De Spaans-Scholastieke Wijsbegeerte op de Noord-Nederlandse Universiteiten in de Eerste helft der 17de Eeuw', *Bijdragen* (*Nederlandse Jezuiten*), 1956, Vol. 17, pp. 26-55, passim) and Dibon (*op. cit.*, pp. 256-7) describe the penetration of his influence in the Dutch Universities. The ambivalent position of Dutch orthodox theology towards Suarez's work is typified by the appearance, at Leiden in 1644, of *Suarez Repurgatus*, the handiwork of Jacobus Revius (1586-1653), Hommius's successor as Regent of the States College, see F. L. W. Posthumus Meyjes, *Jacobus Revius Zijn leven en werken*, Amsterdam, 1895, pp. 172-9.

[120] For Jacchaeus (1578-1628) see Dibon, *op. cit.*, passim. We may note that he was the friend of such scholars as Vossius, Barlaeus and Grotius. Indeed, as he tells us in the Dedicatory Preface to the *Institutiones Primae Philosophiae*, it was the last named who encouraged him to publish the work, 'authoritate Hugonis Grotii, viri incomparabilis, inductus, hanc quam videtis.' In consequence, on the condemnation of the Remonstrants in 1619, he was suspended from office and not restored until 1623.

in the latter's *Institutiones Primae philosophiae* first published in 1616.[121] In the second chapter of the fourth book, entitled, 'On the Infinite Being or God',[122] Jacchaeus had presented a very succinct resumé of Suarez's argument for God's existence, dwelling at some considerable[123] length on the latter's dissatisfaction with the physical argument of Aquinas's first way, 'everything that is moved is moved by something else', ('omne quod movetur, ab alio movetur') for which Suarez substituted that metaphysical axiom which we have noted in Episcopius. The Remonstrant theologian completely ignores this discussion proceeding directly to the latter principle where he clearly follows the outlines of Suarez's extended discussion. Thus as regards the first point to be established from the principle, the former writes,

> 'From that self evident principle I thus conclude that there are created beings in the natural order, therefore there is some being which is uncreated or independent.'[124]

As Suarez argues, the only alternatives to a first uncreated being are an infinite regress or a circular chain of causality, and he proceeds to dispose of the second of these in theses XXII-XXIV,[125] whilst no less than nine such (XXV-XXXIII)[126] are devoted to the refutation of the first. Episcopius duly follows with a paragraph which answers the query, 'You ask, what if there is a circle?' ('Quid si circulo detur, inquies?') thus,

> '... it would be impossible for a being in a circle to be made. For then the same argument recurs: that being which is created is created by some other. It cannot be created by itself ... nor by its effect, for this would involve a contradiction since it would presuppose the priority of its effect, therefore its effect cannot be its cause. Therefore it must be created by something else. And that being which is created must necessarily again be made by another that is created and this again by another, and so on to infinity. Since this is impossible, we must conclude that there is some uncreated being, independent of any

[121] It was reprinted at Leiden in 1628 and 1640. For a brief summary of this work and its relationship to that of Suarez, see Dibon, *op. cit.*, p. 71, where he concludes ' "Abrégé" de Suarez ... certes, mais élaboré par un professeur qui n'a pas les soucis de théologien de son modèle.'

[122] 'De Ente infinito seu Deo.' (Jacchaeus, *op. cit.*, pp. 179-183.)

[123] *Ibid.*, pp. 179-181.

[124] 'Ex isto principio per se noto sic concludo: Dantur entia facta in rerum natura, Ergo datur ens aliquod non factum sive independens.' (*Op. Theol.* I, p. 7.) Cf. Suarez: 'Hoc ergo posito principio sic concluditur demonstratio: omne ens aut est factum, aut non factum seu increatum: sed non possunt omnia entia quae sunt in universo esse facta, ergo necessarium est esse aliquod ens non factum seu increatum.' (*Disputationes Metaphysicae*, Mainz, 1600, Vol. II, p. 19.)

[125] Suarez, *op. cit.*, p. 19.

[126] *Ibid.*, pp. 20-2.

other, indeed a being on which all other created things depend as upon a first being as their cause and principle.'[127]

Episcopius then follows by rejecting the possibility of an inifnite regress:

'The relationship of cause and effect forbids an infinite regress. If there is an infinite regress, there is nothing first and therefore no cause nor a last; therefore no effect; nor are there any intermediate causes between the first and second.'[128]

In particular, he considers the question in relation to the possibility that mankind has existed from eternity and follows Suarez (theses XXXVII-XXXVIII)[129] in considering this to be absurd.

Episcopius's concern to combat certain views arising from Aristotelian naturalism now leads him away from Suarez, since he considers that this first proof does not go far enough.

'For it could be that this independent being produced everything by the necessity of nature and all things depended upon it in this way, moving and living by receiving from it the influx, virtue or power by which they are and exist. And so it does not follow that this independent being is God.'[130]

Further natural principles must be invoked from which it can be shown that the Being demonstrated by the first argument is indeed sovereign over the universe, 'Therefore I add; there are principles in nature from which the ruler and governor of this universe is definitely inferred.'[131] For his second argument then, Episcopius propounds one such, 'All natural beings act for a purpose' ('Omnia entia naturalia finis gratia agunt') and, in doing so, exchanges his Roman Catholic model for a Socinian.

---

[127] '... impossibilis est, si in circulo ens reperiatur quod factum sit. Tum enim redit idem argumentum: Illud ens factum, ab alio factum est. Non potest autem factum esse a seipso ... Nec a suo effecto: hoc enim implicat contradictionem; quia ante effectum suum esse praesupponitur: alioquin effectus sui causa non esset. Ergo ab alio factum sit oportet. Et si aliud illud ens factum est, necesse est ut ab alio iterum factum sit et hoc rursum ab alio atque ita in infinitum. Quod cum sit impossibile, necesse est ut concludamus dari aliquod ens non factum et ab alio independens; imo ens a quo alia facta dependent tanquam a primo ente, causa et principio suo.' (*Op. Theol.* I, p. 7.)

[128] 'Processum in infinitum dari vetat ratio causae et effecti. Si infinitus processus est, non dabitur primum: ergo neque causa nec dabitur ultimum: ergo neque effectus; nec dabuntur mediae causae quia illae sunt inter primam et secundum.' (*Ibid.*)

[129] Suarez, *op. cit.*, pp. 22-3.

[130] 'Fieri enim potest ut ens illud independens naturae necessitate omnia produxerit: atque ita entia omnia ab eo dependeant, recipiendo ab eo influxum, virtutem vel vim per quam sunt et subsistunt, moventur et vivunt. Itaque nondum sequitur hoc ens independens Deum esse.' (*Op. Theol.* I, p. 7.)

[131] 'Itaque addo: Dari principia in natura ex quibus solide colligitur universi hujus Rector ac gubernator.' (*Ibid.*)

In view of the well known, not to say notorious fact of Socinus's rejection of any natural knowledge of God in man, it may occasion some surprise to find that the most gifted theologian of the succeeding generation of his followers[132] has not only reversed the master's position but has provided one of the most extensive defences of such knowledge. The story of the publication of Volkelius's *On the true religion ... five books, to which is prefixed Johannes Crellius' book on God and His Attributes*[133] which, according to Wilbur, was 'the completest and best systematic treatment of Socinianism', is that

> '...Volkelius died in 1618 and it was a dozen years more before it was brought to completion. In fact the first of its five books was found so inadequate that it was finally discarded and replaced by one of Johannes Crellius, to whom revision of the manuscript had been committed.'[134]

A glance at Crellius' first book of this work is sufficient to see just how profound is the reversal of Socinus's position. If we ask the reason for this change from the latter's reliance upon scriptural revelation alone, then Crellius's answer is that such arguments are necessary for use against those who do not accept the authority of the Scriptures.

> 'And even though a satisfactory proof of God's existence may be demonstrated from the disputations to be held elsewhere in this work (book 5, chapter 2) on the authority of Holy Scripture, yet we have decided to make use of other arguments here as well so that God's existence may at least be acknowledged by those who do not yet accept the authority of Holy writ.'[135]

Crellius begins his task in Chapter II, 'God's existence is proved from the universal nature of things' ('Deum esse ex universa rerum demonstratur'), and quickly introduces the argument, 'If all natural things act for a purpose they must be governed by the design of some ruler.'[136] Episcopius takes over the entire remainder of this chapter, often

---

[132] Johannes Crellius (1590-1633), Rector of the College at Racow is described by E. M. Wilbur (*op. cit.*, p. 426) as 'the most distinguished scholar among the Socinians.'

[133] '*De vera religione ... libri quinque; quibus praefixus Johannis Crellii liber De Deo et ejus Attributis*', Racow, 1630.

[134] Wilbur, *op. cit.*, p. 418.

[135] 'Etsi vero ex iis, quae de Sacrarum literarum auctoritate alibi in hoc opere disputabuntur, (lib. 5, cap. 5) perspici satis possit, Deum esse: placet tamen aliis quoque argumentis idem hoc loco demonstrare, ut et illi id agnoscant, qui auctoritatem scriptorum sacrorum nondum admittunt.' (Crellius, *op. cit.*, col. 2) Cf. Vorstius, 'Sed quoniam Athei nec Scripturam Sacram audiunt, nec Spiritus Sanctus energiam sentiunt: ne frustra videamur contra negantes principia disputare, ipsa rerum Natura nobis hic in subsidium vocanda est.' (*De Deo*, p. 3.)

[136] 'Si omnia naturalia finis gratia agunt, necesse est eas rectoris alicujus consilio gubernari.' (Crellius, *op. cit.*, col. 3.)

giving considerable portions of it verbatim. A teleological universe is assumed as axiomatic, 'For nature does nothing in vain',[137] and a few examples are given in illustration. Heavy bodies tend naturally to seek their proper place which is below that of lighter; animals are instinctively driven to seek food and to propagate their species; the sun gives light and heat to the world. It is further stated as abvious that 'Whatever acts for any purpose, must be directed to that purpose either by its own design or that of someone else.'[138] From this it follows that, as so many natural creatures are devoid of understanding, the ends for which they act are determined by another who can only be that independent Being who is their Creator.[139] Even in the case of man who is possessed of intellect there are many natural processes which operate purposefully but without his understanding; the example is given of the wonderful formation of the foetus in a mother's womb. Such processes must certainly be the work of the Author of nature. To counter the insistent objection that natural beings acting purposefully must have at least some knowledge of the end in view, Episcopius gives us all of Crellius' illustrations of the arrow shot at the target, the ship being sailed into harbour, the clock marking out the intervals of time, and the horse ridden wherever its master wishes.[140]

Finally, to the objection that, 'It is nature itself in individual things by whose design the individuals are directed to their purposes', Episcopius replies that since 'there is no common nature apart from individual natures', any attempt to postulate 'some intelligent and knowing substance by whose design individuals are directed', is effectively to acknowledge the existence of God, even if the name is refused Him, 'But this is to make God out of nature, and when you deny God you acknowledge God under the name of nature.'[141]

---

[137] 'Natura enim nihil agit frustra.' (Episcopius, *Op. Theol.*, I, p. 7. Crellius, *op. cit.*, col. 4.)

[138] 'Quaecunque finis alicujus gratia agunt, ea necesse est ut vel suo vel alieno consilio dirigantur ad finem istum.' (*Ibid.*, col. 3.)

[139] 'Forte iidem porci aut asini deliberant quomodo cibus in ventriculo concoqui, quomodo in chylum, chylus in sanguinem verti, et per venas atque arterias diffundi possit.' (*Ibid.*, col. 6.) 'Nec asini nec porci deliberant qua ratione cibus in ventriculo concoquatur, quomodo in chylum, chylus in sanguinem vertatur, etc.' (Episcopius, *Op. Theol.*, I, p. 8.)

[140] Episcopius, *Op. Theol.*, I, p. 8. Crellius, *op. cit.*, col. 4.

[141] 'Naturam ipsam in singulis rebus esse cujus consilio singulae diriguntur in fines suos', .... 'communis natura non est extra singulares naturas', .... 'substantia alique intelligens et cognoscens cujus consilio singula diriguntur', .... 'At hoc est ex natura Deum facere, et cum Deum neges Deum sub naturae nomine agnoscere.' (Episcopius, *Op. Theol.* I, p. 8.) Cf. Crellius, *op. cit.*, cols. 6-7.

Crellius goes on to present the argument from design in wearisome detail in two further lengthy chapters.[142] Episcopius's third argument, 'The whole framework of the world is designed so that all parts of it serve man alone;'[143] also involves him in an extensive appeal to the Design argument, but even though he makes some of the same points as Crellius, as for instance in arguing against the Epicurean view that the natural order came about by chance or the Aristotelian that it has existed from eternity, the form and often the content of his argument is quite different. Once again the familiar axiom is restated near the outset, 'For nature does nothing in vain', ('Natura enim nihil facit frustra'), and the point is made that natural phenomena operate for the sake of others, not for themselves, 'all these things therefore happen for the sake of another' ('Alterius igitur causa omnia ista fiunt.') If we ask, for whose sake?, then the answer is quickly given, 'But for whose? unless for man's, the noblest being of all under the sun?' ('At cujus? nisi hominis, entis omnium inter sublunaria nobilissimi?') The chain of operation is succintly expressed thus,

> '... all heavenly worlds exist for the sake of air and water; air and water indeed for the sake of the earth, the earth for the sake of plants, plants for the sake of animals, animals exist for the sake of man.'[144]

All things then evidently serve man, whilst man himself serves none of them—granted he tills the earth but he does so for his own purposes.

Episcopius has a lengthy and interesting section in which he considers the objection that it is absurd to think that the heavenly bodies in all their vastness should serve man who in comparison is less than nothing in size. He sets out the various figures calculated for the enormous astronomical distances involved in measuring the stars and inter-stellar space; figures which he draws from such authorities as Maimonides and the Dutch Reformed minister and celebrated astronomer whose commentary on the Heidelberg Catechism we considered above,[145] Philip Lansbergen. In passing he notes the opposing views of Ptolemy and Copernicus but makes no choice between them; in any case their differences have no relevance to the point in question. Turning to the refutation of this objection,

---

[142] Chapter III 'Ex mundi hujus opificio Deum esse demonstratur' (cols. 7-22) and Chapter IV 'Pergitur in opifice hujus mundi demonstrando, ut Deum esse intelligatur.' (*op. cit.*, cols. 22-47.)

[143] 'Tota mundi fabrica ista est ordinata, ut omnes ejus partes uni homini serviant.' (*Op. Theol.*, I, pp. 8-9.)

[144] '... coelestes omnes orbes, propter aërem et aquam sunt: Aër vero et aqua propter terram, terra propter herbas, herbae propter animalia, animalia propter hominem sunt.' (*Ibid.*, p. 8.)

[145] See above, pp. 69-73.

Episcopius argues simply that man is of far more worth than all the heavenly bodies be they ever so vast because nobility is not to be reckoned by size but by the quality of a creature's being; 'For the perfection of a being is not to be calculated from its mass and quantity, but from its worth or more excellent capacity', and in consequence, 'Truly an ant or fly is more perfect than the entire earth, sea, sun and moon. For to live and to feel is far better than simply to exist.'[146] Granted the supreme worth of man, then there is no reason why he should not be served by a host of inferiors no matter how much bigger than himself, after all, as we see in human affairs, 'Often several thousands of followers, senates, provinces, kingdoms, armies serve a king, albeit a little man.'[147] It is evident that the ancient concept of the hierarchy of being is fundamental to the whole of this discussion providing as it does the rationale which preserves man's exalted status. Furthermore, Episcopius continues, this subservience of all things to man can only have been effected by the will of the beneficent Ruler of the world since the natural elements have no understanding by which to put themselves in his service and man has no power to command the heavenly bodies. 'What is there left but for us to conclude that this subordination is the work of some wise ruler whom we call God?'[148]

Could this situation have arisen by chance? 'For whatever things arise by the necessity of nature do so at all times and in the same way.'[149] Episcopius scornfully rejects this possibility, pointing out that the wonderful and beautiful arrangement of nature could never have arisen thus.[150] He gives the familiar analogies of the discovery of a painting disclosing the existence of a painter and that of a hut in the countryside which witnesses to man as its builder even if no other evidence of his presence is to be seen. Anyway, supposing for a moment that chance were the creator of our universe, how did it succeed in uniting and sustaining the atoms in their present order? How is it that the atoms of water, being naturally lighter than those of earth, do not swamp the latter entirely? Nor will Episcopius

[146] 'Entis perfectio non est aestimanda ex mole et quantitate, sed ex virtute, sive facultate excellentiori', ... 'Nempe una formica aut musca perfectior est tota terra, mari, sole et luna. Vivere enim et sentire longe melius est, quam simpliciter esse.' (*Op. Theol.*, I, p. 8.)

[147] 'Regi, licet homuncioni, formulantur saepe aliquot stipatorum millia, curiae, provinciae, regna, exercitus.' (*Ibid.*, p. 9.)

[148] 'Quid restat ergo, nisi ut concludamus istam subordinationem esse opus sapientiae alicujus Rectoris, quem nos Deum esse dicimus?' (*Ibid.*)

[149] 'Casu istam subordinationem contingere potuisse, per tumultuarium quendam atomorum concursum, nullo consilio, nulla sapientia.' (*Ibid.*)

[150] 'Tam ordinatam fabricam, tam artificiosam molem, tam pulchram tot diversarum ac sibi invicem repugnantium rerum, et tamen adeo suaviter inter se conspirantium, compagem fortunae aut casui transcribere, ut Deum ejus auctorem non cogaris fateri.' (*Ibid.*)

allow that the universe arose from some eternal necessity of nature ('naturae quadam necessitate, ita evenisse ab omni aeternitate'). He refers back to the arguments of the earlier section where he has shown the absurdity of the notion that man has existed from eternity and, if it is said that the heavenly bodies produce man, then how is it that they do not still do so? As they evidently do not the whole thing is absurd 'For any things which are produced by natural necessity always act in the same way.'[151]

Episcopius's fifth reason, 'From the force and dictate of conscience',[152] is the familiar argument from the various examples of those atheists, for example, Caligula, who, particularly in sickness and at the approach of death, are prompted by the pangs of conscience to display their fear of impending divine judgement. To this Episcopius appends two brief 'ad hominem' arguments against atheism which are, in fact, those of the ancient Stoics, that is, that without religion and belief in God there would be no virtue and no individual or social constraint to prevent licentious violence.[153] So much for Chapter III.

Chapter IV is headed 'The various objections of the atheists proposed and refuted.' ('Variae Atheorum objectiones proponuntur et diluuntur.') These objections turn out to be those raised by the philosophers of classical antiquity. We may not that, in replying to Sextus Empiricus's arguments and in order to make the point that inferior creatures are incapable of comprehending their superiors, Episcopius once more lifts an entire passage practically word for word from Grotius's *De veritate* where it occupies a different context.[154]

When he turns to the consideration of the Epicurean arguments against the wisdom, goodness and justice of God, Episcopius once more has recourse to the argument from design. In response to the objection that there are so many dysteleological features in the natural world, he turns the argument from design on its head and says that if God is the author of these they must undoubtedly have a purpose for Him even if we cannot grasp what this may be.[155]

He draws the analogy of someone entering the office of a surgeon, apothecary or chemist and seeing a whole army of instruments, potions

[151] 'Quae enim necessitate naturae producunt aliquid, ea semper et eodem modo agunt.' (*Ibid.*)

[152] 'A vi et dictamine conscientiae.' (*Ibid.*, pp. 10-12.)

[153] *Ibid.*, p. 12.

[154] *Ibid.*, p. 13, cf. Grotius, *op. cit.*, p. 8.

[155] '... si Deus earum omnium author est, sine dubio finis et utilitatis alicujus causa eas singulas esse voluit, et cui fini serviant optime novit, etiamsi nos istam utilitatem non capiamus aut non adsequamur.' (*Op. Theol.*, I, p. 13.)

and the like the usefulness of which he does not doubt although he may be utterly ignorant of them. It may be, Episcopius continues, that we cannot always see the ends for which various apparently dysteleological features are created but we need look no further than the microcosm of man himself to see purposefulness written in his every member:

> 'Look only at man, the microcosm, there is nothing in all his body, not even the hair which covers his head or the eyelids and the eyebrows which surmount the eyelids, whose use for the body cannot plainly be demonstrated.'[156]

Finally, Epicurus had queried the existence of so many worthless and small creatures such as insects and Episcopius attempts to establish their useful part in a purposeful chain by instancing the fly, 'behold the fly, is it not food for swallows and spiders? and what is more useful than the spider for cleaning the air?'[157]

As we saw earlier,[158] when we considered Trigland's criticism of Episcopius's refusal in the Remonstrants' *Apologia* to advance natural arguments for the existence of God, the latter had there claimed that he preferred those drawn from revelation since they lacked the complexities and difficulties attaching to philosophical arguments. How far does his presentation of the proofs which we have just studied invalidate this earlier claim? First we must note that Episcopius still lays great stress on the appeal to the witness of revelation and accordingly devotes his fifth chapter, 'That there is a God is shown from various revelations of Himself',[159] to a lengthy consideration of this. In his further defence it may be urged that, rejecting as he did the innate idea of God, he was dependent for non-supernatural arguments upon the witness of the book of nature. Here, again as we have seen, unlike Trigland but very much like the more sophisticated Walaeus, he was conscious of the kind of philosophical objections which could be raised against the apparently straightforward appeal traditionally made to it. At the end of the day, however, it must be said that the abiding impression left by Episcopius is that of his stress upon man's free will and rationality.

---

156 'Homo tantum μιχροχοσμος videatur, nihil in toto ejus corpore est, ne pilus quidem qui caput tegit, aut cilia, et quae palpebras vestiunt supercilia, quae non usum praestare corpori demonstrari possit.' (*Ibid.*)

157 'Videte muscam; an non ea hirundinum pabulum est, et esca aranearum? et aranea quid utilius ad repurgandum aërem?' (*Ibid.*)

158 See above, pp. 171-2.

159 'Demonstratur Deum esse ex diversis ipsius patefactionibus.' (*Op. Theol.*, I, pp. 13-16.)

This it is which lies at the root of his objection to the innate idea of God and this it is which inspires the presentation of all his arguments from whatever source. With Episcopius those elements in the Melanchthonian position in accord with such emphases are taken up and the limitations which had hitherto controlled them thrown aside.

# CONCLUSION

At the outset of this study we noted the dispute amongst modern scholars, as to whether, in his discussion of the natural knowledge of God in the opening chapters of the *Institutes*, Calvin could be seen as presenting arguments for God's existence. Even if we accept Parker's case that this was not so, our subsequent investigation has shown that Calvin's followers certainly saw the matter in this light and this to the extent that we have felt justified in referring to a 'Reformation' pair of arguments, the appeal to the innate idea of God and to the order discernible in nature and history.

For Calvin the context was that of the knowledge of God and so long as Reformed theologians concerned themselves with the question of God's existence under this heading, they remained faithful to the essentially Reformation pattern of a twofold natural/supernatural revelation, with the former subdivided into the categories of innate/acquired and the final verdict expressed as to the uselessness of such natural knowledge except to establish fallen man's inexcusability before God.

Thus we have shown that the Barthian charge that the 'virus' of natural theology entered into Reformed thought by way of the 'De Cognitione Dei' articles of the Gallican and Belgic Confessions is quite unfounded. Although, as we noted, Piscator, in the most influential abridgement of Calvin's *Institutes*, did open the door to the use of philosophical arguments for God's existence in the locus, 'De Cognitione Dei', nonetheless it was not through this channel that such gained admission to Reformed theology but through that of the 'De Deo'.

Reformation theologians from Melanchthon onwards had advanced arguments for God's existence but these had been predominantly of the kind that appealed to the same considerations which provided the basis for the 'traditional' pair. Melanchthon had, however, come to add two scholastic arguments to his list but had continued effectively to retain them under the heading 'De Creatione'. With Ursinus's Commentary, Melanchthon's list is transferred to the 'De Deo' section of the Heidelberg Catechism under the conventional scholastic subheading, 'An sit Deus'. That this was not an isolated phenomenon is shown by Daneau's presentation of a very similar list in precisely the same context in his *Isagoges*. We have traced the history of Ursinus's influence in succeeding commentaries on the Catechism and noted the degree to which his successors appear to be redressing the balance in favour of a more cautious appraisement of the status of the natural sources for the knowledge of God.

Although, as we noted at the beginning, Luther rebelled against the scholastic theology and philosophy of his day, it is surely very significant that the setting he chose for his revolt was that of the academic disputation. If we choose to define it simply as a system of instruction, then scholasticism was never absent from the heart of the Reformation's apparatus of higher education, first at Wittenburg, where under Melanchthon it flourished mightily, and then at the other Protestant universities, Reformed as well as Lutheran. In this respect, and although subjected to the kind of modification outlined, for example, by Fraenkel in his study of the academic instruction at Geneva, the medieval tradition continued unbroken. The story of the revival of scholastic philosophy within this continuing framework is well known but it has been particularly interesting to see how its influence was mediated in the matter with which we have concerned ourselves.

For, let us recall, when the theologians of our period came to compose the loci which were the chief means of academic instruction by disputation, those centering upon the topics 'De Cognitione Dei' or 'De Theologia' remained firmly with the traditional reformation fold and always stressed the negative purpose of the natural knowledge of God.

The 'De Deo' locus, however, was a very different matter. This was the realm of traditional scholastic philosophical theology and, it would appear, the pressure of such was sufficient to ensure the penetration into Reformed theology at this point of Aquinas' 'quinque viae' and other even more sophisticated neo-scholastic arguments. That such penetration did not always go unopposed is apparent enough from the example of William Ames' reaction against metaphysics.

Nonetheless, when, in framing their new Confession, the Remonstrants sought in, what any modern scholar with Barthian views on the impropriety of natural theology would surely applaud as, truly Calvinian fashion, to begin with a first article headed, not, 'De Deo', but 'De Sacra Scriptura', they were sharply criticised by the guardians of Dutch orthodoxy for failing to establish God's existence more directly and for being Socinian in the rejection of man's natural knowledge of God. The effect of Socinus's notorious dismissal of such knowledge continued to exercise considerable influence even after his own successors had entirely reversed his position. If in this respect the Remonstrants were apparently truer to earlier Reformation insights than their opponents, in all others they moved further and further away.

Parker urged us to recall the overwhelming importance for Calvin of inexcusability as the sole effect of the natural knowledge of God. In the dispute which we examined on this issue we saw how the Contra-Remonstrants remained resolutely true to the reformer, whilst their opponents came increasingly to emphasize the importance of natural religion and man's freedom and rationality. If Vorstius, whom Episcopius followed in denying the innate idea of God, held an essentially Thomist view of the relationship between nature and grace, with Episcopius and De Courcelles we move appreciably further in the direction of rationalism.

The motive for presenting arguments of any sort for God's existence remained predominantly that of fortifying the faithful in the face of atheists and other doubters. The positive apologetic concern which eventually became such a feature of these exercises is scarcely evident. With the exception of Vorstius, professional academic theologians tended to leave the writing of such works to laymen and our period is dominated successively by those of two such, Du Plessis-Mornay and Grotius.

When at a later date this kind of apologetic became more widespread it was the design argument, fed by the flood of new information about the natural world arising from the growth of science, that eventually came to dominate the picture. By the beginning of the next century Holland had produced Nieuwentyt[1] to rival England's More, Ray and Derham in the exhaustive detail of his account of the wonders of nature. In our own period, the signs of this development are confined to the heterodox works of Crellius and Episcopius, both of which it may be noted presented the design argument under its scholastic colours as the appeal to final causality and it was largely in this guise that it was launched upon its future career.

---

[1] (1654-1718) *Het Regt Gebruik der Werelt Beschouweringen* was first published in 1717. It achieved instant popularity with translations into English and French and was the source from which William Paley drew his famous analogy of the watch and watchmaker.

# BIBLIOGRAPHY

## Primary Sources


*Acta et Synodalia Dordracena*, n.p., 1620.

*Acta Synodi Nationalis ... Dordrechti habitae*, Leiden, 1620.

Acronius, R., *Enarrationes catecheticae: quibus Quaestiones et Responsiones Catechismi Ecclesiarum Belgicarum et Palatinatus methodice, compendiose et dilucide, explicantur*, Schiedam 1606.

Alting, H., *Explicatio Catecheseos Palatinae cum vindiciis a considerationibus Novatorum et Antithesibus Socinianorum*, in *Scriptorum Theologicorum Heidelbergensium*, Amsterdam, Vol. II, 1646, pp. 1-289.

Ames, W., *Christianae Catecheseos Sciagraphia*, Amsterdam, 1635.

——, *Disputatio Theologica adversus Metaphysicam*, Leiden, 1632.

——, *The Marrow of Sacred Divinity*, Leiden, 1642.

Aquinus, T., *Summa Theologiae*, Blackfriars' edition, London 1963-

——, *In omnes D. Pauli Apostoli Epistolas Commentarii*, Vol. I, Liege, 1857.

Arminius, J., *Disputationes magnam partem S. Theologicae complectentes Publicae et Privitae*, Leiden, 1610.

——, *Opera Theologica*, Leiden, 1629.

——, *Catalogus Librorum Viri D. D. Jacobi Arminii quondam in Academia Lugudensi Theolog. professoris*, Leiden, 1610.

——, *The Works of James Arminius*, 2 vols., London, 1822, 1828.

Bakhuizen van den Brink, J. N., *De Nederlandsche Belijdenisgeschriften*, Amsterdam, 2nd. ed. 1976.

Barlaeus, C., *Theses Theologicae de Cognitione Dei*, Leiden, 1605.

——, *Theses Theologicae de modis cognoscendi Dei*, Leiden, 1605.

Bastingius, J., *In Catechesin religionis Christianae, quae in Ecclesiis et scholis tum Belgii tum Palatinatus traditur, exegemata sive commentarii*, Heidelberg, 1590.

——, *Exposition or Commentarie upon the Catechisme of Christian Religion*, Cambridge, 1589.

Beza, T., *Annotationes Maiores in Novum ... Testamentum*, 2 vols., Geneva, 1594.

Bodecherus, N., *Sociniano-Remonstrantismus*, Leiden, 1624.

Bunney, E., *Institutionum Christianae religionis compendium simul ac methodi enarratio*, London, 1578.

Calvin, J., *Opera quae supersunt Omnia, Corpus Reformatorum*, Vols. 29-78, Brunswick, 1863-93.

——, *Opera Selecta*, Vols. 1-5, Munich, 1926-36.

——, *Calvin: The Institutes of the Christian Religion*, Library of Christian Classics, Vol. 20, London, 1961.

*Catechesis Ecclesiarum quae in Regno Poloniae ...*, Racow, 1609.

Chandieu, A. De, *Opera Theologica*, Geneva, 1599.

Coccejus, J., *Opera Omnia*, 10 vols, Amsterdam, 1701.

*Collegium Quartum Disputationum Theologicarum in Academia Lugduno-Batava. Francisco Gommaro, Jacobo Armino et Luca Trelcatio Juniore Praesidibus*, Rotterdam, 1615.

Colonius, D., *Disputationes Theologicae quibus Paraphrasticae et Analytice, Quatuor libri Institutionum Joh. Calvini, in usum studiosae juventutis evolvuntur*, Leiden, 1628.

——, *Catalogus Variorum Librorum Bibliothecae Reverendi Clarissimique Viri D. Danielis Colonii Collegii Gallo-Belg. Regentis et Ecclesiae Lug.-Batav. Pastoris, Quorum auctio habebitur In Officiana Elseviriana 23 September Stylo novo.*, Leiden, 1636.

*Compendium Theologiae Thesibus in Academia Lugduno-Bat ... ab anno 1598 usque ad annum 1605 concinnatum*, Hanover, 1611.

Corstens, C., *Wtlegghinge Des Cateschismi der Gereformeerde Christelicke Kercke in Neerduytslandt*, Leiden, 1598.

Corvinus, J. A., *Petri Molinaei novi anatomici mala encheiresis, seu Censura Anatomes Arminianismi*, Frankfurt, 1622.

[Courcelles, E. De,] *Advis d'un personnage désinteressé* ..., Amsterdam, 1638.

——, *Opera Theologica*, Amsterdam, 1675.

Crellius, J., *Opera Omnia Exegetica*, Vol. I, Amsterdam, 1656.

Daneau, L., *Christianae Isagoges ad Christianorum Theologorum Locos Communes, Libri II*, Geneva, 1588.

Delaune, G., *Institutionis Christianae Religionis a Joanne Calvino Conscriptae Epitome. In qua adversariorum obiectionibus breviter ac solidae responsiones annotantur*, London, 1583.

——, *An Abridgement of the Institution of Christian Religion*, Edinburgh, 1585.

Diest, H. a, *Mellificium Catecheticum continens Epitomen Catechetidarum Explicationum Ursino-Pareanarum*, Deventer, 1640.

Episcopius, S., *Opera Theologica*, Vol. I, Amsterdam, 1650, Vol. II, Rotterdam, 1665.

——, *Apologia pro Confessione ... contra Censuram quatuor professorum Leidensium*, n.p., 1630.

[——], *Confessio sive Declaratio Sententiae Pastorum, qui in foederato Belgio Remonstrantes vocantur, super praecipius articulis Religionis Christianae*, n.p., 1622.

Gomarus, F., *Opera Theologica*, 3 vols., Amsterdam, 1644.

——, *Theses Theologicae De Providentia Dei*, Leiden, 1601.

Grotius, H., *De Veritate Religionis Christianae*, Leiden, 1627.

——, *De Jure Belli ac Pacis*, Leiden, 1631.

——, *Briefwisseling van Hugo Grotius*, Vols I-X, The Hague, 1929-78.

Guedtman, L., *Illustrium Exercitationum, ao 1669*, Leeuwarden, 1669.

Hales, J., *Golden Remains of the Ever Memorable Mr. John Hales*, London, 1659.

Hommius, F., *Het Schatboeck der Christelicke Leere ofte Uytlegginghe over den Catechismus*, Leiden, 1602.

——, *Collegium Disputationum Theologicarum in Academia Leydensi privatim institutarum a M. Simone Episcopio*, Dordrecht, 1618.

——, *Specimen Controversiarum Belgicarum*, Leiden, 1618.

Jacchaeus, G., *Primae Philosophiae Institutiones*, Leiden, 1616.

Junius, F., *Opera Theologica*, 2 vols., Geneva, 1607.

——, *Opera Theologica*, 2 vols., Geneva, 1613.

Junius, J., *Refutatio Praelectionum Theologicarum Fausti Socini Senensis*, Amsterdam, 1633.

Kuchlinus, J., *Oratio ... Joannis Kuchlini ... electi et vocati primi Praesidis Collegii theologici, nuper ... in Academia Leydensi instituti*, Leiden, 1593.

Lansbergen, P., *Catechesis Religionis Christianae quae in Belgii et Palatinatus Ecclesiis docetur, Sermonibus LII explicata*, Middelburg, 1594.

Lubbertus, S., *Commentarius in Catechesin Palatino-Belgicam*, Franeker, 1618.

Luther, M., *D. Martin Luthers Werke*, Weimar, 1883-

——, *Lectures on Romans*, trans. and ed. W. Pauck, London, 1961.

Maresius, S., *Theologiae Elenchticae Nova Synopsis*, 2 vols., Groningen, 1646-8.

——, *Foederatum Belgium Orthodoxum sive Confessionis Ecclesiarum Belgicarum Exegesis*, Groningen, 1652.

——, *Collegium Theologicum, sive Breve Systema Universe Theologicae*, Groningen, 1649.

Melanchthon, P., *Opera quae supersunt Omnia, Corpus Reformatorum*, vols. 1-28, Brunswick. 1834-60.

——, *Melanchthons Werke in Auswahl*, Vols. II & V, Gütersloh, 1952-65,

——, *Annotationes ... in Epistolas Pauli ad Romanos et Corinthios duas*, Nurenburg, 1522.

——, *Melanchthon on Christian Doctrine: Loci Communes 1555*, Trans. and ed. C. L. Manschreck, New York, 1965.

Mornay, P. Du P., *De La Verité de la Religion Chretienne*, Antwerp, 1581.

——, *A Woorke concerning the Trewenesse of the Christian Religion*, London, 1587.

Moulin, P. Du, *Anatome Arminianismi, seu Enucleatio controversiarum quae in Belgio agitantur super doctrina de providentia, de praedestinatione, de morte Christi, de natura et gratia*, Leiden, 1619.

——, *The anatomy of Arminianism: or, The opening of the controversies lately handled in the Low-countryes, concerning the doctrine of providence*, London, 1620.
——, *De Cognitione Dei*, Leiden, 1625.
——, *A Treatise of the Knowledge of God*, London, 1634.
——, *Examen de la Doctrine de Messieurs Amyrault et Testard ... touchant la Predestination et les poincts qui en dependent*, Amsterdam, 1638.
Olevianus, K., *Institutionis Christianae Religionis Epitome. Ex Institutione Johannis Calvini excerpta, authoris methodo et verbis retentis*, Herborn, 1586.
*Orationes Inaugurales*, Leiden, 1620.
Pareus, D., *In divam S. Pauli ad Romanos epistolam commentarius*, Heidelberg, 1613.
Peltius, J., *Harmonia Remonstrantium et Socinianorum*, Leiden, 1633.
Piscator, J., *Aphorisimi Doctrinae Christianae maximam partem ex Institutione Calvini excerpti sive Loci Communes Theologici, brevibus sententiis expositi*, Herborn, 1594.
——, *Aphorismes of Christian Religion*, London 1596, Facsimile edition, Amsterdam, 1973.
——, *Exegesis sive Explicatio Aphorismorum Doctrinae Christianae*, Herborn, 1622.
Polyander, J., *Theses Theologicae De Deo*, Leiden, 1613.
——, *Syntagma Exercitationum Theologicarum*, Leiden, 1627.
Quick, J., *Synodicon in Gallia Reformata*, Vol. II, London, 1692.
*The Racovian Catechism*, Amsterdam, 1652.
Rutgers, F. L., (ed.), *Acta van de Nederlandsche Synoden der Zestiende eeuw*, Utrecht, 1889.
Scaliger, J. C., *Exercitationes Exotericae de Subtilitate*, Frankfurt, 1582.
Schaff, P., *The Creeds of the Evangelical Protestant Churches*, London, 1877.
Socinus, F., *Praelectiones Theologicae*, Racow, 1609.
Spanheim, F., *Disputationes Theologicae Miscelleneae*, Geneva, 1652.
Suarez, F., *Disputationes Metaphysicae*, Mainz, 1600.
*Synopsis Purioris Theologiae*, Leiden, 1625.
Timpler, C., *Metaphysicae Systema Methodicum*, Steinfurt, 1604.
Trelcatius, L. Jr., *Catalogus insignium librorum ex Bibliotheca ... D. Lucae Trelcatii*, Leiden, 1607.
——, *Scholastica et Methodica Locorum Communium S. Theologiae Institutio*, Leiden, 1604.
——, Snr. and Jnr., *Opuscula Theologica Omnia*, Leiden, 1614.
Trigland, J., *Antapologia sive Examen atque Refutatio Totius Apologiae Remonstrantium*, Rotterdam, 1664.
Ursinus, Z., *Doctrinae Christianae Compendium seu Commentarii Catechetici*, Leiden, 1584.
——, *Pars prima Explicationum Catecheticarum*, Neustadt, 1585.
——, *Corpus Doctrinae Christianae*, Frankfurt, 1621.
——, *The Summe of Christian Doctrine*, Oxford, 1587.
——, *The Summe of Christian Religion*, London, 1633.
——, *Volumen tractationum theologicarum*, Neustadt, 1584.
Van Rijssen, L., *De vuile en zielverdervende leer der Nieuwe Remonstranten*, Schoonhaven, 1662.
Voetius, G., *Disputationes Selectae Theologicae*, Vol. I, Utrecht, 1648.
——, *Exercitia et Bibliotheca Studiosi Theologiae*, Utrecht, 1651.
Vogellius, H., *Predikatie vervatende de Belydennisse der ware Christelike Gereformeerde Belgie*, Amsterdam, 1625.
Vorstius, C., *Tractatus Theologicus de Deo sive de Natura et Attributis Dei*, Steinfurt, 1606.
——, *Apologetica Exegesis sive Plenior Declaratio Locorum aliquot ex Libro ejusdem de Deo ... excerpta eique pro erroneis imposita*, Leiden, 1611.
——, *Apologetica Responsio ad ea Omnia quae Festus Homminus nominatim ipsi nuper impegit in eo libro cui titulum fecit, Specimen Controversiarum Belgicarum*, n.p., 1618.
——, *Commentarius in omnes Epistolae Apostolicas*, n.p., 1631.
Walaeus, A., *Opera Omnia*, 2 vols., Leiden, 1643.
Willet, A., *Hexapla, that is a six-fold Commentarie upon the Epistle to the Romans*, London, 1611.

## Secondary Sources

Althaus, P., *Die Prinzipien der deutschen reformierten Dogmatik im Zeitalter der aristotelischen Scholastik*, Leipzig, 1914, reprinted Darmstadt, 1967.

Armstrong, B. G., *Calvinism and the Amyraut Heresy: Protestant Scholasticism and Humanism in Seventeenth Century France*, Milwaukee, 1969.

Bangs, C., *Arminius, a study in the Dutch Reformation*, Nashville, 1971.

Barnaud, J., 'La Confession de foi de Théodore de Bèze', *Bulletin de La société de l'Histoire du Protestantisme Française*, Vol. 48, 1899, pp. 617-33.

Bauer, C., 'Melanchthons Naturrechtslehre' in *Archiv für Reformationsgeschichte*, Vol. 4, 1951, pp. 64-100.

Bernus, A., Le Ministre Antoine de Chandieu, d'après son journal autographe inedit, *Bulletin: Société de l'histoire du Protestantisme Française* Vol. 37, 1888, pp. 2-13, 57-69, 124-36, 169-91, 393-415, 449-62, 561-77, 617-35.

*Biographisch Lexicon voor de Geschiedenis van het Nederlandse Protestantisme*, Vol. I, Kampen, 1978.

*Biographisch Woordenboek van Protestantsche Godgeleerden in Nederland*, The Hague, [1907]-1949.

Bizer, E., *Frühorthodoxie und Rationalismus*, Zurich, 1967.

Cochrane, A. C., *Reformed Confessions of the Sixteenth Century*, London, 1966.

Collins, J., *God in Modern Philosophy*, London, 1959.

Copleston, F. C., *A History of Philosophy*, Vol. III, London, 1953.

Courthal, P., 'Karl Barth et Quelques Points des Confessions de Foi Reformées', *La Revue Reformée*, Vol. 9, 1958, pp. 1-29.

Cuno, F. W., *Franciscus Junius der Ältere, Professor der Theologie und Pastor*, Amsterdam, 1891.

Dibon, P., *L'Enseignement philosophique dans les Universités néerlandaises à l'époque précatesiénne (1575-1650)*, Amsterdam, 1954.

Dowey, E. A., *The Knowledge of God in Calvin's Theology*, New York, 1952.

Eekhof, A., *De Theologische faculteit te Leiden in de 17de eeuw*, Utrecht, 1921.

Erichson, A., *Bibliographia Calviniana*, Berlin 1900.

Eschweiler, K., *Die Philosophie der spänischen spätscholastik auf der deutschen Universitäten des 17 Jahrhunderts*, Münster, 1928.

Fatio, O., *Nihil Pulchrius ordine ... Lambert Daneau aux Pays-Bas, (1581-3)*, Leiden, 1971.

———, *Méthode et Théologie Lambert Daneau et les débuts de la scolastique réformée*, Geneva, 1976.

Félice, P. De, *Lambert Daneau, Pasteur et Professeur en Theologie, 1530-95*, Paris, 1881.

Fraenkel, P., *De l'écriture à la dispute. Le cas de l'academie de Genève sous Théodore de Bèze*, Lausanne, 1977.

Haentjens, A. H., *Remonstrantsche en Calvinistische Dogmatiek*, Leiden, 1913.

Hall, W. Jr. 'The Life of Julius Caesar Scaliger (1484-1558)', *Transactions of the American Philosophical Society*, N.S. 40, 1950, pp. 85-170.

Harrison, A. W., *The Beginnings of Arminianism to the Synod of Dort*, London, 1926.

Hausamman, S., *Römerbriefauslegung zwischen Humanismus und Reformation; eine Studie zu Heinrich Bullingers Römerbriefvorlesung von 1525*, Zurich, 1970.

Hildebrandt, F., *Melanchthon: Alien or Ally?*, Cambridge, 1946.

Hoenderdaal, G. J., 'Arminius en Episcopius', *Nederlands Archief voor Kerkgeschiedenis*, Vol. 60, 1980, pp. 203-35.

Hübner, F., *Naturliche Theologie und theokratische Schwärmerei bei Melanchthon*, Gütersloh, 1936.

Jonge, C. De, *De Irenische Ecclesiologie van Franciscus Iunius (1545-1602)*, Nieuwkoop, 1980.

Kühler, W. J., *Het Socinianisme in Nederland*, Leiden, 1912.

Léonard, E. G., *A History of Protestantism*, Vol. 2, London, 1967.

Lewalter, E., *Spanisch-Jesuitische und Deutsch-lutherische Metaphysik des 17 Jahrhunderts*, Hamburg, 1935.

Manschreck, C. L., 'Reason and Conversion in the Thought of Melanchthon', in *Reformation Studies, Essays in Honour of R. H. Bainton*, ed. F. H. Littel, Richmond, 1962.

Martini, M., *Fausto Socino et La Pensée Socinienne*, Paris, 1967.

Molhuysen, P. C., *Bronnen tot de Geschiedenis van de Leidsche Universiteit* Vol. I, The Hague, 1913.
Nauta, D., *Samuel Maresius*, Amsterdam, 1935.
*Nieuw Nederlandsch Biographisch Woordenboek*, Leiden, 1911-37.
Parker, T. H. L., *Calvin's Doctrine of the Knowledge of God*, 2nd ed. Grand Rapids, Michigan, 1959.
Partee, C., *Calvin and Classical Philosophy*, Leiden, 1977.
Petersen, P., *Geschichte der aristotelischen Philosophie im protestantischen Deutschland*, Leipzig, 1921.
Petit, L.-D., *Bibliographische lijst der werken van de Leidsche hoogleeraren 1575-1619*, Leiden, 1894.
Popkin, R. H., *The History of Scepticism from Erasmus to Descartes*, New York, 1964.
Posthumus Meyjes, E. J. W., *Jacobus Revius zijn leven en werken*, Amsterdam, 1895.
Posthumus Meyjes, G. H. M., *Geschiedenis van het Waalse College te Leiden, 1606-1699*, Leiden, 1975.
——, 'Le Collège Wallon', *Leiden University in the Seventeenth Century*, Leiden, 1975, pp. 111-35.
Rademaker, C. S. M., *Gerardus Joannes Vossius*, Zwolle, 1967.
*Realencyclopädie für protestantische Theologie und Kirche*, 3rd ed., Leipzig, 1898-1908.
Rimbault, R. I., *Pierre Du Moulin*, Paris, 1916.
Robbers, H., 'De Spaans-Scholastieke Wijsbegeerte op de Noord-Nederlandse Universiteiten in de Eerste helft der 17de Eeuw', *Bijdragen (Nederlandse Jezuiten)*, 1956, Vol. 17, pp. 26-55.
Sassen, F., *Geschiedenis van de Wijsbegeerte in Nederland tot het einde der negentiende eeuw*, Amsterdam, 1959.
Schotel, G. D. J., *Geschiedenis van der oorsprong invoering en lotgevallen van den Heidelbergschen Catechismus*, Amsterdam, 1863.
Schrenk, G., *Gottesreich und Bund im älteren Protestantismus vornehmlich bei Johannes Coccejus*, Gütersloh, 1923.
Sepp, C., *Bibliographische Mededeelingen*, Leiden, 1883.
——, *Het Godgeleerd onderwijs in Nederland gedurende de 16e en 17e eeuw*, 2 vols., Leiden 1873-4.
Smid, T. D., 'Bibliographische Opmerkingen over de Explicationes Catecheticae van Zacharias Ursinus', *Gereformeerd Theologisch Tijdschrift*, Vol. 41, 1940, pp. 228-43.
Sprunger, K. L., *The Learned Doctor William Ames*, Chicago, 1972.
Van der Woude, C., *Sibrandus Lubbertus*, Kampen, 1963.
Van Itterson, G. P., *Franciscus Gomarus*, The Hague, 1930.
——, 'De Synopsis Purioris Theologiae, Gereformeerd Leerboek der 17de Eeuw', *Nederlandsche Archief voor Kerkgeschiedenis*, Vol. 23, 1930, pp. 161-213 and 225-259.
Van Slee, J. C., *De Geschiedenis van het Socinianisme in de Nederland*, Haarlem, 1914.
van 't Spijker, W., 'Natuur en Genade in de Reformatorische Theologie', *Theologia Reformata*, Vol. 22, 1979, pp. 176-90.
Warfield, B. B., *Calvin and Calvinism*, New York, 1931.
Weber, E., *Die philosophische Scholastik der deutschen Protestantismus im Zeitalter der Orthodoxie*, Leipzig, 1907.
——, *Der Einflusz der protestantischen Schulphilosophie auf die orthodox-lutherische Dogmatik*, Leipzig, 1908.
Wijminga, P. J., *Festus Hommius*, Leiden, 1895.
Wilbur, E. M., *A History of Unitarianism: Socinanism and its Antecedents*, Cambridge, Mass., 1948.
Wundt, M., *Die Deutsche Schulmetaphysik des 17 Jahrhunderts*, Tübingen, 1939.
Zeeuw J. Gzn. De, *Guido de Brès, opsteller van de Nederlandse Geloofsbelijdenis*, The Hague, 1963.

# INDEX

Numbers printed in italics refer to footnotes